In Nobody's Backyard

Maurice Bishop's Speeches: 1979-1983

A Memorial Volume

Edited by Chris Searle

Zed Books Ltd. 57 Caledonian Road, London N1 9BU

In Nobody's Backyard was first published by Zed Books
Ltd., 57 Caledonian Road, London N1 9BU in 1984.

Copyright © Chris Searle, 1984
Copyright (Introduction) © Richard Hart, 1984
Typeset by Composer Typesetting
Proofread by A.M. Berrett
Cover design by Walter Castro
All photos courtesy of Arthur Winner
Printed by The Pitman Press, Bath

British Library Cataloguing in Publication Data

Bishop, Maurice
   In nobody's backyard : Maurice Bishop's
   speeches, 1979-1983 : a memorial volume.
   1. Caribbean Area — Politics and government
   — 1945
   I. Title   II. Searle, Chris
   320.9182'1   JL599.5

   ISBN 0-86232-248-0
   ISBN 0-86232-249-9 Pbk

US Distributor:
Biblio Distribution Center, 81 Adams Drive, Totowa,
New Jersey 07512

Contents

Editor's Preface

The speeches in this volume were all made by Maurice Bishop in his capacity as Prime Minister of Grenada and leader of the New Jewel Movement, the revolutionary party. Thus they stand not only as his own political testament, but that also of the party and the revolution.

A volume of speeches had been planned to be published by Zed Books as early as 1981, which was to include not only speeches made by Maurice Bishop, but also other members of the People's Revolutionary Government, and Bishop himself had invited Richard Hart, a veteran of the Caribbean revolutionary movement, to contribute an introduction. That collection was never finally realised, ultimately due to the events of October 1983, and this present volume has been compiled as a memorial not only to a man who made a vital historical intervention in Caribbean history, but also to the revolution itself, which he led and symbolised.

> When we hear the news of the Revolution that morning, it was joy come out in the morning! Joy come out in the morning! As if I lifted up that morning! I lifted up above the sky that morning!
> The Revolution make me young again. I young now as if I just in me teens! Me energy come through that happiness of the Revolution. Long live the Revolution! Long live Maurice Bishop and his party! And we praying for them day and night, because they not seeking for one and not for the other, they seeking for all people, from a baby to the old.

Thus spoke a 72-year-old woman about the revolutionary dawn in Grenada of 13 March 1979. Words of joy and a new youth coming from the lips of a people whose experience of resisting attack after attack of imperialist penetration remains unsurpassed and continues more than ever today, and particularly in Grenada, never tamed, always resisting, a green and brilliant bullet lodged in the heart of imperialism, whether coming from France, Britain or the USA.

For the Grenada Revolution was a grasp of joy in the sudden unfolding of the actuality of power for the working people in one island in the one

Caribbean nation, a joy in the discovery that life unfulfilled could and would change, be transformed for a people who had known 400 years of transportation, slavery, colonialism, neo-colonial dictatorship and exportation to the cities of Europe and North America. Joy that the organised genius of ordinary people could at last be applied to develop their own resources for their own future.

There was the joy of education, of seeing your children achieving free secondary schooling and your illiterate mother learning how to read and write, the joy of seeing wasted, unemployed youths forming co-operatives and planting the idle land. There was the joy of free health care, of walking to see a doctor or dentist in your local health clinic and knowing that the few dollars you had would stay in your pocket that morning, the joy of going on a Sunday outing and driving in one of your people's own buses along the runway of freedom, a part of the magnificent airport being built in your own small island, the joy of repairing your own house on a Sunday morning with the voluntary labour of your neighbours, using the materials supplied through the government's House Repair Programme. The joy of seeing your own agro-industrial products, your own mangoes and soursops tinned behind your *own* labels: 'Made in Grenada', of hearing your own poets proudly recite in your own language which your parents and grandparents spoke at your own organs of local democracy that scorned the Westminster imposition and colonial mimicry: all this was the joy that opened the Grenada morning five years ago.

It was 110,000 people's discovery of the world, and the ideas and structures that could begin to make the world live in their island. In political education classes elderly peasants and young workers sat and read Lenin's *To the Rural Poor* together, and seeing their *own* history in his words through their creative application to Grenada's villages and nutmeg estates — 'But man, this is *we*!' In the flashing eyes of Minister of Education Jacqueline Creft, having just read Lunacharsky's *What is Education?* and *The Philosophy of the School and the Revolution*, thrusting the book at me — 'Read this, read this! We need dozens of photocopies. This is us and this is what we must do, but in our *own* way!' Or Maurice himself, furiously annotating an account of the process of socialist emulation in the early years of the Soviet Revolution, his mind open wide to the potential of Grenadian workers developing their own system of emulation and pushing forward their production.

This remarkable *openness* of the revolution to new ideas and messages was epitomised in the character of Maurice Bishop. He was of the world as well as of Grenada. He was, in the words of Fidel Castro, 'a vertical revolutionary', a leader of outstanding qualities. In his very breadth, his friendliness and extraordinary warmth, his capacity to inspire, his wit, eloquence and intellectual depth, he brought the personality and brilliance of his entire Caribbean people into the admiration of the world, like his three great Grenadian predecessors had done before him: Julien Fedon, who, responding to international Jacobinism and the appalling condition of the Grenadian people under slavery, led a massive revolt against British colonialism in 1795, T.A.

Marryshow, the architect of Caribbean federation, and Tubal Uriah 'Buzz' Butler the pioneer trade unionist. Like them he was a man of magnetic energy who achieved a huge empathy with his people. What touched the people, touched Maurice. It was why they loved him and why they felt so proud of him when he defiantly challenged the imperialist giant in the forums of the region and the world. They were also proud of themselves because he *was* them. Thus, when he was so suddenly and bewilderingly arrested, they were arrested too and had to free him to free themselves again.

I can remember going with him one night to visit the parents of a young militant and soldier who had died in a jeep accident. As he entered the yard of the small wooden house and stood next to the concrete cistern which trapped the rain, he embraced the bereaved family, one by one. His modest, humble bearing, a quietness and sad understanding entwined with a message of hope, made him as one with the family.

During those four and a half years it was as if the sea around Grenada did not exist, despite its proud translucence. Insularity disappeared. It was not only the rallies and village discussions reaching out to the people of Vietnam, Chile, the Western Sahara, South Africa, Namibia, El Salvador or Guatemala, not only the internationalist workers from the rest of the Caribbean, the USA, Europe and the Soviet Union, but also the stream of activists, writers and powerfully liberating minds that came to Grenada – from Paulo Freire and Angela Davis to Cheddi Jagan and Harry Belafonte, from George Lamming and Ngugi wa Thiong'o to Samora Machel and Michael Manley. Hazlitt once said of 19th Century imperialist Britain that if you stood at a certain place in London for a year, you would see all the world's most important people pass. During the years of the Grenada Revolution, you would have met in the streets or on the beaches the new and rising world's most radiant spirits, passing through, giving their strength, experience and solidarity to the people of Grenada. This small island was becoming the nexus of a new and burgeoning English-speaking civilisation and the fortress of a proud Caribbean sovereignty.

The life of Maurice Bishop personified this receptiveness and extraordinary energy of open learning and education that was found within the Grenada Revolution, the ability to learn from and imaginatively apply the insights of every process of liberation to the reality of the people's struggle and their achievement in Grenada. He belonged to Grenada and the Caribbean, a revolutionary patriot who became, in the words of Cheddi Jagan 'the measure of the new Caribbean man'. With his comrades like Unison Whiteman, who died with him, he had been a symbol of the national struggle against hideous dictatorship that had murdered many Grenadians, including his father. But he also belonged to the world and his words also belong to the world, all of us. That he had once been a Black nationalist and stayed in the heart of his people and their proud anger during the 1970 Black Power upsurge in the Caribbean which had given popular birth to such new confidence and rejection of colonialist and racist imitation, was as much a part of his stature as his embrace of Marxism-Leninism and hatred of imperialism or any form of oppression of the working people of the world. Despite his death he was a victor over the history of imperialist crimes committed against his Grenadian and Caribbean people.

My enduring memory of him is standing with his fist upraised, roaring out 'Long live the struggle of the British working class!' – The Grenadian, the Caribbean revolutionary who could reject that complex-ridden and blood-soaked division between his own people and the working people of Britain, the old colonising power that had brutally subjected and enslaved his ancestors. It was just one example of the continuous expression of his vision that the common people of our world will triumph together over the forces that threaten to pull us down. This is why the Grenada Revolution through the voice of Maurice Bishop made its great shout for progress the property of all struggling people: 'Forward ever, backward never!' Through the cracking muffler of imperialist occupation it still rings out.

Chris Searle
London, 13 March 1984

Acknowledgements

As the editor of this collection I gratefully acknowledge and thank the following publications, institutions and individuals that have been essential for its compilation: *The Free West Indian, The Crusader* of St Lucia, the *Morning Star, Race Today*, Casa de Las Americas, the Britain-Grenada Friendship Society, the Government Information Services of revolutionary Grenada, Fedon Publishers, Didacus Jules and Don Rojas (Joint Editors of *Selected Speeches of Maurice Bishop: 1979–81*, published by Casa de Las Americas, Havana, Cuba), Merle Hodge, George Lamming, Victoria Brittain and Richard Hart.

My sincere thanks are also extended to Arthur Winner, for his photographs.

C.S.

Introduction
Richard Hart

In the late 1930s the workers in most of the then British West Indian colonies, impoverished and seething with discontent, rose up in spontaneous strikes and demonstrations. Out of these upheavals new trade union movements emerged in many Caribbean islands, but Grenada was relatively unaffected by these events. Two small trade unions existed in the 1940s, catering mainly for urban workers but not succeeding in recruiting appreciable numbers of plantation workers. The awakening of the Grenadian masses did not occur until the end of the decade, around the time of the return to Grenada of two men who had been working at the oil refinery in Aruba. One of these men, Gascoigne Blaize, had been an officer of the Aruba Labour Union and had been deported for his union activities. The other was Eric Gairy.

One explanation of this time-lag may have been the relatively higher level of individual ownership of land among the agricultural workers in Grenada. Another could have been the fact that the cultivation of sugar cane had given way to that of cocoa and nutmegs on most of the big properties, crops requiring smaller concentrations of workers and a less intensive exploitation of labour. Be that as it may, from 1950 onwards the recruitment of agricultural and other workers into the new trade union led by Gairy was rapid and enthusiastic.

Gairy's personality was an inspirational factor in channelling the energy of the workers into militant struggles to obtain increased wages. But from the start he saw the organisation he led primarily in terms of the advancement of a career for himself. I recall a conversation with him when he visited Jamaica in or about 1951 in which this was clearly revealed. I enquired whether his union would affiliate with the Caribbean Labour Congress of which I was then the General Secretary. In reply he indicated reluctance to effect a formal affiliation for fear of offending Mr Bustamante. What stuck in my memory was the way in which he made this point. He didn't say that there was reluctance to affiliate because the Grenada union wanted to maintain good relations with all labour organisations in the area. What he said was that as 'a young man just starting on my career' he had to be careful.

Gairy used the power which the workers' support gave him to further his financial interests and personal political ambitions. He formed alliances with some members of the employing class on whom he bestowed favours, discriminating punitively against others who did not support him. Having been elected to office, he built up by patronage a body of supporters ranging from petty-bourgeois careerists to the criminal thugs who were recruited into his notorious 'Mongoose Gang', modelled on the Haitian 'tonton macoutes'. Thus did he create an alternative power base to the agricultural workers, large numbers of whom were becoming disenchanted and conscious of having been betrayed.

As he consolidated his power, Gairy became a willing, if very minor, pawn of American imperialism. He was also rewarded with a knighthood by the British Government. But perhaps his crowning reactionary achievement was his personal alliance with the Chilean dictator General Pinochet. By 1976 he had clearly lost most of his popular support, but secured his continuance in office by shamelessly rigging the elections. Thereafter, though the repressiveness of his regime increased, so did the popularity of his principal opponents in the New Jewel Movement, formed in 1973. The brutal treatment suffered by several of the NJM leaders at the hands of Gairy's armed forces further enhanced the public support they enjoyed.

The Improbable Revolution

Asked to choose a title for a talk on what had occurred in Grenada during and after the insurrection of March 13, 1979, I suggested: 'the improbable revolution'. Among the improbabilities that a revolution of the type which commenced in 1979 would occur in Grenada the following will be readily apparent:

a) the smallness and social composition of the population;
b) the dimunitive size and undeveloped economy of the islands:
c) the extent to which the people had been indoctrinated with and had accepted institutions and political practices designed by the British;
d) the geographical and geo-political location.

At the time of the Population Census of the Commonwealth Caribbean in 1970 there were 92,775 persons resident in Grenada and its two associated Grenadines. In 1979, according to an estimate contained in the *Abstract of Statistics*, the number had risen to 110,137. A breakdown of the 58.4% of the population over 15 years of age classified in 1970* as engaged in economic activity shows the following percentages for the principal occupational groupings:

---

* There was probably very little, if any, relevant change between 1970 and 1979.

Agriculture, forestry and fishing	33.35
Construction	15.95
Commerce	9.62
Manufacturing	7.97
Transport, storage and communication	5.15
Electricity, gas, water and sanitary services	0.93
Mining and quarrying	0.11
Services †	22.32
Not stated or otherwise classified	4.60
	100.00

It has not been possible, on the basis of the limited statistics available, to determine precisely the percentages of those engaged in agriculture on their own account and those employed in agriculture for wages. The estimate of the number of such employees contained in the *Abstract of Statistics* (less than 5% of employees in all occupations) is not a reliable guide as this was based on Income Tax returns and many agricultural workers will have been employed by farmers who made no such returns. There seems little doubt, however, that in Grenada in 1979 the number of persons engaged in agriculture on their own account exceeded the number so engaged for wages. Many of those working for wages will also have had farms of their own. Grenada probably has the highest percentage of individual peasant proprietors in the English-speaking Caribbean area.

Grenada was the first English-speaking country in modern times in which popular power had been established by revolutionary means. The Grenada Revolution proved that, in the conditions prevailing in the world today, a social revolution is possible even in a very small country with a very small population. The single most important factor contributing to the possibility of such a revolution occurring in Grenada was the existence of the New Jewel Movement, a vanguard party modelled on concepts of party organisation first worked out by Lenin at the turn of the century. Guided by Marxist-Leninist theory, the NJM leaders understood the laws of social evolution and were able to recognise the development of a revolutionary situation and take advantage of it.

The existence of a Leninist vanguard party to provide the necessary orientation at such historic moments is vital for the achievement of popular power. Without such leadership, in times when unrest and dissatisfaction have increased beyond the level of popular tolerance, blind uncoordinated outbreaks of disorder can easily occur which are then suppressed by the armed forces with purposeless loss of life and destruction of property. Such directionless upheavals have indeed occurred over the past half century in other parts of

---

† This lumping together of hotel and other service workers with household servants conceals the fact, so characteristic of under-developed Caribbean societies, that the great majority of these were household servants.

the English-speaking Caribbean area.

The NJM showed exemplary flexibility in knowing when the appropriate form of popular struggle was electoral politics and when the time had come to launch an armed uprising. In 1976 the NJM contested the general elections against the governing party of the then Prime Minister Eric Gairy. These elections were held at a time when, even though it was suspected that Gairy had no intention of permitting a free and fair election in which he might have been defeated, the overwhelming majority of the population nevertheless believed that the possibilities of effecting change through the electoral process had not been exhausted.

In the event, the elections of 1976 were not conducted fairly. Space does not permit a recital of the methods employed by Gairy to ensure victory, but he was nevertheless surprised at how well the opposition coalition did, gaining six of the fifteen seats in the legislature. The results no doubt accelerated his decision to abandon all pretence of adherence to democratic forms. But if the 'constitutional dictator', as he has been called, learned a lesson, so did the people. The brutal behaviour of the Gairy regime brought the majority to an appreciation of the fact that it was no longer possible to effect a change of government by electoral means. That explains in part why there was such a wide social spectrum of approval for the forcible overthrow of Gairy on March 13, 1979.

Having successfully launched the uprising, the revolutionaries took a number of initiatives from which further important lessons can be learned. The first of these was the disarming of the Army and the Police. It is a serious mistake to assume that the armed forces will always remain politically neutral and obediently serve the government of the day, whatever its political complexion. These are disciplined bodies whose officers have, for the most part, inherited the functions and traditions of the oppressive machinery of imperialism. Such forces, if left intact under the command of reactionary officers, may consitute a threat to the survival of a revolutionary regime. But this is not invariably the case. Under the leadership of a progressive group of officers and sub-officers the armed forces in some countries have initiated or supported a popular revolution. The role of the army in Ethiopia is a case in point.

A popular revolution has just as much need of armed forces for its protection as a regime of privilege which has been overthrown. The People's Revolutionary Government, established after the successful insurrection, therefore wasted no time in constituting the revolutionary fighters of the NJM into a regular army and creating its own security forces, though it proved possible to retain the services of some individual policemen.

Another early accomplishment of the revolutionaries was the commencement of broadcasts explaining the reasons for the seizure of power and their immediate objectives and intentions. Not long afterwards, publication of a newspaper commenced. When an existing local newspaper, controlled incidentally by foreign shareholders, began publishing false information designed to create alarm and discredit the Revolution, and continued to do so after a warning, its further publication was suspended. When, subsequently, arrangements were made for publication of a new newspaper, with financial support from hostile elements abroad, that too was prohibited.

That a government serving the interests of the majority can be undermined and discredited by a campaign of media destabilisation has been demonstrated conclusively in recent years. In Chile public opinion was successfully mobilised against the progressive government of Salvador Allende by persistent and deliberate misrepresentations of its actions and intentions in that country's leading newspaper *El Mercurio*. An identical campaign was waged in Jamaica against the government of Michael Manley by the *Daily Gleaner*, which was equally successful. By prompt action the possibility of similar tactics succeeding in Grenada was frustrated.

The Revolutionary regime did not need, and could not have asked for, any higher form of legitimation that the support of the overwhelming majority of the Grenadian people at home and abroad, which it received from the very beginning. Nevertheless, within days of the triumphant insurrection the revolutionary leaders were showing their concern for the institutionalisation of the Revolution. Five days after the seizure of power, at a rally at Queens Park, St George's, some 25,000 persons enthusiastically acclaimed the announcement of the formation of the People's Revolutionary Government. On 25 March 1979, a package of ten fundamental People's Laws were proclaimed and endorsed by popular acclamation at a rally at Seamoon in the parish of St Andrew, attended by 15,000 people. These Laws, together with a number of other People's Laws proclaimed over the course of the next few days, suspended the existing Constitution (though 21 of its III clauses were subsequently revived) and prescribed a provisional governmental structure and system of enacting legislation.

In addition to this formal provisional structure, what might be described as an informal structure for public participation in the affairs of government was developed under the leadership of the NJM. Initially this consisted of 'Parish Councils' in each of the main island's six parishes and in Carriacou, which everyone was encouraged to attend and to which the annual budget and all important new legislation was submitted for explanation and discussion before approval by the Cabinet. Where these Parish Councils were found to be too large and unwieldy they were sub-divided into 'Zonal Councils' and a plan for a further sub-division of some Zonal Councils into village councils was being considered. In addition, there were Parish Councils specifically for workers and for women, and there were the mass organisations – the National Women's Organisation (claiming 7,000 members and 170 local branches), the National Youth Organisation (claiming 9,000 members and 100 local branches), the trade unions affiliated to the Trade Union Council and the Productive Farmers' Union for the small independent farmers. The budget and all important new laws being proposed were also submitted for discussion in these forums. Through these structures it would undoubtedly be true to say that a larger percentage of the population was initially drawn into participation in the affairs of government than in any other country in the English-speaking Caribbean area.

In June 1983 the appointment of a Commission to draft a new constitution to complete the process of formal institutionalisation of the Revolution was announced. This consisted of three lawyers (in whose number I had the honour to be included) and two representatives of the mass organisations. The Commission was required to observe certain guiding principles including the following:

> The widest possible participation by the people in the Country's decision-making process and the day-to-day administration of affairs of the State and of matters affecting their work and their residential communities. The concept of popular democracy should be reflected in the provisions of the Constitution whereby the structures therein contained shall be designed to facilitate continuous popular involvement. Something more meaningful is required than the illusions of popular control by the right merely to enter a polling booth once or twice every four or five years.

Thus it was envisaged that the informal participatory democratic practices, which had been developed under the leadership of the party, would become part of the formal constitutional structure. The Commissioners were required to complete their draft within two years. After public discussion and revision, the final draft was to be submitted to the people for approval in a referendum.

The revolutionary leaders never described the Revolution as 'socialist', nor did they advocate a precipitate transition to socialism. They were agreed that a mixed economy would be appropriate for Grenada's stage of development for some considerable time. The People's Revolutionary Government reflected this in its composition and programme. There were representatives of the private sector in the Cabinet. Though the working class, represented by the NJM, was the dominant partner, the PRG was in effect an alliance with representatives of other social strata prepared to participate in the struggle to free Grenada, politically and economically, from imperialist control. In this national alliance the state sector had already begun to play the leading role in economic development. A co-operative sector was also being encouraged and materially assisted. But the private sector was encouraged to participate in developing the economy, and incentives in the form of tax concessions were offered for a fairly wide range of investments, including investments of foreign capital.

The speeches contained in this volume provide a chronological record of the economic achievements of the PRG during its short period in office. Pride of place among these was the progress made towards the realisation, with Cuban assistance, of the longstanding desire of the Grenadian people for a modern airport capable of accommodating jet aircraft. This project, scheduled for completion by March 13, 1984 and frustrated by the US invasion, would have ensured prosperity through expansion of tourism and the opening up of new markets for fresh fruits, vegetables and root crops.

Also of importance were the modern prefabricated housing plant, the emulsion plant and the stone crushing and asphalt plant, all of which were constructed with Cuban assistance and would have led to an expansion and improvement of housing construction and road building.

Progress had also been made in obtaining new markets for the country's traditional exports. Depressed world market prices for nutmegs had led to the accumulation of considerable unsold stocks. The agreement of the Soviet Government in 1983 to purchase approximately one quarter of the annual production would have assisted Grenada to achieve a steady reduction of accumulated stocks at reasonable prices. Other negotiations, including a proposal for dredging and modernising facilities at the port of Grenville with Soviet assistance, were in progress when, following the US invasion, relations with the USSR were terminated.

The establishment of the Marketing and National Import Board deserves special mention. This institution not only purchased locally grown food-stuffs for export and for the local retail trade, but was also used as a means of controlling and in some cases reducing the prices of essential imports. Fertiliser was imported for resale to farmers at reasonable prices, and likewise cement for the building trade and cheaper rice for wholesale and retail distribution. Expansion of the MNIB by erection of refrigerated storage space and other warehousing facilities was envisaged. The Government's agro-industrial plant for the canning of fruit juices and other agricultural produce was another impressive development.

Grenada's economic growth was consistent throughout the period. Gross Domestic Product rose in 1979 by 2.1%, in 1980 by 3.0%, in 1981 by 3.0% and in 1982 by a record 5.5%. In 1982 an unexpectedly large (EC$6.5 million) surplus in the Government's recurrent Revenue and Expenditure Budget was partly the result of greater prosperity in the private sector than had been expected, with the result that the anticipated income tax returns were exceeded.

Economic growth was achieved despite the hostility shown by the Government of the USA. US hostility was an important factor in destabilising and bringing about the defeat of the progressive government of Michael Manley in Jamaica in 1980. Fortunately for Grenada, only a relatively insignificant part of its exports have traditionally gone to the USA and no major enterprises in Grenada were owned by US citizens. So far as the International Monetary Fund and the Banks whose assistance was required were concerned, the PRG was a model client. It successfully balanced its budget and needed to allocate only 3.7% of its foreign exchange earnings in 1982 for servicing and repayment of its debts.*

---

* *Report on the National Economy for 1982 and Budget Plan for 1983* presented by Bernard Coard, Minister of Finance on 24 February, 1983. By way of contrast, Jamaica has had to set aside approximately 27% of its foreign exchange for this purpose (*National Economic Survey*, 1982)

Despite the commitment of the PRG to the development of a mixed economy and the fact that the private sector was sharing in the relative prosperity, there was no mistaking the determination of the NJM to ensure that state power was used to protect and advance the interests of the workers. The commitment of the party and government to the protection of working class interests is indicated in the speech entitled 'In the Spirit of Butler'. It may also be helpful, by way of illustration, to give some practical examples of how the workers benefited from the manner in which state power was exercised.

Soon after the insurrection in 1979 there was a dispute between the Commercial and Industrial Workers Union and the holder in Grenada of the franchise to bottle Coca Cola. Negotiations over the dismissal of two employees were referred to the Labour Commissioner, whose adjudication required their reinstatement. The employer refused to reinstate the men, deciding instead to close the factory. Perhaps he believed that, having demonstrated the impotence of the union, he would be able to offer re-employment to selected employees.

The workers responded by taking control of the factory and resuming production. The employer then requested the Police to eject the workers, but this did not happen. Instead the Government opened an account for the business under the supervision of the Ministry of Finance. The workers continued to operate the factory, and did so so successfully that the business continued to make a profit. This continued until the employer agreed to reinstate the dismissed employees. Control of the factory was then returned to the owner, together with the accumulated profits.

In other countries in the English-speaking Caribbean area it is usual for the state to recognise rights of property as taking precedence over the rights of the workers. In similar circumstances the probabilities are that the police would have attempted to eject the workers and restore the factory to the employer. The PRG's attitude was that, unless the employer respected the worker's rights, his rights would not be protected by the state. The workers' rights were regarded as the primary consideration. Indeed, in this particular case, some of the workers were disappointed that they were required to surrender control of the factory, but, given its commitment to the mixed economy, the PRG did not consider that the circumstances justified expropriation.

The outcome of the Bata company strike in 1983 was another illuminating example, if not of the actual use of state power at least of how it was anticipated by the parties that it would be used. Bata are notorious internationally for their anti-trade union attitude. In Grenada, however, they were prudent enough to recognise the union in accordance with the requirements of the Trade Union Recognition (Amendment) Law of 1982. But negotiations for a new contract reached a stalemate when the company refused to include a profit-sharing clause. Such clauses had by that time been accepted by many of the major employers and the union remained adamant. All the other matters in dispute were agreed but the negotiations broke down on this point.

The union called a strike which dragged on for several weeks. With no prospect of an accord in sight the union then publicly notified the company that if a settlement was not reached within one week the company would be regarded as having abandoned its business in Grenada and appropriate action would be taken. This notice was given full publicity on Radio Free Grenada. Its language was subtle but the meaning was clear. No doubt remembering what had happened at the Coca Cola plant, the company got the message. Within a week agreement had been reached on the profit-sharing clause and work had been resumed.

Within the parameters allowed by its primary concern for the interests of the working class the PRG, in keeping with its mixed economy commitment, not only permitted the private sector to operate but rendered it considerable assistance. Commerce continued, virtually undisturbed, in the hands of the merchants, though the MNIB successfully competed with them by importing fertiliser, rice and cement. Only two individuals had their property expropriated without compensation – the deposed Prime Minister Sir Eric Gairy and his deputy Derek Knight – both of whom were accused of having acquired their wealth corruptly and by abuse of their official positions. All other compulsory acquisitions of privately owned property for public purposes were carried out under a colonial statute, the *Land Acquisition Ordinance 1958*, which required payment of market value compensation.

There were, however, limits on the extent to which state power was used in support of the workers. When a group of persons led by a former supporter of the Revolution, who was allegedly planning to organise them to grow ganja (marijuana) for export, seized a plantation at River Antoine, the PRG insisted on the land being returned to its owners. But the Agricultural Workers' Union, led by a prominent NJM member, negotiated the inclusion of a profit-sharing clause for the workers in its contract with the employer.

An example of the PRG's helpful policy towards productive plantation owners was what occurred in December 1982 at Douglesdon, the largest banana plantation. Faced with an immediate requirement for capital, the owners requested permission to sub-divide and sell off in plots an area in excess of 100 acres.* This was refused for reasons explained in the footnote below, but the Government assisted the owners to raise the required capital by guaranteeing repayment of a loan from the Bank, which was in turn secured by an option, if the owners defaulted, to purchase a share in the ownership.

The attitude to non-productive land-owners was, however, quite different.

---

* Under the *Land Utilisation Law* no sale of more than 100 acres of land could be made without permission, a requirement devised to discourage fragmentation of lands used for export crops, which might then be used for subsistence farming thereby causing a decline in export earnings.

Under the *Land Utilisation Law 1981* the Minister of Agriculture was empowered to take a compulsory lease of any agricultural land which was not being brought into cultivation. The land so leased could then be sub-let for development either as a state farm under the Grenada Farms Corporation or to farmers willing to form a cooperative.

Deserving of special mention are the achievements of the Revolution in public health and education, referred to in this volume in the speeches entitled 'Health For All' and 'Education is a Must'. But perhaps the greatest achievement of the Revolution was the extent to which, for the first time in the history of the English-speaking peoples of the Caribbean area, the masses of the people were encouraged, and given the opportunity, to participate in the affairs of state.

US Hostility

On October 25, 1983 the Government of the USA launched a massive invasion of Grenada, effectively destroying the Revolution and re-establishing imperialist control. Why was the mightiest imperialist power in the world so concerned about the Grenada Revolution? Needless to say, the PRG's working class orientation and the leading role it assigned to the public sector in economic development would not have endeared it to the capitalists and their political representatives in the American bastion of private enterprise. But, given the insignificant size of Grenada and the negligible level of US capital investment in and trade with the islands, the US government could have lived with that. What the American imperialists could not abide was revolutionary Grenada's defiantly independent external relations policy.

To avoid American displeasure developing countries in general and Caribbean and Latin American countries in particular are required to tailor their conduct in international affairs to the requirements of Washington. At his first meeting with the revolutionary leaders the US representative informed them that his government would disapprove of relations being established with Cuba and threatened that Grenada's tourist trade would suffer if this occurred. There is an account of this encounter in this volume in the speech entitled 'Nobody's Backyard'.

The Reagan administration in particular sees the national security of the USA in terms of its capacity to control the policies of other governments. The PRG's determination to pursue the best interests of Grenada regardless of US disapproval was perceived as undermining this concept. Grenada was the living proof to other small states (and few states could be smaller than Grenada) that, by establishing good relations with the socialist and other self-respecting non-aligned countries, reliable markets and alternative sources of capital goods could be found which would considerably assist economic development. Even the World Bank had to admit that, while the economies of other countries in the region were stagnant or declining, Grenada was achieving considerable economic growth. To Reagan's advisers this was a cause for alarm.

On March 10 and again on March 23, 1983 Reagan informed the American people, in speeches broadcast nationwide, that Grenada was a threat to US national security. The ridiculous nature of the suggestion that tiny Grenada could threaten the mighty USA was overcome by alleging that the PRG was an agent of the Soviet Union, on whose behalf Grenada and Cuba were falsely alleged to be building an air base and a naval base.

That the decision to invade Greanda had been taken by March 1983, if not before, is no longer in doubt if indeed it ever was. The operation had been well rehearsed during the NATO exercises in 1981 when forces were landed on Vieques Island, Puerto Rico. The scenario for that practice operation could not have been more explicit: to occupy an imaginary Caribbean island state called 'Amber and the Amberines' (read 'Grenada and the Grenadines'), rescue American citizens resident therein and replace its hostile government by one friendly to the USA.[1] All that remained to be decided was the timing of the invasion and possibly the creation of some incident which could be publicised as the immediate provocation. It is possible that Reagan and his advisers had intended to allow the Cuban and Grenadian workers to complete the surfacing of the runway for the new airport so as to save the US Government that expense. But the events which occurred in Grenada in October 1983 provided too good an excuse and opportunity to be missed.

From Reagan's point of view the killing of Maurice Bishop, the Grenadian Prime Minister, and several of his ministers, on October 19, 1983, was ideal. Whatever the level of CIA participation may have been (a matter not yet clarified) it appeared that Grenadian revolutionaries themselves had removed from the scene the national leader most capable of inspiring the Grenadian people to resist, and of arousing the maximum international opposition to a US invasion. Caribbean public opinion had been shocked and outraged to the point that obliging politicians in a number of Caribbean states felt confident that they could, without forfeiting much popular support in their own countries, give the US Government the 'fig-leaf' cover it required. The prime ministers of several other small islands in the Organisation of Eastern Caribbean States quickly joined Jamaican Prime Minister Seaga and Barbadian Prime Minister Adams, the principal collaborators with US imperialism in the Caribbean, in requesting the US Government to invade. Grenada's Governor General, who accepted US 'protection' aboard a warship, completed the conspiracy by signing a letter of invitation back-dated to the day before the invasion.

The Revolution: Destroyed from Within?

There were, in fact, no substantial differences of opinion within the NJM as to the policies to be pursued by the PRG. Suggestions in the media to the effect that there was within the party an ultra-left group favouring some kind of instant socialism, or that some were opposed to the establishment or maintenance of normal relations with other states (including the USA), or that there were those who were opposed to the formal institutionalisation of the Revolution and the holding of elections under a new constitution are entirely unfounded. To understand what happened within the revolutionary ranks in October 1983, we must understand the nature of the party organisation and the context in which it was operating, and examine the party's records.

A characteristic feature of party organisations based on the Leninist model is their 'democratic centralism', a concept which, in the context of the events which occurred in Grenada, deserves discussion. The democratic aspect of this concept is that, at all levels of the party, decisions should be taken after full discussion in which all the participants enjoy equality of status and everyone agrees to be bound by majority decisions. The centralism of the concept implies that the lower organisms of the party are bound by decisions arrived at by the higher organisms.

The highest organism is a meeting which represents the entire membership. In most countries this would be a meeting of elected representatives of the local party organisations, but in a very small country, such as Grenada, the entire membership attended. In between sessions of the highest organism, the governing body of the party is its Central Committee. The Central Committee does much of its work through its sub-committees. The principal sub-committees of the NJM were the Political Bureau, which was responsible for policy, and the Organising Committee.

This structure, designed to ensure equality of status in the decision making processes to all who have been admitted to membership, does not however detract from the degree of influence exercised by leading members of the party. Nor does it preclude the party from projecting the personality of an individual leader, should it decide to do so. Most political parties, whether or not structured on the Leninist model, have considered it advisable, in response to the expectations of the public, to project the personality of a party leader. In this respect the situation in Grenada was not exceptional and it was to be expected that the NJM would follow the usual practice.

There is another concept of a Leninist vanguard party which requires explanation. This is the concept that the party is the party of the working class. What does this mean in practice? A working-class party is a party consisting of persons who recognise that in the modern world it is of all classes the working class which is the instrument most capable of effecting social change. Only the working class is capable of achieving the revolutionary transformation of a capitalist economy into a socialist economy. This concept is elastic enough to admit the possibility that individuals whose social origins are outside the working class are, nevertheless, eligible for membership of the working-class party, provided that they have recognised the role of the working class and pledged themselves to the task of organising the workers to fulfil that role. History provides us with many examples of persons of middle-class origin who, with more or less consistency, have become genuine leaders of the working class.

In the context of Grenada it is not difficult to see that the NJM, as a working-class party in a society in which small farmers and petty traders outnumbered the wage earners, was in a vulnerable situation. If it failed to maintain its unity and exemplary qualities of revolutionary leadership, there was always a danger that it would lose its position of leadership of the Revolution. The whole course of the revolutionary development would then be changed.

In Maurice Bishop the NJM had a party leader who also admirably filled the role of a national leader. By any standards he was a remarkable man. A lawyer by profession from a comfortable middle-class background, his sympathies were nevertheless with the underprivileged masses. The initial emotional stimulus which he had received from the Black Power movement of the 1960s had ripened and matured during the 1970s on a more secure intellectual basis as he familiarised himself with Marxist-Leninist theory. Sentiment, theory and practice had combined to mould him into a dedicated revolutionary. He possessed to an extraordinary degree the ability to articulate clearly the objectives of the Revolution and to inspire support for it internally and regionally. His analytical mind and capacity for simple explanation helped the people to understand and share his convictions. His personality was magnetic.

Sometimes Bishop found it difficult to make decisions. I experienced this on occasion when I needed instructions in the performance of my responsibilities. He described his style of leadership of the party as being 'by consensus'.* It was his practice to engage in the widest possible informal consultations with his comrades before making up his mind. There is, of course, much to be said for this method; it is always better to proceed by agreement, resolving differences which are not fundamental by compromise. But this works best as a prelude or supplement to discussion within the formal committee structure, not as an alternative to it as appears all too often to have been the case in the NJM.† Also, when an urgent or early decision is required, there comes a point when the attempt to arrive at a consensus must be abandoned.‡ Good chairmanship involves knowing when to terminate discussion and resolve outstanding differences by majority vote.

---

* Minutes of the NJM Central Committee, September 14-16, 1983

† That the practice of making decisions informally outside the appropriate party committees had developed was acknowledged by Bishop at a Central Committee meeting held on August 26, 1983, the Minutes of which record him as saying:
'There is reasonable basis to share the concern that many key decisions of the party, if not the majority, have been made informally outside of higher organs'.

‡ The vital decision to attempt the seizure of power at 4 am on March 13, 1979, was taken on a majority vote. The four members entrusted with deciding whether or not the insurrection should be launched (Bishop, Bernard Coard, Hudson Austin and another) being equally divided, a fifth member (George Louison) was added to their number. Voting with Coard and Austin, Louison resolved the deadlock in favour of launching the attack.

To place the events of 1983 in context it is necessary to appreciate that whilst revolutionary Grenada was achieving reasonable economic progress, popular expectations were nevertheless running somewhat ahead of what was being achieved. Despite the spectacular growth of the economy and the reduction of unemployment from allegedly 49% of the adult population in 1979 to 14% at the end of 1982, the latter figure is still indicative of the fact that many people were without work. Also, despite improvements in wages and social services, the great majority were still enduring a very low standard of living. Indeed, the NJM leaders themselves acknowledged that they were to blame for not emphasising sufficiently what a long slow climb the ascent out of poverty would be and the fact that, while the foundations for future prosperity were being laid, a low standard of living would have to be endured for a long time to come.

It is also important to appreciate that, inevitably, in such a small and underdeveloped society, the level of efficiency was appallingly low. Thus, the best laid schemes for improvement could easily fail to realise anticipated results. The fact that the party is composed of the most dedicated revolutionaries who are willing to devote themselves to the service of the community and to act in unity, is not in itself a guarantee of success. Its capacity to lead and inspire the masses will be seriously impaired if it fails to operate efficiently. Such a party is obliged to set itself and its members realisable tasks and keep a constant check on the fulfilment of those tasks. It must ensure that its members do not attempt to do all that needs to be done by themselves. They must constantly encourage the masses to participate in improving their work, their work-places, their residential districts and the economy of the country. The success of such a party ultimately depends upon the extent to which it can inspire the people to take their future into their own hands.

There were three categories of membership of the NJM: full members, candidates and applicants. Full membersip was achieved only after a member had served in and progressed through the lower categories, studying to improve his or her understanding of the laws of social change while carrying out assigned tasks in the service of the people. The applicant who accepted the programme, policy and principles of the party and demonstrated his or her ability to study conscientiously, perform assignments efficiently and make personal sacrifices of time and energy, could expect promotion to the higher categories of party membership. With such high standards to be maintained, the membership of such a vanguard party is inevitably small. The total membership of the NJM was in fact under 500, of whom about 65 had achieved the qualification of full membership.

However, although the actual membership of a vanguard party of this type is small, this does not mean that it is undemocratic. Indeed, if it is observing Leninist principles correctly it should be more democratic than many very much larger parties which require their members to do no more than sign an application form. Parties of the latter type are, for the most part, run by a handful of leaders, the rank and file members exerting little or no influence on party decisions and being little more than followers in a game of 'follow my leader'. In a vanguard party which practises Leninist principles, active participation in the making and execution of decisions is a requirement of membership.

In or about September 1982 the problem of how to maintain the internal efficiency of the party led to an unexpected development. Bernard Coard resigned as a member of the Central Committee of the NJM and of its sub-committees — the Political Bureau and the Organising Committee. As his resignation had to do with his dissatisfaction with the internal workings of the party, the Central Committee met from October 12–15, 1982, to look into the whole matter. The Minutes of this meeting are very interesting. They show that the party had held several meetings over the past year to try and improve its efficiency, but little or no improvement had in fact been achieved.

Among Coard's reasons for resigning was a complaint about the slackness of the Central Committee and the failure of members to speak out frankly when things went wrong. He had always been outspoken on such occasions while other members had remained silent. As a result he had been suspected of seeking to discredit the leadership and been accused of seeking power. As he was not prepared to have personality clashes with the Chairman (Bishop), he had decided to resign. This, he had argued, would also have the effect of forcing members to make their own criticisms when they thought something was wrong, as he would no longer be there to voice their criticisms for them. He offered the rationalisation that this would help them to develop.

Having decided to accept Coard's resignation, the Central Committee went on to discuss ways and means of improving their efficiency. They collectively assessed their respective individual performances and as a result, decided to remove one veteran member from the Political Bureau and Central Committee because of his 'lack of political work, extremely bad attitude to study and deep seated individualism and petty bourgeois opportunist attitude to criticism'. But the Committee also decided to conceal from the other members of the party the fact that Coard had resigned and the reason why the veteran member had been removed — a concealment which was to cause a storm of resentment when it leaked out nine months later. Throughout this period Coard co-operated in not disclosing the fact that he had resigned and continued to discharge his state functions as if nothing had happened.[2] It was, indeed, remarkable that the secret was so well kept for so long. Working closely on numerous occasions with both Bishop and Coard, I did not know that Coard was not still in the party leadership, nor were the leading members of any of the fraternal parties in other countries aware of this development.

Over the following nine months the continuing deficiencies in the work of the leading organs of the NJM began to have their effect on the morale of the party members and affected the quality of the party's work among the masses. This was clearly recognised by all members of the Central Committee and can be perhaps best summed up by reproducing from the Minutes of meetings of the Central Committee of the NJM some of the conclusions stated by Bishop.

At the CC meeting on 26th August, 1983 Bishop is recorded as saying that he was 'in agreement . . . that we are faced with the threat of disintegration' and 'agrees also with the analysis that comrades of the party are afraid to raise criticisms.' He felt that the Central Committee members 'should reflect on the individual strengths and weaknesses of all CC members' and 'should also think about the specific responsibilities of CC comrades both at the party and state levels — this should be in writing'.*

At the meeting of the Central Committee held in the middle of the following month Bishop spoke even more frankly about the inefficiency and ineffective leadership given to the masses by the party. Though the Minute-taker's command of the English language on this occasion leaves something to be desired, the meaning is clear. He records Bishop as concurring with the view expressed by other speakers that 'the main problems lies in the Central Committee', and saying:

> The lack of proper application of strategy and tactics has led to our party paying no significant attention to the views of the party and the masses; there is clearly no channels for communications which has led to a breakdown of collective leadership . . . Decisions were taken outside of the CC, we have not set up systems for implementation and verification . . . The CC has made a number of mistakes over the past 18 months because of weak links with the masses we became bureaucratic and too formalistic in our approach. Visits to work places have disappeared, increasing non attendance at zonal councils and parish meetings, visit to communities to meet the people at an informal level, decrease in the number of discussion and meetings with people in all areas of work, failure to participate in public activities, village meetings have disappeared. We have not paid sufficient regard to the material base in the country. Changes in the economy, changes in social wages and the predominant Pb [petty bourgeois] character of the masses and society as a whole. Our propaganda positions have consistently fed economism [a term used in Marxist literature to describe being concerned entirely with securing material improvements within the existing system]. We have failed to point out to the masses that this period requires a number of sacrifices and if we are not prepared to build the economy through hard work we will not make it. We have to take the blame for the over economic expectations of the people . . .
> (Minutes of the NJM Central Committee, September 14-16, 1983)

The Minutes show that Bishop went on to refer to the mood among the farmers and agricultural workers as 'very low'. Summarising the state of affairs, after further discussion, Bishop is recorded as drawing the following conclusions:

* Minutes of NJM Central Committee, August 26th, 1983

1. There is a state of deep crisis in the party and revolution.
2. The main reason for these weaknesses is the functioning of the CC.
3. The crisis has also become a major contributing factor to the crisis in the country and the revolution and the low mood of the masses.
4. The crisis has also been compounded by the weakness in the material base, electrical block cuts, bad roads, retrenchments and jobs as an issue.

However, although in agreement with other members of the Central Committee concerning the low state of morale in the party and among the masses, and willing to concede that the main reason for these weaknesses was the inefficient functioning of and poor leadership given by the Central Committee itself, Bishop was uneasy at this meeting when he heard the solution proposed by a member of the Committee, a solution which a substantial majority of the Committee favoured.

This proposal, put forward by Liam James, was premised on a criticism of the quality of the leadership which Maurice Bishop himself was providing as sole leader of the Party and Chairman of the Central Committee, and its two main sub-committees: the Political Bureau and the Organising Committee. James is recorded as saying:

> The most fundamental problem is the quality of leadership of the Central Committee and the party provided by Cde. Maurice Bishop. In his view the Cde has great strength, his ability to inspire and develop cdes, his ability to raise the regional and international respect for the party and the revolution; he has the charisma to build the confidence of the people both in and out of the country and to put forward clearly the positions of the party. Today these strengths alone cannot put the party any further in this period. The qualities he lacks is what is needed to push the revolution forward at this time.

James went on to list the qualities he felt that Bishop lacked:

1. A Leninist level of organisation and discipline;
2. Great depth in ideological clarity;
3. Brilliance in strategy and tactics.

The discussion sparked off by these criticisms seems to have come as quite a surprise to Maurice Bishop. No one had hitherto criticised him personally, except Bernard Coard, and Coard was no longer on the Committee. Following the lead given by James, no less than 9 others of the 13 members present [there were 17 Central Committee members in September 1983] voiced similar criticisms. Basically, what they were saying amounted to this: the comrade leader is an outstandingly good mobiliser, inspirer and articulator but he is a poor organiser. Unison Whiteman, the Minister of Foreign Affairs (who had himself been criticised at the meeting in October 1982) is recorded as putting it in this way:

> . . . the weaknesses mention[ed] of the Cde. leader are correct. Since October there have been some improvements in scheduling and study but these improvements are not fundamental enough. He said that the Cde. Leader had not [given] enough time to the fundamental but we have to be careful that we don't shift too much blame from the CC collectively. We need to have a commitment on the CC to new norms, prioritisation, greater reflection, better style of work. We have to build up Comrades, e.g. Cde. Leader, we have to assist [insist?] on higher standards from him which he is capable of.

Bishop's reaction to these criticisms, as recorded in the Minutes, is interesting:

> Cde. Leader thanked the Cdes. for their frankness in their criticisms. He said that Cdes. in the past have given serious thought to the question of leadership and failed to raise it for diplomatic reasons which was not good. He is dissatisfied over the fact that CC Cdes. have not raised these points before with him frankly, though a couple of non CC Cdes. have done it. He picked up an overwhelming sentiment that the qualities required are not possessed by him. He agreed that the points are correct, especially correct application of strategy and tactics which cannot be achieved except the other qualities are fulfil[led]. He had found difficulties in finding a relevant material to study the question of the functioning of the PB [Political Bureau] and CC which reflects a weakness, he don't think that he had given adequate leadership to bodies. He had several problems over the years especially the style that entails consensus, and unity at all costs which can result in blunting class struggle. He had tried to keep a certain kind of relationship with Cdes. even though it is not what it used to be before. He also questioned his approach as regards to collective leadership, he said that there is not enough participation and discussion. Too much decisions are taken by smaller and smaller organs which affect collective leadership. On the question of crisis and problems it is correct as the maximum leader to take the full responsibilities. He needs time to think of his own role and to give a more precise response to the problem addressed . . .

After a break for lunch Bishop put forward some ideas as to how the problems could be overcome:

> To develop and maintain links with the masses the leadership must personally get on the ground among the people, step up participation in zonal and parish councils, visit schools, monitor and push production. The role of the CC must be worked out in this regard. Develop mechanism for accountability, and to review constant feedback from

the membership and to ensure channels of communication with them. The CC must do a constant evaluation of the progress by members, receive reports from the OC [Organising Committee] on the re-rationalisation of the work, prioritise the work of Cdes. on the CC and set targets to be achieved on a weekly monthly and yearly basis.

As the debate proceeded, however, it became clear that what James had in mind was a far more fundamental solution to the problems created by the leader's generally acknowledged weaknesses. James' proposal went further than simply helping Bishop to overcome these weaknesses. What he proposed was joint leadership of the party:

> Cde. James . . . proposed a modle [model] of joint leadership, marrying the strengths of Cdes. Bishop and Coard. He went on to define the responsibilities of the two cdes.
>
> *Cde. Maurice Bishop*
> (i) Direct work among the masses, focus on production and propaganda;
> (ii) Particular attention to the organs of popular democracy, working class, youth masses, visits to urban and rural work places;
> (iii) Militia mobilisation;
> (iv) Regional and International Work.
>
> *Cde. Bernard Coard*
> (i) Party organisation work;
>   Chairman of the OC [Organising Committee];
> (ii) Party organisational development and formation of cdes.;
> (iii) Strategy and tactics.
>
> The CC must discuss and ratify all proposals and decisions sought by the Cdes. CC meetings must be monthly, chaired by Cde. Maurice Bishop. PB [Political Bureau] weekly chaired by Cde. Bernard Coard. The both Cdes. will write quarterly reports to the CC for review. The membership must be told of this decision.

Later in the debate James made it clear that his proposal was confined to the internal working of the Party and did not involve alteration in the state functions of the comrades: 'Cde. Bishop will be Prime Minister and Commander in Chief, he will sign all documents of the CC'. He made the further point that he was not proposing that Coard's authority in the areas of strategy and tactics should be unlimited:

> this does not mean that he will decide strategy and tactics all by himself. However, he will chair all commissions to determine strategy and tactics. The CC will discuss and ratify all proposals brought forward . . .

This proposal for joint leadership of the party was a novel one. Everyone recognised that Coard was the most efficient and organised member of the party and welcomed the idea that he should be required to return to the Central Committee and its principal sub-committees. But the suggestion of joint leadership instead of sole leadership did not have unanimous approval at this meeting of the Central Committee. George Louison, the Minister of Agriculture, heatedly opposed it. Whiteman had reservations. So too, obviously, did Bishop. It did, however, have the approval of a substantial majority of those present. Bishop's cautious reactions indicate fears on his part that the comrades had lost confidence in him. He acknowledged that:

> The party must utilise all strengths and talents of Cdes. in the party . . . He has never had any problem with sharing power, or even a bad attitude to criticisms. He had worked very well with Cde. Bernard over the years from school days, they share a lot of policy decisions, they both wrote the manifesto [of the NJM proclaimed in 1973 and published in 1974], the peoples congress enditement [indictment] of Gairy.* He referred to 1977 when Cde. Bernard was accused for aggressiveness and wanting to grab power,† he had defended him. His position is that he or [neither he nor?] anybody has the right to be leader for life, he favours cooperation over competition. He feels that Bernard can come back to the PB because of his skills and intelligence. Cde. James' breakdown of responsibility is very useful, however his concerns is the operationalisation of strategy and tactics. His own idea of his role falls into what Cde. James had outlined. He feels that school visits should have been included under his responsibilities.

Bishop then stated some of his reservations. He said 'He would like to know what is Cde. Bernard's view of the situation and response', and posed the question 'If he do not agree what will be the views of the CC?' He also needed 'to get some answers on the operationalisation' of joint leadership, and he wanted to know 'how we will articulate this to the party and the masses.' He said: 'His personal concerns are; image of leadership, power struggle, imminent collapse of the revolution.'

Bishop went on to say: 'The formulation of Cdes. criticisms have indicated a clear note of no confidence' and that 'he cannot inspire the masses when he have to look over his back or feel that he does not have the full confidence of his comrades.'

This last reaction caused considerable disquiet in the Committee. One member expressed this in the following way:

> Cdes. were very frank, they criticised themselves for not being brave

---

* In 1973 a public 'trial' of Gairy for his many abuses of power was organised by the NJM.

† When Coard, in 1977, successfully proposed the establishment in the NJM of the 'Organising Committee' some persons had accused Coard and others, including George Louison, of wanting to establish a rival power base.

enough to do so before. This frankness is critical for the development of an ML [Marxist-Leninist] party. It will be sad if the meeting concluded that this was a vote of no confidence. This was done in the interest of the party and revolution, what we are solving here is a problem that we experienced for years.

Another member said: 'the meeting was one of unprecedented frankness and boldness by all Cdes., it was done through the spirit of great love for the revolution and Cde. Leader.'

There is, however, no avoiding the conclusion, after studying the Minutes, that Bishop's initial reaction to the proposal for joint leadership was one of resentment and suspicion. But that was not how the Committee saw things. When the vote was finally taken as to whether or not to adopt the joint leadership proposal, nine members voted in favour, one (Louison) opposed and three abstained. Those abstaining were Bishop and Whiteman and also Hudson Austin, General of the Army, who gave the fact that he had come in late and missed the greater part of the discussion as his reason for abstaining.

Following the vote, which was taken on September 16, one of the members proposed that they take a break and 'ask Cde. Coard to come to the meeting for the decision to be put to him'. Bishop opposed this, as the Minutes record, 'because of the fact that he has to make a personal reflection on the issue.' He proposed that the CC meet with Cde. Coard in his absence. He suggested that the CC meet Cde. Bernard tomorrow while he will be leaving for St Kitts' [independence celebrations]. In answer to the argument that it was important for both of them to be present, Bishop said that 'based on his personal position to sit down with Coard for productive discussion, it will have no usefulness, it will be counter-productive.' He said it was critical for him to know 'Bernard's position' (how Bernard felt about the proposal). 'This will even help him in his own reflection'. The Minutes record that 'Sister Phyllis Coard* then questioned what will the CC say to Cde. Bernard in the absence of Cde. Bishop'. This, however, was not addressed.

The Committee adjourned until the following day, as Bishop had suggested. to ascertain Coard's response to the decision. In the light of persistent allegations in the media and elsewhere that there was a struggle by a group led by Coard to obtain control of the party, Coard's reactions to the proposal are of the utmost interest. Informed of the decision of the previous day, the Minutes record that Bernard Coard raised four points:

1. He would like to see the minutes of the meeting.
2. The position of those opposed or abstain and what are the reasons.
3. Were other options examine[d], what were these options and why were they rejected.

---

* Bernard Coard's wife who in her own right was a member of the Central Committee.

4. Why was not this meeting schedule[d] so that Cde. Bishop could be present.

Having heard what the members present had to say about the proceedings of the past three days, the Minutes record that Coard:

> reminded Cdes. of his reasons for resigning last year . . . He said that he was tired and sick of being the only hatchet man and critique [critic]. The failure of CC comrades was to speak up freely, as a result he concluded that he was the main fetter to development of the CC because everyone was depending on him for everything, especially in the area of the economy . . . He said he had detected a feeling of wanting him to undermine the Comrade Leader's position. He would not like to return to the CC and PB, any tasks given to him he will do it. He even used the struggle of the formation of the OC [Organising Committee]. Cdes. Louison, Strachan and himself was accused for organising another seat of power in the party . . . He was seriously affected by the accusation of wanting to undermine the leadership so he resigned from the OC.

Though Coard was frankly critical of Bishop's shortcomings, he expressed his reluctance to return to the leadership. This is what he is recorded as saying:

> The Cde. Leader found himself vacillating between the ML [Marxist-Leninist] trend and the petit bourgeois trend on the party. This worsened as the CC was not aware what was going on and the situation was slipping and because Comrades were not thinking, therefore the severe drift and disintegration was not seen . . . [If] he was an ordinary member he would have manners* the Cde. leader years ago. Because of his position as deputy leader and the extent that Cdes. will think that he is fighting for leadership, if he comes back and Cde. Bishop falter he would be afraid to criticise him and will resign again. For it to be left for him to manners the leader, he is not prepared to deal with this. He admit that this is on his part a Pb [petty-bourgeois] conduct.
>
> However, he had tried to give the party his best support in strategy and tactics, he would prefer to operate as in the past year. He also is prepared to take all responsibilities the CC offers him, but off the CC. He cannot take emotional conflict situation that saps his energies. He wants this to be clearly put to the party.

* 'Manners', used as a verb in this way, is an expression, originally popularised in Jamaica, meaning to discipline someone — to put them under manners.

The Central Committee, however, showed no disposition to go back on its decision of the previous day. On September 25, 1983 a meeting of the full members of the NJM was convened to consider the Central Committee's decision. The meeting got off to a bad start because Bishop, who said he had not completed his reflections, was reluctant to attend. Coard, too, expressed his own reluctance to be present if Bishop was not there. Eventually, however, the members having required the attendance of both, they both arrived and the meeting proceeded.

At this meeting of full members on September 25 the proposal for joint leadership, which had been so exhaustively discussed by the Central Committee, was debated all over again. Bishop participated in the discussion but Coard refrained from speaking until after the matter had been amicably resolved. At the end of 15 hours of debate a resolution approving the proposal for joint leadership was unanimously adopted. Only two members of the Central Committee had been absent (out of the country): George Louison who had voted against it and another member who had voted in favour. The Minutes record an emotional ending to this meeting:

> The members then called on Cdes. Coard and Bishop to speak.
>
> Cde. Bernard Coard said that today is indeed a historic day in the life of the party (applause). He said that the CC meetings he attended from Monday 19th September surprised him because unlike the past every CC member was putting forward well thought-out, clear and reasoned positions on the way forward for building the party and transforming it into a genuine Marxist-Leninist party. He said that in the past most CC members would be silent in CC meetings and seem not to have ideas on how the party and revolution is to be built. However, now he witness a qualitative difference . . . He said that in his opinion the members have spoken from both their heads and their hearts. Their words have been sincere and it shows a genuine commitment by the members to struggle for socialism and lay the basis for the eventual building of communism. He repeated that a qualitative lift has taken place in the CC as well as among the membership, thus he is deeply confident in the future of building socialism and communism (applause). He pledged to the party that he would put every ounce of effort in building the process and that he knows that Cde. Bishop would do the same. He said he had known and work together with Cde. Bishop and that they both owe it to the party, revolution and the Grenadian working people to do all that is possible to build the revolution (applause).
>
> Cde. Bishop stands and embraces Cde. Coard. Cde. Bishop said that it was correct for him to come to the GM and stay and hear the views of the party membersip. He said that reflecting in isolation would not have been correct for him since he would have seen things in a lopsided manner. He said that the entire GM had accepted the CC analysis and decision and this has satisfied his concern. He admitted to the GM that

his response to the CC criticism and decision was petit bourgeois. He said that the GM has rammed home that the criticism was correct and so too was the decision. He said, 'I sincerely accept the criticism and will fulfil the decision in practice'.

Cde. Bishop went on to say that his whole life is for the party and revolution and the difficulty he had was because so many things were going through his mind. He said that he agreed with Cde. Moses Jeffrey that he had not shown confidence in the party. But all these things are now behind his back. He said that the party comrades are maturing and are capable of taking strong positions. He said that his desire now is to use the criticism positively and march along with the entire party to build a Marxist-Leninist Party that can lead the people to socialism and communism. He pledged to the party that he would do everything to erode his petit bourgeois traits. He said that he never had difficulties in working with Cde. Coard and joint leadership would help push the party and revolution forward (applause).

At the end of Cde. Bishop's speech the entire GM broke into singing the Internationale and members filed past to embrace Cdes. Bishop and Coard.

On the following day Bishop left for Hungary and Czechoslovakia. He left behind him a happy band of party members, confident that they were well on their way to solving every difficulty, reviving morale and regaining the entire confidence of the masses.

However, not many days were to pass before the members of the Central Committee still in Grenada began to suspect that all was not well.

Whilst he was out of Grenada Bishop had had second thoughts about accepting joint leadership and had decided to reopen the matter. What exactly it was that brought about this change of heart may never be known. All that can be said with certainty is that before his return home from Czechoslovakia, via Cuba, on October 8, and for whatever reason, Bishop had changed his mind and was no longer prepared to accept the new form of party leadership. This may have been formally announced to the Central Committee at its meeting on October 12. No Minutes of that meeting (if indeed Minutes were prepared) have as yet been found, but the Minute-taker's copious hand-written notes of what took place on the following day at a meeting of all party members (full, candidate and applicant) are available. These notes disclose an atmosphere of widespread distrust and hostility towards Bishop, very different to the atmosphere of concern and comradely criticism apparent at the meetings of September 14-17 and September 25. What had happened to poison the atmosphere?

My own analysis of these events suggests that, having ascertained the unwillingness of the Central Committee to reopen the matter, Bishop had decided to employ a strategy somewhat similar to what the late Chinese leader Mao Tse-tung decided to do when he lost control of the Central Committee of the Chinese Communist Party — go directly to the masses over their heads and rally them to his support.* But what appears to have enraged the membership of the party was the disclosure of the bizarre tactics Bishop had decided to employ. This plan, which had begun to be put into effect on October 12, was disclosed by one of Bishop's two personal security guards upon whom he had relied in part to put it in motion.

This security guard had given a statement to his superiors to the effect that Bishop had informed him that Bernard and Phyllis Coard were plotting to kill him (Bishop). Bishop, he said, had given instructions for a list to be drawn up of persons to be informed of this plot and had personally approved the list. This, the security guard now repeated orally on October 13, in Bishop's presence, to all the members of the party.

On October 12 word was in circulation concerning the alleged plot. One immediate effect had been that a group of persons, led by an insurance agent from the St Paul's district where Bishop's mother lived, collected firearms at the local Militia headquarters and set off to defend the Prime Minister. Having been alerted by the security guard, the security forces intercepted them. The other security guard was also taken into custody and interrogated.

Whatever the merits or demerits of the decision to seek a reopening of the decision of September 25, the spreading of such a rumour was a particularly desperate and dangerous course which could have endangered the life of the man chosen by the party members to be their joint leader. At the meeting of party members on the night of October 13 Bishop denied responsibility for the rumour, speaking at length in his own defence. But having heard the evidence given to the meeting by the security guard, the overwhelming majority of the members believed that Bishop was guilty. On that same night (not on October 12 as has been suggested by some persons) Bishop was placed under house arrest. Though the overwhelming majority of those present had applauded demands that Bishop be expelled from the party, a final decision on the matter was left to the Central Committee.

Over the next few days the Central Committee, no doubt conscious of an upsurge of mass support for Bishop, endeavoured to work out a compromise with him whereby he would have resumed the exercise of his state functions and remained a member of the party. Four members of the Committee met with him directly and at their request a trade union leader from Trinidad came to Grenada to act as a conciliator. But up to the time of his release by a crowd led by Whiteman and others, on the morning of October 19, Bishop had not given his answer to the proposals put to him, proposals which he

* In 1966 Mao Tse-tung, the revered leader of the Chinese Party, launched the so-called 'cultural revolution'. The youth masses were encouraged to form 'red guards' which, with Army support in many areas, physically removed from office and humiliated persons in authority. In this way the authority of the Central Committee of the party was destroyed and for a time Mao was able to exercise personal control.

had told the Trinidad intermediary he would 'sleep on'.*

Bishop's release from house arrest set in motion events which were to lead to his being killed at the Army headquarters at Fort Rupert, which he had taken over with the assistance of the crowd which had freed him. To what extent the American Central Intelligence Agency participated in the events leading up to the killing of Bishop is not yet clear. That 'agents provocateurs' were at work in Grenada is evident from the sudden and well organised appearance among the crowd of anti-communist placards. Some read: 'C is for Coard, Cuba, Communism'. The involvement of the CIA in the removal of political leaders disliked by the US Government is too well established for the probability that its agents had a hand in the events leading to Bishop's death to be discounted, but at what level it is difficult to determine. It is alleged that the shots which killed Bishop, and others who died with him, were fired by soldiers of the People's Revolutionary Army.

The circumstances in which Bishop died at Fort Rupert occasioned a flood of rumours and allegations of responsibility. These circumstances will no doubt be the subject of evidence during the course of the trial of criminal charges which have been laid against a number of members of the PRA and the Central Committee of the NJM who are being held in detention. It would, therefore, be quite improper to add to the speculation. The trials may not, however, be conclusive in establishing the facts. In a country still dominated by the presence of foreign armed forces, where the accused persons have been tortured to extract 'confessions', it seems unlikely that the persons charged will receive a fair trial.

But wherever the responsibility may lie for Bishop's death, the fact remains that the revolutionary leaders themselves set the stage for the imperialist intervention in Grenada by their failure to find an acceptable solution to the problem of what form the direction and leadership of the party should take. When Bishop changed his mind about accepting the party's decision on joint leadership, he was violating a fundamental principle of the NJM – democratic centralism. This principle committed every party member to accept majority decisions, whether or not he or she agreed with them. The disappointment and resentment of party members is, therefore, understandable. But the Marxist approach requires that all the circumstances of a given situation be taken into account.

One aspect of the situation, which the Central Committee does not appear to have taken sufficiently into account, is that such was Bishop's popularity

---

* Many persons have asked why, since I had worked closely with and had the confidence of both Bishop and Coard, I was not asked to assist in the process of conciliation. The only explanation that I can think of is that my position must have been compromised by the fact that my name appeared on the list, approved by Bishop, of persons who were to be informed of the alleged plot to kill him. This may have created the suspicion that I was conspiring with Bishop to overturn the decision of the party.

and personal influence that if he would not abide by the party's decision and was determined to take the matter to the masses, the masses would support him rather than the party. Given Bishop's determination not to implement the joint leadership decision, the prudent course for the Central Committee to adopt, their disappointment and resentment notwithstanding, was to explore other options for improving the structure and quality of the leadership of the party until a compromise formula had been found which both Bishop and other members of the Central Committee could accept. There was no sensible alternative. Any other course was bound to bring the party into conflict with the masses.

Bishop's position in Grenada was pivotal. His popularity with both the workers and the masses of the peasantry and petty bourgeois elements generally, and his capacity to articulate the aims of the Revolution and inspire popular co-operation was one of the factors which ensured that the Revolution could survive and move forward under the leadership of the NJM. But without the guidance of a vanguard Marxist-Leninist party the leading role of the working class in the revolutionary process could not have been maintained. These two complementary elements were essential for ensuring that petty bourgeois influences did not become predominant and divert the Revolution away from the ultimate objective of establishing a socialist society.

An aspect of the Grenada situation to which insufficient consideration has been given is what would have happened if Bishop had succeeded in rousing the masses against the Central Committee and the party, and had established personal control. Without the support of the party he would have had to rely heavily on the support of petty bourgeois elements. Without a Marxist-Leninist party to guide and lead the Revolution what orientation would it have taken? However sincerely Bishop may have believed that the survival of the Revolution depended on his maintaining his position as sole top leader, would it not, without the guidance and direction of a Marxist-Leninist party, have lost its working-class socialist orientation? Did Bishop take this problem into account when he decided to defy and, if necessary, destroy the party? And did the other members of the Central Committee appreciate the danger that failure to reach agreement with Bishop would have the effect of putting the party in conflict with the masses and destroying its capacity to keep the Revolution on course? Whichever way we look at the matter, the conclusion is inescapable that the revolutionary leaders, from Bishop downwards, displayed deplorable immaturity in failing to resolve their disagreement and preserve the unity of the party. Had they done so, they could have united the overwhelming majority of Grenadians to defend their country and the Revolution against any imperialist attack.

We have already discussed the preparations which the Government of the US had been making for the invasion of Grenada. There was always the possibility that, if no other excuse was available, a 'Gulf of Tonking' type of incident would have been fabricated to justify an attack. President Reagan was obviously looking for an opportunity to win a victory somewhere after the succession of failures of US foreign policy from the Vietnam war onwards. As the forces were so unevenly matched, it would not have been possible for the people of Grenada to defeat the invaders. But had they faced a united people they would certainly have paid more dearly for their victory and the burning hatred of the people for the invaders would have made their occupation difficult.

Psychological Warfare Since the Invasion

A particularly odious aspect of the US invasion, which has so far received less attention than it deserves, is the presence and continuing work of the Psychological Warfare Department of the US Armed Forces. These brain-washers had established their headquarters at Marryshow House, a building of historical significance for the peoples of the English-speaking Caribbean area. Marryshow House is the former home of the late T.A. Marryshow, an outstanding Grenadian who has been described as the father of West Indian nationalism. For some years it has been in use as the headquarters in Grenada of the Extra-Mural Department of the University of the West Indies. The presence of these professional deceivers within its walls defiled the memory of a great West Indian patriot. The University did not succeed in getting them to leave until January 1984.

A principal task assigned to the Psychological Warfare unit is to distort the achievements and destroy the reputation of the Grenada Revolution and persuade the people that they have been liberated from oppression. Their aim is to revive the feelings of inferiority which the Revolution had taught the people to overcome and to prepare them mentally for a future of subservience to US imperialism. Initially their plan was to destroy the reputations of all the revolutionary leaders. As Mark Krischik, a propaganda specialist from the US embassy in Buenos Aires, seconded to Grenada, informed all who would listen at the Seascape Inn in December 1983 'Bishop was as much of a God-damned communist as those God-damned communists in Richmond Hill prison, and our job is to make the Grenadians understand this'.[3] Later, when they discovered how deeply the love for Maurice Bishop was embedded in the hearts and minds of the people, they changed their tactics, concentrating their attacks on those NJM leaders who were still alive and imprisoned.

Forced to make concessions to Bishop's popularity, these brain-washers are now trying to make out that he was not a communist after all, but a misguided pragmatist who had allowed himself to be surrounded by communists. But as a precaution against the possibility that this deception may not succeed and that Bishop's ideas may become a rallying point for resistance to American domination, the US Government has refused to return Bishop's body to Grenada, alleging that the body they took away for positive identification cannot be identified as his.

These psychological warfare experts are hoping to create, in Grenada and elsewhere in the English-speaking Caribbean area, a state of mind which will lead people to conclude that the Grenada Revolution was a negative experience, or at least a mistake, which should never again be attempted. The discrediting of Marxist-Leninist ideas is their most important but not their only objective. They are also hoping to create a state of mental, and consequently physical, resignation to the domination of the region by imperialism.

The imperialists and their agents are aware that there would have been no revolution in Grenada had there been no disciplined Marxist-Leninist vanguard to organise and lead the insurrection and therefore guide and inspire the revolutionary developments. They are equally well aware that a renewal of the revolutionary struggle will not occur unless this vanguard, shattered by the invasion and the military occupation, is able to regroup and reorganise. That is why the destruction of the NJM and the adoption of measures to frustrate its revival have been given such high priority, and why most of the full members of the NJM are being held in prison. It also explains why every effort is being made to prevent those in prison from being adequately represented legally, with the expectation that the judicial process can be used to physically eliminate them or at least secure their permanent incarceration.

The Task Ahead

The task of reviving and reorganising the NJM as a Marxist-Leninist party will not be an easy one. There will be other difficulties in addition to those created by the military occupation and the incarceration of the majority of the full members. The first of these difficulties arises from the fact that during the four and a half years of the Revolution the NJM did not do sufficient political education among the masses, explaining the leading role of the working class in the anti-imperialist struggle and the need for a Marxist-Leninist vanguard party. Nor did they sufficiently widen the membership base of the party.[4] The second difficulty, increased by the first, is that the present atmosphere in Grenada favours the growth of opportunism.

Marx, Engels and Lenin often found it necessary to combat the emergence of opportunist tendencies within the working-class movement. Lenin defined opportunism as a sacrificing of the fundamental interests of the masses to the temporary interests of an insignificant minority of the workers and the interests of the petty bourgeois politicians. The fundamental interests of the masses in Grenada lie in the direction of a renewal of the struggle against imperialist domination and concretely against US occupation and influence.

The highest expression of opportunism is already evident in the promises now being made by a number of political aspirants that, if elected, they will offer the US Government whatever facilities it may require in the way of military bases. Politicians who would offer such facilities can easily be exposed as servants or would-be servants of imperialism and betrayers of their country's sovereignty. What is not so clearly understood is that politicians whose consciences would never permit them to consciously surrender their country's sovereignty, may nevertheless be tempted to pursue a less obviously opportunistic course. One such possible course would be a repudiation, either explicitly or by implication, of Marxism-Leninism and an attempt to replace the NJM by an old-style electoral party such as the people were accustomed to long before the Revolution.

The argument would not be over the question of whether or not elections should be contested. A Marxist-Leninist revolutionary party contests elections in the same way as a social-democratic non-revolutionary party, when the circumstances make this method of struggle appropriate. The NJM, as we have seen, contested an election in 1976. Similarly, members of such a party are always actively engaged in giving leadership in the day to day trade union struggles of the workers and other mass struggles. But a disciplined party based on Marxist-Leninist principles is able to evaluate the situation and know when the time is ripe to go over to alternative forms of struggle; when to lead the masses forward to the revolutionary seizure of power.

Arguments in favour of pursuing the opportunistic course of substituting a social democratic, purely electoral, type of party for the NJM and repudiating Marxism-Leninism, are that in this way the hostility of the US Government and the occupation forces might be avoided, and that such a party might escape the adverse effects of the current wave of anti-communist propaganda. Persons who found the high standards of discipline required for membership of the NJM irksome, or who never understood the need for a disciplined vanguard party, will find these arguments particularly attractive. When these supposed advantages are analysed, however, it soon becomes apparent that they are such as will accrue to politicians, not to the worker and peasant masses. Poverty and unemployment will continue to be the scourge of the masses until there is a revolutionary restructuring of society. The fundamental interests of the masses therefore lie in the speediest possible recovery and reorganisation of the NJM as a Marxist-Leninist revolutionary party.

Though the fight for progress in the English-speaking Caribbean area has suffered a reverse as a result of what happened in Grenada in and after October 1983, these events, tragic as they are, must be seen in perspective against the tremendous advances which have occurred in other countries. Revolutionary developments during the contemporary period in Ethiopia, Angola, Mozambique, Nicaragua and elsewhere, the steady consolidation of the revolutionary gains in Cuba, Vietnam, Laos, Kampuchea, Yemen, Afghanistan and Algeria, and the ever increasing strength and capacity of the USSR and the other longer established socialist societies, give a sufficient guarantee of the ultimate defeat of imperialism. Only a nuclear holocaust could rob mankind of a free prosperous and peaceful future.

As for the anti-communist propaganda, as important strategically in the arsenal of the imperialists as their conventional weapons, this can be overcome only by patient and consistent popular education. To endeavour to deal with this problem by climbing on to the anti-communist bandwagon, by repudiating Marxism-Leninism or by remaining silent, is to call one's integrity into question. To engage in such unprincipled conduct would be an insult to the memory of Maurice Bishop and a repudiation of the tremendous contribution he has made to the struggles of the Caribbean peoples. The life and work of Maurice Bishop, his human frailties notwithstanding, was guided and inspired by Marxism-Leninism.

The Bolsheviks of Russia did not furl their revolutionary banners and adopt a course of opportunism following the defeat of the 1905 Revolution. Fidel Castro and his comrades did not give up the revolutionary struggle in Cuba when their attacks on the Moncada and Bayamo barracks failed in 1953 and many lives were lost. There are many other examples of revolutionaries who have regrouped their forces and renewed the struggle, undeterred by temporary reverses and confident of final victory.

There are lessons to be learned from every revolutionary experience, whether or not it has ended in defeat. The Paris Commune of 1871, suppressed after the workers and their allies had held state power for less than three months, is a classic example. It was studied closely by Marx, whose writings on the subject enriched theoretical and historical studies of class struggles and the state. The Grenada Revolution, too, contains important lessons. If honestly and carefully recorded and analysed these will add to our understanding and improve our capacity to struggle more effectively against imperialism.

Maurice Bishop was, in many respects, a personification of the Grenada Revolution. His speeches, so much a part of the revolutionary developments, increase our understanding of its nature and accomplishments. His premature death in the fortieth year of his productive life is a tragic loss for Grenada, for the entire Caribbean area, for the Americas and for the world. But the memory and inspiration of his contributions to the anti-imperialist struggle will live for ever.

Richard Hart
April 1984

1. A final rehearsal, in which airborne troops subsequently used in the invasion were involved, took place at Ephrata municipal airport, Washington State, USA, during the week commencing September 23 1983. The object of this exercise was to practise capturing the airport and rescuing hostages on terrain very similar to Point Salines. *Cleveland Plain Dealer*, September 1983, cited in *Grenada, Whose Freedom?* Latin American Bureau, London, 1984, p. 79.
2. During the period he was out of the Party leadership, Coard continued to perform his state functions as Deputy Prime Minister and Minister of Planning, Finance & Trade. He also played a leading part in the Party's educational work. The same meeting of the Central Committee which accepted his resignation decided that he should conduct an eight-week crash course in Marxism for leading comrades (including Whiteman and Austin) whose grasp of theory was weak.
3. *Latin American Newsletter*'s Caribbean Regional Report, December 9 1983, no doubt referring to the same remark, says Krischik described Bishop as 'a Communist no better than the men in Richmond Hill prison'.
4. At a meeting of the Central Committee on September 30 1983, before word that Bishop had changed his mind had got back to Grenada, a proposal by Coard was adopted to endeavour to recruit to membership of the Party 500 women from the NWO, 3-400 youths from the NYO and 4-500 workers from the Party Support Groups. *Minutes NJM Central Committee*, September 30 1983.

Maurice Bishop Lives

Address by George Lamming at the Memorial Service for
Maurice Bishop and Colleagues at Trinity Cathedral, in
Trinidad, December 1983

It is the tragedy of a whole region which has brought us here.

The landscape of Grenada and its people are the immediate victims, the
arena and the symbol chosen for a unique experiment in murder. But all of
us are now the casualties of the American invasion. The United States has a
long and consistently brutal record of arbitrary invasions within this hemisphere. But this is unique, since we, in the English speaking Caribbean, may
have been the first to facilitate that intention to invade by actual invitation.

We can share the panic and grief which a small gang of native military
killers inflicted, and which forced the people of Grenada to respond in-
stinctively to the American presence as a promise of relief, and to welcome
what they genuinely felt to be relief. But time, and their gradual recovery
from mourning may yet reveal that what appeared to be rescue will later be
experienced as a new form of colonial and racist subjugation. And Grenada
will respond again, as she has done in the past, from the deepest resources
of her pride and self-esteem.

Those Caribbean leaders who now luxuriate in the applause of the American
aggressor will sooner or later become the targets of a different and more
devastating kind of scrutiny by the historians, the novelists, the poets and all
other intellectual and cultural workers from among their own people; men
and women for whom the name, Maurice Bishop, will blossom into one of
the most fertilising symbols of creative expression in the culture and politics
of this region. It is their judgement, not Mr Reagan's, which will be decisive.

It is to the credit of Trinidad and Tobago that its Prime Minister, Mr
George Chambers, has, throughout this tragic time, and in his quiet and
steadfast way, displayed a regional patriotism which can remain a model for
all who struggle for the political and cultural sovereignty of the Caribbean.
This gathering should have no reservation in recording their admiration and
their gratitude for the solitary battle he has fought on our behalf: the battle
to hold this broken region together, and to defend its sovereignty at all
costs.

It is my view that the late Dr Eric Williams would have taken exactly the
same principled stand. There is some evidence for this in his major address
to the People's National Movement on its 25th anniversary in 1981. He is
describing the character and the motives of those he calls 'marauding sharks',

1

and who ask to come to our rescue in times of peace. I quote:

> Five years tax holiday not enough. 'We offer you 10 years.' Still not
> enough. I will pull out of your country and go next door, unless you
> give me, that, this and the other. I need a guarantee of 99 years tax
> holiday. I need a guarantee as I got elsewhere on a strike-free holiday.
> I need a blanket clearance for all my expatriate personnel; all goods
> must be duty-free, no with-holding tax etcetera, etcetera . . .

This was Williams at his patriotic best. Today, as before, the soldier clears
the way for the entrepreneurial sharks.

A calendar date, be it in January or June, whatever the year, bears no
relation to the actual process of a people's history: the struggle to transform
their natural environment into a human world which their children will
inherit. Here in Trinidad you have been fighting that battle long before
1962. On sugar estates, in the Oilfields, among the most determined workers
in the public and domestic services of the land, this struggle has continued;
and 21 years after the formalities of Independence, it remains your continuing
assignment with destiny. And this is the point which enshrines the name,
Maurice Bishop.

The history of a people's culture is first and foremost the history of that
process of labour on which such a culture is built; and a history of degraded
labour will reflect itself in the distortions of a people's cultural formation.

This was a central theme of Bishop's struggle, and he required no text-
book, no sterile list of abstract principles, to recognise where his duty lay.
His head found a home in the hearts of his people at mass level; and he tried
to move forward from his concrete experience of their reality.

If the analyses of our social and political problems appear complex, the
truth of our reality is fairly simple. The poor remain neglected. The new rich
have learnt to be as vulgar, and destructive in their vulgarity, as this type has
always been in other cultures at similar stages of its arrested development.

Those who so eagerly prepare themselves to be what's called modern
consumers never reflect on the meaning of this word, consume. Its original
meaning is to destroy, to use up, to waste up, to exhaust; and this meaning
has survived centuries to become most relevant to that increasing herd of men
and women who no longer seek and use the things they need.

They consume and are, in turn, consumed by the barbarous appetites
which an aggressive advertising industry has elevated into a philosophy of
our times: 'To exist is to consume. I do not exist if I do not consume.'

A whole mode of production we call capitalist rests on that philosophy
and its survival depends on multiplying across the face of the globe vast
armies of working people who are seduced into the belief: 'to exist is to consume. I do not exist if I do not consume'.

Rodney and Bishop were the gifts of a generation that set out, from their
own small corners, to fight that philosophy.

But the simple things are always the most difficult to achieve. And we have failed, collectively, to make a decisive and fundamental break with that old colonial legacy which left us tenants of the very ground which the hands of our ancestors have humanised and made fruitful for hostile strangers; and which, out of habit, we call home.

A society is as free as its poorest citizens. This was a fundamental truth recognised and shared equally by Walter Rodney and Maurice Bishop. They were of the same generation, and had enjoyed, as you would say, similar privileges of education and social opportunity. In a region where these emblems of success were scarce and difficult to achieve, they could earn access to that minority kingdom which normally views the world of men and women from down below with habitual contempt.

It had always been the function of our institutions to create this division in the ranks of our society; and to ensure that the social function of the professional and technocratic classes would be to reinforce and stabilise this social division of labour and status.

But Rodney and Bishop gave the word, ambition, a new virtue, by making the central ambition of their lives a commitment to break, in a decisive way, with the tradition which had trained them to approve and supervise the intellectual enslavement of their own people. They broke away; and they became subversive traitors to that tradition which could so easily have bestowed on them the blessings of those who proudly identify themselves as affluent consumers.

It was this betrayal which would ultimately cost them their lives. They had learnt to respect the world of men and women from down below; they had learnt that their own freedom depended on the liberation of that world; and that their personal destinies had to be identified with the future of that world of men and women from down below.

They were, in this sense, among the rarest gifts their generation has so far offered to this region. And that is why they remain alive. Rodney lives. And Bishop lives. And Creft, and Whiteman and all the committed dead we remember today; they live.

In Guyana, Walter Rodney, a political activist and historian had sought to show that those Indians in that category of indentured labour had always waged heroic struggle against that condition (31 strikes in 1886 and 42 in 1888). This investment of labour and resistance had made them equal partners with their African brothers and sisters in a struggle to liberate a people and a region from the imperial encirclement of poverty, illiteracy, and self-contempt.

Rodney fought to help dismantle a tradition which, before and after Independence had used the device of race to obscure and sabotage the fundamental unity which marred the destinies of Indian and African workers through their common experience of labour. A democratic future for Guyana rested, above everything else, on the recognition of that historical fact, and the means whereby this could be absorbed and experienced as the most important truth of their daily lives, the characteristic feature of all their social relations.

3

Difference in cultural heritage is not an objective obstacle to such an achievement. Indeed, this cultural difference can only be accepted, respected and cherished after the artificial conflict of race had been abolished by that unifying force which derives from their common experience of labour. It was this possibility which alarmed Rodney's executioners.

I did not know Maurice Bishop intimately or over a very long period of time. But he had that very rare gift of making you feel that the history of your relationship went much further back than your first encounter.

In personal conversation, on formal occasions, at the public rally, he spoke directly, almost spontaneously; and he spoke of a particular vision which embraced the dead and gave immediate inspiration to the living, especially the youth of his country. It was a vision which was founded on the principle of work as a liberating force in man's life; and it reminded me always of a passage from the Cuban, Jose Marti, the real spiritual ancestor and patron saint of Fidel Castro:

There is only one magic wand at whose stroke all rocks yield springs of water; it is work.

Let every man learn to do some item of what the other needs. The curse of unemployment which Bishop and his colleagues had inherited really hurt; and he shared that pain publicly, by letting it be known what he could not do. In an address given in June 1982 he said:

> As an honest, democratic and revolutionary government, we cannot give unproductive jobs to our unemployed simply for the sake of giving them jobs and then watch them dig up holes in the road and fill them up again, and then declare that we have finished with unemployment. Nor do we have the capacity to or the desire to serve out a weekly dole or freeness to the unemployed.
>
> We can only honestly seek to solve unemployment by seeing it in the context of economic construction, of the drive for greater production . . . of the necessity to work harder and harder in order to build our country . . .

He had felt that since unemployment was a mass problem it required a mass solution; that the people themselves, the unemployed, had to be fully engaged in finding the remedies that would cure joblessness in the society once and for all. He was concerned here, not only with increase of productivity and increase in trade activity – the sole criteria of philistine economists; he believed that genuine human development had to do with the social organisation of production, the process in which those who were called upon to work were themselves the organising and directing agents of the work they discovered they had to do.

And he and his colleagues had reason to rejoice at the popular response to this message. They saw people from many villages take Sunday mornings off to clear the drains and culverts of accumulated sewerage. Grenada saw its sons and daughters repair roads and bridges, wash and redecorate their walls.

It was a voluntary response which saved the country millions of dollars in what would have been the cost of labour. As Maurice said in that same address:

> We saw the maroon coming alive again in Grenada. A new attitude had developed towards work. Work changed its very nature as the Revolution revealed its true meaning for us. . . . We were realising a truth that was new to us, that work is a liberator, work is what unites us, builds us, develops us and changes us. . . . When our work is against us, only serving others who exploit and scorn us, we fall into despondency and frustration. But with work on our side we build a new world, a world which will truly serve all workers of the world . . . and that is why we have to set out on this long process to ensure that every single one of our people can proudly say: 'I am a builder of Grenada, I am part of that fuel that will drive my country forward.'

But he also had a capacity to admit failure. The seasonal cockfight we call elections does not easily allow a leader to speak to his country on that level of candour. It doesn't allow leadership to learn the value of error. For to concede error in the exercise of Government is not an expression of defeat; but rather a renewal of the social contract with your people on behalf of truth.

What is the nature of this contract and the role of Labour in its fulfilment? In his encyclical on Labour Pope John Paul made this challenging reflection. It could have been the theme of the Grenada Revolution.

> Property is first of all acquired through work in order that it may serve work. This concerns in a special way the ownership of the means of production. Isolating these means as a separate property in order to set it up in the form of 'capital' in opposition to 'labour' and even to practise exploitation of Labour . . . is contrary to the very nature of these means and their possession.
>
> They cannot be possessed against labour, they cannot even be possessed for possession's sake, because the only legitimate title to their possession — whether in the form of private ownership or in the form of public or collective ownership — is that they should serve labour, and thus, by serving labour that they should make possible the achievement of the first principle of this order, namely, the universal destination of goods and the right to common use of them.

This could have been the theme of the Grenada Revolution.

These martyrs died in good faith. If rage sometimes twisted their faces and made their voices harsh, we must remember they lived their revolution in an environment of increasing hostility. They tried to the very end, to lay the foundations of friendliness with their neighbours and they were not allowed to be friendly. And so we send them this message of commitment and love from the Guyanese Poet, Martin Carter:

5

Dear Comrades
if it must be
you speak no more with me
nor smile no more with me
nor march no more with me
then let me take
a patience and a calm
for even now the greener leaf explodes
sun brightens stone
and all the river burns.
Now from the mourning vanguard moving on
dear Comrades I salute you and I say
Death will not find us thinking that we die.

President Machel of Mozambique, accompanied by Maurice Bishop, talks to Cuban workers at the Point Salines International Airport site.

1. A Bright New Dawn

First Address to the Nation on Radio Free Grenada (RFG) at 10.30 am, 13 March 1979

This is Maurice Bishop speaking. At 4.15 am this morning the People's Revolutionary Army seized control of the army barracks at True Blue.

The barracks were burned to the ground. After a half-hour struggle, the forces of Gairy's army were completely defeated, and surrendered.

Every single soldier surrendered, and not a single member of the revolutionary forces was injured.

At the same time, the radio station was captured without a shot being fired. Shortly after this, several cabinet ministers were captured in their beds by units of the revolutionary army.

A number of senior police officers, including Superintendent Adonis Francis, were also taken into protective custody.

At this moment, several police stations have already put up the white flag of surrender.

Revolutionary forces have been dispatched to mop up any possible source of resistance or disloyalty to the new government.

I am now calling upon the working people, the youths, workers, farmers, fishermen, middle-class people and women to join our armed revolutionary forces at central positions in your communities and to give them any assistance they call for.

Virtually all stations have surrendered, I repeat. We stress, resistance will be futile. Don't be misled by Bogo DeSouza or Cosmos Raymond into believing that there are any prospects of saving the dictator Gairy.

The criminal dictator, Eric Gairy, apparently sensing that the end was near, yesterday fled the country, leaving orders for all opposition forces, including especially the people's leaders, to be massacred.

Before these orders could be followed, the People's Revolutionary Army was able to seize power. This people's government will now be seeking Gairy's extradition so that he may be put on trial to face charges, including the gross charges, the serious charges, of murder, fraud and the trampling of the democratic rights of our people.

In closing, let me assure the people of Grenada that all democratic freedoms, including freedom of elections, religious and political opinion, will be fully restored to the people.

The personal safety and property of individuals will be protected. Foreign residents are quite safe, and are welcome to remain in Grenada.

And we look forward to continuing friendly relations with those countries with which we now have such relations.

Let me assure all supporters of the former Gairy government they will not be injured in any way. Their homes, their families and their jobs are completely safe, so long as they do not offer violence to our government.

However, those who resist violently will be firmly dealt with. I am calling upon all the supporters of the former government to realize that Gairy has fled the country, and to co-operate fully with our new government. You will not be victimised, we assure you.

People of Grenada, this revolution is for work, for food, for decent housing and health services, and for a bright future for our children and great grandchildren.

The benefit of the Revolution will be given to everyone, regardless of political opinion or which political party they support.

Let us all unite as one. All police stations are again reminded to surrender their arms to the people's revolutionary forces.

We know Gairy will try to organise international assistance, but we advise that it will be an international criminal offence to assist the dictator, Gairy.

This will amount to an intolerable interference in the internal affairs of our country and will be resisted by all patriotic Grenadians with every ounce of our strength.

I am appealing to all the people, gather at all central places all over the country, and prepare to welcome and assist the people's armed forces when they come into your area. The Revolution is expected to consolidate the position of power within the next few hours.

LONG LIVE THE PEOPLE OF GRENADA!

LONG LIVE FREEDOM AND DEMOCRACY!

LET US TOGETHER BUILD A JUST GRENADA!

2. In Nobody's Backyard
National Broadcast on RFG, 13 April 1979

Today, one month after our historic People's Revolution, there is peace, calm and quiet in our country. Indeed, there has been a tremendous drop in the crime rate since our Revolution. Foreign residents in the Levera/Bathway are feeling so comfortable and safe nowadays that they have advised the Commissioner of Police that he could close down the sub-Police Station in that area. An unusually high number of tourists for an off-season period are presently enjoying the beauty of our land and the warmth of our people, and this is so in spite of the fact that we have just had a Revolution and that a real and present threat of mercenary invasion is faced by our country. In fact, it is almost impossible to rent a vehicle or to find an empty cottage at this point.

Tourists and visitors to our country have all been greatly impressed by the discipline of our troops, and the respect that has been shown for the lives and property of local and foreign residents and visitors. From all over the island the same report have come to us that the tourists are commenting on the warmth, friendliness and discipline of our people and the People's Revolutionary Army. The same comments are being daily made by the hundreds of medical students studying in Grenada.

The annual boat race from Trinidad to Grenada took place as usual last night with a bigger than ever participation. The great sense of relief and happiness of our people are obvious to all. In fact, it is clear that there is no sense of panic here or hesitation by the tourists who daily continue to stream into Grenada.

Big Stick and Carrots

For this reason we want the people of Grenada and the Caribbean to realize that if all of a sudden tourists start panicking and leaving the country, or stop coming to our country, then they should note that this came after veiled threats by the United States Ambassador with respect to our tourist industry. The Ambassador, Mr Frank Ortiz, on his last visit to Grenada some days ago, went out of his way to emphasise the obvious importance of tourism to our country. He argued that as Grenada imported some $32 million a year in goods but exported only $13 million, we had a massive trade deficit of some $19 million, which earnings from the tourist industry could substantially lessen. His point was, and we accept that point, that tourism was and is critical to the survival of our economy. The Ambassador went on to advise us that if we continue to speak about what he called 'mercenary invasions by phantom armies' that we could lose all our tourists. He also reminded us of the experience which Jamaica had had in this regard a few years ago.

As some of you will undoubtedly recall, Jamaica at that time had gone through a period of intense destabilisation. Under this process the people of Jamaica were encouraged to lose faith and confidence in themselves, their government and their country and in the ability of their government to solve the pressing problems facing the country and meeting the expectations of their people. This was done through damaging news stories being spread in the local, regional and international media, particularly newspapers, aimed at discrediting the achievements of the Jamaican government. It was also done through violence and sabotage and by wicked and pernicious attempts at wrecking the economy through stopping the flow of tourist visitors, and hence much needed foreign exchange earnings of the country. The experience of Jamaica must therefore remind us that the economies of small, poor Third World countries which depend on tourism can be wrecked by those who have the ability and the desire to wreck them. In his official meetings with Minister of Finance Brother Bernard Coard, and then with me on Tuesday of this week, and in his unofficial discussions with a leading comrade of the People's Revolutionary Army at Pearls Airport on Wednesday, the Ambassador stressed the fact that his government will view with great displeasure the development of any relations between our country and Cuba. The Ambassador pointed out that his country was the richest, freest and most generous country in the world, but, as he put it, 'We have two sides'. We understood that to mean that the other side he was referring to was the side which stamped on freedom and democracy when the Amriecan government felt that their interests were being threatened. 'People are panicky and I will have to report that fact to my government', he advised us. However, the only evidence of panic given by the Ambassador was the incident which took place last Monday when the People's Revolutionary Army, as a result of not having been warned beforehand, shot at a plane which flew very low, more than once over Camp Butler. He calls that panic. The people of Grenada call it alertness.

At the end of our discussion on Tuesday the Ambassador handed me a typed statement of his instructions from his government, to be given to us. The relevant section of that statement reads, and I quote:

> Although my Government recognises your concerns over allegations of a possible counter-coup, it also believes that it would not be in Grenada's best interests to seek assistance from a country such as Cuba to forestall such an attack. We would view with displeasure any tendency on the part of Grenada to develop closer ties with Cuba.

We Are No One's Lackey

It is well established internationally that all independent countries have a full, free and unhampered right to conduct their own internal affairs. We do not, therefore, recognise any right of the United States of America to instruct us on who we may develop relations with and who we may not.

From day one of the Revolution we have always striven to have and develop the closest and friendliest relations with the United States, as well as Canada, Britain and all our Caribbean neighbours — English, French, Dutch and Spanish speaking, and we intend to continue to strive for these relations. But no one must misunderstand our friendliness as an excuse for rudeness and meddling in our affairs, and no one, no matter now mighty and powerful they are, will be permitted to dictate to the government and people of Grenada who we can have friendly relations with and what kind of relations we must have with other countries. We haven't gone through 28 years of fighting Gairyism, and especially the last six years of terror, to gain our freedom, only to throw it away and become a slave or lackey to *any* other country, no matter how big and powerful.

Every day we fought Gairy we put our lives on the line. On the day of the Revolution we started out with almost no arms and in so doing we again put our lives on the line.

We have demonstrated beyond any doubt that we were prepared to *die* to win our freedom. We are even more prepared to die to maintain that freedom now that we have tasted it.

We feel that people of Grenada have the right to know precisely what steps we have taken in our attempts to establish relations at various levels with the United States, and the response which we have so far received.

From the second day of our Revolution, during our first meeting with American government representatives in Grenada, we were at pains to emphasise the deplorable and ravished state in which the Gairy dictatorship had left our economy and our country. We pointed out then that massive assistance, technical and financial, would be required in order to begin the process of rebuilding the economy. The American Consul-General told us that he was not surprised to hear this, and assured us that he would encourage his government to give us the necessary assistance, particularly as he had been so impressed by the bloodless character and the self-evident humanity of our prompt assurances in the first hours of the Revolution that the safety, lives and property of American and other foreign residents were guaranteed. Indeed, he freely admitted that his American residents had all reported to him that they were happy, comfortable and felt secure. However, one month later, no such aid has arrived, It is true that the Ambassador did point out — and correctly so — that his Government generally grants aid on a multilateral basis through the Caribbean Development Bank. It is also true that he said his government would prefer to maintain that approach rather than help directly, despite his admission that red tape and bureaucracy could cause delays of up to one year in receiving such multilateral aid.

It is also true that he advised us that his Government is monitoring movements and that it is against United States law for Gairy to recruit mercenaries in the United States of America. This we appreciate.

US $5.000 Is Not The Price Of Our Dignity

However, we must point out that the fact is, that in place of the massive economic aid and assistance that seemed forthcoming, the only aid the American Ambassador has been able to guarantee that he could get to Grenada in a reasonably short time would be $5,000.00 (US) for each of a few small projects.

Sisters and brothers, what can a few $5,000.00 (US) do? Our hospitals are without medicines, sheets, pillowcases and proper equipment. Our schools are falling down. Most of our rural villages are in urgent need of water, electricity, health clinics and decent housing. Half of the people in the country who are able to and would like to work are unable to find jobs. Four out of every five women are forced to stay at home or scrunt for a meagre existence. $5,000.00 cannot build a house, or a health clinic. We feel forced to ask whether the paltry sum of a few $5,000.00 is all that the wealthiest country in the world can offer to a poor but proud people who are fighting for democracy, dignity and self-respect based on real and independent economic development.

Let us contrast this with the immediate response of our Caribbean brothers. We will take two examples: Guyana and Jamaica, countries thousands of times poorer than the United States of America; countries, indeed, like ourselves, poor, over-exploited and struggling to develop. These two countries have given us technical assistance, cheaper goods, and are actively considering our request for arms and military training. This assistance has included a shipment of rice which arrived two days ago, a six-man team of economic and other experts from Guyana presently in our country, and the imminent arrival of Mr Roy Jones, Deputy Governor of the Bank of Jamaica and Professor George Eaton, a leading authority on public service structures. And notwithstanding these concrete and much appreciated acts of assistance and solidarity they have never once attempted to instruct us as to the manner in which we should conduct our own internal affairs or as to which countries we should choose to develop relations with.

The American Ambassador is taking very lightly what we genuinely believe to be a real danger facing our country. Contrary to what anyone else may think we know that the dictator Gairy is organising mercenaries to attack Grenada in order to restore him to his throne. We know the man Gairy. Nobody knows him better than we the people of Grenada and we recognise the meaning and implications of the evidence which has come before us.

We say that when Frank Mabri Jr. and Mustaphos Hammarabl, Gairy's underworld friends, write to him indicating how much and what kind of arms are available, and when Gairy says on radio broadcasts and in newspaper interviews that he will never give up and that he intends to return to Grenada as prime minister, that he can only mean that he will use force in order to achieve these ends. And because our Revolution is a popular one, supported by the vast majority of our population, and because many of our patriots are armed, force here can only mean getting another country to intervene on his behalf, or hiring mercenaries to do his dirty work for him. And this in turn could only mean the mass killing of thousands of innocent Grenadians, regardless of which political party they support. It is in these circumstances, and because we have an undoubted freedom that we called on the Americans, Canadians, British, our fellow-countries in CARICOM, like Guyana and Jamaica, Venezuela and Cuba, to assist us with arms.

And we reject *entirely* the argument of the American Ambassador that we would only be entitled to call upon the Cubans to come to our assistance *after* mercenaries have landed and commenced the attack. Quite frankly, and with the greatest respect, a more ridiculous argument can hardly be imagined. It is like asking a man to wait until his house is burning down before he leaves to buy a fire extinguisher. No, we intend if possible to provide ourselves with the fire extinguisher before the fire starts! and if the government of Cuba is willing to offer us assistance, we would be more than happy to receive it.

We Are Not in Anybody's Backyard And We Are Definitely Not For Sale

Sisters and brothers, what we led was an *independent process*. Our Revolution was definitely a popular revolution, not a *coup d'etat*, and was and is in no way a minority movement. We intend to continue along an independent and non-aligned path. We have stayed in the Commonwealth, we have stayed in the Organization of American States and in CARICOM; despite pressures we have stayed in the Eastern Caribbean Common Market and in the expanded West Indies Associated States Organization (WISA). We have applied to join the Non-Aligned Movement. We will be applying to join the International Labour Organization – the ILO.

We are a small country, we are a poor country, with a population of largely African descent, we are a part of the exploited Third World, and we definitely have a stake in seeking the creation of a New International Economic Order which would assist in ensuring economic justice for the oppressed and exploited peoples of the world, and in ensuring that the resources of the sea are used for the benefit of all the people of the world and not for a tiny minority of profiteers. Our aim, therefore, is to join all organisations and work with all countries that will help us to become more independent and more in control of our own resources. In this regard, nobody who understands present-day realities can seriously challenge our right to develop working relations with a variety of countries.

Grenada is a sovereign and independent country, although a tiny speck on the world map, and we expect all countries to strictly respect our independence, just as we will respect theirs. No country has the right to tell us what to do or how to run our country, or who to be friendly with. We certainly would not attempt to tell any other country what to do. We are not in anybody's backyard, and we are definitely not for sale. Anybody who thinks they can bully us or threaten us, clearly has no understanding idea or clue as to what material we are made of. They clearly have no idea of the tremendous struggles which our people have fought over the past seven years. Though small and poor, we are proud and determined. We would sooner give up our lives before we compromise, sell out, or betray our sovereignty, our independence, our integrity, our manhood and the right of our people to national self-determination and social progress.

LONG LIVE THE REVOLUTION!

LONG LIVE GRENADA!

3. Organise to Fight Destabilisation

National Broadcast on RFG, 8 May 1979

On Sunday last, the 6th May, elements opposed to our Revolution moved to a new and higher level in their attempts to discredit and destroy our Revolution. When the news came that two fires, set within one hour of each other, had burnt down a Carifta Cottage at Morne Rouge in the heart of our tourist belt, and a building on Church Street in the heart of the capital of our country, this would have come as no surprise to those Grenadians who remember what I had said in my Good Friday address to the nation. As you will recall, in that address on 13th April, when our Revolution was just one month old, we warned that the process of destabilisation, which the people and government of Jamaica had gone through during 1975 and 1976, could soon begin in our own country.

Referring to that troubled and difficult period in Jamaica's history, I said the following:

> Under this process the people of Jamaica were encouraged to lose faith and confidence in themselves, their government and their country and in the ability of their government to solve the pressing problems facing the country and meeting the expectations of their people. This was done through damaging news stories being spread in the local, regional and international media, particularly newspapers, aimed at discrediting the achievements of the Jamaican government. It was also done through violence and sabotage and by wicked and pernicious attempts at wrecking the economy through stopping the flow of tourist visitors, and hence the much needed foreign exchange earnings of the country.

What is Destabilisation?

Sisters and Brothers, destabilisation is the name given to the most recently developed (or newest) method of controlling and exploiting the lives and resources of a country and its people by a bigger and more powerful country through bullying, intimidation and violence. In the old days, such countries — the colonialist and imperialist powers — sent in gunboats or marines to

15

directly take over the country by sheer force. Later on mercenaries were often used in place of soldiers, navy and marines.

Today, more and more the new weapon and the new menace is destabilisation. This method was used against a number of Caribbean and Third World countries in the 1960s, and also against Jamaica and Guyana in the 1970s. Now, as we predicted, it has come to Grenada.

Destabilisation takes many forms — there is propaganda destabilisation, when the foreign media, and sometimes our own Caribbean press, prints lies and distortions against us; there is economic destabilisation, when our trade and our industries are sabotaged and disrupted; and there is violent destabilisation, criminal acts of death and destruction, such as we witnessed on Sunday night with the fires. All of these vicious tactics have been used before, in the recent past, in countries close to us, and in countries far away. As we, people of Grenada, show the world — clearly and unflinchingly — that we intend to remain free and independent — that we intend to consolidate and strengthen the principles and the goals of our Revolution — as we show this to the world, there will be attacks upon us.

We must be ready to defend ourselves against these attacks. But to defend ourselves, we must know the enemy — for that is the best defence, the best preparation. The People's Revolutionary Army is diligent and on the alert, but the PRA and all the people of Grenada must know what to look for, what to expect.

It is one thing to prepare against an attack by a band of cowardly mercenaries send by Eric Gairy. It is easy to recognise this kind of enemy. But destabilisation is a different kind of enemy. It is much more subtle and much more deceptive. But it has a great weakness, a fatal flaw. Destabilisation can only work when it goes unrecognised — like a thief in the night. Destabilisation can work only when the people do not know that it is happenning.

It is a total failure when it is exposed and when the people see it for what it is. The people of Grenada must learn what this destabilisation is, because then we cannot be fooled by it.

What is Propaganda Destabilisation?

You know the facts about Grenada — you know what is happening here. You know what the People's Revolutionary Government stands for. You know why we fought and what we are trying to do. You have known and been involved with our programmes and our principles for many years. So what do you see when you look at a newspaper and see *lies*? What do you hear when you turn on a radio and hear news from other neighbouring countries which you know is not true. You are seeing destabilisation; you are hearing destabilisation. These are the lies printed and broadcast to try to destroy our Revolution — *your* Revolution.

On this question of propaganda destabilisation, you will recall the numerous distorted, untruthful articles being written by some newspapers, particularly by one weekly Trinidad newspaper, *The Bomb.* You will remember also that a Grenadian resident in Jamaica made numerous telephone calls to members of his family in Grenada trying to persuade them to write letters to him stating that people were being murdered and raped in Grenada. But that was only the tip of the iceberg. The real propaganda war has now begun. The lies that are being spread about our Revolution are not new restricted to one or two newspapers or one or two people abroad but have now spread to several newspapers — local, regional and international — and even to prime ministers and other ministers of Caribbean countries.

Just in the past week there have been several different, false, distorted and malicious stories about what is happening in Grenada appearing in different newspapers in Grenada, the Caribbean, Latin America and the world. During this period one pewspaper claimed that there were several hundred Cubans living in Grenada and training the comrades of our People's Revolutionary Army. Another report claimed that there were 5,000 Cubans in Grenada. We have requested, and will of course, be happy to accept assistance from Cuba in any area in which we have needs, but as Grenadians living here you know these reports are lies.

Yet another of their ridiculous reports claimed that we have missiles in Grenada pointed at neighbouring islands in the region. And not satisfied another news story claimed that there is a Russian submarine base in our sister island of Carriacou. Can you believe that? The people of Carriacou who are listening can surely expose this for the wicked and mountainous lie that it is! Another newspaper has claimed that there is a war going on in Grenada, that the country is a pitched camp and that several Cuban ships are at present tied up alongside our docks.

Not to be left out, the Prime Ministers of two independent Caribbean countries, and the Minister of Education of a non-independent Caribbean island have joined in the malicious and distorted attacks. One Prime Minister has claimed that no Chilean arms were discovered in Grenada after the Revolution, despite the fact that the world press actually photographed the arms discovered in the Chilean crates marked Medical Supplies. This same Prime Minister appears to be ignorant about the fact that Gairy did have soldiers trained in Chile and that Gairy's military gang of Mongoose men, Secret Police, Army and the criminal elements in Gairy's Police Force did in fact terrorise and brutalise the people of our country. But how can he be ignorant of these facts? Is he saying that our murdered comrades, Jeremiah Richardson, Harold Strachan, Rupert Bishop and Alister Strachan got struck by bolts of lightning from the skies or were murdered by UFOs? What is he saying? The people of Grenada remember that a former Prime Minister of that particular country once described Gairy as a political bandit, a description with which we fully agree. But we certainly have no memory of this present Prime Minister ever speaking about the tyrannical ways of Gairy. One wonders, therefore, what is the basis of his new-found confidence and new-found knowledge, and his sudden willingness to speak out on the internal affairs of Grenada, having regard to the fact that he remained silent for so long during the years of the Gairy dictatorship?

We wonder from whom or from which country he gets his information or, more accurately, shall be say mis-information, that he can state with such confidence that there were no Chilean arms found in Grenada?

We are confident that the views of one or two misinformed individuals in the area are not shared by the vast majority of the people of the Caribbean who fully support our Revolution and want to see us go forward to the achievement of genuine independence and social progress.

The second Prime Minister confidently asserts that some $5 million worth of arms have been sent to Grenada by an unnamed country, and expressed the view that this poses a threat to the security of the region. According to this gentleman, who only a week before had indicated his interest in coming to Grenada for an informal visit to hold discussions, the region was too closely tied together for him to stand like Pontius Pilate and say that any unusual occurrences in one state are solely an internal matter and of no concern to another Caribbean state.

We wonder how this Prime Minister can stay several hundred miles away and know how much, if any, arms the people of Grenada have? We wonder how come, given his professed concern for regional security, and for unusual occurrences in particular CARICOM countries, that he remained so dumb and silent, not only during Gairy's reign of terror in Grenada, but particularly with regard to Gairy's Chilean military connections.

The Minister of Education of a particularly oppressive CARICOM regime with South African connections, which takes pleasure in jailing teachers, dock workers and political activists and denying them bail, had the nerve to claim that Brother Kendrick Radix, our Attorney General and Minister of Legal Affairs and also our Ambassador to the United Nations and to the United States of America, was banned from his country before the Grenada Revolution, because he was involved in a 'communist plot' to overthrow his Government.

Grenadians will recall that Brother Radix had been picked up, detained, made to sit on a chair all night and deported the next morning. His crime was that he had gone to that island to defend the leader of the Teachers' Union and the leader of an opposition political party, both of whom had been charged with the ancient and forgotten offence of 'watching and besetting' while taking part in a workers' demonstration. It seems to us that the only plot involved was the plot to deny the workers and people of that island their basic and fundamental human rights.

The Torchlight – A Local Agent of International Reaction

A local newspaper, *The Torchlight*, has also jumped on to the bandwagon by attempting to discredit the People's Revolution. Grenadians should reflect on the fact that *The Torchlight* gave front page treatment to the diplomatically offensive and unusual cable sent by the United States Embassy in Barbados directly to *The Torchlight* recently, replying to my Address to the Nation of April 13. *The Torchlight* failed to carry in the first place any report of the address itself. Then, last Sunday's issue of *The Torchlight* carried a number of malicious and distorted articles, some of them potentially damaging to national security.

Under big banner headlines on the front page *The Torchlight* carried a story repeating the libellous propaganda relating to a so-called 'communist plot' by Brother Kendrick Radix to overthrow the government of Antigua.

It is significant that although this story was some five days old, *The Torchlight* never chose to contact Brother Radix or any other member of the government for a comment and response.

It smacks of destabilisation that a five-day-old story, which had been beaten up and down the radio stations throughout the region should take up almost the entire front page of the newspaper.

Not satisfied with page 1, page 2 gives banner headlines and photograph treatment to the slanderous statements of Messrs Compton and Adams, again without asking for any response from the government. Yet another long article entitled 'Cuban's Trojan Horse' and signed 'Voice in the Wilderness' contains classical CIA planted anti-communist propaganda. On the back another article with banner headlines stated 'Grenada Government Owes UWI $4 million.'

The real news for the people of Grenada, which is that the new government has paid $300,000.00 to the University within the first two months of the Revolution, while Gairy had consistently refused to pay, is buried in the middle of the article.

At another point, *The Torchlight* stated that another soldier was reported shot last Thursday during training exercises. This story is completely untrue. It is clear that the objective was to panic readers and create a feeling of tension on the island. We ask, how can a newspaper be so reckless and irresponsible on a matter of such seriousness?

The other front page story called 'Click, Click, Got Ya' shows the extent to which Acting Editor of *The Torchlight*, Nick Joseph, was prepared to go in order to try to discredit the People's Revolutionary Government. In that story Mr Joseph recalls his attempts at trying to photograph the security men who were accompanying me, on May Day. It will be obvious that in order to provide effective security for the leadership of the country, especially at this time when it is widely known that there is a danger of paid assassins striking, that it is necessary to avoid publicity of our security men. It must be obvious that if photographs of security men are taken, then this will make it a lot easier for hit-men to achieve their murderous objectives of wiping out the leadership.

Because of the People's Revolutionary Government's well known desire to encourage a free press, we did not prevent Mr Joseph from taking photographs, We had hoped that he would have put patriotism and concern for the safety of the leadership of the country above cheap journalism. We have certainly noted the irresponsibility of the Acting Editor and his newspaper in publishing these pictures. It should be noted that America, Britain and virtually all other countries in the world do not generally permit the photographing of security personnel, especially the systematic attempt to do so. It should be further noted that the British government, for example, has a system of what they call D-notices, whereby with the full co-operation of the press the British government issues notices to the press preventing the publication of anything which the British government deems to be a danger to national security. We sincerely hope that a similar attitude of responsible journalism with respect to national security matters will be observed by *The Torchlight* in the future.

The Pyramid Plan Of The CIA

Five days ago we received a visit from a leading economist and adviser to several governments, who has very close contacts with individuals in the United States State Finance Department. He advised us that he had received information from his contacts inside the State Department that the Central Intelligence Agency (CIA), had drawn up a plan to turn back the Grenada Revolution. According to this person, the plan was drawn up in the shape of a Pyramid. At the bottom of the Pyramid was a plan to destabilise the country by planting false reports about Grenada in newspapers and on radio stations, and also by encouraging prominent individuals, organisations and governments in the region to attack our Revolution.

The first part of the plan was aimed at creating dissatisfaction and unrest among our people and at wrecking our tourist industry and economy. A second level of the Pyramid involved the use of violence and arson in the country. And if neither of these methods in destabilising the country worked, then the plan was to move to the stage of assassinating the leadership of the country.

It is clear that the first and second phase of this plan are already in operation. It is now up to us to ensure not only that the third stage is avoided but that we also take steps to crush the first and second stages and move forward to build our Revolution in our own way. We must make sure that these tactics of destabilisation do not succeed.

The two fires on Sunday, coming on the heel of the propaganda campaign outlined earlier, suggest that both stages one and two have already begun. Sisters and brothers, we are not a violent people, and when we see violence, we must look hard and deep to see whose hand is behind it. In Jamaica there was unleashed a flood of violence in 1976 — to try to cause the defeat of Prime Minister Michael Manley. Guns appearing in the hands of thieves and gangs who never had guns before. Who was sending them these guns? Who was encouraging the violence? Certainly not the people of Jamaica. In Jamaica there was a terrible Orange Lane fire when dozens of innocent people were killed and hundreds left without homes. Who was responsible for the fire? Certainly not the people of Jamaica whom it hurt.

Just this week we have seen the same development in our country. One fire was set — deliberately and by admission — outside of town. And then, a few minutes later, when the fire trucks rushed to the first fire, another one broke out in the heart of town, a fire that could have destroyed a large part of town, a fire which endangered hundreds of lives, a fire which was undoubtedly caused by arson, as the comrades of the People's Revolutionary Army and the firemen who went into the building came out smelling very strongly of kerosene. Fires planned by the enemies of Grenada tell us that we are dealing with a monster — with a soulless monster who would kill and destroy to create fear. Indeed, we must note that both the fires could have a bad effect on the tourist industry. This is so, because one of them occurred in the heart of the tourist belt, and the other destroyed the building of the leading travel agency and tour operator in our country. As a matter of fact, we received information this morning that a tour operator in Barbados actually cancelled a trip to Grenada yesterday — apparently as a result of the fires.

Our Vigilance Will Crush The Enemy

But the people of Grenada must not be afraid; they must be vigilant. They must not be terrorised; they must be determined. They must not be unprepared; they must be on guard. The people of Grenada will not be destabilised; we will not be fooled.

We must also remember that in the exercise of their disruptive activities, those hostile forces will always require local agents and local opportunists. The people should, therefore, not be surprised in the coming days if they discover opportunist elements trying to foment unrest. One should always expect that there will be those who will rush to echo the propaganda lines being fed to them by forces whose objective it is to sabotage the gains made by the Revolution now and in the future.

(1) Report at your nearest recruiting station to join the People's Militia. We shall be opening a number of centres within the next three or four days. We believe that it is precisely our people in uniform and our people without uniform, represented by the People's Revolutionary Army and the People's Militia, who will be our best safeguards of our Revolution.

(2) Phone up or otherwise contact the People's Revolutionary Army if you notice any suspicious behaviour or strange persons around the areas.

(3) Keep your eyes on what is happening in the economy.

We stress yet again that never in history has there been such a humane and lenient Revolution. Freedom of the press and all other freedoms have been fully protected and guaranteed by the Revolution. At the same time, no one must mistake our leniency for weakness, and no arsonists or saboteurs must expect any mercy from the people and the people in uniform — the People's Revolutionary Army. As a people we have made great sacrifices in

21

the past. We have never succumbed to the violence of any bully. We shall not be bullied today. When people are conscious, when people are alert, when people are organised, and when people are prepared to fight in a united way, they cannot lose. We have no doubt that in the same way that we were able to decisively defeat Gairy, we shall undoubtedly crush all the attempts to disrupt and destabilize our country.

4. Beat Back Destabilisers

National Broadcast on RFG, 18 September 1979

Today our Revolution is six months and five days old and even our worst enemies have been forced to concede that during this period the Revolution has made impressive gains on all fronts.

More of our people have been able to find jobs over the past six months than at any previous period in recent times; in fact, over 800 new jobs have been created by the government during this period. Some 20 miles of main roads and feeder roads have been repaired or built during this period, three new community centres are being built, 50 young farmers are right now being trained at our Mirabeau Agricultural Training Centre and we hope to train another 150 in the next coming months.

Over the next six months we expect that about 100 of our youths will be trained as fishermen on board the fishing vessel given to us by the Cuban Government; 38 students are also about to leave for Cuba to pursue university studies there for degrees in Civil Engineering, Mechanical Engineering, Agriculture, Medicine, Dentistry, Veterinary Science and so forth. Scholarships in the fields of Agriculture and Veterinary Science, including modern techniques of artificial insemination, have also been obtained from the government of Kenya. The government of Tanzania has also given us scholarships in the fields of finance management. On top of this, because of repayments made by the People's Revolutionary Government (PRG) over the past six months to the University of the West Indies, 20 Grenadian students will be able to pursue studies at that University in October and we will also be paying the economic costs for 25 more students who are already at the University.

All this means that something like 109 students will be receiving university or higher education this year — an undoubted record for us. This works out at one in every 1,000 of our population going off to university in a single term. Locally, we have increased by 56 the number of Secondary School Scholarships for our Primary School children and have reduced Secondary School fees by one-third, down to $25.00 this term. In approximately half of all primary schools, children are already receiving lunch. All children under five, and all primary school children, are now receiving free milk.

Food Prices Coming Down

The National Importing Board has also begun to have some impact on the high cost of living, and food prices of some commodities have begun to come down, rice by between 8-10% and sugar by between 16-20%, depending on which part of the country you live.

We have also been able to dramatically improve the extent and quality of health care for our people. The 12 Cuban doctors and dentists kindly loaned to us by the Revolutionary Government of Cuba have made a most dramatic impact. Already these outstanding doctors and dentists have attended to well over 7,000 patients in Grenada, Carriacou and Petit Martinique. And, on top of this, we have been able to attract new Grenadian doctors, nurses and public health personnel back home. Our hospital at last has medicine, sheets and basic supplies. In fact, we were even able to send some medicines to our hurricane-stricken Dominican sisters and brothers.

The women of our country have already begun to benefit from our proclamation of the principle of equal pay for equal work for women. And all sections, classes and strata of our population have benefited immensely and released a hugh sigh of relief at the ending of brutality by minority elements of the Police Force, the Secret Police, the Mongoose Gang and the old Gairy Army. On top of this, crime and violence in our communities have been dramatically reduced — in fact, by some 75%.

At the same time, the previously forgotten and abandoned sister islands of Carriacou and Petit Martinique have also been receiving our attention. Carriacou's new airport is three quarters finished and its electricity supply has been vastly improved, Petit Martinique now has a resident nurse and visiting doctors, and we are working on providing electricity and communication facilities for that island.

Workers are now protected under the Trade Union Recognition Laws passed by us, and for the first time in the history of our country working people have the right to form or to join a Trade Union of their choice. Having abolished the right to exploit, the people of our country are now protected from big profiteers and prices are being carefully watched. At the same time, job victimisation and the shameful practice of sexual exploitation of our women in return for jobs have been abolished.

Our people now know that in return for hard work, increased productivity and greater sacrifice, the rewards for all of us would be cheaper food, more work, better health care, more roads, more schools, more community centres and more scholarships for our children. The people have therefore responded magnificently to our revolutionary call to join with the Government through voluntary work to build the communities, and the evidence of this can be seen in every parish and in most villages throughout the island at this time, where more and more of our people are uniting and organising to build the new Grenada.

We have Kept our Promises

We have also made good our promises to remove Gairy's repressive and dictatorial laws from the law books: the Newspaper Amendment Act which required the payment of $20,000.00 before newspapers can be published has been abolished; the Public Order Amendment Act, which had in effect banned the use of loudspeakers at public meetings, has been abolished; the law banning the importation of progressive reading material, which severely restricted the right of Grenadians to read, has also been repealed. The Essential Services Act which in real terms took away the right to strike for eleven of the most important categories of workers in our country has also been thrown into the dustbin of history. Thus, not only have the basic human rights of Grenadians been restored, but, indeed, new rights, particularly social and economic rights, have been introduced.

Naturally, progressive internal changes must also have a progressive external reflection. Grenadians are justifiably full of pride at the fact that for the first time in our history and our country now has a well defined, principled and honest foreign policy which has gained for our country tremendous international respect during the past six months. No longer are Grenadians laughed at as being from the UFO country — the land of flying saucers and crazy politicians who believe that they are mystics. Now, when Grenadians speak abroad, people want to hear our message, and they listen.

Following our successful impact at the Commonwealth Heads of Government Conference in Lusaka, Zambia, which led to a historic state visit to our country by one of Africa's greatest sons, President Kenneth Kaunda of Zambia, we made an even bigger impression at the Non-Aligned Movement Conference recently held in Havana, Cuba. There, our country was selected as one of the Vice-Presidents of the Conference; we were elected to the Bureau, the executive arm of the Non-Aligned Movement, and Grenada was one of only five countries (out of the 91 full member countries participating) which was called upon to move a vote of thanks at the end of the Conference.

New Respect For Our Country

Because of the new respect with which our country is now held we were also able to conclude successful bilateral discussions with the Presidents of Iraq, Algeria, Syria, Panama, Tanzania, Ethiopia and the Foreign Minister of Libya, among others at the Havana Conference. The results of these discussions, and also of discussions held with President Fidel Castro of Cuba, will soon be seen by all Grenadians.

Our call for closer Caribbean co-operation, greater movement of Caribbean peoples to each others' countries, and a firm, independent and non-aligned posture in our relations with the rest of the world, have had a deep and resounding impact on the people of the Caribbean. This is why the Mini-Summit of the governments of Dominica, St Lucia and Grenada called by our government, and the 'Declaration of St George's' which it produced, has touched a chord in the minds and hearts of the people of the Caribbean. This is also why, in spite of hostility from the reactionary elements of the Caribbean press and hostility from a few Caribbean governments, the working people, progressive intellectuals and technocrats of the Caribbean have continued to pour into Grenada to see in what ways they could make a contribution to the building and consolidation of our Revolution. Like the people of Grenada, the people of the Caribbean also understand that a new experiment, a new process is being attempted in Grenada which can bring social and economic justice and a new way of life for the over-exploited and oppressed masses of Grenada, and thereafter the Caribbean.

Yes, sisters and brothers, we have made tremendous strides in the past six months. The new sense of freedom, dignity and national pride is undoubtedly felt by all Grenadians. And without doubt we will continue to go forward to gain more and more successes.

Not Everyone Is With Us

But, we must never forget that there are those in and out of Grenada who would wish to see the Revolution derailed, to see our efforts turned back. These counter-revolutionaries, these saboteurs, these destabilizers are without doubt among us, and have used and will continue to use different tools to try to turn back the Revolution.

There are those who have begun to dismiss and lay off their workers, so as to give the impression that although a Workers' Government, a People's Government, is now in power, the government can do nothing to protect the right of workers to job security. There are also those, like the Manager of Buy Rite, who will begin to harass and intimidate their workers, even to the extent of physically searching their bodies in an absurd attempt to pretend that managers are still above the law.

These and similar activities are calculated to make working people lose confidence in their government and in the ability of their government to protect them against continued acts of harassment and exploitation. In this way, their willingness to continue to work hard to build the country and safeguard the Revolution will be considerably weakened. Let me say at this point that we simply wish to advise all such persons that *the full weight of the Revolution will be brought to bear on them.*

Conscious Destabilisation by the Press

It is now more than ever clear that some newspapers and radio stations in the Caribbean have abandoned all pretence of fair and objective reporting in so far as the Grenada Revolution is concerned. One good recent example of this, out of several possible choices, is a recent report of an interview with me by the *Jamaica Gleaner*. In that report the *Gleaner*, which is a well-known destabilizing influence in Jamaica, claims that I said that one of the first acts of the People's Revolutionary Government was to pass a Law requiring that newspapers pay $20,000.00 before being able to publish; when what I said in fact, and what is by now well known to everyone in the region, is that one of the first acts of our government had been to repeal and abolish Gairy's Newspaper Law which had required newspapers to pay $20,000.00 before having the right to publish.

In my view, there is absolutely no chance that this lying report could have been the result of a mistake by the *Gleaner*. My comments on this were made at an airport press conference in Kingston, Jamaica on Sunday 2nd September, while on my way to the Non-Aligned Movement Conference in Havana. There were several reporters present who accurately reported what I had said and, so far as I know, only the *Gleaner* had hearing problems. When a so-called free and responsible newspaper can go to such extremes to lie, distort and fabricate, some idea can be had of the vicious nature of the destabilizing campaign which is being directed against the Grenada Revolution by reactionary and backward agents of imperialism in the region.

Grenadians must understand that the Grenada Revolution is seen as a threat to newspapers like these. Under their concept of a free and responsible press, the press had the right to distort, to fabricate, to print and reprint libellous and scurrilous material from inside and outside, to refuse to publish the views of the broad masses, to ignore the work and achievements of progressive governments and to openly and unashamedly carry the line of reactionaries and other elements serving the interests of imperialism, foreign domination and exploitation.

Vested Interest in Exploitation
Several of these newspapers in the region are owned by the same big businessmen and corporations with a vested interest to maintain the cruel, unjust, exploitative and profiteering system that we live under. For example, the *Trinidad Express* which has been attacking us quite consistently over the past several weeks is one of the two main owners of the Grenada *Torchlight* newspaper, They must, therefore, oppose majority rights, they must oppose attempts to end profiteering and exploitation, they must oppose all attempts at progressive or socialist reconstruction of our societies.

Let us again use the *Torchlight* to illustrate this point. Compared to the 50 to 100 shares which most shareholders in *Torchlight* own, one man, Mr D.M.B. Cromwell, owns 6,902 shares and the Trinidad Express Newspapers Ltd owns the next highest bloc of shares, 4,606 shares. Thus, between the two of them they are able to exercise effective control over the company and therefore over what goes into the papers. That being so sisters, brothers and comrades, would you expect the *Torchlight* and the *Trinidad Express* newspapers, owned, controlled and run as they are by these big businessmen, to support the Grenada Revolution, to publish the achievements of our Revolution, to honestly explain how our Revolution intends to bring social and economic justice to the masses of the people, to take a sympathetic view of our intention and determination to pursue an independent, sovereign and non-aligned path, to agree with us when we oppose imperialism, that is, foreign control and domination of our economy by a few big overseas companies? Can we really expect them to oppose precisely those things which are responsible for their own wealth, comfort, influence and privileged status? Obviously none of this could be expected. This would be like asking the slave master to voluntarily give up his slaves; or like asking the big imperialist multinational corporations to give up their profits; or like asking the racists in South Africa to voluntarily give up their system of apartheid: or like asking the mass murderer Hitler to agree that he was a criminal and a murderer.

The People's Revolutionary Government of Grenada wants to make it perfectly clear that we are totally and completely opposed to minority control of the press, that we are totally and completely opposed to a press which fabricates and distorts, that we are totally and completely opposed to a press which refuses to publish the reality about what is happening in our country, to a press which refuses to publish the views of the overwhelming majority of the broad masses, to a press which believes that its freedom to publish gives it the right to print and reprint libellous and scurrilous material. That is our position and we are willing to stand by it.

We remember only too well the destabilizing role played by the newspaper *El Mercurio*, and the extent to which it helped to lay the basis for the vulgar, cowardly, murderous and criminal overthrow of the progressive and duly elected Allende Government in Chile by General Pinochet and his gang of fascists in collusion with imperialism. We are not going to let the same thing happen in Grenada. That had better sink home because it is a fact.

Rumours: The Greatest Threat at this Time

Another powerful agent of destabilization which is being used by the enemies of the Grenada Revolution and which at this time perhaps represents the greatest threat to the Revolution, is the spreading of false and malicious rumours. Sometimes we take rumours for granted and dismiss them as the innocent pastimes of idle people and sometimes of course this is true. But we must never forget that rumours can be, and often are, used in a systematic and scientific way by our enemies as a method of spreading confusion, creating fear and panic and deteriorating and destroying the image of our government and its leadership.

Let us consider some examples. The early rumour, for example, that I had been bitten by a bee, and was no longer able to see, was meant to suggest that Gairy's mystical and obeah qualities had begun to work on me, and was clearly an appeal to the backward and superstitious beliefs of some of our people. The later rumour that my colleague and brother, Comrade Bernard Coard, had cuffed me was meant to suggest that there were serious divisions in the leadership of the party and government, and that a power struggle was taking place.

The further rumour that the Government was conducting a house-to-house survey and asking questions about the people's ownerhisp of beds, chairs, sheep, cows, goats and so on was used to suggest that we are going to divide and share up people's property in order to make sure that nobody had more than one bed, or one sheep, or one goat, or one chair. The other rumour, that the Cuban doctors who have worked so hard and so impressively with us in Grenada were really only male nurses and had not been trained to be doctors, was clearly aimed at discrediting the fantastic work being done by these doctors and to try to get Grenadians to be afraid to go to them for treatment.

Another recent rumour that ordinary level and advanced level results had arrived in Grenada but could not be published until I had returned from Cuba, so that I could decide who had passed and who had failed, was aimed at giving the impression that the Gairy system of corruption and favouritism was still continuing. And the most recent rumour, that the People's Revoluitionary Government had given instructions that nobody between the ages of 18 and 40 years would be allowed to leave Grenada, is clearly aimed at creating panic in the minds of that section of our population hoping to travel abroad.

These Rumours Have Been Carefully Organised

We have no doubt that most of these rumours are carefully worked out by vicious but clever minds in our country who understand the importance of propaganda warfare. It is significant that the 18 to 40 year rumour is aimed at the young people who are generally regarded as constituting the very core and heart of the support for our Revolution. It is also significant that this particular rumour was released simultaneously in Grenada and America, so that we actually received a query from our Embassy in New York a few days ago asking us to confirm whether this rumour was true or false. The destabilizers not being content simply to attempt to destabilize Grenadians in Grenada are also aiming to destabilize Grenadian nationals abroad.

Following the imperialist-inspired and CIA-organised overthrow of the Allende government in Chile, surviving Chilean patriots put out a document entitled *Psychological Warfare Against The Popular Government* which carefully detailed the different forms of psychological warfare which had been used against the Allende government. This document quotes quite extensively from the sections of the Handbook published by the US Army and CIA dealing with psychological warfare entitled *Field Manual of the Department of the US Army*. The document shows that the intention of the destabilizers is to keep the nation in a state of commotion, to promote malicious rumours and other forms of false propaganda constantly, to create a general social situation of instability and crisis, to manipulate people's natural feelings of terror, hatred and hope, to destroy the image of the

29

leadership, the party and the government so they will no longer be able to govern and will appear weak, uncertain and defenceless. The document explains with great clarity that the procedure for carrying out psychological warfare combined both direct political action by reactionary politicians and false propaganda in the local newspapers and other forms of the mass media. It also points out that rumour-mongering and malicious telephone calls played an important part in this destabilisation process. What the above tells us is that these rumours are not just the work of local reactionaries working alone, but local reactionaries being guided by and working hand in hand with imperialism, the CIA and other reactionary forces outside of Grenada.

We Must Unite To Beat Back Destabilisation

Sisters and Brothers, we must learn from the experiences of others. We must recognise the destructive role that economic sabotage, malicious and irresponsible press reporting, arson, violence and malicious rumour-mongering can play in attempting to destabilise our Revolution, to turn back the gains which the poor and working people are only must beginning to enjoy after so many years of bitter suffering and terrible deprivation.

It is vitally important that such activities should be nipped in the bud. It is vitally important that you should remain alert, vigilant and watchful. Anyone caught spreading malicious rumours or attempting to engage in other acts of sabotage or arson must be reported immediately to your nearest PRA Camp or Police Station, or better yet, should be communicated directly to anyone answering telephone number 2265.

I give you our firmest assurance that those found committing such activities will be jailed, will be severely dealt with. The Revolution will not be slowed down or stopped by the activities of counter-revolutionaries, saboteurs or destabilizers. In spite of attempts to turn back the Revolution, the Revolution will go forward.

In the words of the Bible, we say very firmly that *justice will come to the poor and the meek shall inherit the earth*, whether or not the exploiters and destabilizers are against this happening.

Let us unite to beat back the destabilizers!

Let us constantly struggle to raise higher and higher the consciousness and commitment of our people!

Let us organise and mobilise to build our Revolution!

5. New Martyrs, New Patriots
National Broadcast on RFG, 19 June 1980

A Savage, Brutal and Cowardly Blow

Today, imperialism struck its most savage, its most brutal, its most cowardly blow against our Revolution. Today a monstrous crime was committed by imperialism and its local agents. Today is a sad day for our country. Today is a day when we gather together to commemorate, as we have been doing, another important Anniversary: on this occasion the Anniversary of Butler and Strachan, two of our national heroes. But before the day was ended, and even while we were commemorating the lives of these two outstanding comrades, we find now that in the future, on the 19th of June we will also be commemorating new martyrs, new heroes, new patriots of our People's Revolution and of our struggle.

At this time two young comrades of our country — two young sisters — are dead; murdered by these cowards, murdered by these vicious beasts of imperialism. At this point two more people of our country are gone. The way in which this incident took place was that a bomb was planted at the foot of the steps of the pavilion of the Queen's Park. It was planted in such a way that it was directly below the point where the leadership of the country was sitting. It was timed to go off at 3.00 o'clock and at 3.00 o'clock, it did go off. The fragments which were collected by our Security Forces indicate that the clock was connected to sticks of dynamite, and indicate also that it was done in a very sophisticated way. In a way that indicates very clearly that they received training. This is not local technology. This is not the way of our Grenadian people.

Plan Not Only to Kill Leadership but also Ordinary Grenadians

We must know too, that this was not just an attempt to kill the leadership of our country. Important as that would be, important as it would be for any of these reactionaries and these murderers to wipe out the entire leadership at one time, we must note that the plan here went even beyond that. Because in the attempt at trying to wipe out the entire leadership of the country, these murderers were prepared to kill dozens, hundreds, perhaps thousands

31

of ordinary Grenadians. In our situation only imperialism could be responsible for this.

Can one think of an ordinary Grenadian counter-revolutionary being prepared entirely on his own to wipe out hundreds of innocent Grenadians, while at the same time trying to kill the leadership? Can one think of an ordinary Grenadian agreeing to plant a bomb in a rally of thousands of Grenadians? When we consider the list of those who have died, those who may yet die and those who are injured, some very seriously, some in a critical way, you can get an idea of the point I'm making.

At this point, two young women of our country, 13-year-old Laureen Phillip of River Road, and 23-year-old Laurice Humphrey of Byelands, are dead – murdered – blown to pieces by this bomb. At this point also, two other young children, two other young people of our country, both Baileys, both of the River Road/Tempé area, one eight years old, one 15 years old, are lying in a very critical condition. One has lost her leg, the other one has serious injuries to the back and buttocks, blown off by this deadly bomb. (Fifteen-year-old Bernadette Bailey has since died.) Two more people are also in a serious condition; in fact, in the last few hours, our valiant doctors and nurses have performed six operations and we hope and pray that no one else will die as a result of this savage attack. Thirty-eight more of our citizens are right now hospitalised, lying in our St George's Hospital, unsure whether they would live or whether they would die. Several dozen more people have been treated and have been discharged, and we hope that their injuries will not prove to be serious.

Chile, Jamaica, Cuba, Vietnam – Now Grenada

Today's events brothers and sisters, Comrades, remind us of the history of other countries like our own which have faced the might and the fury of imperialism. Today's events remind us of Chile, remind us of the time when the Pinochet fascist gang killed hundreds and thousands of innocent Chileans in September 1973. We remember the football park in Chile where innocent people who were on a hit list prepared by Pinochet and his imperialist allies were rounded up and brought to this park and there brutally murdered. We remember the torture which followed, torture which extended not just to the workers, not just to the fighters and the leaders of the Party but extended to the middle classes, extended eventually even to priests and nuns. Torture knew no bounds. No one was safe from these criminals. We remember too, our brothers and sisters in Jamaica. We think of the Orange Lane fire of May 1976 in Jamaica, when dozens of people were shot; when a fire was started and when children were being carried out of that fire the gunmen shot them back into the building to roast. We recall that just a few weeks ago on the fourth anniversary of the same Orange fire, another fire was started in Kingston, Jamaica; this time the Eventide Old People's Home when more than 150 old people were burnt out, were killed. Who was responsible? Only imperialism and their local reactionary agents.

We think of our comrades in Cuba at this time. We remember the many struggles, the many trials, the many tribulations of our Cuban comrades. We think of their heroic sacrifices; we think of their courage. We recall 'The Bay of Pigs' when US imperialism trained Cuban exiles in Miami and backed them up and sent them to Cuba with the intention of turning back the Revolution. They were routed by the brave heroic people of Cuba. We think of the blowing up of the ship Coubre. We think of the October 1976 Air Cubana disaster when 73 innocent people travelling on a Cuban plane were blown out of the skies in order to appease the revenge and the thirst of imperialism. We think of the 'pirate ship' attack on Cuba. We think, too, of the dozens and dozens of unsuccessful assassination attempts on the Cuban leadership and, in particular, on our friend and comrade, Fidel Castro. Comrades, we think of Vietnam where thousands and millions of people were killed and massacred by US imperialism. We think of the My Lai massacre in the early 1970s, when innocent people were rounded up during that notorious war and brutally murdered, women and children, all innocent people.

Revenge on the Masses. They Cannot Win

Tonight, it is important for us to try to put into context what today's events mean, because today's events did not just drop out of the skies by accident. Today's events are part of a total unfolding plan aimed at the destruction of the Grenada Revolution; aimed at the wanton devastation of our country, if we choose not to continue along the old submissive and exploitative path that Gairy and his minions pursued. We think of the history of US imperialism. We think of the days when the gunboats ruled the world; when you landed marines in someone else's country; Arbenz in Guatemala in '54, Dominican Republic in '65 and dozens of other examples. We think of the occupations and the annexations of other people's territories, particularly in our region, in Latin America and the Caribbean. We think of the assassinations of Sandino the Patriot of Nicaragua, of Allende, the hero of Chile, of so many other martyrs of this region who had to die at the hands of imperialism.

We think of the scientific way in which they have evolved a new concept which they have called destabilisation; sabotage; a concept which, when it fails, eventually leads to terrorism. We think of the attempts to use local opportunists and counter-revolutionaries — people who try to build a popular base, people who fail in building that popular base, and people who, as a result of having failed to fool the masses, then turn to the last weapon they have in desperation; the weapon of open, naked, brutal and vulgar terror — having given up all hope of winning the masses, these people now turn in their revenge on the masses. They now seek to punish tha masses, to murder them wholesale; to plant bombs in the midst of rallies; to try to break the backs of the popular support of the Revolution; because imperialism was frightened and terrified by the Grenadian masses on March 13 1980 when 30,000 of our people gathered in one spot to celebrate one year of People's Victory, People's Progress, People's Benefits. They were terrified by that, and as a result they now seek to intimidate, to bullpistle, to browbeat, to frighten and terrorise the masses to get them to be afraid to assemble, to get them to be afraid to continue to build their own country in their own image and likeness. We think of the October/November plots last year. We remember what De Raveniére and his gang had in mind for our country, the slogans they were using, calling upon NATO — NATO, which our people know nothing about, calling upon the CIA. We remember their plans to try to bring back the dictator Gairy. We remember their plans to try to burn down St George's, to slaughter innocent people, to use the very same bomb that today some of them were able to use. We remember the Budhlall gang which surfaced a few months ago; their pretence at being honest people, their pretence at being in support of the ordinary working and poor masses, their pretence at being revolutionaries. We think of this gang that believes our Revolution is like instant coffee, where overnight changes can come. This gang that pretends that no benefits have come to the masses, when in fact, their real aim was to take over the country in order to spread their own ideas, in order to push a marijuana society. We think of this crowd. We think of their weapons. We think of the plan they had to take over one of the PRA camps to try to subvert and influence some of the Comrades in the People's Revolutionary Army. We think of their counter-revolutionary demonstration. We remember that only last week, one of them, Russell Budhlall, elder brother of Kennedy and Kenneth Budhlall, when his home was searched by Security Forces, hundreds of bullets were found; AK 47 bullets, M16 bullets, sticks of gelignite; only last week, brothers and sisters.

The Fascist Alternative — A New and Higher Stage

We think too, at this point, of the numerous death threats, some on the telephone, some in letters, directed to different members of the leadership. Threats so vulgar and so gross, that half the time we are unable to even finish reading these notes. We think of people like Stanley Cyrus, who continue to try to plot and plan and scheme and who hope that one day they will be able to return this country into the hands of imperialism. People who are willing to use any amount of violence and bloodshed to try to overturn the Revolution, because they recognise, and recognise quite clearly, that the people are the Revolution, and that the Revolution is the people, that the Revolution is popular and strong and deeply rooted in the masses. They understand that reality. They know that after tasting 15 months of people's participation and people's benefits that the people will fight back. And, therefore, the only alternative to the Revolution at this period in our history is bloodshed, terrorism, open, naked, violent fascist dictatorship; that is the only alternative.

We think of those who have called our Revolution a temporary obstacle in their path. People who choose to campaign at this time on the question of Grenada. We think of those who have referred to Grenada and Suriname as 'temporary obstacles', and just weeks after that statement, our Suriname brothers and sisters find that their country has been invaded. We think of all these things.

We think of the Solid Shield 1980 exercises which were planned by the Americans; plans which included the use of more than 350 ships, several planes, more than 20,000 marines, plans which included invading the territory of Cuba, going on to Guantanamo to stage the operation, plans which included learning and practising how to mine the Caribbean Sea so as to be able to block off our country, and other progressive and revolutionary countries in the region, in any kind of situation. We think of the recent nuclear war alert that took place in the United States when, because of a mistake in a computer — a mistake which took four minutes before it could be discovered — the world came very close to nuclear destruction and nuclear confrontation. We think of the warmongers, of those who recognise the crisis now afflicting international capitalism, of those who see their super-profits being drained away, of those who recognise that only if they are able to get a war economy moving again, to build more and more armaments and weapons of destruction, only in this way will their super-profits rise, and in pursuit of dollars — in pursuit of more and more profits — they are willing to destroy innocent children, innocent women.

Comrades, we have to recognise that this is a new stage, we have to recognise that what we are seeing, what we saw today represents a new and higher stage in the plans of counter-revolution. Their desperation is now complete. This act and exhibition of gross and naked and vulgar terrorism which we saw today was aimed at frightening and terrifying our people into submission. What we saw today comrades, was aimed at trying to reduce us to cowards, was aimed at trying to force us to return to the old days when they were able to dominate and exploit our country.

Who Does the Revo Benefit?

We must note very carefully that our Revolution was for justice, for food, for health, for housing, for clothing, for pipeborne water, for education, for people's control of our resources, for people's participation. Our Revolution was and is anti-imperialist. We are against the naked exploitation of our own resources for the benefits of a small minority of big multinational corporations and their backers in the big powerful governments. Our Revolution was and is anti-colonialist. Our Revolution was and is in favour of the National Liberation Movements, in favour of the New International and Economic Order which aims at bringing social and economic justice to the poor and over-exploited countries of the Third World.

This means that our Revolution is for the poor in our country, for the working people in our country, for the youths and women in our country, for the middle classes in our country, for the small and medium businessmen and farmers in our country, for the fishermen in our country. In fact, as we have said over and over again, this Revolution has room for all of us, once we are patriotic, once we are prepared to end our exploited days.

Think of who has benefited from the Revolution. What has the massive distribution of free milk to all children under five years meant, the massive distribution of milk to children in schools, to mothers in homes – islandwide; who has this benefited? What about the increase in scholarships, the 109 university students who are now studying abroad to become doctors and engineers, to become agricultural scientists and what not, who is benefiting from that? The fact that secondary education fees have now been chopped from $37.50 to $12 a term. Who will benefit? The extra scholarships given to secondary school children; the fact that the debts that Gairy owed to the University of the West Indies are now being repaid, who will benefit? Look at our recent People's Budget. If one-third of our people no longer have to pay taxes, many of those earning up to $510 a month no longer have to pay taxes, who is benefiting from that? We are to think of these questions sisters and brothers. Twelve million dollars is being spent in this year's budget on health and $9,000,000 on education. The National Commercial Bank which now aims at utilising the savings, the financial resources of our people in our own interest – who is going to benefit from that? The National Importing Board has so dramatically reduced the price of sugar and cement and kept that price stable, because while we sell sugar today at 50¢ a pound, in several territories in this region the cost of sugar has gone to beyond $1 a pound. And if it were the same old monopolist still controlling sugar, Grenada's sugar could not be selling for less than $1.20 a pound. It is the masses, it is all of the people, except the tiny handful of exploiters that you could count on one hand and their foreign imperialist backers, apart from this tiny minority, it is the masses of our people who have benefited and are benefiting.

They Will Attack – We Must Fight Back

Imperialism is afraid of this situation. They are worried about their profits because dollars is the only god that they worship. They are afraid of the example of the Grenada Revolution and what it can do by way of indicating what a small and poor country with a small population and limited resources can do for its people, if the people are serious about their own development, if they are willing to take their destiny into their own hands, if they are willing to stop looking outwards to the imperialist world and instead look to the problems, the needs, the resources of their own people and their own country, and willing to use those resources to benefit their people. They are afraid of the loss of control and the exploitation which they were able to bring in the past. That is why our country is being attacked. That is why the

United States considered, in the first few weeks of the Revolution, having a naval blockade against our country. That is why the ex-Ambassador, Ortiz, tried to organise a 'human rights campaign', as he called it, against our plan that the CIA had worked out, a plan of destabilisation, a plan of assassination, a plan of bringing terror to our people.

But this country is our country. These resources are our resources. We have a right to choose how we are going to build our country. We have a right to determine who our friends are. We have a right to end exploitation in our country. We have a right to bring justice to the poor, and food and work to the poor people of our country. We have a right to use our labour and our resources to build our country. That is why we must fight back. That is why we cannot sit down and accept the plans of imperialism and local reaction.

Sometimes, sisters and brothers, a people are called upon to fight back, to draw on hidden or inner reserves of strength that they do not know that they have, to demonstrate extraordinary courage in the face of adversity, to fight back against what might appear to be impossible odds. Sometimes people are called upon to do these things. We are confident that as a result of today's monstrous crime our people will emerge stronger, more united, more vigilant, more powerful than imperialism and its local terrorists and stooges. We are confident that a united and determined people can never be turned back. We are confident that a well organised and conscious people can never be frightened, can afford to be brave, can afford to stand on our feet and face the world. In any event, revolutionaries do not have the right to be cowards. We have to stand up to fight for our country because this country is ours. It does not belong to anybody else.

Our first task in this new situation is to protect, to consolidate, to defend our Revolution. We have warned over again of the danger that our country faces, we have pointed out on hundreds of occasions that imperialism will, not 'may', but will attack our country. We have pointed out that there is absolutely no doubt in our minds that imperialism and local reaction will keep plotting and scheming. We have said that Revolution has laws; that one of the laws is, that the more progress the country makes, the more benefits that are brought to the ordinary masses of the country, the more resistance you will see from the counter-revolutionaries and from imperialism. Some have doubted this. Some have felt that we are spending too much time talking of imperialism, that we are spending too much time looking for counter-revolutionaries, that we are talking too much about the possibility of our country being attacked and our people being murdered. Some disbelieved the word of the Revolution, but now they know, now they understand. Imperialism and local reaction, know no boundaries. They draw no lines. They make no distinctions between killing people and killing animals. It is the same to them. The mercenaries they hire are quite correctly called 'dogs of war'. Because when they come they do not look to see if it is a man or a woman or a child, they do not look to see if it is a soldier in uniform or a cripple on a bed, or an infant resting in its mother's arms. They do not make these distinctions.

Only the Beginning

And we have to be honest tonight comrades, and point out that this is only the beginning; what we have seen today can happen again; that is a fact of life and because it is important for our people to always know the truth, to face the facts, we must point it out. Remember that just as Bloody Sunday in November 1973 was a signal to our country, that worse was to come and worse did come; 21st January, 1974 Horror Monday, when our people were massacred, when one man Rupert Bishop was murdered; June 1975 when our Comrade Kendrick Radix was brutally beaten in the streets; 1977, 19th June when young Alister Strachan, another patriot of our Revolution in our cause was murdered because he chose to stand up for his rights. Think too of that connection Gairy was building with the Chilean fascists. Now, when we remember Bloody Sunday forewarned us of all of this, in the same way, we must realize that today 19th June, 1980 is like a warning and an indication to us of the possibility and the likelihood of more attacks, more desperation, more terrorism by imperialism and local reactionaries and counter-revolutionaries.

And it must also be a signal to us of a greater need for more and not less vigilance, for more and not less alertness, for more and not less preparations. Now more than ever our people must be the eyes, the ears and the noses of the Revolution. Now more than ever our people must redouble their efforts at vigilance, must be more and more on the lookout for the opportunists, the reactionaries, the counter-revolutionaries. Now more than ever our people must look out for imperialist attacks, for the possibility of more and more planes flying over our air space in open violation of international law, as if they own our country. If we had a plane and sent it to fly over their countries they would shoot it down. But they believe they have a right to just come to our country and fly over as they wish. But we repeat the warning tonight that the comrades in the PRA are able to use their anti-aircraft weapons and when unauthorized crafts fly over our lands, without permission, we reserve the right to do what they would do, shoot them out of the skies.

Tonight, we must be conscious of the need for us to continue to patrol our beaches and our lands, not just broadly and roughly speaking, but every square inch of soil that we have in this country must be carefully watched. The only way in which we can avoid a repetition of what happened today is if we are more alert, if we are more watchful of suspicious activity, if we keep looking at people with parcels, for example, that seem to be behaving in an odd way. If we re-double our look-outs on important buildings in our country, if we greatly increase, not by doubling or tripling, but increasing by a hundred times the Militia that we now have in our country; if we step up and strengthen on the popular defence forces of our country, not just the People's Revolutionary Army, not just the People's Militia, not just our people in uniform therefore, but all of our people must now prepare for a people's war to defend our country against local attacks and foreign invasions.

All people who love our country must be willing to defend our country.

Revolutionary Firmness

Today we saw signs of the greatness of our people. We saw signs and reminders of the courage, of the discipline, of the vigilance of our people. We saw that today. We looked at the orderly way in which our people left Queen's Park after the bomb attack. We noted their concern for the leadership of the country, the number of our people who came and surrounded us and made sure that we got out. We noted the deep concern of our workers for the women, for the children, for the elderly. We noted most of all today, the fact that the people of our country came forward with information telling us what they observed, who they believed put the bomb, when they believed the bomb was planted; important intelligence information on which the security forces have acted and right now are still acting. Several arrests have already been made. Interrogations are right now going on, and in fact, as I speak to you a number of our soldiers, policemen, militia comrades, members of the security forces are presently in St Paul's in Mt. Airy at the headquarters of counter-revolution, at the home of a man called Strachan Phillip, the present leader of the counter-revolutionary gang in our country.

Acting on information which we received in Queen's Park, and also on previous surveillance of Strachan Phillip and his tiny minority band of counter-revolutionaries, our security forces went to arrest Strachan Phillip tonight and were greeted with a hail of bullets. Our soldiers, our security forces had to duck and run for their lives at first, and then of course, they fought back. And up to when I left to come down here to make this address that fight was still going on. That battle of our forces, of our people in uniform against the forces of counter-revolution was still being waged. We must be conscious of this because something that you do not yet know, which I will say tonight, is that we have firm evidence of a direct link between these local counter-revolutionaries and a number of other counter-revolutionaries and agents of imperialism residing abroad, some in countries not too far from here. We have a fair amount of details of the plans of these elements. And what we say to them is, let today be a warning, that whenever they choose to come to land in our country to try to turn back the People's Revolution they are going to be wiped out. They are going to be dealt with without mercy. The same lack of mercy that today they showed when they planted their bomb, that same lack of mercy, that same firmness, but on this occasion revolutionary firmness, will be used to deal with them.

Only the People Can Defend the Revolution and Build the Country
Starting tomorrow, recruitment teams will be going around to all work places, to all villages, to all schools. These recruitment teams will be aiming to recruit at least 20,000 more Grenadians to become members of our Militia, to mobilise our people for a state of war, to put our people on a war alert, to

put them in a situation of serious preparation for defence of our country. We expect and look forward to the fullest co-operation of all teachers, of all employers, of all our people generally, as we start this massive recruitment drive, because at this stage the only guarantee against external attack and internal sabotage and subversion and terror is if our people are ready, able and willing to fight to defend our country. We need to defend our schools. We need to defend all our key buildings, we need to defend our coastlines against any attacks. And the PRA and the Militia as presently constituted cannot do that by themselves.

All of our people now need to move to the centre stage of learning how to defend the country with guns in our hands. So when any of them land in this country with the intention of overturning our Revolution they will understand that what they will meet is a fighting and combative people, a people prepared to die, to defend their country. So if they must win, what they will inherit is a barren and scorched country. We must be prepared to defend our country. Only the people can do that, only the people can defend this Revolution and defend this country because this country belongs to the people, this Revolution belongs to the people. But even as we put outselves on full alert it is necessary in this year of Education and Production that we continue to pay a lot of attention to building our country, to producing more, to bringing all of the idle lands that we have under heavy productive measures, to get the marriage of idle lands and idle hands going. The bridegroom of idle lands with the bride of idle hands must produce the children of more production, more food, more skills, more jobs, more dollars for our country. We must not allow ourselves to fall into the trap of beginning to relax, because that is also one of the plans of imperialism, to use terror, to frighten and to intimidate, and to make us forget about production. We have to continue to produce.

Imperialism Must Not Succeed

Our martyrs, the past martyrs Alister Strachan and Harold Strachan and Jerry Richardson and Rupert Bishop, and our present martyrs, Laureen and Laurice, they all expect us to continue to struggle to make sure that their deaths were not in vain. They expect more discipline of us, more production. They expect an end to corruption, an end to inefficiency. They expect a Militia of 20,000 or 30,000 people prepared to wage a people's war to save our country and to protect it and to defend our Revolution.

As we sympathise tonight, sisters and brothers, comrades, with the Phillip and Humphrey families, as the entire nation hopes and prays that the young Bailey children will survive, we must at the same time redouble our faith and conviction that imperialism must not succeed. We must, as a people, be prepared to fight back, we must as a people, even as we sympathise and condole with the families of those who have been robbed of their children tonight, never forget that the greatest honour any patriot can pay to himself or his country is to die for his country. There is no honour greater than that. So yes, we sympathise, but at the same time we note that new national heroes have emerged, that new national heroes have sprung up out of the struggle of our people, and the funerals of these young martyrs will be our people's response. We must assemble in our thousands to honour those who died today and to show by our numbers, not just the quantity, but in terms of the quality of our response, give imperialism and reaction the answer that they will not be expecting; that we have not been cowed, we have not been frightened, we have not been intimidated. But we are prepared to continue to struggle in the recognition that the struggle of the freedom-loving people of Grenada, that the struggle to build the Grenada Revolution is a historic task which our country is shouldering, which we are doing not just for ourselves in Grenada but for the entire region, for the entire Third World, because freedom and struggle and revolution and social progress are indivisible, cannot be separated.

Freedom-loving people throughout the Caribbean and Latin America are looking forward to the Grenada Revolution, want to see it succeed. Deputy Prime Minister of St Lucia, Brother George Odlum, rang me a few hours ago and expressed the deepest solidarity of the people of St Lucia. They have expressed the solidarity in words and they plan to back it with deeds. Comrade Bobby Clarke of Barbados, well known to Grenadians is at this very moment in Barbados at a Rally in remembrance of Walter Rodney, expressing solidarity and support with the Grenada Revolution. The Antigua Caribbean Liberation Movement and the leadership, under Tim Hector, have already sent us two cables of firm solidarity. There is no doubt that the freedom-loving people of the Caribbean want to see our Revolution go forward.

Those Murderers Will Pay

Let imperialism, let local reaction, let counter-revolution hear this from the people, that for every one of us they kill 10,000 more will come forward to carry on the struggle. Today, as we commemorated young Alister Strachan's murder, and as we stood by the graveside in Calivigny thinking of the young comrade who was murdered three years ago, we saw passing before us 25 more young pioneers who came forward to continue the struggle — 25 more young pioneers ready to fill the place of that young comrade. When will imperialism learn? Yes, they can kill our bodies but they can never kill the spirit of a people fighting for their liberation, they can never kill the spirit of a people fighting for their country and fighting to push their country forward.

Next year, on this same date, as we commemorate the anniversary of Tubal Uriah ('Buzz') Butler, of Alister Strachan, of Laurine and Laurice, two newest martyrs, we know that instead of 25 pioneers we will have 25,000 more pioneers, more members of the National Youth Organization, of the Militia, more and more of our people will come forward in order to

41

ensure that our struggle continues.

Before the end I want to say that I have just been passed a cable which has come from Jamaica from the People's National Party expressing its deepest shock at the assassination attempts and also its deepest shock at the the murders, these fould and cowardly and gross murders of our young Grenadians committed today. We thank these comrades as we thank the other comrades.

We think of the other families who are right now praying and hoping and begging for the lives of those on the critical list in our hospital, but most of all we think of the courage of our people and we know that the sacrifice that was made today will not go in vain. Those murderers will pay for what they have done. Imperialism will see us fight back. They will learn to respect the will and the fighting spirit of the Grenadian people and the Grenadian Revolution.

DOWN WITH COUNTER-REVOLUTION!

DOWN WITH IMPERIALISM!

THE LIVES OF THESE NEW MARTYRS MUST NOT BE WASTED. THEIR BLOOD MUST BE FURTHER MANURE AND FERTILIZER TO PUSH OUR REVOLUTION FORWARD.

REMEMBER – A UNITED, CONSCIOUS, ORGANIZED, VIGILANT PEOPLE CAN NEVER BE DEFEATED.

FORWARD EVER, BACKWARD NEVER!

6. Health for All — A Right of the Caribbean Masses

Feature Address at the Sixth Meeting of
CARICOM Conference of Health Ministers in
St George's, July 1980

In the name of the people of Grenada it gives me very real pleasure to welcome you all to our country. It is particularly pleasurable to do so because this meeting being hosted in Grenada is a meeting of CARICOM Ministers of Health, and in line with our very deep commitment to the CARICOM Movement, and to Caribbean and regional integration generally, it is always a pleasure for us to have here in our country our friends, our sisters and brothers from the Caribbean countries.

It is also particularly a pleasure because this, in our mind, is a very important meeting on a very important subject with important agenda items. This meeting can certainly help to influence the future course of our region as proper health to us is a key to the all-round development of any country. Clearly, our working people will be unable to be fully productive, a goal that all of us desire, if they are unhealthy. Clearly, likewise, the children of our region will not be able to receive or to benefit from the educational opportunities open to them if they are hungry, if they have poor eyesight, or if they are otherwise similarly disadvantaged. Thus, any serious meeting on this question of improving the quantity and quality of health care must be an important meeting.

We have observed that there are 45 agenda items and all of them appear to us to be relvant to the full development of the regional health strategy and to the smooth continuation of the process of improving the quantity and quality of health care for the people of this region — a matter we are sure that undoubtedly concerns all governments in the Caribbean community — a matter on which all of us have yet to make significant progress or at least have much more to achieve.

As a result of our common history of colonialist exploitation and continuing imperialist domination we all share a number of disadvantages. An economic system that taught us to look outside of our own countries for solutions to our problems, an economic system that has perpetuated the rule of a privileged local elite working in the interest of, and as the hand-maidens of rapacious external forces; an economic system that has left us poor, underdeveloped, over-exploited, with a very open, very dependent economy. This legacy has also left us an educational system that has prepared a tiny elite to be masters while condemning the broad majority to perpetual self-contempt, derogation and poverty; an educational system, moreover, that has trained this tiny elite to measure progress in terms of dollars, and hence to be unpatriotic and uncaring for the suffering of others; to get rich quickly and thus to seek fortunes abroad if and when the local environment does not allow for sufficiently rapid advance; an educational system that did not stress service but stressed rather personal individualist advancement. Hence a system that made it very difficult for the certificated elite to be willing to put their talents at the disposal of the masses, to work as part of a team with people deemed to be their 'inferiors', and to be unwilling to make any personal scarifices or concessions in the interests of the deprived and oppressed masses. This legacy has also left us a political, social, moral and psychological climate that has deformed our perspectives and priorities. That has left us thinking that development and progress should not be measured in terms of meeting the basic needs of our people, with regard to jobs, with regard to more housing, with regard to better food, with regard to pipeborne water, with regard to decent health care, with regard to clothing, with regard to education. It has instead left us measuring progress in terms of how many of us can become new millionaires or new members of the middle classes. This experience past and present has, therefore, left deep scars and greatly affected our capacity for achieving genuine development and social progress.

Our Health Problems Reflect the Colonial Legacy

In the area of health there are many ways in which this can be seen. Firstly in the area of the serious manpower shortage. With the doctors in most of our countries unwilling to work for any length of time for wages that societies can afford to pay, the result is a continuation of the brain-drain, a resumption or a turning in the first place to private practice, or an insistence on the right to use tax payers' time and money to supplement public employment with private practice. Furthermore, in the case of many of our doctors, we see a great unwillingness to move out of the confines of the hospital system and into the communities, into the medical clinics, the health centres, the day-care centres — in other words, into those areas where precisely the vast majority of our people are needing medical attention. It has left us, too, with a legacy of a serious shortage of nurses; many ill-trained, and also many with an incorrect approach to the whole question of developing a community approach to solving our medical problems. It has left us with a serious shortage of trained public health workers. It has left us in many cases with not even a single paramedic, so important if we are serious about developing the concepts of primary health care.

A second broad area of concern arising out of this legacy is in the area of the serious management and planning problems that we face. In many cases in our countries there are not even health planners, and there are very limited attempts at scientifically devising a national health plan. And again, precisely because training historically has been seen as unimportant, the whole question of community participation in improving the quality and quantity of health care have also been sadly neglected. Food and nutrition councils are still the rare exception in the region. The possibility for mobilising communities to unblock drains, cut overhangings, thus helping to deal with the serious problems of disease communicated by the mosquito — these possibilities have, by and large, been relatively untapped.

This legacy has also left us inadequate and in some cases non-existent facilities. We are faced with a shortage of basic medicines, a shortage of important items of equipment. The situation with regard to pipeborne water, for example, remains a serious problem and this is certainly a very large contributing factor to the continuing problems of gastro-enteritis and diarrhoeal diseases. These two problems certainly continue to be a substantial cause of death for children under two years. In many of our hospitals X-ray machines do not function, specialised services — for example provision of eye clinics, provision of dentists — these continue to be missing. In the area of environmental health, the serious lack of trained health inspectors and even junior inspectors, the necessary equipment for dumping sites, bulldozers, spreaders, the refuse trucks, the garbage bins, all of the basic and very important facilities are missing in several of our territories.

Changing the Situation is Within Our Means

It seems to us, sisters and brothers, that for societies like ours, it is important to identify all the possibilities for improving the quality of life, especially when this quality of life can be improved without a substantial capital expenditure. We believe that two areas where it is possible to bring benefits without perhaps spending a great deal of money, are precisely in the areas of health and education. We feel this is so for the following reasons at least.

Firstly, the possibility to attract assistance from outside, from friendly countries, from regional and international institutions, these possibilities in our view are more readily available for these two areas of education and health than for several other areas. In the case of education for example, the possibility of getting scholarships from friendly countries and friendly institutions is undoubtedly a reality. In the case of health, the possibility exists for attracting financial assistance to improve the water supply in our country, to obtain much desired and vital equipment, the possibilities for getting technical assistance, the possibilities, indeed, for devising suitable project proposals that form part of an overall national plan.

Secondly, this is possible in our view because of the possibility to rationalise the allocation of our scarce resources. For example, improvements can certainly be made in areas such as our nursing schools, in the area of in-service training there are limited possibilities there for bringing about improvement without a great deal of additional expenditure. We can consider seriously and begin to implement the possibilities of cutting back on wasteful expenditure, looking for example, for cheaper sources of drug supplies. This is one of the areas in which regional co-operation must certainly move decisively.

Finally, in this area we can begin to ensure a more proportionate use of the budgetary allocations in health. We have found in Grenada for example that in 1978 something like 70-75% of the health budget was being spent on the three General Hospitals, while the remaining 25-30% of that budget was being spent on the service of the 35 Health Centres and Medical Clinics around our country. The obvious disadvantage of this approach is that the three areas of greatest spending were precisely the areas that were attending to a very small percentage of those in our country who need medical attention.

A third possibility, it seems to us, is to begin to exploit more the opportunities for involving our communities, for involving the masses of our people in participating in this programme of improving on the health needs of our country. In the area of education, we found in Grenada that in January, for a period of two weeks, by calling on the communities, we were able to get something like 65 primary schools around Grenada repaired, refurbished or renovated. And this of course amounted to a massive saving for tax payers.

In the area of health, similar possibilities exist. There seems to be no good reason why community centres could not in some cases also be used for bringing health care to our people. Our clinics and health centres can certainly be repaired in part, by community involvement and assistance. The unblocking of drains, the stepping up of public health education, the establishment of village health committees not only look to the question of repairing and maintaining public health buildings, of unblocked drains, but also of monitoring the quantity of health service that the people receive, all of these it seems to us must represent important possibilities in this area of health care.

Health: A Right of All Our People

We feel confident, sisters and brothers, that our efforts and goals are in keeping with the oft repeated policy statements issued by the CARICOM Ministers of Health. These statements have stressed among other things, that health is a right for all people and as such maximum health opportunities should be provided with fees taking secondary place rather than priority. These statements have also stressed the need to deliver health opportunities to our rural population, and the need to reduce inequalities in the provision of more housing and other such amenities that have a direct or indirect relationship to the question of proper health care. These policy positions in turn are in keeping with the specific objectives of CARICOM in the field of health. As long ago as 1977 at the Third Ministers of Health Conference in St Kitts, these objectives were listed as follows:

Firstly, the development of comprehensive health services. Secondly, a proper health care for mothers and children. Thirdly, a proper strategy for food and nutrition. Fourthly, control of communicable diseases. Fifthly, control of non-communicable diseases. Sixthly, proper environmental health, and finally, the development of adequate supporting services.

Many of these objectives are being tackled and I understand that today the Secretariat can report that there is a clear declaration on a regional health policy, that there is an ongoing management development project, which is helping to train over 700 personnel in our region; that there is a serious thrust in the field of health manpower development. The community is also developing the ability to monitor and to survey the outbreak of epidemics. There is a clear environmental health strategy. There is a comprehensive, maternal and child health strategy. There is great progress towards the creation of a food and nutrition strategy. This could become a reality, I am told, by the end of this year. There is also a dental health strategy which is in need however of urgent implementation.

I am advised further that the regional pharmaceutical policy is in the process of preparation, and that progress is being made in the field of disaster prevention, preparedness and relief. No one can seriously say that these are not important advances, but nonetheless we must also recognise that we still have, individually and collectively a long, long way to go. Accordingly, we in Grenada have begun to develop a national health plan, aimed at dramatically improving the quality and quantity of health care ino our country.

A Rational Health Policy Is a Vital Part of National Development Plans

The People's Revolutionary Government of Grenada views health as a basic human right and as a fundamental prerequisite for the formulation of a sound economic policy. Further the People's Revolutionary Government is aware that health for all can only be attained through national political will, and through the co-ordinated efforts of the health sector and the relevant activities of other social and economic development sectors, since health development both contributes to, and results from social and economic development. Health policies must form part of an overall development policy, thus reflecting the social and economic goals of government and people. In this way, strategies for the health, social and economic sectors will be mutually supportive, and together can contribute to the ultimate goals of our society.

Everywhere people are more and more coming to realise that the motivation in striving to increase their earnings is not simply greater wealth for its own sake but the social improvements that increasedpurchasing power can bring to them and their children, such as better food and housing, better education, better leisure opportunities and of course better health. Only when they have an acceptable level of health, can individuals, families and communities enjoy the other benefits of life.

Health development is, therefore, essential for social and economic development, and the means for attaining them are intimately linked. For this reason, efforts to improve the health and socio-economic situation of our nation must be regarded as mutually supportive rather than competitive. Discussions on whether the promotion of health consumes resources or whether it is an economically productive factor contributing to development belong to the academic past. We fully accept our responsibility to provide our people with adequate health care as a matter of right. It is imperative, therefore, at the time when resources are scarce, to ensure that comprehensive social and economic planning be implemented. And in this regard, it is mandatory for Grenada and the region's developmental efforts to give separate and special priority to a health strategy particularly designed to reach the poorest of the poor in our respective countries.

Our Plan for Realising Better Health Care

In order to effect such changes in the health care system the following minimum positions have been recognised and agreed upon. Firstly, our Government has recognised Health Planning as a function of the highest level of decision-making. This is essential to ensure the appropriate delegation of responsibility and authority, the preferential allocation of resources to health care, and the proper location of the supporting services so that they are accessible to the communities they are to serve. And since the planning of health care involves political, social and economic factors, multidisciplinary planning teams are needed especially at the central level. Central planning will aim at enabling communities to plan their own health care activities. It will therefore, provide them with a clear idea of the part they have to play in the national health care strategy and in the overall development process at community level.

In Grenada health care services are not now sufficiently accessible, or sufficiently readily available to a majority of the population. A nationwide plan of action to overcome the problems of availability and accessibility has therefore been initiated. The main components of this plan are: firstly an investigation of existing health care services – manpower, supplies, equipment and facilities; secondly, an investigation into the basic needs of the population; and thirdly, the question of linkages and referrals. It is necessary to thoroughly research the present health delivery system to ascertain exactly what components are presently being offered, to whom are these services available, by whom are they provided, at what time are they available, and at what price, both to the consumer and the government.

The object of this research will be to serve as the platform from which a comprehensive health delivery system can be planned. It will address such problems as poor or uneven quality, and inadequate and inaccessible health care. Intersectoral co-ordination between health and some or all other sectors such as finance, education, agriculture and water resources, will also be sought and established.

Community Support and People's Participation — A Key Factor

It is our firm belief that all genuine democratic processes rest on, promote, and are strengthened by a mass movement. The active participation of the popular masses in all such processes is essential for the realisation of these goals. At the Alnia Ata Conference, members clearly recognised that primary health care was the means of attaining health for all. And, in order to make primary health care universally accessible in the community as quickly as possible, maximum community and individual self-reliance for health development is essential. To attain such self-reliance requires full community participation in the planning, organisation and management of their health care. Such participation is best mobilised in our view through appropriate education which will enable communities to deal with their health problems in the most suitable ways.

Substantial community support is therefore a key factor in the success and continuity of a primary health care system. We certainly believe that all organisations and groups in our country, be they or workers, farmers, youth, women, business — all of them should be involved in planning and monitoring of this system. The fundamental tasks which are hoped to be developed on an intersectoral level are the raising of the health education level for the entire population; obtaining the effective support of the population on health programmes; strengthening community service and doctor/patient relations; and increasing and strengthening the communities' confidence in their health services.

Curative medicine, although it is continuously perfecting its techniques, cannot alone assure the maintenance of the population's high health level. The promotion and protection of health are activities which are priorities when it comes to offering the community a high level of health. The national health system being developed in our country will encourage medical practice to take a preventive/curative approach, and allow for the development of programmes for the lessening and eradication of diseases. This activity will be based on the integration of the preventive and curative activities of the Ministry of Health.

We are also actively looking at the question of administrative reform and we are publicly committing ourselves, as government, to bring about the necessary health reforms that are essential to convert a goal into a reality. It is clear that the full development of the primary health care programme and the achievement of its fundamental purposes is a long-term process. The strategy will need to be constantly adjusted in the light of new information, day-to-day experiences, and social changes taking place. However, while the primary health care approach itself is universal there is no universal recipe for primary health care programmes, each one being a national endeavour specific to the country's concrete situation. What succeeds in one country cannot necessarily be trasnplanted and have the same results everywhere. However, we firmly believe in the words of the 1977 draft resolution, which was proposed at the 1977 St Kitts Ministers of Health Conference, that in the Caribbean Community the question of health is geographically indivisible. That to the extent that any of us are able to make progress in this important area of improving on the quality of health for our people, it must be of benefit to the rest of us in the region, to the extent we are so closely connected and linked together by different forms of transportation, by regularity of travel and in other such ways.

Primary health care would be a more acceptable and easier way of delivery of health care. To make the community the focal point of the whole system, to look for the relevant technology that our countries can accept and afford and to aim at the universal accessibility of health care is in many ways revolutionary.

Primary health care would be more acceptable and easier to implement for all countries, if we all realise that others are successfully using this approach. For this reason, regional and international, political, moral, technical and financial support are important. Our government has recognised the fact that with the availability of basic health techniques and opportunities, the provision of food, education, decent housing, more pipeborne water, and assistance in improving productivity, the health of communities can improve dramatically and in a way that ensures the potential for continuing and continuous change. We have acknowledged that it is our duty to provide the population with a health care system which is available, accessible, affordable and of a high quality. And although we are fully aware of, and limited by financial and human constraints, we are determined to achieve the goal of health for all by the year 2000, through primary health care. And we believe that this should certainly continue to be the aim of all of us in the Caribbean community and in the region.

May I therefore once again welcome you to our shores, wish you a very successful Conference and ask that while you are here with us that you take the time off to enjoy our hospitality, our friendship and the beauty of our country and people.

7. Education is a Must!

Speech to Inaugurate the National In-Service
Teacher Education Programme (NISTEP) at the
Grenada Teacher's College, 30 October 1980

As everyone before me has said, I know I must now repeat it, today is undoubtedly a red-letter day in our country. It's a day that in more senses than one, our country is once again making history. Today is undoubtedly an important day because what it signals is the start, not in a symbolic but in a real sense, of a very important experiment. It is an experiment which for us will be the first of its kind in our country, and if the truth be said without any boasting whatsoever, the very first of its kind — having regard to its scale — in the entire English-speaking Caribbean. We're embarking, therefore, on a massive project, an ambitious project, a project which has its problems even now, a project which took several months of very serious sacrifice to initiate, very determined hard work by many comrades led by our remarkable, hard-working and disciplined Minister of Education, Comrade George Louison.

Today is going to see the start of a more systematic, a more scientific, a more planned approach to the question of the training of our teachers. In the past, what we were able to do in this very building where we are sitting and standing right now, was train, over a period of two years, something like fifty teachers. Now, out of that figure, as we know, there was a large leakage factor of teachers who received the training but nonetheless caught the first flight they could out of our beloved country, heading north to the colder climates.

New Values, New Attitudes, New Habits

What we hope to start today is a programme that will reverse that trend in more ways than one. A programme that, because our country is poor, will have meaning to the further material development and the better spending of our limited resources. A programme that instead of aiming to teach or train teachers on the basis of only 50 every two years, now aims to train that this land is ours, that we alone can build it, that if we think in terms of catching a plane or boat out of it then the country will never be developed. Because in the final analysis only *we* can build it, and we certainly would hope that over the three years, because of some new inputs into this programme, because of the greater emphasis now on instilling new values, new attitudes, new habits, new approaches to the question of education, of integrating the theoretical aspects of education with the practical aspects, of ensuring that the people receiving this training are in fact being prepared for the real world that they are going to have to live in, then our teachers will be able to pass on to their students an appreciation of understanding that education is *not* primarily about certification. There are many certificated fools in the world. Education is really much, much more about preparing us for life and preparing us for the *real* world.

That is the point of receiving an education, and the sooner we grasp that, the quicker we will be able to develop an approach that says that work and study are part and parcel of the same dynamic, the same process, the same dialectic. We shall then aim in a serious way to make each one of us become worker and student from day one of our existence until the day we die. That is what life must be like in a poor, developing country such as ours. We really cannot afford the luxury of compartmentalising people into these separate categories, and then pulling them off the shelf, rubbing the dust off them and saying: 'Right! You're a graduate now, you're no longer a student, you're a worker. When you're working, you stop reading.' Or while you're a student, your parents and family are so concerned that you fill up your head with all of this 'Education', that even during the long summer vacation some parents are afraid to let their nice children go outside lest they stomp their toe, and stomping their toe their head might get affected! Afraid to let them take a job, afraid to let them go by the land and pick up a cutlass, afraid to let them go by a mechanic's shop and learn something about the repairing of vehicles, afraid to let them go down by the International Airport project site to see what is happening down there. That is the way we have been indoctrinated, that is the way we have been brain-washed and socialised — not just for the last 40 years, but for centuries.

Education for the Elite — A Colonial Legacy

The history of our country, as with the history of Latin America and all Third World countries generally, has been a history that has said that education is for the elite, for a tiny few who get certificates and then use those certificates to lord it over the others below them. That has been the historic point of education. That was the way our history was developed consciously by the British colonial masters. That is why after 350 years of British colonialism we only have one secondary school — the Grenada Boys' Secondary School on top of the hill. They never even thought of building a second secondary school because they didn't want the masses to have an education. The masses were supposed to remain uneducated, ignorant, backward, superstitious, diseased and poor. That was colonialism's plan. And in that way they could continue to exploit us forever, to pull out our raw materials from our land and encourage us always to look to the metropole, to look outside of our own country, our own economy and look only to *their* country to find jobs for their people, to use our surplus to build their ports and their industries while we got the crumbs.

But of course, with the coming of the Revolution all that has come to an end. Now we can truthfully say in our country that we have begun the process – it will be a long, hard one – but we have taken the first steps of reclaiming our land, reclaiming our resources, reclaiming our people, and we are now beginning the historic task of ensuring that all of our people receive all the education that they are willing to receive. That is one of the most important meanings of the Grenada Revolution.

Problems for the New Programmes

So that is another reason why I am saying that this is a historic day for us. For after all, when you really sit down and think about it seriously in terms of all the massive problems – many of them real, genuine problems that did need solving – problems, for example, associated with what we are going to do with all of the children in the schools on the days when we take 259 teachers from these four parishes and bring them to St George's. Or what are we going to do with the children of the other section of the island when we take their 190 teachers from St Andrew's and St Patrick's and bring them to the teaching centre in Grenville? Or, of course, the same problem in Carriacou. These are real problems, nobody can deny that. When teachers were raising difficulties centred around the question of what was being described as 'overwork' – *how am I going to be able to do all of this extra amount of work?* When other teachers were raising the problem of the bond and trying to put this argument in the context of our consensus and voluntary and democratic spirit – in other words, 'if I don't want to learn how to teach properly, nobody has a right to force me, and if on top of forcing me how to teach properly you want to make me sign a bond, that is slavery!' Remember all the arguments that were coming out? Other arguments centred around the question of vacation time. Teachers were saying 'how am I going to lose X number of weeks in my vacation to take part in this course, especially if I don't see the value of it and I don't want to take part in it.'

All of these objections were coming forward comrades, as you know. And one person throughout that entire period that I know of, who kept saying that these objections were ones you must expect, that these objections in one sense were only natural, that to a great extent they were going to be fuelled by the rumour-mongers, by the counter-revolutionaries, by those who do not want to see progress, by those who want to create confusion and division – so therefore if we hold dialogue with the teachers, if we continue to reason and to rap with them, to ground with them and show them the objective value of this programme, then in fact all of them are going to come around. And I must say that the early results of the survey which has been done over the last two days have shown conclusively that the vast majority of our teachers are expressing their fullest support for the programmes and are willing to go forward to make it into a massive success. That shows the calibre of teachers that we have in Grenada.

Comrades, whatever we do there'll be problems. The Centre for Popular Education, as you know, was a programme where we had tremendous early problems. It's a programme which still has problems, but which has gone forward and is now undoubtedly the most publicly-known programme that the Revolution is involved in, and to a great extent it is the most successful. So we have come from a tradition where we can truthfully say that when we recognise problems and difficulties and obstacles, without allowing ourselves to sink into idealistic optimism, nonetheless we can realistically face our problems, engage in dialogue with our people and make serious attempts to bring them into participation in these programmes, involve them at every step, mobilise them at every step, organise them at every step and let them come up with their own creative ideas as to how to solve the problems. In that way we are confident that any programme that the Revolution embarks upon, any realistic programme, can and will succeed. That has been the secret so far, and once again that approach has been proved correct in relation to this particular programme.

The Real 'Firsts'

Our country has always been a country of firsts — and I'm not speaking about the kind of firsts in the way in which the old dictator used to use the term. No, I'm not talking about first in building roundabouts, I'm not talking about first in planting flowers, I'm not talking about first in riding UFO and I'm not talking about first in winning Miss World! What I *am* talking about is firsts in the real sense, in a sense that brings real value to our country and our people. That is why it was Fedon, a Grenadian, who led the insurrection in 1795, that is why Marryshow was called the Father of Federation, that is why Butler was the most important Caribbean trade unionist of this century, that is why Mighty Sparrow is the World's greatest calypsonian, that is why we in Grenada led the first revolution in the English-speaking Caribbean! So, comrades, when we look at our history we can truthfully see ourselves as the descendants of Fedon, Butler and Marryshow. We can recognise what we were able to do in the past, and so no In-Service Teacher Education Programme can ever be too big a task for this Revolution. We are going to make it move forward more and more, we are going to make it succeed in a massive way.

Over the 19 months there has been progress in education in a number of different areas. If you look at it carefully you will see that from pre-school right up to university and thereafter in the area of adult education, there have been tremendous advances. Advances in the area of improvements in physical facilities, in greatly increased educational opportunities, advances in the sense that more and more of our people coming from all different walks

f life and involved in all different sectors have access to more and more
raining possibilities, advances in the serious work that has been started on
a new curriculum — and finally and most significantly, advances because we
are now instilling into our people and our teachers this new approach, this
new sense of values and attitudes to the question of education. These are
undamental areas of progress. Some might appear intangible, all, nonethe-
ess, are of great importance.

Advances in Primary Education

n early childhood, for example, we have seen that over the last 19 months
more teachers have been trained to work full-time in that area of the three
o five year bracket and the infants category. A lot of work has been done,
not just among the teachers but also in the improvement of supervision and
facilities. This is one of the areas that we regard as being extremely
important. In the overall area of primary education we have also made many
advances. From the time that the Curriculum Development Unit was estab-
ished last October, a whole number of programmes were worked out which
had an immediate impact on our primary school syllabus. We can see that in
erms of the workshops and discussions which were held, the new reading
materials that are being developed and most of all, once again in terms of
his *dialogue* which has been taking place between the officials at the Ministry
of Education and yourselves, the primary school teachers. A large part of
hat dialogue, on a mass scale, took place in January when the schools were
closed down for two weeks for that historic National Teachers' Seminar. Most
fundamentally, it has been the day-to-day and week-to-week work done by
he comrades from the Ministry of Education, who have been going out there
on a regular basis and rapping with you at your schools and in different
centres, trying to see if *with* you, this new approach to education can be
developed. If change is seen as coming from above it will never really succeed.
But if we look at the question of trying to get change going by approaching
and involving the people — particularly those who are involved in the specific
area where change is being sought — then there is a great chance of success.
You are the ones who stand up in the classroom, you are the ones who teach.
Therefore, your ideas on teaching must be fundamentally important, your
deas on how you can create new approaches to what you are doing, your
deas on how you can improve your methods of communication with your
students *must* be important, your ideas on how you can simplify and
elucidate the content of your teaching tasks. That is why the programme has
tressed from the beginning that *you* are involved, that *you* understand, that
you approve, that *you* help to develop, to shape and to mould the programme.
We think that this is essential to whatever success we are going to continue
o have.

Advances in Secondary Education

In the area of secondary education, comrades, there again the Revolution ha
made a number of important steps forward. The question of the reduction
of school fees was basic to the poor working masses of our country. If you
can imagine the situation of the average agricultural worker. Still today these
brothers and sisters form the largest sector of our people, our working class
notwithstanding the fact that over the last 20 years it has been cut by half
The average sister working as an agricultural worker can expect to take home
$50 a fortnight, which is $100 a month. When you have worked out how
much it costs to eat, how much it costs to send your child to school, how
much it costs for recreation or to use the transport system that we have, then
obviously $50 a fortnight cannot go very far. So by reducing secondary
school fees from $37.50 a term to $12.50 has made a real difference, and
made it a lot easier for those sisters and brothers constituting the poorest
of the poor in our country to ensure that their children can either continue
to go to school or have access for the first time to secondary education.

The number of scholarships from primary to secondary school has also
substantially increased. That is going to mean that more and more children
now have the opportunity of attending secondary school and doing so free
of cost. But perhaps even more important than that is with the opening of
the Bernadette Bailey Secondary School in Happy Hill, more places are
available for children at secondary level — and this is, of course, only the
second secondary school to have been opened by any government in Grenada
over 400 years! That is the reality. The British gave us *one*!

Developments in FE and the Productive Sectors

The Institute of Further Education, which now has over 250 students, has
the biggest ever number of students in our country, at one time, studying
for 'A' levels. The reasons for that are obvious. With more and more oppor
tunities for going abroad to study on a university scholarship, it means that
more and more children who have previously dropped out of school have now
found it necessary and valuable to go back to school and study again. The
student-teacher ratio has also improved dramatically, moving from 45-1
under the Gairy days to 1-31 at the present. This means that the problem
of overcrowding in our schools is gradually being relieved. This also means
that the approach generally that our students and teachers have had to the
question of Education should also improve. In the past, many students going
to school would have seen a classroom with such numbers as being like a
nursery, and a teacher might well have been forgiven if instead of teaching
she or he felt as if they were child-minding — because with that number of
children in a class and nobody being able to hear what the next one is saying
that is not seriously a school.

In the productive sector we have also started training programmes fo sisters and brothers involved in different aspects of the economy. In agriculture, we have re-opened the Mirabeau Farm School and last year there were 50 graduates. Likewise, in the various Agro-Industrial plants which are being established right now, training programmes for the workers have been progressing and are continuing. We now have in our country a fishing school, where our fishermen will now have the opportunity of learning more modern techniques of fishing. We have opened a Co-operative Training School, where the youth, whom we are encouraging to go back to the land, will receive education and training in co-operative principles and practices so that the lands that they will be working can be run along those lines. We have also opened a hotel training school, so that the workers of that important sector of the economy will be receiving training for the first time in the history of our country. These are four or five key areas in the productive sector in which we have been trying to develop training programmes.

In-Service Programmes

In the in-service area a number of other programmes have also been developed. Apart from this teacher training programme there is an ongoing in-service programme for nurses. Only two days ago I opened the annual week of activities sponsored by the Grenada Nurses Association, and while I was up there with the nurses and talking to the sisters, a number of them were saying that they had been waiting for something like eight years after they had qualified, for a midwifery course. Those courses had been closed down under the dictatorship, but now again they are running and the nurses were overjoyed about that. Our Police also are engaged in an in-service training programme. Tomorrow at Gouyave, the first police to have been trained under this programme will have their 'passing out' graduation ceremony. Between 25 and 30 police will be graduating, and several more have gone on extended courses overseas, to places like Guyana and Panama. The public service workers in our country have also begun an in-service programme, as yet mainly in the area of top and middle management, but an overall programme to be started early next year will aim to bring all civil servants in our country into this programme. In the state apparatus, comrades from the Information Department, External Affairs, Statistics, Planning, in the Computer Centre and several other sectors are involved at different levels of training, some on an in-service basis and some abroad in countries which have the particular skills which we do not now have. The militia has a continuous in-service course. There is a permanent militia school which runs a programme every two months. So my point is that both inside and outside the productive sector there are more and more opportunities for training developing, so that all of our people will have the opportunity of doing whatever they have chosen as their career to the best of their ability. We believe this is central to the success of the Revolution, that it is going to be impossible to push the country forward and build a national economy, if our people are not trained, if our people are not given skills and shown what are the best and most scientific ways of doing whatever they are involved in.

At the tertiary level, the government has been able to pay off most of Gairy's debts to the University of the West Indies, and, therefore, Grenadians are once again, after several years, able to go back to the UWI at the subsidised rate. So that has made a lot of difference to our university students and those engaged in trying to enter university for a degree course. We have also been able to obtain many new university scholarships. Last year 109 of our young people were able to go abroad and study, and there are more this year. The main problem that we are discovering now is that we have moved to the stage where we have more university scholarship offers than we have qualified students who can fill the places. So that is another reason why we must ensure that more and more of our children have a sound base at primary level, so that by the time they reach secondary level they will be able to more easily absorb the material they will be taught. In turn that will make it easier for them to pass their 'O' level and 'A' level exams and get university scholarships to go abroad.

The Centre for Popular Education

Of course, the most fundamental area in our Education sector which we have undertaken is our CPE [Centre for Popular Education] programme, which is really an adult education programme. It is aimed in this first phase, first and foremost, at reaching those people who are altogether unable to read and write. Acquiring these skills is essential, not only for personal and individual development, but also because of its significance to the development of our economy. If we are going to modernise our economy and bring science and technology to bear on greater production, if we are going to be searching for more appropriate and creative technology to deal with our situation, we do need a skilled and educated workforce. At a minimum we certainly need a workforce that can read and write. It is also going to have a tremendous relevance to the success of building a deeper and greater sense of national unity, and raising the national consciousness of our people. If all our people are able at least at a minimum level to read and write, it will be much easier for them not to be misled, and to understand more and more of what is happening in their country, in their region and in the world. It will be so much easier for them to understand this word we use so often, that we call *Imperialism*. It will be much easier for them to understand what we mean when we talk of *destabilisation*, what we mean when we say that the Revolution is for the people, and that the people *are* the Revolution. It will be much easier for them to understand why the Revolution came in the first place and where we are trying to go. Therefore the CPE programme is certainly the most fundamental part of the overall drive we are making in the area of education. It will not stop once we have taught *all* our people how to read and write; it will continue. We see it as not just a centre for Popular

Education but a Centre for *Permanent* Education. After the phase of basic literacy we shall move on to the phase of popular education, of continually raising consciousness and passing on more and more knowledge of mankind to more and more of our people. For as I said at the beginning, our approach to education is that it is a process which begins from the time you are born, and ends the day you die. It cannot be compartmentalised into two or three or 10 or 20 years of your life. It has to be an ongoing process, and if that is so, a Centre for Popular Education is an institution that has to remain forever as a permanent necessity.

There have also been important strides forward made in raising the cultural awareness of our people, as well as increasing the *formal* educational opportunities for our people. In the formal area, many more film shows have been shown around our country, panel discussions, seminars, rallies, Health Workshops — all these have a basic educational content. In sport too and physical education, our co-ordinator has been doing an excellent job in building a community-based support for sport, and the National Youth Organisation is developing a programme aimed at creating new areas for sport. They are going around the country now identifying present activities with a view to improving them, and seeing what new areas and complexes are required for the future. They are obtaining the necessary materials from the Ministry of Public Works, and mobilising the youth in the particular villages to help create the facilities themselves.

No one could have failed to notice the great outburst of creative and artistic activity that has happened in Grenada over the last 19 months. Think of the number of new skits and plays you have watched. Think of the development of the Workers' Enlightenment Theatre Group, the Theatre Group of the National Youth Organisation, the dozens of groups putting on plays that have been springing up all around the country. At the CPE emulation monthly sessions you would have been impressed by the quality, content and enthusiasm of the young comrades from all over the country, coming forward to stage their productions. Think of the number of poems that have been written and published — they are all a part of this same upsurge of creativity since the Revolution. As a part of culture — and I put it here deliberately — we have seen the development of new habits, new attitudes and new values in our people, particularly among our women. That is one of our healthiest developments. The ending of sexual discrimination and victimisation of our women with regard to jobs has meant that women have been able to integrate much more easily into the society. The provision of equal pay for equal work and its introduction into government estates and farms has created a certain climate and basis for ending the discrimination against women and removing the artificial distinction that has separated our men from our women. Yesterday I had a telephone call from our comrade sisters, led by Sister Phyllis Coard, from the Dominican Republic, where they are attending an international women's conference of the ICAW, the main women's organisation of the Organisation of American States. There are 26 countries represented at that conference and five had to be elected to an

Executive Committee. Our women made a further stride forward yesterday morning, when Grenada was elected.

Related to this question of culture, comrades, are our eating habits. People sometimes do not see this as being a question of culture, but of course it is. This whole question of what we eat: you know, some of us are waiting for Christmas because we want to buy an apple! Or a turkey! And then people like my friend in the front row, Brother L.A. Purcell, might make a few more dollars selling turkey and ham! But this whole question of developing a new approach to what we ourselves produce is of the greatest importance: to think local, buy local, to eat local. The fact of the matter is that to some extent we *are* producing our own food now. Of course, we have a long, long way to go, but if you come out of the cutlass technology of the 17th Century, you can't rush into the space-age technology of the 20th Century in a night. But in some areas progress has been made. We now have our own nectars, our own jams, jellies, juices and mango chutney. These things are being processed right here. We now have our own saltfish and smoked herring. A lot of people used to say, 'We can't produce that!' But we can and are producing these things, and we have the responsibility as part of this *overall* educational process to begin to see what we produce as what we should buy. And let me tell those who haven't tried it yet, that the saltfish being produced in Grenada by the Ministry of Fisheries is a lot better than the saltfish we used to import — you want to try it, it has a *lot* of juice in it.

Knowledge in the Service of Production

As a part of this educational process, I want to mention science and technology. If we are going to go forward and solve problems of diseases or pests that affect our crops, if we are going to find ways of growing more without using chemicals — because they cost a lot of money, if we are going to get more yield out of every acre without at the same time putting more acreage under cultivation to produce the same old amount, then all of these things are going to require that we bring science and technology to bear on what we do. We need to find the appropriate technology that we can use and adapt for every situation. That is an important task, and that is one of the prime reasons for this work/study approach to the question of education. For in using this approach you are showing your students what the *real* world in Grenada looks like, and not just what the classroom walls look like. Where they can really go out now and *see* what the agricultural workers are doing, when they can come down and see what the agro-industrial plant looks like and how it works, visit the saltfish plant, see how the fishing school is operating and how the comrade fishermen are catching their fish and what hooks they use to catch the different fish. Over the past few weeks, for example, we haven't been able to catch many sharks, although we have them in abundance out there. The reason — we didn't have the correct hooks, we only got a shipment of them this week. We need to have our young sisters and brothers of the future understanding these things. For apart from knowing how to read, write and understand history, they need to know what a nutmeg tree looks like, they need to know something about crop fertilisation, about grafting plants, about the kind of yield you can expect from an acre of nutmeg or cocoa, or bananas and sugar cane – and what the possibilities are for increasing on that yield. Then for the first time they would be able to address their minds, even at their young age, to how they can use the little learning they are getting to further develop their country, and how they can find new, scientific, technological and *creative* ways of lifting production without involving a lot of dollars.

Cutlass-Technology and Worker of the Year

Look at the Cuban comrades helping to build our airport, for example. The main base for the explosives they are using right now is the bagasse from the sugar cane. This means a big saving in fuel so that the cost of blasting all the earth at the airport site is perhaps half the price of the explosives we would otherwise have to buy from Canada, America or Britain. That is a concrete example of the Cubans, in a situation of difficulty because of their poor economy, applying their creative minds and coming up with a scientific and cost-reducing answer. Let me give you an even better example. There's a brother living in St David's who works on a government estate. He's in his fifties, he can't read or write, he's a poor, agricultural worker. He's been working on that same estate for over 15 years. It's a cocoa-producing estate of 127 acres. Now, you know our cocoa is suffering from a lot of diseases and pests. The main pests are beetles. So this man kept walking around his estate over the years, trying to find some way in which he could eradicate the beetle without having to spend all this money on expensive chemicals. So what this poor 'uneducated' comrade did was to follow the beetle from place to place to see what other trees it liked to lie down upon. He found that apart from the cocoa tree, the beetle liked the African breadfruit. So the brother chopped down a few branches of an African breadfruit tree and he made a trap and covered it with nine little sticks from one of the branches. He put three at the bottom, three across and three more at the top. Then he put these traps under different cocoa trees all over the estate. He had 40 or 50 traps scattered all around the 127 acres, and every day after that he would walk around the traps below the cocoa trees to see if any beetles had settled on them. Then, when he discovered them, he would pull them out and put them into a bottle. In one day he caught 205 beetles, and no amount of chemicals had ever done that! Now, if you are looking for a man who should not only be worker of the year but *man* of the year in Grenada, it should be this man for what he has done. That is what I mean be creatively applying science and technology. The only technology that this brother – his name is Brother Coonyahr – knew was cutlass technology. Yet here he is discovering in this creative way a solution to a problem that saves the country masses

61

of money. So we don't have to use these chemicals now – and a lot o
farmers in the private sector are also seeking the services of Brother Coonyah
because they want his trap. He's become a kind of hero! That is the kind o
spirit we have to inject and instil into our young ones. That is the kind o
enthusiasm and searching, the new approach and attitude we have to ge
across. That is what is going to build this country, and that is what this new
educational thrust is going to be all about.

Comrades, the internationalism in our country has also greatly developed
and that too we see as a crucial part of the educational process. That too, we
believe, cannot be separated from what we do in the classroom, whether i
is what we teach or what we learn. We are living in a world, we are living in
a region – the Caribbean. We are *not* cut off, we are a part of this region and
a part of this world. Therefore, whatever happens in any part of this region
or this world *must* be of concern to us. And if there are other people in othe
parts of this region or this world that are seeing trouble or are being
oppressed or are having to put up with injustice, then it is our right as a free
and revolutionary people to express our firmest support and solidarity with
them and give them our fullest material backing. That is our duty and respon
sibility. That is why we have to develop this internationalist approach. Tha
is why two of our comrades are right now in Nicaragua, helping the Nicar
aguans with *their* literacy programme, two young Grenadians carrying ou
their internationalist assignment. That is something we should justly be very
proud of.

The Threat of Imperialism

How much time, for example, have we spent over the last week thinking
about what is happening in Jamaica today? Elections going on. Ten dead
20 dead, 30 dead, 40 dead. Papers and radio have been talking about it. Every
night it is clearer and clearer that imperialism does not respect the right of the
people of Jamaica to choose their own government. Every night it is cleare
and clearer that imperialism is trying to seek to dictate to the people o
Jamaica how they must build their country and who they must use as thei
leader. Every night imperialism is giving us the great lesson of recent time
over and over again: that they have no respect for any people, that they don'
care what amount of violence and murder and killings they have to do to ge
their way. They don't care if they are on an electoral path or a non-electora
path. You know they always telling us in Grenada, 'Call election!' Americ
always shouting, 'Call election!' *They* take 13 years after *their* revolution
in America to call election, yet they want us to call ours in 13 days! The
same America likes to say:'If you had elections, there'd be no bombs in
Queen's Park.' I want to know how *they* explain what happening in Jamaica
Election been called, and every demand Seaga makes on an electoral level
he gets. Elections holding, but that'ent stopping Imperialism, they'ent waiting
for the election result. They trying to kill Manley even *before* the elections

That is what these hypocrites mean when they talk of 'elections'. But there are no elections in Chile, or Paraguay or El Salvador! No elections in South Africa, no elections in Namibia! You never hear about imperialism talking about 'hold elections there' when it is their allies and their friends! Are we able to talk about *that* to our students in the classroom? What when they hear about elections in Jamaica and they hear '40 dead'? Can we tell them about that? Can we understand about that? Can we develop that consciousness if we ourselves do not have an internationalist outlook?

The Need for Internationalism

We have to think about all these things, comrades. This is our region, this is our land, and nobody has the right to tell us what to do in our region and our land. That is why we keep saying that the days of interventionism, of hegemonism, of invasionism, or backyardism — all of them days gone. And we have to be able to explain that to the students in front of us when they ask us. That is why all this internationalist activity, all of this concentration on the radio, in the newspaper, in all these panel discussions and rallies — the rallies we've had for El Salvador, Zimbabwe, Puerto Rico, Jamaica, Vietnam, Chile, for the Polisario Front. Our masses don't know nothing about El Salvador or the Polisario Front, but the fact of the matter is that what they don't know they must get to know. It is our duty and responsibility as revolutionaries to understand what is happening in the world and to back those processes of liberation. We can only do that if we raise our internationalist consciousness. That is why, comrades, we have had so many visits and conferences in our country over the last nineteen months. Have you thought about that? Michael Manley, the very man fighting Seaga and them today, he was here for the Festival of the Revolution in March. Ortega, the number one leader in the Nicaraguan Revolution, he was here for March too. Kaunda was here last year. We've had visits from people like C.L.R. James, Paulo Freire, George Lamming — and Cheddi Jagan also comes from time to time. John Stockwell, the ex-CIA man who wrote his book *In Search of Enemies*, detailing his experiences in Angola and how the CIA were trying to overthrow the Angolan Revolution. All of these visits are for good reasons, so our people can have their consciousness raised and be informed about what is happening in the world.

Conferences and Seminars

That's also why we have had so many conferences here: International Union of Students, conferences on Agriculture, Agro-economics, on Tourism and Planning. Next week we are starting two more such conferences, both very important. One is organised by the Energy Institute of the region, and it will consist of a month of workshops in our country — and after that we're going to have two Bio-gas plants. And Bio-gas can supply all the cooking gas we need over a small area. The other conference is sponsored by an OAS agricultural organisation and is on fruit tree production, one of the key areas of our agricultural diversification over the years to come. As well as cocoa, bananas and nutmeg we shall be going further into the cultivation of tropical and exotic fruits. Already mango is becoming more and more of a hit from the point of view of the farmers. Mango in the old days, remember? You took one bite and threw away three-quarter? You'd catch one and throw away the next – mango was a joke! Now mango is being sold and mango farmers are getting a mango bonus! Nutmeg bonus this year will hardly be more than 50c,cocoa bonus will hardly be more than a dollar and mango bonus might be the same dollar a pound. Imagine that! The mango we used to throw away and kick and laugh at! So all of these conferences and seminars have a great value to our country. We need to involve ourselves as teachers, and involve our students in understanding these things and seeing their importance.

The Visa Mentality

So comrades, these are some of the points I wanted to make to you on this very important day. I am sure that as teachers of our country who are dedicated, patriotic, democratic and progressive, you understand the nature of the responsibility you have to shape the minds of our country's future. We have nearly 40,000 children in school here. That is a big, big figure and a big, big responsibility for you. So whether they learn what I had to learn in primary school – do you remember those days? 'Cow jump over the moon'? 'Hickory, Dickory dock'? And all the rest of it. Whether they learn something more sensible, and how to integrate what they are picking up in the book with the real world, that is to a great extent going to depend on you. Whether they learn that what they are really doing in school is preparing themselves for making a contribution that they will later put at the service of their people and use unselfishly the skills they acquire, not seeing education as something only for the benefit of an elite, something to make themselves into millionaires, something to use to try to get themselves a visa for America – that too is your responsibility. The Visa Mentality, the Transient Mentality, all of that we have to get out of our people. For if all of us run, nobody going to be left to build the country. Every time we run, what we are doing is helping Imperialism to get richer and stronger.

To get all of these things across to your students, comrades, will be your job. I know you definitely understand the importance of getting the best possible training for getting that message across. The technical things you have to teach in Mathematics, language arts or whatever else you have to communicate, all of these require from you constant study, constant dedication, discipline, sacrifice and work. Most people don't like work, except to look at it. Everybody like to look at work! But the fact of the matter is, if we don't work we can't build the country. If we don't make the sacrifices this year, the problems will still be with us next year. The more we give ourselves skills and training this year, the less we will have to do three years from now. That is what is real, and the reason why we must be willing to make sacrifices and work harder this year.

Comrades, I'd like to compliment you on the seriousness in which you are approaching this task. I would like to congratulate and compliment the Co-ordinator of the programme, Sister Judith Bullen, and the hard-working, very qualified and experienced teachers who are going to be the mainstay of this programme. I want you to observe too, yet another aspect of what we mean by internationalism. When you look at these tutors you're not only seeing Grenadians. You're seeing an American, an Englishman, a Trinidadian, you're seeing people from around the world and from our region. For when we don't have the skills here, but there are people abroad who have the correct out-look and are willing to come to our country to help to make a contribution to build our country and our Revolution, we must welcome them with warm, open arms and thank them for the contribution they are making.

May I also on your behalf, comrades, end by once again formally express-ing the greatest appreciation of the Revolution to the outstanding work that Comrade George Louison has been doing in the Ministry of Education. I'm sure you recognise that work, and the fact that were it not for this comrade a lot of these programmes, whether it's the CPE, the In-service Teacher Training or the Curriculum Development Unit, would either have not gotten off the ground or would be much further back in the planning process. Although I know he doesn't like compliments and praise, therefore I don't want to overdo it, I think it is necessary that we make the point of the tre-mendous work that the comrade has been doing.

Document History as History is Being Made

Finally comrades, I want to make one small suggestion. I want to suggest that you all think seriously about putting aside materials that are being developed as a part of this programme. Things like the questionaires that have been circulated and all materials in all areas of work, whatever they are. Then use those materials to create a mini-museum that will be a permanent record of this important programme you are starting today. The comrades organising the CPE, for example, are now gathering the necessary materials for the same kind of archive. In many countries of the world, in all kinds of programmes — some far, far less important than this one you are embarking upon, people have kept permanent records. Then that would not only be a permanent attraction for interested people coming to our country, but also the young teachers of the future will be able to see what happened at this particular stage of our country's educational development, to see who were the main participants, how it took place, what the problems were, the kind of materials that were used — they would have all the information at their dis-posal. That is yet another crucial aspect of the work we have to be engaged in more and more in the future: the permanent documentation of the history of our country as that history is being made.

So comrades, may I wish you a very successful three years of hard work and study, and at the end of that time I have no doubt that the vast majority of you, if not all, will receive your certificate. Equally, I have no doubt, and I hope, that the vast majority of you will still be in our country, and will not use the excuse of the certificate as your stepping stone and ladder to get a visa to go to somebody else's country. The country is ours, we have to build it.

8. Work Towards Integrated Agricultural Development and Regional Co-operation

Opening Address at the Regional Workshop on Fruit Tree Crops in St. George's, 10 November 1980

It is really a pleasure for me this morning to be able to welcome you to our country. Particularly, it is a great pleasure because of the number of countries and regional and international organisations which have managed to come to this workshop. In fact, we have 18 countries and 12 regional and international organisations present and that of course is a very significant thing. Because it does say that a lot of people in the region are concerned, not just about agriculture in the sense of the traditional crop, but also about finding ways of diversifying agriculture and moving more and more into new areas of production. This whole business of fruit trees has not been one of the more popular areas, certainly not in the English-speaking Caribbean.

I am also very happy this morning because what we have represented here today is not just our sisters and brothers from the English-speaking Caribbean, but also from the wider Caribbean and from Latin America in general. In fact, there are not only people who speak the English language, but French, Dutch and Spanish, and that is very important to us. Because part of the thrust of the Grenada Revolution has been precisely in the area of trying to develop and to widen contact with our sisters and brothers throughout the entire region, regardless of what language they speak or which country they come from.

Agriculture is the Motor of Our Economy

The third reason, of course, that makes this morning significant is because we are dealing with extremely important areas and this workshop hopefully will help us to analyse in some depth, in some detail, some of the problems facing traditional and potential fruit crops in the region. We do hope that out of this period of analysis and evaluation, this period of assessment, will come the beginning of some solutions for the problems faced in each area. And I am sure that over the next few days the countries are going to spend a lot of time looking at the question, because there is a field component to this workshop, there will also come some very useful suggestions for our own development of fruit tree crops in Grenada.

May I make two apologies, Sisters and Brothers. The first is for the absence of Comrade Unison Whiteman, our Minister of Agriculture, who is unfortunately out of the country. He had to leave at fairly short notice, and I know he very much would have liked to be here with us all this morning. The second is the absence and lack of translation facilities and I do hope this will not mean that some of you are not always able to understand what is being said.

Agriculture is the motor and the heart of the Grenada economy. This fact is of course, true for many countries in the Caribbean and indeed Latin America. For us it means more dollars, more earnings for our countries, more foreign exchange. For us it also means more food for our people. These are all very important reasons why agriculture is so very important to the economy. It is also as we see it, the base, the natural base for any industrial-isation that will take place in our country in a serious way.

We see it, therefore, as being the source and the future for the develop-ment of the economy and in general the development of our country. But agriculture, of course, has had its problems over the past years. Last year, for example, we imported $57,000,000 worth of food and food-products. But in that same year with earnings from nutmegs, cocoa and bananas mainly, we were able to receive $58,000,000. In other words, a balance in our favour of $1,000,000 — which is ridiculous.

We Must Break this Economic Dependence

More than that, last year the overall imports into our country were valued at $117,000,000 so we had an overall deficit of $60,000,000. This had to come from remittances from nationals abroad, from earnings in the tourist sector, and also from external grants.

If we are to break this dependence of our economy, because we do have an open dependent capitalist economy, then it is for us to greatly improve pro-duction in agriculture over the next several years. We see the growing of food in particular, as being a key component of any agricultural strategy, because I am sure that you will agree that if anybody on a desert island, for example, was asked to come up with a short list of items of products that he had to have to survive, the top of that list would surely have to be food.

We have found that the state sector in agriculture has been largely depen-dent on export crops and mainly on the tree crops of nutmegs, cocoa and bananas. The sector in our country comprises some 30 estates and the average is about 150 acres to each estate. The total acreage on all of these estates is just over 4,200 acres. It is relatively small, but yet it has been subject to tremendous deterioration over the years.

In 1978, for example, operating costs were in the excess of $1,000,000, while revenue that came in was somewhere around $250,000. By that it is clear that the tax payers had to subsidise the agricultural sector, the state sector in agriculture, to the tune of something like $ ¾ million.

Important Incentives for Agricultural Workers

Last year we were able to reduce that deficit somewhat. In fact, earnings went up to about $700,000 and some state farms were able for the first time to make small profits. We believe that by a series of incentives for the workers it will be possible to go on to increase these earnings for the state in the agricultural sector even more.

We have introduced, for example, a profit sharing scheme under which the agricultural workers for the first time will be able to share in part of the profits which they make. The basic plan is that of any profits made $1/3$ will go back to the state, $1/3$ will be used on the estate or farms for the purpose of further increasing production and providing more inputs on the particular farm, and $1/3$ will be shared among the workers. That incentive of course will be an important one.

Likewise, we have introduced the policy of equal pay for equal work for women on the government estates in the country and we certainly hope that the private sector will folllow this example as rapidly as possible.

An emulation scheme also has been introduced, under which every month the agricultural workers get together and discuss the problems on the farm, look at the question of projections and targets, discuss why they are not reaching their targets, or if they are reaching them how and why they did reach them. In other words, the policy is to fully involve them and to encourage them to participate in the running of the particular state farm, because our principle is that there must be no secrets from the workers of our country. Everything that is taking place in a particular work place and in the economy of our country as a whole, must be open and subject to public and national scrutiny and debate. And as part of this emulation process these workers choose, or will be able to choose, where that process has not yet begun, a worker of the month for each State farm.

In small areas like that, we believe it is going to be possible to make some impact and begin to push forward at a more rapid and more meaningful pace to further development of agriculture in our country.

Too Much Unutilised Land

In so far as the private sector is concerned, in the area of agriculture, you will find that all agricultural land holdings in our country, total about 40,000 acres, and about half of these agricultural holdings fall in the bracket of 100-500 acres.

In our country, we have something like 87,000 acres of land and there are, as I said, 40,000 in agricultural holdings. We estimate that perhaps 55,000 acres are cultivable but in fact a lot of it is not cultivated. Somewhere around 15,000 acres would be unutilised or grossly under-utilised. So you have this picture of half of the land holdings falling into this particular bracket (110-500 acres), but at the same time it is precisely in that section of ownership of agricultural holdings in the same country that the greatest amount of uncultivation and under-cultivation can be found.

The figure that we have from about four years ago indicate that 32%, just about $1/3$ of all the land in the bracket 100-200 acres is unutilised. At the same time, in the bracket of 200-250 acres, some 68% of all the land is unutilised. This is bad enough. But what compounds it to make it even more unacceptable, is that we have had a continuous decline over the years in the amount of land being cultivated. This drop has been quite frankly, dramatic.

In 1961 for example, there were over 60,000 acres of land or 71% of the total land undercultivation. By 1972, 11 years later, this figure fell to 56,000 acres or 66% of the land being cultivated, and by 1975, the figure had fallen to 46,000 acres of land or 54% of the land being uncultivated. At the same time, the pressure for the land and the population/land ratio in the country generally, has equally continued to get worse.

In 1961, there were 140 Grenadians to every 100 acres of land that we had. By 1972, 11 years later, this figure had become 151 Grenadians to every 100 acres. By 1975, three years later, this figure had become 218 Grenadians to every 100 acres, and now by 1980, our estimate is that perhaps there are about 270 Grenadians to every 100 acres of land. That just tells us that not every Grenadian who would like to own his own piece of land is going to be able to achieve that ambition. Because, apart from the over 100,000 Grenadians in Grenada, there are well over 400,000 Grenadians scattered throughout the metropolitan centres and different countries in the Caribbean, and all of them also have deep aspirations — patriotic aspirations — to own a piece of their mother land, but obviously that is not going to be possible.

Bringing This Idle Land Into Production

That just means that part of our strategy is going to have to be to find a way of bringing all of the idle land in our country under production, and this strategy in fact we have begun in a serious way.

Our intention, which has been publicly announced on several occasions is to encourage the private owners to bring their land that it unutilised or under-utilised back into production. We are willing of course to provide as much assistance and incentives as possible. This we have been doing through the extension officers, through the provision of greater marketing facilities and possibilities. We are working more and more on developing a common pool of services which include tractors and what not, and we are also hoping that more and more farmers from the private sector will take advantage of the training possibilities and training facilities which have been established or re-established since the Revolution.

We also believe that utilising this idle land is one way also of solving, or at least reducing the problem of unemployment therefore in our country. We established some months ago, a Land Reform Commission, which was charged with the task of identifying how much idle land we had in the country and how many unemployed people in the country are willing to join together in co-operatives to work that idle land. We were in effect, seeking to bring about a marriage of idle hands and idle lands so as to end unemployment, so as to increase production, so as to earn more foreign exchange for our country.

NACDA: A Package of Services

And I can tell you that the Land Reform Commission at this point has identified well over 4,000 acres of land, though we know the reality is that there must be nearer 10,000 acres of idle land. Consistent with this policy and in order to fully implement it we have at the same time established a National Co-operative Development Agency called NACDA, and this organisation NACDA, is really a package of services. It does about six different things. On the one hand, once unemployed people identify lands that they are willing to work, a study is done first of all to test the question of feasibility and capability of the particular land to do what the people hope to do. We then as government, begin negotiations with the particular owners to see if it is possible to arrange either freehold or leasehold purchase of the particular land. The land is in turn then given to the particular co-operative in leasehold form.

Thirdly, NACDA at the same time begins a programme of training of the young co-operators and this is to teach them the principles and practices of co-operative management and to instil in them in a deep and concrete way, the importance of agriculture to our country.

Fourthly, the question of funding then arises. NACDA makes available loans for seeds, for fertiliser, for tools. Then technical assistance comes into the picture and the question of the consistent use of the extension officers and also the co-operative officers attached to NACDA, who then work with the particular co-operative to ensure that production continues.

Finally, NACDA is involved also in assisting these young farmers to get the best prices for their products. In other words, assistance in the area of marketing. Our overall view of a way forward for agriculture in our country is, first of all, to maintain the present acreage we have in the traditional crop, but move rapidly to increase the yield per acre. We also move rapidly at the same time to increase the amount of production per worker. That is the first part of the strategy.

Being Released from the Clutches of Foreign Control
The second part is to move more and more into the area of food crops/cash crops. That for obvious reasons for effecting import substitution, for ensuring that the base of the economy widens so that the open dependent nature of the economy that now exists is gradually eliminated as we disengage from the clutches of foreign control.

The third area is precisely the subject of today's seminar. The area of fruit crop production, which we see as being an essential component of the future of agriculture in our country, and hence the particular importance for us of today's conference.

The fourth area is the question of agro-industrialisation, the question which the Director General himself has spent so much time in stressing in a very brief but important address a while ago. We also believe that agro-industrialisation is a large part of the key to any strategy that is aimed at promoting, at developing and strengthening the agricultural sector in our countries in this region.

We of course have many problems which still need resolutions. There is the burning problem of pest and disease control, a problem which many of the officials in the Ministry would characterise as the biggest problem of all. There is, secondly, the problem of praedial larceny, a problem which many farmers in our country would characterise as being the biggest problem.

There is the question of marketing, which some of us in government believe to be just about the most important problem, because if agriculture is about people and the development of these people, and the improvement of their quality of life, then one of the key questions, if not the key question, must be the question of the price. If the price is such that the farmer, the agricultural worker, is not able to enjoy a decent standard of life, then agriculture must collapse. So a large part of whatever strategy we employ for developing agriculture, must have a long and hard sustained look at the finding of better markets, of obtaining prices so that the quality of life of the farmer, and in turn of the agricultural worker, would dramatically improve.

More Seeds and Plants for our Farmers

A fourth problem of course, relates to the provision of some of the key inputs that are necessary for agriculture. Insufficient quantities of fertiliser, insufficient quantities of seeds and plant materials. These are also problems with which we will help. In fact before cocoa propagators in our country were in such a sad state of disrepair, that much of our work for the first year had to be centred around just bringing them back up to some level, from which a take off would be possible. Fortunately, this has been reasonably achieved and we are now able to embark more seriously on phase two, that is the provision of much larger quantities of seeds and plants for the farmers.

A fifth problem, the question of inadequate and very often insufficiently trained expertise, whether in the area of extension officers, whether in the area of training facilities that we have, or research facilities that are available, or whether in the area of appropriate technology that is possible in our particular condition. In all of these areas too, we find that our country has been suffering in common of course, with most countries represented in this room.

The sixth factor is intangible. But it is a very key intangible that we really have to begin to address more and more in a serious way if we are to tackle this problem of finding the best ways of planning, in an efficient and effective way for our agricultural development; and that is the question of hurricanes and bad weather. That is something in our limited state of technology which we have not been able to do very much about. And, of course it has been increasingly a problem.

The Great Problem of Natural Disasters

Last year, for three months, for example, we had very severe rainfall which played havoc on our crops. In one month alone, the month of November last year – we had 23 inches of rainfall – which is as much as some countries get for the entire year. We found too, that hurricane Allen which struck these islands a few months ago, although only the tail winds got to Grenada, just the tail of the hurricane was enough to throw down 19% of our crops in cocoa, 35% in nutmegs and 40% in bananas. You would hardly wish to think what kind of damage it must have done to our sisters and brothers in St Vincent, St Lucia and most of all Dominica, where they had three such occurrences in the past year alone. This problem of hurricane and weather control is of course a typical one and perhaps as part of our general concerted effort to get the New International Economic Order going, one of the key answers in this area must be for us to press the developed countries to put aside money for a fund, and out of that fund will come on a pro-rata basis, assistance to countries that are in fact inflicted and afflicted by hurricanes and problems of weather generally. That call we ourselves have made most recently to the United Nations, at a special session to look at the question of a New International Economic Order, and it is certainly a call in which we believe that everybody should join.

But we feel too, that there must be some possibilities here for co-operation among ourselves. That these countries that are hit the least find it somehow or the other possible, to give immediate assistance to those countries that are really badly hit. We feel that this is an extremely important thing. Particularly, we feel it is important for us not to allow the opportunity of damage done by hurricane or weather, to allow any policies that divide and rule to emerge in our region.

Maintaining a Consistent, United Policy

We notice recently for example, that USAID was making feverish and desperate attempts to keep Grenada out of the assistance to WINBAN (Windward Islands Banana Association) following Hurricane Allen. Notwithstanding the fact that the approach was made by WINBAN as one organisation comprising four countries. To the credit and integrity of our sisters and brothers in Dominica, St Vincent and St Lucia, they have in fact spoken up against this divisive policy and have insisted that Grenada in fact be part of any assistance to WINBAN. I am sure that is the problem that is going to arise in the future and it is necessary for us to ensure that we always maintain a consistent, united policy on these matters.

Our policy is to try to deal with these six problems which have arisen over several years. On the one hand of course, we have spent a lot of time on the question of training. We have reopened the Mirabeau Agricultural Training Centre. We are desperately trying to find the necessary funding to open at least two more agricultural training centres. We have established NACDA which I have spoken about already; we are training the workers who are going to be employed at our Agro-industrial plant to be opened in the next few weeks, and we have also opened a Fisheries School. In this school our fishermen are now able to learn something about the more modern techniques of fishing. At the same time of course, we have been seeking scholarships and training assistance in countries abroad. We have received offers and now have students studying for example in countries like Kenya, Cuba, Jamaica and Hungary, in institutions like the University of the West Indies and the Eastern Caribbean Institute for Agriculture and Forestry. So we do see training as being a key component in the way forward for the development of agriculture in our country.

There have also been substantial improvements in the area of plant propagation in general and most specifically in the area of cocoa propagation and rehabilitation. We have now been able to increase our annual output from about 150,000 upwards to 400,000 trees a year. And our plan is with the assistance of CIDA and the Canadian Government to replant some 1,000 acres per annum over the next seven years.

In the area too, of pest and disease control, we have been working for the eradication of these problems. The FAO has given us the sum of US$105,000 to help to fight the Moko disease in bananas. The nutmeg wilt disease – we have also received some assistance in that area. In the area of cocoa, particularly to deal with the thrips and beetles we have also been attempting to obtain assistance so that our programme in this area can be rapidly stepped up.

I can tell the Director-General as of now, that one approach we are certainly going to be making to IICA is for technical assistance in the area dealing with control of pest and disease.

Planting more Sugar Cane

We have also been once again making a drive to produce sugar in our country, because the monthly increases in the price of that commodity has continued to be a source of great headaches to our people, all of whom need sugar. We intend, therefore, over the next few months to double the acreage presently under production, and quite a sum of money has now been set aside for the Sugar Rehabilitation Programme in our country. In the area of reforestation likewise, the plan is to plant or replant over 2,400 acres of our forest land over the next 15 years. We expect that once that process is completed we ought to be able to get at least 1,000 boardfeet per annum and that will represent just about 1% of our estimated needs at that time.

International agencies of course have been very important. It is precisely because we recognise the importance of technical assistance and other forms of assistance from these agencies that we have joined IICA, we have joined IFAD, we have joined OLADE, over the past 18 months. We continue of course to work with CARDI, DARDATS, with the Caribbean Food Corporation, the Caribbean Conservation Society, the Caribbean Food and Nutrition Council, the Caribbean Development Bank, University of the West Indies, CARICOM itself, the OAS, FAO, the United Nations and several other regional and international organisations and agencies, and we have found in practice that this work has been extremely important and has brought many benefits for the country.

Apart from this workshop being opened today for example, tomorrow another workshop and seminar will be opened in Mirabeau; this one by OLADE, and this one will be concentrating on the whole question of bio-gas and the possibilities in that area for developing a source of alternative energy. And that also will be an extremely important workshop.

From IICA iself, we have been able to get quite some assistance in the very short time we have joined that organization. Only last month we received a study done by IICA which analyses our markets and marketing systems of fruits and vegetables in Grenada and that study is of the most fundamental importance to us, and I am sure that participants at this workshop will find it very useful to thumb through that study to see what might be there of any value for your own countries.

The Importance of Tree Production

So, sisters and brothers, this workshop is of the greatest importance. The whole question of tree production is central to the development of our own strategy and I have no doubt the strategy of several other countries in this room. As possibilities for food, agro-industrialisation, provision of more jobs, alternative energy possibilities, the possibilities of developing feeds out of waste parts of the fruits – we see the question of fruit tree production as having a lot of value to all of these areas. In our own country the production in this area is small. It tends to be scattered and dispersed over several different estates. We have found in fact, that most people who are into fruit tree production have been doing this more in the form of backyard gardening more than anything else. It is therefore more by a combination of chance and of fertile soil and favourable growing conditions that any fruits are grown at all in the country. We are sure that out of this workshop more of our people will find new incentives, new material reasons why we should see this area of production as being key and as having possibilities for material benefits for themselves.

I hope therefore that over the next four days that you spend in our country, not only on our field trip, but in your moments of leisure, you may perhaps enjoy our beaches and the friendliness, the warmth and the hospitality of our people, that you are able to enjoy yourselves. I hope as a result of that you would wish to return on some future occasion for a holiday. We certainly would like to thank IICA and the the other sponsors and contributors for allowing us the privilege and the honour of hosting this conference in our country.

We also want once again to thank you the participants, for coming from your own countries, for being here in our country. We are certainly very pleased to see you and hope to see you again very soon.

9. In the Spirit of Butler, Unionise! Mobilise! Educate! Democratise!

Address by Comrade Maurice Bishop, on the Opening of the Third Trade Union Conference for the Unity and Solidarity of Caribbean Workers, at The Dome, St. George's, 18 November 1981

Comrades, if we were to study the history of this country, Grenada, we would find that the central theme that has characterised the lives of our people over the centuries has been *resistance*. Our people have struggled at many times and in many ways.

From the stubborn refusal of the Grenadian Caribs to accept any colonial stranglehold over their island, through the consistent pattern of slave revolts which culminated in the mass upsurge led by Julien Fedon in 1795 which for two years brought Grenada a determined, militant independence, through the years of anti-colonial agitation and the eloquent leadership of T.A. Marryshow, through the two great popular uprisings of 1951 and 1973-4 to the climax of our struggle in the March 13th Revolution of 1979 – Grenadians have always resisted domination, injustice and exploitation. Our great Caribbean poet, Edward Kamau Brathwaite, himself a Barbadian, has likened this spirit of permanent struggle to the dramatic and sublime peaks which tower along the spine of our island. And it is into this tradition of resistance that we must place the growth and development of our trade union movement.

We have produced here in Grenada perhaps the greatest, the most brilliant and audacious of pioneer Caribbean trade unionists – I am referring, of course, to *Tubal Uriah 'Buzz' Butler*, that huge, monumental igniter of the spirit of the Caribbean masses, who, born in Grenada, moved to Trinidad to accomplish his great deeds of leadership of the burgeoning Caribbean working class. His volcanic influence there sent our entire region throbbing with a new will and resistance which soon broke out through all our islands. But let it also be said that we produced Eric Mathew Gairy, perhaps the most degenerate and decadent manipulator and corrupter of the trade union movement that our islands have ever spawned.

Butler vs. Gairy: to say them with the same breath makes one choke! But we have seen both their traditions *and* disciples alive in our Caribbean. Our duty now is to strive to emulate the one and make certain that the other will never be re-created! Certainly we must also remember how Butler was sought, hunted and hounded by British colonialism and the employing class that saw him as their greatest menace, how they imprisoned him, interned him but could never smother or even dim his enormous determination and lustre! And certainly we must also remember how his opposite lied, bribed, bludgeoned and murdered in his path to power, and how the consequences of that misrule strewed hurricane wreckage through our nation and working people that he claimed to represent, so much so that nearly three years after the Revolution that ended his sordidness forever in our country, we are still clearing up the devastation he caused to our national life and economy.

So we have known only too well this type of bogus trade unionism in Grenada, and we have lived through the ghastly damage it caused to our country and people. And we also know how much our real, genuine, patriotic trade unionists fought against such deformity when its political arm came into power with the Gairy neo-colonial dictatorship, which lasted for over two decades here in Grenada. For right through these years of struggle, our militant, selfless trade unionists fought gallantly against Gairy's terror, squandermania and neglect of the rights of workers, even though he could also count through that period, upon certain sections of the trade union leadership to sell out the masses at crucial points of their struggle, as he had done himself in 1951, and as the conciliators did again in April 1974.

Trade Unionism Against the Dictatorship

Gairy's neo-colonial dictatorship introduced several draconian laws that were clearly anti-worker and were aimed at muzzling and straitjacketing any threatening action from our trade unionists. The *1974 Public Order (Amendment) Act* prohibited trade unions, as well as other organisations, from using public address systems. The next year he passed the *Newspaper (Amendment) Act* which, without just cause, effectively forbade trade unionists and other workers' organisations from publishing their own newspapers. Then the *Essential Services Act* of 1978 was passed particularly against the prospect of members of the Technical and Allied Workers' Union taking direct industrial action. Significantly, the leadership of this union, notoriously inactive, did nothing to challenge the passage of a law which was designed to render them impotent. This was hardly surprising when we understand that the leadership of this union was in the hands of the same man who acted as the 'Research and Education Officer' of the American Institute of Free Labour Development in the Eastern Caribbean. But other unions and the political leadership of the NJM fought on behalf of their brothers and sisters in this union, comrades, and when Gairy tride to extend the law to include the dockworkers — who proved to be the most militant section of the urban working class under the dictatorship — they never allowed the amendment to be implemented. For it was a common feature of those years that the workers themselves would take industrial action *in the absence of or in defiance of* their conciliatory leadership. This was perhaps best seen in the 1973-4 period when the workers had to *force the hand* of their leaders to strike, and simultaneously resist the propaganda and persuasion techniques of the AFL-CIO.

Repression Was Total

Comrades, it is important to note that all this activity and struggle within our trade union movement was taking place against a backdrop of massive repression that was building up in our country, in all aspects and spheres of the people's lives. The dictator was making a systematic and comprehensive attack on all the rights and freedoms that our people had campaigned for and won over the years of British Colonialism. The freedom to express ourselves, the freedom of assembly — in fact the freedom to live any sort of decent life, all this was being ripped from us. The elections that were organised were rigged and farcical: a mockery of the democracy that our people truly aspired to reach. When we moved to protest or organise against the decay of life we saw around us, we were hounded by paid bandits who battered, bruised and murdered some of our most valued and courageous comrades. Life itself was being torn away from us, piece by piece, in the growing fear and reality of repression.

Our youth saw desolation around them in a hopeless search for jobs. Our women faced sexual abuse and exploitation in the daily struggle to keep their dignity. A youth like Jeremiah Richardson was shot, point-blank, in the streets of Grenville because he sought to question a policeman's abuse. A boy, Harry Andrews, was killed because he climbed over a wall in a calypso tent. Harold Strachan, Alister Strachan, Rupert Bishop all heroically sought to challenge this ebbing away of freedom and the right to live, and they all fell before the horrendous rule of terror and corruption which characterised our country during those years. Our people lived in an ethos of death and tyranny, when honest people disappeared mysteriously, the fate of Inspector Bishop of the Carriacou Police, or the four youths tending goats on Frigate Island. Comrades, to be an active, combative and militant trade unionist during that portion of our history was to court this danger and violence. Militancy meant a challenge to death and an assertion of everything that was that was hopeful and positive and which could reconstruct life and happiness for our people.

The Workers Fought Back

But as the dictatorship tried to tighten its grip on the lives of the Grenadian people, more and more democratic and progressive fighters were elected to the leadership of our trade unions. By 1978 the Executive of the Commercial and Industrial Workers Union was demonstrating this and Gairy was answering by trying to crush the union. Resolutions were being passed by the Executive against Gairy's ties with the butchers of Chile and the visit of Pinochet's torture ship, *The Esmeralda*, to our shores. The dictator realised he was not dealing with the previous pattern of pliable and opportunistic leadership. The only price of these new comrades was freedom! So he went directly to the employers, trying to persuade and bribe them to compel their workers to join *his* union, even though these employers had already signed agreements with the Commercial and Industrial Workers Union [CIWU].

He also attempted to force CIWU members directly to change unions, but because of the respect they had for the consistent and principled hard work and positions of the new CIWU leadership, they were not moved.

Over the years our Caribbean trade union movement has constantly been the target of that most unscrupulous arm of imperialism: the Central Intelligence Agency. We had had *rare* instances of our trade union leaders *consciously* selling out to their silky bribes and offerings, but more usually the CIA, with its sophistication and enormous financial resources, has succeeded in manipulating and infecting unwitting trade unionists who may well have been continuing with their work with the best of intentions. In doing this, the CIA has sometimes directly infiltrated and controlled some sections of our movement, and thus forced the leadership of some of our unions to actually take anti-worker positions. This has happened, we know, in Grenada, and more and more of our workers are becoming conscious of this danger to their hopes. We saw how the CIA actually succeeded in turning back the progress of the organised workers' movement in Chile, by both open and covert activity, and we in the Caribbean must be particularly *vigilant* in recognising their position and subversion of the workers' cause, for *imperialism will never rest* in its resolution to crush the onward march of the progress and emancipation of our struggling people.

For on the day that the Revolution triumphed, March 13th 1979, trade unionists from all over the country showed direct support for and involvement in the revolutionary events. The Telephone Company workers, for example, were contacting and radioing our security forces to tell them of the whereabouts of Gairy's ministers, and trade unionists and workers generally all over the country left their work-places to take up arms to end forever the power of oppression that had constantly tried to thwart the free aspirations and genuine and constructive organisation of our Grenadian workers.

Since our revolution most of the old, corrupt union leadership has been thrown into the dustbin of history, for because of their growing consciousness, our workers can now contrast and see who is bringing benefits to them and who is not, who is desperately trying to maintain the old pattern of dictatorship and who is in the forefront of the struggle to bring more democracy into our trade unions.

What we are seeing more and more in Grenada is that the objectives of the Revolution and the objectives of the trade union movement in our country are one and the same. Thus, any antagonisms between them are gradually lessening and disappearing, for the Revolution has *set free* the opportunities for the trade union movement to accomplish its tasks of building the emancipation, security and prosperity of the working people, the identical will of the Revolution itself.

Membership and Democracy

Let us consider the massive rise in membership since the Revolution, of the most militant and democratic unions. On March 13th 1979, the Bank and General Workers' Union had some hundred members. It now has about 3,000. It has spread out from its birthplace at Barclays Bank to the banana boxing plants, the nutmeg pools, the restaurants and hotels, the factories and workshops. Its tradition of honest and consistent struggle on behalf of its members has made it the largest union in the country. The Commercial and Industrial Workers' Union has had over 50% increase in membership, the Technical and Allied Workers' Union a 60% increase and the Agricultural and General Workers' Union has risen from scratch to its present level of 2,300 members. We had a huge, symbolic demonstration of our increased trade union membership and power in this year's May Day celebrations. It was the biggest ever May Day turn out in the history of Grenada, and the seemingly endless procession of organised workers wound around the steep streets of our capital.

Along with this sudden explosion in the membership of our unions is the emphasis the new leadership is putting on their *democratisation*. This is very much allied to the general thrust in democracy right through our society since the Revolution, in all structures of mass organisations, community groups and the other organs of our people's power. As we have seen, before the Revolution there was a tradition in some unions of few or no General Meetings.

Following the Revolution we have seen a massive new interest in trade unionism as Grenadians saw new hope and strength in co-operative and collective democratic solutions to their problems. At the first General Meeting of the Commercial and Industrial Workers' Union after the Revolution, in July 1979, there was over 100% increase in the attendance. Two hundred and ninety members came and voted 246 to 44 in favour of a militant, democratic leadership as against the previous conciliatory and conservative type, even though the latter had organised and conducted the elections.

What is happening now in our country, is that everybody is becoming affected by the dialectic of democratic participation that is sweeping through our villages and workplaces. Involvement in one organisation or meeting leads directly to involvement in another. A worker who attends a Workers' Parish Council hears something which he wants to bring to his trade union. So he goes to the meeting of his union, although he may not have attended one for years. And when he finds, quite surprisingly, that his union is taking a vibrant, democratic direction, he involves himself in one of its new committees or structures for fund raising, sports or planning for educational seminars. His confidence is raised through all this activity and the speaking and organising that goes along with it, and his appetite is whetted to join one of the mass organisations – the local Party Support Group, the Militia, House Repair Programme, or for the sisters, the National Women's Organisation. Each organisation feeds strength, power and confidence into the next, and all of them, including the trade unions, grow in real potency and democratic advancement.

And now we see Workers' Parish Councils splitting into Zonal Councils, in a new sprouting of decentralised democracy right through our nation, a reflection of a similar tendency that is happening within our progressive trade unions.

New Legislation

The People's Revolutionary Government has been swift to take legislative action in favour of the trade unions. All Gairy's anti-worker laws were repealed and two months after the Revolution, in May 1979, People's Law Number 29, the Trade Union Recognition Law, was passed. For the first time in Grenada's history, our workers had the opportunity to join the union of their choice, and the employer was compelled to recognise the trade union, once 51% of his workforce were financial members. Under this Law, the Ministry of Labour has to respond within seven days of the Union's application for recognition, and then call a poll of workers. If the majority is shown to be members, then the union must be certified as the bargaining agent for the workers. For, apart from Barclays, before the Revolution there were other grotesque examples of non-recognition of trade unions. The workers at the Red Spot Soft Drink Factory had a 100% financial membership of the Commercial and Industrial Workers' Union in 1978, but the company still refused recognition, and it took the workers at Bata some 17 years of struggle before they finally won recognition. So this law has changed all those old abuses and given the workers real and genuine security in making their trade unions effective bargaining agents on behalf of their workers.

For the sister trade unionists, the 1980 Maternity Leave Law has made an enormous difference to their working and personal lives. Every working woman now has the right to two months' paid maternity leave over the period of the birth of any child. An the trade unions were involved, together with the mass organisations, particularly the National Women's Organisation, and the churches, in the widespread consultation conducted all over the nation before the bill was finally passed. The Equal Pay for Equal Work Decree in the state sector has also had a profound effect in improving the wages of the sisters and levelling them up with those of their brother workers throughout Grenada — as well as increasing their general confidence to organise and struggle, side by side, with their brothers. For now both men and women are sharing equally in the improvement in wages and conditions being brought about since the Revolution. The old, appalling working conditions and lack of facilities like no drinking water or workers' amenities in workplaces, compulsory overtime without pay and no job security are now doomed. The recent successful strike of agricultural workers in the St Andrew's Parish, waged by members of the Agricultural and General Workers' Union, is proof of this. The comrades achieved their demands of holiday and sick leave pay under the new democratic leadership of their new union.

At this moment arising from a decision of the St George's Workers' Parish Council, and based on requests from trade unions, the Ministry of Legal

Affairs has prepared two pieces of legislation — a Rent Control Law to ease the burden of high rent costs for our people and a new Workmen's Compensation Act, both of which will be circulated to our unions for their comments before enactment.

New Attitudes

Of course, you would know how closely higher productivity and trade union organisation are connected. More than two decades of Gairyism produced in our workers many negative attitudes. The new trade unionism in our country is now helping to transform such attitudes by helping to apply new incentives.

Before the Revolution our agricultural estates brought in absurdly low returns. They were making only a quarter of a million dollars, even though their yearly expenditure was nearly three million. Now, from being a national liability they have become profitable, and the workers themselves have shared in that success, taking one-third of the profits made. This new attitude has grown through the spirit of emulation that the workers have adopted as a result of those seminars. The Age of Cynicism is gone in Grenada.

Workers in a revolutionary country like ours, who are under a progressive and democratic leadership in their trade unions, do *not* see Trade Unionism solely in a narrow, economistic sense. They do not see their responsibilities stopping only at these fundamental tasks of improving their members' wages and working conditions. They see themselves deeply involved in *all aspects* of the social and political life of their country, their region and their world. Our unionised workers have consistently shown solidarity with all other struggling workers of the world. They see this as an internationalist duty to all trade unionists organising for their rights and fighting for social and political justice, be they in Chile, El Salvador, Southern Africa, the Middle East or any part of the world where the producers of wealth are exploited and oppressed. They see their responsibility, likewise with other trade unionists of the Third World, in pressing for the New International Economic Order that will create more favourable terms of trade between rich and poor nations and transfer wealth and technology for the benefit of the masses in countries such as ours.

The Need for Trade Union Unity in the Caribbean

Comrades, it is clear that the growing economic crisis of world capitalism is having a dynamic effect in the Caribbean. Throughout our region we see the employing class united in its attack upon trade unionism. There have been newspaper advertisements in Barbados calling upon workers there to abandon their trade unions. There have been incidents of multi-national companies in St Vincent forcing workers to sign documents, pledging that they will

83

leave their trade union. Clearly, the employers are trying to *de-unionise* their workforces to make them more pliable and exploitable, so we, throughout the Caribbean must go beyond all our political and ideological differences and forge the essential *unity* of our regional trade union movement to combat this reactionary offensive by the employers. This is why we have to work towards the *total unionisation* of our workers and the *maximum democratisation* of our unions, to ensure that they are vigilant and active in the struggles against the employers, and to guarantee that the negativism and passivity that arise from undemocratic trade union structures are forever finished in our region.

We consider that in Grenada we have a critical role to stimulate and achieve this unity, because our Revolution has emancipated our trade union movement to fully serve the country and help to build it, along with our party, the mass organisations and other democratic community structures. For we are benefiting, not only from increased wages and better working conditions, unlocked freedoms and an explosion of democracy, but also from a massively *increased social wage* which makes more and more sure and profound the security of our working people, one of the prime objectives of trade unionism. Free medical treatment, primary health care, an eye clinic, free milk distribution, more doctors and dentists than we have ever had before, new low cost housing and house repair schemes, free secondary education, de facto free middle level technical and university training for all our untrained primary school teachers, a Centre for Popular Education, cheaper basic food through our Marketing and National Importing Board, loans for productive purposes through our National Commercial Bank, a vastly improved water supply system, cheaper electricity rates and less tax to pay for the poorest workers, a new International Airport, a national Public Bus Service on the way — all this has been achieved in the last 30 months. Such concrete benefits are what true trade unionists have always struggled for, and we see our trade unionists too taking a greater and greater part in this huge process of national reconstruction.

For the first time in our history, and as far as we know this step is unique in the CARICOM section of our region, our trade unions have been involved in the exercise of framing the national budget. The Public Workers' Union, the Grenada Union of Teachers and the Technical and Allied Workers' Union were all involved in this process last year, and this year and in the coming years more of our unions will be involved. Proposals for the 1982 Budget will be circularised by the Ministry of Finance in a booklet, and 50,000 of these are being printed, to be given among others, to the workers at their workplaces for them to study and add their comments and suggestions. This, of course, is an extension of the already-existing policy of our government of *opening all our books to our workers during wage negotiations* with trade unions, giving them *access* to all accounts and files, so that they can see for themselves what the national budget can afford to give them, and so they can make their own assessment of what could be a realistic and equitable wage demand. This is the absolute antithesis of Gairyism, a total transformation.

This process will underline yet again that the trade union movement must be involved in *all* aspects of national development. This means planning, production, management, distribution of foods, working in the literacy campaign through the Centre for Popular Education, in the House Repair Programme, the School Repair Programme, the community work and the creation of democracy in *all* our popular and democratic programmes to *ensure* that the benefits of the Revolution reach not only its own members, but all the people of Grenada.

Finally and crucially, there is the question of National Defence, particularly at this juncture when we are facing so many threats from a belligerent and vulgar imperialism. Our trade unions and their members are becoming more and more involved in our People's Revolutionary Militia, and the Trades Union Council itself, in response to the US 'Amber and the Amberines' provocations and manoeuvres in Vieques Island in August, issued a call for all trade unionists to join the militia and be prepared to defend the homeland from imperialist military attack.

Call to the Delegates

So comrades, what is the way forward? What are the challenges ahead of us and how must we respond? We would not want to leave this conference without having clear ideas and proposals in our heads to secure greater bonds and solidarity between us. What concrete steps can we make as a result of our discussions?

For a start we must exchange information, insights and experiences to make more profound the trust between us, and more unified the causes and strength that bind us. And let us pledge that in the spirit of trade union democracy we hold more regular assemblies and meetings such as this one to combine in a more coherent and purposeful way, to consolidate our power and unity, and to co-ordinate our strategies to beat back the offensive against us. Our enemies are intensifying their unity, as has been seen in the recent general inter-Caribbean meetings of Chambers of Commerce, and even more pointedly, in the meetings of various army and police chiefs, with external representatives also involved.

The violence of this offensive has also been made clear in the imperialist-dominated campaign of lies, slander and disinformation – the deliberate manipulation of half truths and fabrications – which has been principally directed at the revolutionary countries in our region: Cuba, Nicaragua and Grenada, and against the progressive movement of workers generally throughout the Caribbean. This campaign intensified to a particularly blatant level in May this year, when the United States International Communications Agency (USICA), the propaganda arm of the US State Department, organised a conference in Washington, to which were invited the editors of all the major English Language Caribbean newspapers. The editors were counselled and lectured to by reactionary congressmen, and slick American journalists taught them techniques of propaganda destabilization, with 'How to Deal with Grenada' as an unlisted item on the agenda. Within two weeks of this conference we witnessed in the region signs of a co-ordinated approach by all of these newspapers, in their propaganda attacks against the Grenada Revolution. Articles and editorials were swapped and reprinted, and this process descended to its most vulgar depths with the appearance in five regional newspapers – the *Jamaica Gleaner*, the *Barbados Sunday Sun*, the *Barbados Advocate*, the *Trinidad Guardian* and the *Trinidad Express* – of identical front page editorials, calling upon the governments, peoples and workers of the region to isolate Grenada and expel us from all regional groupings and organisations. The magnates and warlords of the Caribbean media are about to start yet another campaign against Grenada. While the Jamaican *Daily Gleaner's* Hector Wynter travels to Trinidad to plan strikes with his fellow *Trinidad Guardian* and *Express* blood-suckers, his compatriot and twin brother in lies and hypocrisy, Ken Gordon, is in Jamaica shamelessly announcing yet another plan of orchestrated propaganda destabilization against our Revolution.

It seems that these clowns do not yet understand that the game is up, that they have been fully exposed before the Caribbean people and before their own workers, who so valiantly stood up to them in September, and condemned them for their dishonesty and vulgarity, after their front page fiasco.

It seems like these Judases, who are willing to trade the journalistic integrity of their own workers and the limited value of their own depraved souls for a few dollars more, are in need of yet another slap on their bottoms from the workers of the Caribbean.

Let them continue to attack. The more they do so, the more they help the cause of the working people. For they are the best possible proof of the decadence, corruption and nasty stench of unmitigated, free enterprise capitalism, and its twin sister of rotting, hypocritical, saltfish journalism.

Comrades, this propaganda campaign continues unabated until this very day. We would therefore like to call upon all the delegates here, representing as they do the most active and conscious leaders of the working class movement in our region, to condemn this monopoly control of the Caribbean media by unprincipled press magnates in league with imperialism, and support the struggle of media workers all over the world for a *New International Information Order* to serve our movement and our peoples, which can only be made possible through the struggle to achieve the New International Economic Order, the creation of which will be of particular significance to all workers in the Caribbean and Latin America.

Comrades, very importantly we must express that all the workers of our region must have a clear understanding as to why PEACE is in their interest and why WAR is such a high priority on the agenda of Reagan and the ruling circles in the USA.

At present the world capitalist system is in the midst of a serious crisis. Runaway inflation, compounded by ever-rising unemployment has meant hat for millions of workers in the industrialised capitalist economies, the cost of living keeps going up, seemingly beyond control, while job security is weakened.

Almost as daily routine factory after factory is closed down, business after business declares bantruptcy resulting in hundreds of thousands of workers losing their jobs. Those workers fortunate to retain jobs, find that their wages remain stagnant, their unions attacked and undermined by the monopolists, their rights abused and their hard-won gains eroded.

And as the international capitalist crisis intensifies it generates increased imperialist aggression, spearheaded by the most reactionary circles of imperialism's military industrial complexes who feel that the solution to this crisis is the build-up of arms, the provocation of wars and the creation of tension spots around the world, the Caribbean region being no exception.

The struggle carried on by the world's workers for peace is strongly linked with the effects of the crisis of capitalism on their living standards. Thus one can say that the economic and social gains won through such struggle are a contribution to the consolidation of world peace, because these gains are an expression of the change in the balance of forces against the roots of all wars: monopoly capitalism and imperialism.

Ignoring the new realities brought about by this change in the world's balance of forces however, the military and conservative circles of imperialism are trying to return the world to the cold war period and intensification of the arms race with the planned deployment of many more nuclear warheads in Western European countries, with mad talk of limited nuclear war, and right here in our region with stepped up military manoeuvres and exercises and preparations for military invasions of Cuba, Nicaragua and Grenada, along with massive intervention in El Salvador.

The present level of military efforts puts on the shoulders of Caribbean workers and workers all over the world a very heavy burden of sacrifice exposing the very existence of humanity to the risk of a catastrophic disaster. High military expenditures are damaging to economic stability, slow down the rate of development and make unemployment more acute. The contemporary capitalist crisis and the arms race are directly connected with each other. In many capitalist countries, arms contracts provide the motive force for the industries connected with arms manufacture.

But workers must not be intimidated or resort to pessimism in the face of this bleak scenario. Hope still exists and it resides in the struggle of all peace-loving forces for disarmament and world peace, which will make it possible for science and technology to be put fully to work for the material and spiritual enhancement of humankind.

The working class of the world constitutes the principal force of peace. Because of its role in the crucial sphere of social life and production, the working class is also the principal force of social progress.

Thus, there is a direct connection between the historical role of the working class and the struggle for peace and disarmament. The Caribbean Trade Union Movement cannot fulfill its mission of emancipating the working people of the region in a situation where imperialism is attempting to make the Caribbean into a theatre of war. Genuine social and economic progress can only be achieved in an atmosphere of peaceful co-existence, co-operation goodwill, mutual respect and understanding among the region's peoples. It is therefore, an urgent imperative that the Caribbean trade union movemen strongly condemns all efforts by imperialism to bring unnecessary tension to our region and in equally strong terms supports the call for the Caribbean to be declared a Zone of Peace.

Caribbean and Latin American workers employed by capitalist companies who do not own the means of production because they are an exploited class have no stake in war or in the profits deriving from the manufacture of weapons, as in the case with the transnational corporations. Peace is the workers' ideal. Historical experience shows that in the imperialist wars it is the working people influenced by the ideological hegemony of imperialism who are the victims, who shed their blood and sacrifice their lives. But it is also the working people who have always fought against wars of aggression and who now find themselves in a common front in the struggle for peace.

In fighting against the monopolies, against the transnationals and the military industrial complexes, the working people of the Caribbean and Latin America carry out a direct offensive against the roots of war. In this context, the workers and their trade union organisations have a fundamental role to play. In defiance of the imperialist merchants of death, the Caribbean and Latin American trade union movement must make a clear and consistent response to Washington's aggression in this region by the unity and common action of all the trade union forces. In these times there is an urgent need, comrades, for unity and co-ordinated action, for co-operation and direct alliance between the region's democratic trade unions, some with different ideological tendencies but all with the same class interests and with similar economic and social aspirations. Warmongering in our region can only be stopped by a united and decisive workers' struggle for peace and disarmament. Workers of our region can be heartened and even inspired by the forthright resistance demonstrated by millions of workers, who have taken to the streets of European capitals in recent weeks to say a loud 'no' to the war policies of the Reagan Administration.

So our message today comrades, to all our workers in our island and throughout the Caribbean, is: in the spirit of Butler, Unionise! Mobilise! Educate! Democratise! Dynamise the trade union movement throughout our region! Let the spirit of Butler fire and inspire us! Let us seek to emulate his cause and dedication to the most sacred commitment of all — the emancipation and freedom of our working people.

We in Grenada pledge to continue to put our trade union movement at the centre of the process in our country to link all our workers in an organised relationship with democratic structures and practices, and so pump with ever-increasing vigour the vibrant blood that runs through all the organs of our Revolution.

10. Emulation is the Seed that Brings the Fruit of Excellence

Feature Address on National Emulation Night in St. George's on 29 October 1981

Our Revolution has already proved to be a Revolution of real deeds and actions. As we look around us and see the transformations actually in process, we can be in little doubt of that. But have you also ever thought of the new *words* we have brought into public and popular use, words which express ideas and ways of acting and organising that were completely unknown to our people before the Revolution? One such word, which expresses a totally new concept that the last two years have brought alive for Grenadians, is *emulation*. We have seen this *emulation* in action in the Centre for Popular Education, in the National Women's Organisation, in the National Youth Organisation, in the Pioneers and National In-Service Teacher Education Programme.

How many of us had previously counted this word in our active vocabularies before the Revolution? Now we meet it as a common word on the lips of our people all over Grenada. And through our actual practice of the process of emulation we are learning what exactly the word means. For it means we are recognising the best among us, not to glorify them personally but to raise the *collective* level of consciousness and production. And in doing that, comrades, we are automatically drawing comparisons between the stronger and weaker aspects of our national life, stimulating a sense of the value of criticism and self-criticism, identifying and analysing our problems, and, as a result, creating the resolve to move forward. For in those old colonial and neo-colonial days, the recognition of excellence only came about as a result of individual contest. But the old concepts of competition were built around the dominance of the individual *over* his peers, where separate competitors used each other's heads as rungs in a ladder. The new concept of *emulation* gives us models and symbols for inspiration, increases the group effort and production drive — and thus contributes to nation-building and the construction of our economic and political independence.

Importance of Emulation

In *emulation* we still recognise individual achievements and progress, but our cause is different. The individual is a *participant*, a *contributor* to our new

89

society, and we recognise him or her for that contribution, and *not* to exalt individualism for its own sake. Education — as we have been saying with some regularity of late — is production too! Teaching and studying are both arms of production. The teacher is producing young workers, patriots and intellectuals who will become our scientists, our engineers, our agro-industrialists, our agricultarists, our administrators, our technicians of the future. The student is producing in himself or herself the capacity to conquer and transform nature by that knowledge he or she develops, the capacity to solve the myriad of material problems which beset and harass our people, and the capacity to produce the wealth and riches from the soil, which can offer our people a new life which will realise all their vast and beautiful potential. Our teachers and students *are* producers too, and it is in their ability to *produce* that they will best serve our people. Teacher and student together are planting seeds for the future — they are a part of that *same* future and clearly there should be no antagonism or contradiction between them.

In the People's Republic of Mozambique, a country which shares many similar concrete problems with us, and whose government also shares a strong commitment to the principles of emulation, there is a simple poem, written by an ordinary worker for other workers, which begins to illustrate what emulation is all about. I want to read a section of that poem for you. It starts in this way:

> If you put two seeds into the ground,
> I'll put three — to see if you'll put four,
> So that I'll put five in afterwards,
> In the challenge of emulation.

With that attitude, comrades, we could see the kind of harvest we could reap! We are recognising the excellence around us in the sphere of education tonight, so that the seeds that have been planted in our schools and colleges by our comrade teachers and students will be doubled, trebled, quadrupled over the next year — the first year in our history when secondary education will be free for our students — so that we would all taste the fruit of that harvest! And when our students return from their higher studies to fully integrate themselves and their expertise into our economy and national development, they too will increase our production, teach and inspire others and produce yet greater harvests in future years. That is the whole point of emulation, comrades; it is not a *static* recognition, it pushes our process forward, it is the very *motor* of our advances. It *challenges* and *motivates* us at every juncture. That is why we have put so much importance upon it and that is why it is one of the constant and recurrent themes of our Revolution. It is much more than a new word adopted by our people, it is a characteristic and a watchword of our unity and progress.

It is also in a way a strange contradiction, that in our national embrace of the idea of emulation, we are seeking — and quite definitely finding — excellence and extraordinariness in the *ordinary*. We are discovering in the hardened agricultural worker, in the disciplined fisherman, in the industrious teacher, in the skilful carpenter, the conscientious mason, an excellence that has never before been recognised and acclaimed in our country, although, of course, it always existed, it was always there. We can remember awards and scholarships for a tiny elite in the days that are gone. Do you remember those island scholars who went away every year and just about never came back? And we were told that excellence was the property of the few, the monopoly of the privileged and the fortunate. It was a badge that separated the powerful from the mass of the people. Now we are discovering through our emulation processes that excellence truly belongs to the masses, to the ordinary people — to the 12-year-old boy in Carriacou who is an exemplary literacy volunteer, to the 71-year-old woman in Carriacou, who is his exemplary student and at that age learns how to read and write for the first time in her life — and soon she will set about reading information that will tell her how to more effectively fertilise the soil of her backyard garden so that it will produce more food. Excellence also belongs to the worker on the cocoa estate who, with extraordinary creative insight and mental stamina, discovers a simple device to catch pests that have for generations devoured the products of his land, to the unemployed sisters who unleash the expertise hidden inside themselves to start and develop their own co-operative bakery. This is the spirit of excellence in our working people that has been unlocked through the Revolution and through the recognition of their power and inventiveness by themselves and their fellow comrades. All this energy has been set free by our national grasp of *emulation*, the same spirit of emulation and recognition of the excellence amongst our people that we are sharing in tonight.

Emulation at the Work-Place

Having considered some of the main features of emulation, let us now look practically at how emulation can assist us in our efforts to develop our country. Most importantly, of course, emulation is vital to the development of production — to the development of our agriculture, our agro-industries and our tourism. Though some elements of an emulation system have already started — you will remember that last year we had a 'Worker of the Year' for the first time in our country — there is still need for much more development. Let us take the example of how emulation might work on one of our government farms.

Firstly, for an emulation system to be set up, management and workers would have to come together and examine all the information about the farm — how many acres it has, what crops it now grows, how much profit it now makes. Having done this, workers and management would have to agree on production targets on the farm, and each worker would have his own personal target at which to aim. This process is important not only because it would clearly result in an increase in production, but also because by being involved in all this the worker would at the same time be raising his educational and cultural level and also effectively become part of the management of the farm.

Each Worker Participating

Secondly, for a successful emulation programme the workers and management would have to examine together the way in which things are organised on the farm and to look to see what can be done to improve it. They may discover for example, that you do not really need four people to do weeding – three can do that, but the group doing drainage can use one more because maybe the ground keeps a lot of water in it, bogging down the plants. This again would mean that each and every worker would be participating in the discussion of what is going on in the farm. Each worker would know why his own work is important and why the whole farm will suffer if one person falls down in his task.

Thirdly, a successful emulation programme would mean that when the crop and the targets are examined, the people to be emulated would not be big shots or people with money or degrees from fancy universities – it would be the ordinary worker himself. It would be an ordinary worker like 'Coonyah' – our worker of the year in 1980 – who through his invention of the improved beetle trap was able to remove a particularly destructive pest on the Marlmount Farm and therefore contribute to increasing production. It would be the ordinary worker who would be getting the medal and whom everybody would be applauding and recognising. Think of how important such a person would feel and how many other people could be spurred on knowing that if they too increased their efforts, the next time it could really be them up there receiving the recognition.

Fourthly, and most importantly of all, comrades, the workers must know that when they increase their efforts the people to benefit will not be some small group of people in St George's who want to drink champagne and entertain their friends at Evening Palace. The people to benefit will firstly be able to get their piece of the increased profits to take home, and secondly the nation as a whole will benefit because when the state farms make more money, the government will have more to spend on free health care, on free milk distribution, and on better education for our children, so that more and more of them can achieve the kind of success like those being emulated here tonight.

Emulation Can Transform Education

Comrades, just as it serves to dynamise the process of production and self-management, emulation can play, and ought to play, a central role in the transformation of education. In every major area of the life of the school and the educational life of the nation as a whole, we must move to establish emulation. Emulation in education must exhort our youth to learn more and study better. It must urge greater participation and broader organisation of the student body – in every school there must be a vibrant student council sharing responsibility for the efficient running of the school, sporting clubs, debating societies, agricultural associations, cultural groups, pioneers, and contributing to the patriotic and full development of character. Emulation in education contributes also to the better *administration* of the school because it sets standards for the pursuit of excellence, it requires continuous assessment, it evaluates the main activities of the school. Within the educational system, emulation on the one hand recognises achievement, uses these as the measure for higher collective and individual standards and on the other hand, evaluates and criticises, identifies shortcomings, encourages and motivates to resolve these difficulties. In short, emulation in our educational system is about challenging student and teacher to new levels of achievement, greater discipline and more initiative.

Concrete Successes of Emulation

Those of you, parents, teachers and undoubtedly many youths here who attended the Emulation Celebration of the National Youth Organization Youth Camp, 1981 will recall the extraordinary enthusiasm of the youth, their intense spirit of pride, their militant participation in the Heroes of the Homeland Manoeuvre. Never before in our history has such enthusiasm been demonstrated by the youth of our country. Yet this enthusiasm was not a mood which mysteriously and spontaneously appeared — it was in large part the result of *emulation*. The leaders of Youth Camp 1981 have an instructive story to tell about what was described as 'the total youth experience'.

The first two weeks of Camp 1981 was a difficult period for them because it involved the setting up of camp structures, the organisation of the youth in the many camp activities and the establishment of camp discipline. By the end of this period, the camp leadership was totally exhausted. Comrades were literally falling asleep in the middle of meetings. They were almost defeated because they — a small leadership core — had taken on single-handedly the task of organisation and discipline. Given the history and characteristics of our youth, the answer to these difficulties had to be one which challenged the youth to new standards of discipline and participation. The 'magic' word was emulation!

A thorough system of emulation covering all the major aspects of camp life was put into effect, and one week later the situation in all camps had qualitatively changed. Youths who were refusing to wake up at 5.00 am for camp assembly and Physical Training were now the first in the assembly area! Friendly competition, (one of the three ingredients of emulation) between brigades gave a new sense of purpose, challenged the youth to improve their individual performance as a contribution to the success of their brigade and on a wider scale, the success of their camp. The more disciplined youth criticised and helped (a second main ingredient of emulation) the less disciplined members of their brigade to improve themselves. Discipline was no longer supervision from the top but encouragement/criticism/supervision by fellow brigade members. Competition was transformed from the virtues of selfishness to one of working together, struggling together. The excellence of a brigade or camp gave honour to all of its members and the outstanding individuals within it were the symbols of that pride and honour — they set the example of the best. And for this they were recognised and awarded (third major ingredient of emulation).

Emulation Unlocks Creativity
In this great challenge of emulation, youth who (because they had never bee provided with such a challenge) would not ordinarily have been viewed a outstanding were able to unlock new founts of creativity, discover a dee sense of responsibility and receive higher levels of training (a fourth mai ingredient of emulation). In two camps in particular, Camps Che and Fedon among those emulated were harbour boys and former 'delinquents'. They faced with this challenge, had earned the respect of their peers for thei performance.

The experience of the National Youth Organization Camp 1981 and th results of their emulation programme have direct implications for our edu cational system because it demonstrates concretely the possibilities an the value of emulation among our youth.

During the literacy campaign, we again saw the value of emulation i education. The Centre for Popular Education, parish emulation activitie played a valuable role in changing the public understanding of the nature o illiteracy. For the CPE students themselves, it raised both their continuin confidence to develop their literacy skills *and* to apply and practise then consistently, thus consolidating their strengths. Some of our CPE student spoke out publicly with new pride and determination in speeches which the made for our emulation ceremonies.

Likewise, the National Women's Organization, through emulation tech niques of setting specific goals – in their case 5,000 members by the end o 1981 – sought to rapidly increase their membership. What the sisters foun was that because this goal was met over two months before its deadline (i fact on 23rd October) they had to produce a supplementary goal of 3,00 more members before the end of the year, thus setting a new overall targe of 8,000 members by the end of 1981! The emulation process had been s successful that it was necessary for them to produce a secondary goal (fifth main ingredient of the emulation system) to retain the massive momen tum that the membership drive had generated amongst women throughou the country.

Thus, comrades, we can see from the National Youth Organization Cam that emulation produced a huge *qualitative* improvement in the disciplin and organisation of the camp, and thus in the consciousness of the youtl themselves; and from the National Women's Organization membership drive it is clear that the quantitative results had an equal burst forward, due to th use of *strategies of emulation* by our sisters.

Through emulation, through the system of friendly competition to achiev agreed targets, with mutual assistance and friendly co-operation, with du recognition for achievement, with more training to achieve skills, know-how and greater efficiency and through the additional or supplementary target once the original targets have been reached, a dramatic increase i productivity, efficiency and performance can demonstrably be achieved in our country in all spheres.

The Role of Educators

Comrades, when we speak in terms of production and emulation among teachers, what do we mean? We mean that we are recognising *models* who will inspire us in our own daily work, models who will serve as examples for us today in our schools in every village of Grenada, Carriacou and Petit Martinique.

As model, I can think of no better an example than F.F. Mahon, an ex-Principal of River Sallee Government School. This ordinary, yet extraordinary man was Principal of this school for 42 years, from 1888 to 1930. Just reflect on the years he lived through, comrades, the years he worked through, a term of principalship longer than the lives of the majority of us here, including myself. Think of the thousands of children through that period who passed under his tutelage and care! All from the same village and its surroundings. Think how many working hands and brains he nurtured and produced, how many skills he made sharp and useful, how many ideas he started ticking. Can you imagine such dedication over the fantastically long period of 42 years? If you can, then you would have some idea of the massive achievement and great merit of Brother F.F. Mahon of River Sallee.

And yet, after this retirement in 1930, in fact precisely four days after his retirement — he died. That fact, of course, puts both his sacrifice and his example into even sharper perspective. Here was a teacher whose entire working life was dedicated to the uplifting of the intelligence of a single one of our villages. When we look for heroes of production among our teachers, as among our other workers, we can see Brother Mahon shining like a star. And yet, comrades, let us note, this man held no degree from Oxford, Cambridge, New York or Washington. This man had published no esoteric thesis on who-knows-what academic topic. He was no professor or dean of students of member of some elite scholarly society. He was a simple, ordinary, elementary school principal in a small village of our country. It is for that fact that we remember him and take such value in his example. And it is for his selfless service and dedication that we honour him, for his huge contribution to the production of our country, and thus our present and future, that we recognise him tonight.

A Mirror of Emulation for All of Us

I have selected Brother F.F. Mahon to concentrate upon for what I hope are fairly obvious reasons. His life ended when he ceased to be a teacher, in fact just four days after he ceased being a teacher. His career was exemplary, and as such a mirror of emulation for all of us. In his image, as teachers and workers, we look at ourselves and our own work and we measure our own contributions and standards. If we do not measure up to him, let us try, let us drive ourselves to reach his excellence — not just as individuals but as a united and organised body. If we all put in even half of his service, think how our country would grow, would bloom, would blossom.

But we are talking about emulating the brother, of doing as well or even better than he did — do you see how far we have to reach, comrades? Think how the man must have resisted and put aside the temptation to emigrate and abandon his schools and his pupils — for if we study our history carefully we would know how common a feature constant emigration has been for our people, and in particular for our teachers. It is clear that his village was no prison to him. It was his venue for performance and for achievement. For there was nothing small about the man F.F. Mahon — clearly, he was professionally a giant and a very sincere and dedicated human being. Neither is there anything insignificant about spending a working life serving the people in a village like River Sallee. For any community where people live, produce and love each other is a theatre of achievement and great human deeds. And once they are performed, in the spirit of emulation they drive us forward and inspire us towards further excellence in the same — and in other new and transformed venues — which we must build for ourselves.

Thus, we recognise the F.F. Mahons of our country not as mere excellent individuals to extol their virtues and say how *different* they are from the mass of our people, but we recognise them instead as symbols to show how much *common genius* and patriotic commitment exist among *all* our working people, in particular, tonight, our teachers. If only they would realise it and exercise it to the full, like the brothers and sisters we are honouring through this event.

May I also say that while F.F. Mahon has been singled out for particular mention, that the encormous contribution of other greats such as J.W. Fletcher, F.H. Ireland, P.I. Taylor (all immortalised tonight by the 'O' level gold, silver and bronze awards) and other outstanding educators listed in the programme and written about in your profile are worthy of special praise and recognition. In fact, I want to emphasise that while we are not about the task of singling out of over-singling out specific individuals, these greats do indeed deserve a special place in the history of education in our country. And it is for this reason that I give them special and particular mention.

And because people should be recognised while they are alive, may I also repeat the names of the living greats who all came on stage earlier: Mr C.A. Martineau, Mr Cresswell Julien, Mrs Maude De Coteau, Mr H.D. Baptiste, Mr R.O. Palmer, Mr Renalph Gebon — these outstanding educators stand as a living tribute to the work of our professional educators over the years. May we once again recognise them.

Role of the Church

The history of education in our country, as in the rest of the Caribbean, is a history of partnership between church and state. The churches we must recognise were the pioneers of education in the Caribbean. Formal education can be said to have begun when missionaries came to christianise African slaves. Then when slavery was abolished and the colonial government decided that it should do something about educating the black population, they simply gave the job to the missionaries. The money allocated for education (The Negro Education Grant as it was called) was handed over to the churches. That was in 1835. It was the beginning of a partnership that can be likened to the traditional marriage contract – the church looking after the children and the state providing the money. It is not much different today.

The alliance between church and state did not produce an education system that was as egalitarian as Jesus Christ himself would have designed because the church had to work within the context of a state that did not wish its citizens to develop any fancy ideas about the equality of human beings. Today, one of our tasks is to combat the legacy of elitism in education: to create equality of opportunity, to make the highest quality education available to every single citizen, all the way from pre-school to tertiary.

In this endeavour, and in all of our efforts to change the education system for the better, we rely upon the collaboration of the church, indeed, today's partnership between church and state in Grenada must certainly be a more comfortable one for the church than the historical situation where it had to be the accomplice of slavery, of colonial exploitation, and of one generation of naked political repression: the regime of Eric Matthew Gairy.

Deepening Relationship Between Church and State

As we honour the contribution that the church has made in the past to education, we look forward to a deepening relationship between church and state in the task of educating all of our citizens for a better future and to an even greater sharing of church and school facilities.

In the secondary sector the role of the church is particularly noteworthy, for, as you know, in our history the church had massively outstripped the colonial state in the provision of facilities for secondary education. In fact, the great majority of the teachers and students being honoured here tonight are from schools set up by religious bodies.

We know that the educators who are the heart and soul of these institutions welcome the advent of free secondary education and support the goal of secondary education for all. We know that you will warmly receive every new secondary school into the fold. We know that the old church schools will combat vigorously any tendency on the part of any section of our society to view your schools as elite or prestige institutions and the newer schools as second best, as has happened, unfortunately, in several of our sister Caribbean territories.

In fact, we are extremely proud to report that here in Revolutionary Grenada this trend has not shown any sign of emerging. The proof of this is that in the short space of one year, the Bernadette Bailey Secondary School, the school of the Revolution, has established such a high reputation that in the placing of successful common entrance candidates this year, this new school was the choice of an overwhelming number of parents and students.

A Salute to the Outstanding

Sisters and brothers, comrades, I want to end these remarks by congratulating all of our award winners — the students, those who received school-leaving prizes, common entrance examination prizes, those who received awards for being outstanding performers in the field of sports, those who received awards for making the most vibrant contributions to their school. I especially offer my congratulations to those who received the Fletcher, Ireland and Taylor gold, silver and bronze awards for 'O' level results, the medal awards for outstanding 'A' level results. I also congratulate the 13 schools that received awards tonight and the educators — those who have passed on and those who fortunately are still here with us and whom we feel confident will be around for a long time to come.

May I also extend congratulations to the Ministry of Education for the excellent work that they have been doing over these two and a half years. But, most of all, I congratulate and salute tonight all of our hard-working and courageous students who over the years, not just the past two and a half years, but over the past decade in particular, have engaged in consistent struggle to ensure that their own educational standards were maintained and uplifted, while at the same time being engaged in the forefront of the struggle for a new and just society.

Emulation Will Bring Excellence

Comrades, as Comrade Didacus Jules, the Permanent Secretary in the Ministry of Education, has indicated, this will be an annual ceremony. We hope that through this annual emulation, all students and educators will reach an even greater excellence through setting targets, competing with each other in friendly competition, assisting, helping and co-operating with each other to ensure higher standards through greater training.

We also hope that this emulation exercise will oblige our students and educators to keep setting new targets as their original targets are achieved. We must recognise and never forget that it is only the best among us who set targets — as most of us live from day-to-day most of us do not have a weekly or a monthly or a yearly plan — some do not even have an hourly or daily plan. The business of setting targets is a serious business that only the more serious, disciplined and conscious among us undertake. But it is one thing to set targets. It is another thing to reach these targets. And if it is true that only the best set targets and the very best reach these targets, then it must be even more true that it is only the super-best who having set targets and reached these targets then go on to set additional or supplementary targets.

It is these standards of the super-best that we must all aim to achieve. It is these super heights of excellence that this system of emulation is hoping to spur all of our students, all of our educators, all of our workers, all of our farmers, all of our women, all of our youth, all of our people to reach as we move rapidly towards building the new and just Grenada.

LONG LIVE THE STUDENTS OF GRENADA!

LONG LIVE THE MEMORY OF OUTSTANDING DECEASED EDUCATORS!

LONG LIVE THE WORK AND CONTRIBUTION OF LIVING EDUCATORS!

LONG LIVE THE SYSTEM OF EMULATION!

LONG LIVE THE DRIVE TOWARDS EXCELLENCE!

FORWARD TO EDUCATION!

FORWARD EVER, BACKWARD NEVER!

11. Forward to 1982 — the Year of Economic Construction!

New Year's Address to the Nation, Made on Radio Free Grenada and Television Free Grenada, 1 January 1982

On behalf of our Party and Government I bring you warm, revolutionary greetings on the first day of 1982, and wish you all peace, good health and success for the New Year.

At the beginning of every year it is necessary to plan, to make resolutions, to project our vision and chart the course for the upcoming 12 months. As we stand shoulder to shoulder on the threshold of a new year let us, therefore, prepare ourselves for the many challenges that the national construction effort will pose for us. Let us continue to cultivate more revolutionary ideas, values and practices and let us recommit ourselves and our nation to the world revolutionary process and the international anti-imperialist movement which is struggling to bring about a more just and happy life for the vast majority of men, women and children of our globe.

Comrades, it is also important that before we enter the doorway of the New Year we should pause to look back at the road we have travelled over the past 12 months, take stock of our successes ans setbacks and to evaluate those efforts, projects and processes which were begun in 1981 and which must be continued and strengthened in 1982.

1981: Year of Agriculture and Agro-Industries

In January of last year our People's Revolutionary Government declared 1981 as the 'Year of Agriculture and Agro-Industries'. We did this because we recognised the urgent necessity to undo the tremendous destruction wrought on our land by 29 years of Hurricane Gairy and to begin repairing what we have come to call the motor of our economy, the pillar and bedrock of our entire economic system: agriculture. At that time we also understood that the model of industrialisation which would provide most jobs and income for our people could only be possible as an offshoot of a national and productive agricultural sector.

Thus, Comrades, our Party and government clearly recognise the close interrelationship between agriculture and agro-industries, hence the declaration for the year 1981 and our progress in these areas last year has fully justified this declaration.

The Revolution was convinced 12 months ago that we had to move rapidly to give agriculture a new role in our development as well as to bring a new standard of living to the workers and farmers in that industry.

Agriculture – Motor of the Economy

We perceived agriculture to be the main supplier of food for our people, as a major earner of foreign exchange, as a weapon against unemployment and as a means for increasing our self-reliance based on the full development of our main natural resource – the land.

In 1981 the Revolution began the serious task of meeting these objectives by building state companies for commercial production and marketing and ensuring that the state sector plays the leading role in the development of commercial agriculture in our country. In addition, we moved to establish the Ministry of Agriculture as a vital force giving material support and advice to small and medium farmers struggling with problems of production and organisation. Comrades, to give you an indication of the social and economic importance of agriculture to our nation consider that 40% of our gross domestic product and 50% of all foreign exchange earnings come from agriculture.

Almost 7,000 of our countrymen work full time in this field and given that the average Grenadian household consists of five people it means that 35,000 sisters and brothers – one third of our total population – depend directly and solely on the soil for a living. Therefore, in order to build the Ministry into an effective tool capable of planting the seeds of rapid agricultural growth, the Revolution started a large number of new programmes to solve the multitude of problems inherited from the Gairy dictatorship.

Between recurrent and capital expenditure the Revolution is now spending 54 times more money than Gairy ever spent on agriculture. We are now experimenting with and introducing new methods, new crops, new varieties. Pest and diseases are daily fought and destroyed and proper methods of conservation and field sanitation are being employed so that we may not lose our precious resources of soil, water and plants.

Our agriculture is gradually becoming green once more and we must ensure that in 1982 it will be much greener.

In the coming months, for example, the Mardigras Soil and Water Conservation Project, which now represents the most impressive agricultural innovation in our country, and possibly in the Eastern Caribbean, will continue to bring into full production land that was previously useless scrub and steep hillside.

It is important to note here Comrades, that the agricultural programmes of the Revolution do not only come under the Ministry of Agriculture. A big slice of the Budget of the Ministry of Communications and Works is earmarked for agricultural development. For example, the many new feeder roads under construction and the massive $10 million Eastern Main Road Project will mean that a vital new link for agriculture will materialise in the coming year, thus facilitating the cultivation of more land and easy transportation of crops to markets and to ports. Increasingly, the application of science and technology to agriculture is overcoming old barriers and opening the way for greater production and full use of all our land.

In this regard, training has become a key element of our agriculture. In the early months of the Revolution we re-established the farm training school and have now moved from 50 students a year to 150, and this was done in spite of a devastating fire which destroyed the Mirabeau Training School early last year.

1981 also saw the youths of our country playing a part in agricultural development. Before the Revolution, the average age of a Grenadian farmer was 62 years but the recent agricultural census shows the average age of the farmer is now 51 years. This indicates that more young people from the ranks of the unemployed have since become involved in agriculture. This is undoubtedly a hopeful sign for the future, and we eagerly look forward to a significant increase in this youth involvement in 1982, particularly in the agricultural co-operatives which our National Co-operative Development Agency (NACDA) will be continuing to establish. Let us then move rapidly in this new year to make a reality out of the popular slogan 'Idle Hands and Idle Lands Equal an End to Unemployment'.

With our Revolution now providing opportunities for our youth as never before in our history — free secondary education, hundreds of university scholarships, more training opportunities, more employment — we must work towards ensuring that all of them fully understand the tremendous possibilities that are now available and make the maximum use of them.

The Colonial Legacy

Comrades, part of the colonial legacy from which our country and our sister countries in the region still suffer, is that we have always been primary producers, producers of raw agricultural products. Our production of sugar cane made the imperialist countries of today strong and powerful and paved the way for their industrial development in the 19th Century, and after slavery was abolished we became exporters of agricultural commodities — in our case cocoa, nutmegs and banana. In turn, we imported and still import food and other industrial products at very high prices from the same countries that our exploitation helped to make wealthy and powerful.

Consequently, this unfair and unjust trade relationship left us with little or no industry. In our case, Grenada's Industrial sector contributes only 4–5% of our entire domestic product.

Before 1981 our true industrial potential remained untapped. The Gairy dictatorship failed to formulate any kind of meaningful industrial development policy or strategy. Critical questions such as the kind of industries we need, their linkage to other areas of the economy, or an investment criteria were never seriously examined in the past. Consequently, industrial activities were disorganised and often out of tune with the nation's interest.

However, Comrades, conscious of the need for structural change in the economy, our government has been promoting a strong commitment towards the principle of industrial development compatible with our national interests.

Instead of the dying 'Industrialization by Invitation' approach, our government advocates a policy of industrialization based on the greater use of our natural and human resources, particularly our agriculture.

This strategy in 1982 and beyond will call for a vigorous and leading role for the public sector within the economy, joint ventures with local and foreign interests and the provision of incentives and assistance to the private sector.

Our government accepts the principle of a mixed economy and invites the participation of local and foreign private and co-operative sectors. To this end a draft investment code outlining the policies which will guide the role of the private sector has already been partially circulated and will soon be circulated to all the mass organisations in our country for them to study and comment on.

Agro-Industries and Fisheries

Early last year we established a Ministry of Agriculture, Agro-Industries and Fisheries (now called Industrial Development) to deal specifically with the promotion, implementation and monitoring of industrial activity. During the year also we formally opened our million dollar Agro-Industrial Plant which at present employs some 27 persons full time and 71 part time, a plant which daily produces thousands of units of Mango Nectar, Tamarind Nectar, Paw Paw slices, Guava-Banana Juice, Nutmeg Jelly, Hot Sauce, Chutney and even Guava Cheese. And we are happy to say that at the Bulgarian International Trade Fair last year our nutmeg jam won a gold medal for its excellent quality.

After just a few months, our Agro-Industrial Plant has been able already to provide some $59,000.00 in revenue to 800 small farmers and 18 of our State Farms.

Spice Isle Coffee, now being processed in our country for the first time, has shown a healthy economic return on investment and we look forward to its continuing growth this year.

In 1982, our new Ministry of Industrial Development has plans to begin the manufacturing of nutmeg oil, the processing of spice products, and large-scale production of high-quality ice cream, reconstituted milk products and fruit juices.

The Ministry also intends to formally open a new sheep and pig farm which, over a period, will add to our stock of cheaper and good quality meat and provide us with the capacity to move into the area of ham, bacon and sausage production. Of course, the Agro-Industrial Factory at True Blue will also be expanded during this year to meet the ever-increasing demand for its high quality products.

Utilising the six modern fishing trawlers given to us by the Revolutionary Government and people of Cuba, the National Fisheries Company has caught over 55,000 pounds of fish in the last six months. Some of this has been sold fresh on the market and to selected institutions, and the rest has been smoked and salted and sold in our shops and supermarkets; our saltfish is even being exported to neighbouring countries. We expect that in 1982 the total catch will increase substantially thereby bringing more protein-filled food to our people and more foreign exchange to our nation.

Our handicraft industry took a giant leap in 1981 with the opening of Grencraft, a retail outlet which buys and sells a wide variety of quality products from our local craftsmen.

Our sugarcane industry also made significant progress as our efforts to revive this industry yielded good results in 1981. As you know, this industry is no longer owned by a private company of plantocrats. It is, today, substantially owned by the government for the benefit of the workers and last year, despite inclement weather, the factory was able to pay sugar farmers $61.00 a ton for their cane — a record for our country.

Objective Economic Difficulties

Comrades, this list of economic successes and achievements in 1981 is more impressive when looked at in the context of the tremendous objective difficulties that have confronted the efforts of our government.

In the two years and nine months of the Revolution we have had to contend with natural disasters such as hurricanes, floods and freak wind storm, all of which brought considerable destruction to our cocoa, nutmeg and banana crops and to our roads and bridges.

Years of neglect under Gairyism have brought serious disease problems such as Leaf Spot and Moko to our banana cultivation, Witches Broom, beetles and thrips to our cocoa fields and wilt to our nutmeg plantations. In fact, Moko disease has meant that this year alone over 120 acres of banana cultivation had to be destroyed.

One of the harsh realities of being tied in a dependency relationship to imperialist economies is that when these countries suffer crises we, in Grenada, and, indeed, much of the Third World, suffer disasters. As we say in the Party, when their economies sneeze, ours catch the cold and when their economies have a bad cold, as they do now, we face fatal pneumonia.

In fact, the ups and downs of world market prices provide us with daily lessons on how imperialism operates. For example, cocoa and nutmeg prices have collapsed over the last two and a half years on the world market and we are literally powerless to do anything about the situation. Millions of dollars in vital foreign exchange have been lost as a result.

The normal yearly production of nutmegs in Grenada is about five million pounds, yet for the last year we have had in storage in different warehouses some seven million pounds, unable to find buyers on the world market for them. And to make matters worse, our farmers as a result of increased effort and the application of new methods of husbandry last year produced the largest nutmeg crop in our history — some six and a half million pounds.

With bananas, we share the same fate as the other Windward Islands in the virtual collapse of the industry in recent times. At present, our banana farmers receive the abominably low price of .12c per pound from the British multinational company, Van Geest, yet the price per pound for the box in which the bananas are transported is .10c, and the cost of production per pound is estimated at about .18c. Added to this, the cost of imported fertiliser to the farmer is massive and the cost of a cutlass or a hoe or a fork keeps going up while Geest moves merrily along buying more ships from their ever-increasing profits.

In the area of tourism, because of the world capitalist crisis virtually all Caribbean countries have suffered significant declines in the number of visitors and the amount of money spent by them. Here, too, Grenada has been no exception and we have had to carry the additional burden of an orchestrated world-wide propaganda campaign against our Revolution carried out by US imperialism. Needless to say, this campaign did some damage to our tourism but because of our fighting response we are optimistic that when the first phase of our International Airport comes into operation tourism will experience a revival. And we are confident that our hoteliers and other investors will commence construction activity in 1982 out of their recognition of the tremendous future for tourism in our country.

Our People Have Defeated Imperialism

In a sense, Comrades, 1981 can be described as the year of the all-out assault by imperialism on our people and our nation. We can recall the endless propaganda bombardment, the frenetic, vulgar, aggressive and economic pressures, the sinister and threatening military manoeuvres. But for every vile salvo imperialism launched at our Revolution our fighting people resisted and responded with greater determination and with more creative counter-attacks, and we were victorious.

When imperialism tried to stop different countries from attending the European Economic Community Co-financing Conference to raise money for the completion of our new International Airport it failed. The Conference was a success and we have been able to raise the vast majority of the remaining funds. Our International Airport with all its facilities including a large modern Terminal building is being built on schedule and it will be completed on schedule.

When US imperialists attempted to get the EEC to cut back on its general economic assistance to our homeland, the EEC in fact increased its assistance in all aspects over the next five years — another humiliating defeat.

When US imperialism sought to block a $19 million loan we had applied for from the IMF we mounted a massive diplomatic effort successfully mobilising 90 member countries of the IMF. We ended up getting a loan in the amount we had applied for, and imperialism got another kick in its pants.

When they tried to pressure the Caribbean Development Bank [CDB] to stop funding various projects in our country, they again failed. The CDB and our sister CARICOM nations refused to accept a US grant that carried terms and conditions that were in conflict with the laws of the CDB. Their neocolonial attempt at divide and rule failed miserably.

When US imperialism, using a corrupt and unpatriotic gang of 26 plantocrats, lawyers, businessmen and saltfish journalists attempted to revive the *Torchlight* under the guise of a counter-revolutionary ragsheet arrogantly misnamed the *Grenadian Voice*, the Revolution moved swiftly to put it under [teach it] manners. Another setback for imperialism as they were reminded that our Revolution is popular and must be respected.

When in September the anti-Grenada propagandists in the US State Department instructed their bell-boy lackeys who run the newspapers in the region to publish identical front page editorials attacking the Grenada Revolution, their own media workers were outraged at this blatant violation of journalistic ethics and condemned the editorials in the strongest terms. And when the attempts at economic strangulation and the propaganda onslaughts did not bring the desired results, imperialism in a move of desperation, began the infamous 'Amber and the Amberines' rehearsals for an invasion of our beloved homeland.

But even in the face of this most ominous, illegal and intimidating threat, our courageous people and all democratic and peace-loving peoples of the world found the correct and appropriate response.

In our historical 'Heroes of the Homeland' manoeuvre thousands of ordinary Grenadians demonstrated to Reagan and his warlords that they were ready and able to defend this country, and to give their lives if necessary, for the preservation of our glorious Revolution. And together with the worldwide condemnation of this vulgar and cowardly action, imperialist plans to turn back our process were dealt another serious blow.

Imperialism and Reaganism have also failed miserably, Comrades, in their vulgar diplomatic efforts to isolate us from the international community, and to prevent us from conducting a principled foreign policy based on peace, co-operation, mutual respect, non-interference and friendship towards other nations and peoples.

The hugely successful International Solidarity Conference recently held at the Dome in St George's is a brilliant testament to the failure of imperialism's isolationist policies. When 107 delegates representing 80 delegations from 40 countries and all continents of the world said in a clear and resounding voice that they strongly support our Revolution and will continue and increase their solidarity with the Grenadian people, imperialism received a hard slap in the face.

Comrades, as we stand on the threshold of a New Year we can state confidently that no amount of imperialist threats or pressures will shake the Grenadian people's uncompromising opposition to all forms of racism, fascism, colonialism, neocolonialism or imperialism. We will continue to speak out loudly against exploitation and oppression in any part of the world whether it be in El Salvador, Haiti, Chile or South Africa or by Zionist forces in the Middle East and we will remain firmly committed to the struggle for world peace, disarmament and a new International Economic and Information Order.

We will continue in 1982 to play an active role in the many international organisations and groupings to which we belong. And we certainly look forward to and repeat our consistent calls for the early convening of a CARICOM Heads of Government Meeting this year. As always, our CARICOM partners can be assured of our deep commitment to the regional integration process for the benefit of all of our people. Our country will always stand by our deeply held principles of mutual respect for sovereignty, non-interference in the internal affairs of other states and friendly co-operation for mutual benefit – particularly with our closest neighbours in CARICOM.

The highly successful trade union, Socialist International Ecumenical and Small States Conference held in Grenada last year, our successful state visit to Mexico, our diplomatic initiatives at major international Conferences and for all indicate that the Grenada Revolution enjoys the respect and admiration of the world community and it shows that imperialism has failed to tarnish our good image abroad.

But, Comrades, let us not get carried away by our victories. Let us not fall prey to false illusions of security. Indeed, some battles have been won but the war against our implacable imperialist enemy is not over. It will continue in 1982 and we must prepare ourselves for the struggles that lie ahead.

Failures and defeats will not stop the enemy trying again. As we have said so often, imperialism never rests and so we must continue to be on our guard, continue to be vigilant, continue to expand and strengthen our revolutionary People's Militia. We must keep our eyes open for new tricks, for new variations of the enemy's plan, for new devious twists and turns on the propaganda, and on the economic and the military fronts.

Benefits of Revolutionary Democracy

Patriots, Friends, Comrades, 1981 has proved to be a year of a great explosion of popular democracy in Free and Revolutionary Grenada. It has been a year of the real fulfilment of our 1973 Manifesto pledge when we said, and I quote:

> To replace the political system with a truly democratic and grassroots system in which the people of every village and parish and of the island

as a whole will be able to exercise power on their own behalf, in their own interests, in order to build a bright future for our children.

Comrades, when we conceived of that future in 1973, we knew that we were not just dreaming a crazy or vapid dream. We had always *concretely* and *genuinely*, built our entire political process and reality around the *participation* of our people, firstly in building the strength and determination to crush the dictatorship, and secondly, once that had been achieved in March 1979, to build real and solid structures of democracy that would be the *bone marrow* of our growth and advancement.

Indeed, *people's* participation has, is, and always will be the guarantee of our democratic development, and 1981 has been the year when we began to consolidate our people's power. Halfway through the year, we took the virtually unprecedented step in the English-speaking world of creating a Ministry of National Mobilization. Many of our people were asking: why, such a Ministry, and what was its function? The answers to these questions have been spoken time and time again over the last few months, by every working man and woman who has risen in a parish, zonal, or workers' parish council and poured out their criticism and suggestions to their Comrades and workmates, in the presence of the Revolutionary leadership; by every brother or sister, who for the first time in their lives, have strode forward from the middle of a public assembly, approached a microphone, and uttered sentences that have helped in their every word, to push our country forward; by every Grenadian who has cast aside the nervousness and timidity forced upon them by colonial and neo-colonial systems, that held their contribution to our national life to be nothing, to be meaningless and worthless; by every grasp of confidence and power that has made our people speak out and speak up, expressing in each statement:

> I am a Grenadian, and this is the place where I was born and I live, this is my country, the country I love and the country I will transform along with my sisters and brothers.

For this is the true meaning of revolutionary democracy. It is a growth in confidence in the power of ordinary people to transform their country, and thus transform themselves. It is a growth in the appreciation of people organising, deciding, creating together. It is a growth in fraternal love, and this is what has been happening in our country in 1981.

Consider again our women and their National Women's Organization. From the membership of 1,300 at the beginning of the year our women burst forth and have more than quadrupled their membership. The National Youth Organization has visibly been growing more and more muscle week by week and by the time of its jubilant congress a few weeks ago had also quadrupled its membership from January 1981. Comrades, of course we must associate our young people with growth, but this year it is as if we have been spectators of the blossoming of a great national bloom of youth, with every petal an NYO member or a pioneer. Our democracy is not pampering or fussing over our children, it is building their strength, stamina and creativeness. For this year our children too have become a *vibrant social force in their own right*. And with the strides made by our Pioneer Movement, our children are already developing the maturity and creativity that will steam our country forward over the next decade. Have you heard their choirs, their poets, their calypsonians, their debates and discussions? Have you viewed their confidence and organisational ability in their television programme? If you have, then you are looking at the seeds of our future, you are experiencing the energy that will spark our country, pull it out of underdevelopment and drive us forward. And that too, is the result of the democratic power we have unleashed this year, for our mass organisations have all taken succour and strength from the motive force of mass mobilisation which we have been generating as a national priority.

For we have always declared that the mass participation of the people in all the major decisions that affect their lives, from budget to bananas, from planning to pest control, is the vital component of our development. People's participation is the blood supply of our Revolution, not only because it seeks to release our people's submerged potential, creativity and genius, but because it is the only *viable way in which our economy can grow*. Our economy can only become strong if our people's input into its organisation is equally strong. We can only produce together if we also plan together. We can only increase our collective investment in that wealth. Our soil is rich, but its yield will only match that richness if we understand that we must create production targets *together*, agree on planning procedures *together*, achieve exemplary punctuality *together* and finally share in the profits and prosperity of our organisation *together*. For economic growth is our second pillar of development and it is bound absolutely to the ways we find of democratising our society and organising its growth. *Every worker has a voice, has creative suggestions, has his portion of genius*. Let us extract it all and put it at the service of our economic growth, for with that great flame of workers' energy and culture to drive us forward our possibilities are infinite.

This is why we are saying that in 1982 we must extend our democracy even further, so that it encompasses every aspect of the work place. This means our workers must become more and more involved in the participatory re-organisation of our trade unions, to ensure that any stagnation of the past is stirred into democratic motion. In doing this, we are asking our workers to use their own organisations, their trade unions, to call for production committees at every work-place throughout our country, so that democracy and efficiency can work side by side in our economy, creating a massive increase in production. And in the same way that our workers must be democratically involved in planning the budget, they must also, through their trade unions, *be at the other end of the process*, monitoring and identifying price increases and consumer problems, investigating unreasonable, inconsistent and profiteering price rises, and calling upon their own democratic organisations to be vigilant and to speak up for them.

The Manoeuvre Will Never Over

Our third pillar of development, *national defence*, also has a vital link with democracy. For when we ask of our people to step forward to defend the gains and benefits of their Revolution, we are using no pressure, no compulsion. We are saying in effect 'this is your Revolution, it is your democratic right to defend it'! For as we know, democracy brings *responsibilities* and *rights* in equal measure, and our people, in their huge and patriotic response to join our People's Revolutionary Militia and in their understanding of the full impact of our slogan *'The manoeuvre will never over'* are clearly realising this. They are making the profound and proud choice of a free people; to hold fast to what is theirs, and it is theirs because they are *involved*, brain and muscle, action and speech, in the building of a new vibrant and loving Grenada.

A Strong Economy Means More Benefits

Since our Revolution, we have seen a remarkable growth in capital expenditure on infrastructural developments that have benefited all Grenadians, but in particular our poor and working people. This growth has clearly laid the basis for genuine economic transformation and diversification in the future. In the last year of Gairy, the capital expenditure was $8 million. In 1979, the first year of the Revolution, we drove it forward to $15 million, in 1980 that more than doubled, to $32 million, and in 1981 it doubled yet again to over $73 million. Every dollar of this rising spiral of national expansion has benefited our people, and has formed an integral part of the *social wage* of our people, which makes our dollar so much more valuable than just about any other dollar in our region. Massive infrastructural projects, such as the huge acceleration of the building of our International Airport, the laying of whole new systems of pipes for our water, the renovation of our electricity generators, the establishment of our asphalt plant and new quarry, and the virtual reconstruction of the Carriacou road system, and the introduction of the first public transport system in our sister island. We shall soon see the beginning stages of a new telephone system as well as a new cement plant, new ice-making plant and new warehouses to accommodate our increasing production and expansion. Our other sister island, Petit Martinique, will soon have its first health clinic, with a residential nurse, and already has its own branch of the National Marketing and Importing Board.

We shall also be energetically seeking new markets all over the world, and further diversifying our crops and produce. The marketing of egg-plants [aubergines] will be stepped up in the coming months, and we shall be introducing, in a serious way, the production of English potatoes. In

Carriacou, black-belly sheep are fast becoming a common sight on the potentially rich pasture lands of that sister island.

Our new economic institutions, created by the Revolution, have been
bringing real benefits to our people. The Marketing and National Importing
Board, which is unique in Carriacou, has directly brought vital produce
to our tables at much reduced cost, as well as keeping down the prices of
staple food commodities like rice and sugar. The National Commercial Bank
and the Grenada Development Bank have continued to expand and make
profits for the benefit and investment of our masses, providing vital loans to
our farmers and fishermen to increase their economic and productive possibilities.

Thus, our *social wage is permanently increasing* with the development of
our Revolutionary institutions and programmes. Our money is worth more
every time we gain a concrete benefit — when we build an Eye Clinic, when
we institute free secondary education, when we introduce free public health
care, when we open the primary health programme, when we give out free
milk or free school books and uniforms, when we provide free mass adult
education, when we expand our low income housing project, when we
expand our house repair programme for the poorest workers; for our social
wage is a guarantee of an improvement of our *quality of life* and *social
security*, which, in most of the countries of our region, must be bought with
hard-earned dollars.

1982 — 'Year of Economic Construction'

As you know, since the Revolution we have given names to our years of
progress. 1979 was named and correctly named, the 'Year of National Liberation'.

1980, because of our thrust in those two areas, became 'The Year of
Education and Production' and 1981 was the 'Year of Agriculture and Agro-
Industry'. We have never viewed these slogans as ornaments or mere symbol-
isms or pretty names. For us, they summarise the *thrust* of the particular
years, without neglecting or abandoning all the thousands of other
component parts and essential energies that also compose those years. Of
course, *every year* is a year of agriculture, agro-industry, education, production and national liberation. But we need to create *emphasis* in our process,
so that we can give *even more* to the direction we are underlining. So our
slogan once it has been chosen becomes the *key focus* and *major priority*
of the year.

For these reasons, 1982 has been declared by the People's Revolutionary
Government as '*The Year of Economic Construction*', and when we examine
this title, we must not see just words, but real and concrete economic achievements. Economic construction will be the major area of struggle for all our
people, because of its importance to the future building of our Revolution.
Thus, together with the continuing move from strength to strength of our

111

mass organisations, our organs of popular democracy like our parish and zonal councils, and our firm and disciplined Militia, we must resolve also to carry on the struggle to build the priorities of 1981, our agriculture and agro-industries. These still remain the cornerstones of our economic advance and construction, *and in no way* must we de-emphasize their continued and crucial significance. But, in addition to these we shall also see other vital emphases.

The second phase of the Centre for Popular Education, the adult education programme for the functionally illiterate, will be launched for the benefit of the mass of our people, and this must coincide with a greatly increased momentum in the organisation of workers' education classes through all our work-places, particularly in our rural areas. This twin thrust of mass education must lay the base for a hugely increased raising of consciousness nationally, which in turn will have its effect in a much greater understanding of, and commitment to, the cause of economic construction. And notice Comrades, that we are talking about national *construction*, not *reconstruction*, for we are entering a new phase in the development of our country's productive capacity that has *never* before been conceived of or approached.

The Worker and Economic Construction

What will the year of economic construction mean to our workers? What challenges will it throw out to them? What benefits will it bring to them? Firstly, we must say that there must be no contradiction between those who are involved in the economic construction and what will be constructed. For the construction will be the *work* of our people, and will also be the *cause* of their progress. Our people are the *constructors*, and will also be the beneficiaries of what they construct. This is why we must have more and more involvement of our workers in the planning and decisions affecting their work, as well as in the work itself. This is why we need more forums for discussion, more seminars, more committees to set targets, more structures of emulation. For in all this democratic activity we shall not only be achieving greater production and output, sharper efficiency, the elimination of waste and corruption, but also, as a direct consequence, a much improved social wage and range of national benefits, all coming as a direct result of workers' participation and democracy. This is why we need to understand that people's democracy is not just a satisfying and dignifying human activity, it is also the watchword of economic advance and social progress.

Farmers, Businessmen and Economic Construction

So, when we bring more democratic energy to bear upon our farming or our tourist industry, we are calling upon our farmers, our hoteliers, our local businessmen *and* those foreign investors who respect our goals of national development, *all* to contribute to our year of economic construction. As our new Airport nears its completion, and the Terminal building takes shape with its two storeys stretching across one and a half acres of land, we are creating more avenues for economic construction in the duty free stores and terminal shopping facilities that are needed, and in the new hotels that must be built, and in the existing ones that must be expanded so as to accommodate our new tourist arrivals.

Eat What We Grow

And as we *expand* in the many areas of economic construction, we also need to be conscious that we must *conserve* energy and work hard to *cut out* unnecessary consumerism. With the unfortunate but unavoidable new increases in the price of gasolene and diesel, as of today — accompanied by a decrease in the price of kerosene — we must be more and more careful not to waste fuel or to use unnecessary electricity. And, together with this, we must understand the need to develop a new approach to eating habits, which should be, basically, *producing to feed ourselves*. We must grow what we eat and eat what we grow. We shall not be able to afford large import bills for items we can produce and eat for ourselves, from our own resources, our own land, our own work, our own economic construction.

End Corruption, Waste, Abuse and Indiscipline

As you know, today is traditionally a day for resolutions. Often, New Year resolutions are seen as a joke, but for us they need to be serious. Let us resolve that this year, 1982, will be the year when we attack any vestiges of *corruption* at our work-places and make them a thing of the past; let us resolve to combat any *bureaucratic abuse*, any arrogance of power by those who use their desks, forms, rubber-stamps or positions as barriers against our people's progress; let us save money at a national level by pooling and co-ordinating our large-scale buying at a department or ministerial level, to *economise* in all purchases, from tractors to aspirins; let us make war on waste, for everything we save and put back into the national Treasury will eventually come back to us through that same conomic construction and profit-sharing. In short, let us become more economy conscious.

We must vigorously resolve to struggle against all forms of indiscipline, laziness, inefficiency, clock-watching and unproductivity in the bureaucracy and in our work-places, all of which are cancerous and must be stamped out.

Let Us Make a Start Together

To ensure the fullest implementation of our plans and aspirations for 1982, we — all of us — must make an early start. And perhaps the best start that we could all make would be to begin immediate discussions in our unions, organisations, groups, clubs and at our work-places aimed at identifying what contribution we can make to building our economy, what contribution we can make to the building of the four pillars of our economy, agriculture, agro-industry, fisheries and tourism; what contribution we can make towards cutting out waste, indiscipline, corruption, inefficiency; what contribution we can make in the area of building democracy and participation at the work place, and to examine the need for *production committees* that would set production targets, *discipline and grievance committees* that would deal with genuine problems and difficulties and *emulation committees* that would on a regular weekly or monthly basis salute, recognise and reward the achievements of our outstanding workers.

We of the People's Revolutionary Government have already made a start through the commencement of widespread discussions in the public service, and outside of it, around the one year *National Plan* which for the first time in our history we intend to implement this year. We certainly urge you to invite us, and particularly, our Comrades in the Ministry of Planning, to come to your trade union, organisation, group or work-place to discuss this National Plan and to share with you our and your ideas on how *together* we can achieve our goals of economic development and make this year — 1982 — truly the 'Year of Economic Construction'.

12. Not One Human Right Has Ever Been Won Without Struggle

Opening Address to The American Association of Jurists' Conference: St. George's, 10 March 1982

I want to join with Comrade Kenrick Radix, our Minister of Justice, in extending a very warm and fraternal greeting to all of the comrades who have come to our country for this very significant conference. We certainly appreciate very much your presence here with us on this occasion, for several reasons. Firstly, of course, because you have chosen our country as the site of your conference and for us that is always very important and we believe is a reflection of the support that many of you have for the political process which is developing in our country or at least an expression of the open-mindedness of all comrades present here.

Come See for Yourself

This certainly falls in line completely with one of our main slogans in the country, 'Come see for yourself' — come to our country, and after you have seen, then make a judgement on what you have seen and not judge the situation in our country based on the adverse propaganda which is sweeping the region and many parts of the world.

We are also very happy that you are here today, comrades, because as we understand from Comrade Deborah Jackson, this conference is a run up, preparatory conference to one that will be held by the American Association of Jurists next year again in St George's and of course we look forward with great anticipation to your presence at that conference also.

Certainly by that time we will be more organised, we will be better prepared, our country would have gone through more progressive developments and, therefore, your visit on that occasion we certainly hope will be even more congenial and fruitful.

Comrades, we are also happy that you are here today because of the variety of countries that are represented: countries from the Caribbean, from Central America and of course from North America, from the United States and Canada, and from the United Kingdom. We feel it is extremely important for lawyers who are engaged in active practice in so many different parts of the world to have the opportunity of getting together and holding discussions in an atmosphere of friendliness, where very critical questions can be openly discussed, where views can be freely exchanged and where, hopefully, a consensus can emerge.

I am happy, too, comrades, because as a former practising lawyer myself, it is very good to see so many of my old friends, and several comrades whom I have had the opportunity of working with in different cases, particularly what one can, I suppose, call public interest, human rights and political cases over the years.

Finally, comrades, we are happy to have you in Grenada at this time because you have come at an extremely important time for our people, at a time when we celebrate what we regard in Grenada as being the most important event to have ever occurred in the history of our country: our glorious March 13th Revolution which took place three years ago.

Comrades, the theme of your conference, 'Human Rights in the 80s, a Caribbean Perspective' is an extremely important theme for us all to be discussing at this time and for us to develop a perspective that is relevant, that is rooted in reality, that has a concrete relationship to what is happening in the real world, to what is happening in our region and in the wider world outside. Having the opportunity, therefore, of giving in a few words a view from the People's Revolutionary Government of what our own broad perspective is on this question, looked at from the point of view of lawyers, is, for us, very significant and we certainly hope that these brief remarks will have some bearing on the discussions which you will be holding over the next two days.

Only Struggle Brought Human Rights

By far the most important point I want to make is that human rights have always come only after struggle. There is nothing that I will say today that will be more important than that. Not one single human right has ever been won without struggle. Notwithstanding the mythology of the law, that laws come naturally, that some laws exist from birth and some rights exist from birth, the truth of the matter is that every single important right under the law, which are today are taken for granted in many countries, (and in many more countries these laws and these rights still do not exist) every single one of those rights only came after a struggle by the ordinary working people.

Struggles of the Slave Ended Slavery
Certainly, this can be seen from the historical epoch classified as slavery. It was not as a result of anybody's kindness, or anybody's change of heart, not as a result of any new, sudden development in philosophy that slavery was abolished; slavery was abolished when and only when the struggles of the slaves themselves forced the slave masters to make a new calculation, to decide whether it was worth while being killed, whether it was worth while risking on a nightly basis a new slave uprising. Further, slavery only came to an end when the economic realities of the age made it more prudent and

116

more desirable to move to a new form of exploitation, that known in history as feudalism.

Only Struggle Wiped Away Feudal Rights
Similarly, comrades, under feudalism, the oppression of the serf did not end overnight but only came about as a result of hundreds of years of concrete struggle and development of new economic realities.

For example, the right to sleep the first night with the wife of the serf, which the Lord of the Manor for several years regarded as his exclusive right, did not disappear because one night a nice Lord of the Manor decided it was no longer nice to sleep with the wife of his serf. It disappeared because of struggle by the serfs to end that particular form of oppression as, indeed, other forms of oppression under fuedalism. It was the same with the rights assumed by the Lord of the Manor to appropriate the fruits of the labour of his serf. That did not end because the Lords decided one morning that they no longer wanted to collect their ill-gotten gains. That ended because the serfs rose up in revolt. That ended because the new economic reality which began to emerge, the new reality of capitalism, made it imprudent and unwise for the relationsnips under feudalism to continue.

Laws Did Not Suddenly Emerge
That is why it is no accident, comrades, and as lawyers you will know this, that the law of contract, for example, the law recognising enforceable bargains, the law sanctioning agreements, did not emerge overnight. That simple law of contract which today we all take for granted, and can quote millions of legal precedents, customs and practices to argue in favour of or against one aspect or another of its many dimensions — that simple law took hundreds of years to emerge. The law of contract arose out of the crucible of life, out of the real struggles of the emerging capitalists who were at that time a revolutionary force demanding the right of free trade, insisting on an easier form of exchange for the goods that they were selling, insisting that the laws relating to barter were too cumbersome, that they were not prepared to walk around with a wheelbarrow full of wheat in order to obtain a shirt or something else but were determined to struggle for a new legal relationship based on trade, so that they could fully exploit the potential and possibilities of the embryonic free enterprise, capitalist system.

Subversive Capitalist Rights

But the relationships that the emerging capitalists in feudalist times were fighting and dying for were relationships that were subversive to the whole feudal system, because if you had a right to contract, if you had a right to engage in free trade, then it must mean that the 'divine right' of the king to certain privileges being given to him on a regular basis by his Lord with the Lords in turn being entitled to exact similar privileges and entitlements

117

from their serfs, must be destroyed.

This would happen because, if the serf was free to buy what he wanted, if the serf was free to engage in a contract and to reach a legally enforceable agreement, then the whole system of relationships under feudalism would collapse. That is why the emerging capitalists of the 17th Century were killed so often. That is why the different kings declared that these people were bandits and robbers and were open game for anybody who wanted to kill them. That is why when this question of an enforceable contract reached before the Ecclesiastical Courts in the beginning they were always rejected.

Prevailing Economic Realities

What all of this says, comrades, and says very clearly, is that the law developed around the prevailing economic realities and struggles of the age. The law is really a system of legal relations with a direct bearing and relationship to the material relations in the society. *The Law, therefore, is first and foremost an expression of the balance of forces between the oppressor and the oppressed, between the exploiter and the exploited.* That is what the law is first and foremost.

Expression of the Balance of Forces

The question of what laws get on the statutory books is always a question of the strength of the oppressed. The question of what laws are enforced on a regular basis is always, in part, an expression of the balance of forces between exploiter and exploited. That is why the right to vote did not come automatically after modern day slavery was formally abolished in 1834, but for most countries in the Caribbean that right only came in 1951. The right to vote, universal adult suffrage, came as a result of concrete struggles by our working people, struggles which they led because they felt they had a right to have a say in what was going on in their country, and under the prevailing system of democracy the right to vote was the key way to giving expression to this demand for participation, this ancient call of no taxation without representation.

That is also why comrades, the right to form trade unions did not suddenly descent on us one morning in the 1840s or 50s, or 60s, but only came gradually as the result of dozens of years of struggle by workers, not only in the Caribbean, but by workers throughout the world. And as comrades know, May Day itself, International Workers Day, is the institutionalisation of the day when many workers were sacrificed because of their boldness in demanding trade union rights under the law. That is why in the 1920s, 30s and 40s, Caribbean workers had to consistently struggle for such rights because these rights were never handed down or given gladly.

Trade Unions Dangerous to Exploiters

The exploiting class, the ruling class, always had a very, very clear understanding of the fact that a trade union was, and is a dangerous thing; that if you have trade unions, that if workers have the right to gather together collectively, that if workers have the right to declare a bargaining agent on behalf of themselves to meet with the employer, then the employer's ability to keep wages at starvation level, the employer's ability to divide and rule, the employer's ability to put one worker against the other would be substantially reduced. The employing class always understood this point and this is why the workers had to fight for that right.

The right to form political parties, the right to speak at public meetings, the right to hold demonstrations, every single one of those rights only came about as a result of concrete and often bloody struggle. And therefore, comrades, what I want to suggest at this time is that because the law is an expression of the balance of forces between exploiter and exploited, a reflection of the existing material economic reality in any particular country, the way in which laws are consolidated, the way in which laws that exist are checked or changed and the way in which new laws are brought into existence are always dependent on a number of critical questions which need examination.

Four Key Questions

Firstly, which class is in power? Is it the working class or the representatives of the working class? Or is it the ruling class?

Secondly, how strong are the opposing forces? What is the respective balance between exploiter and exploited in the given society? What is the size of the particular class? What is the level of organisation? What is the level of unity prevailing? What international links and connections do they have? These are some of the concrete questions which determine the strength of either side.

Thirdly, the prevailing economic reality: is there recession? What is the situation with jobs? What is the attitude of the trade unions in the particular country at the given time? Are trade unions on the retreat because of weak, cowardly, or vacillating leadership, or are trade unions standing up? Are they negotiating cut-backs with the bosses, or reduced pay, or are they struggling for even more rights for their workers?

Fourthly, the political outlook of the executive, or the particular leadership in the country. At one level, the point looks like the same point as the first point, which class is in power, but in a deeper sense there is a difference and I think the difference can be illustrated if one compares, let us say, a Carter with a Reagan. Under a Carter in the United States, there is some hope for limited justice under the law and limited justice in general. There is some hope that the rights which women have won over centuries of struggle might

119

be maintained. There is some hope that the rights which workers have won over centuries of struggle might be maintained. There is some hope that the rights which minorities have won over centuries of struggle might be maintained.

What would certainly be in question under a Carter is how these rights could be expanded; but, at least certain rights could be maintained. Certainly, too, with a Carter in power there is always a much greater possibility of peace in the world because of a particular attitude and particular philosophical outlook.

Reagan Rolls Back Rights

But with a Reagan in power, comrades, what are the prospects for any of these things? Is there any realistic basis for any optimism at all that the rights of women, that the rights of workers, that the rights of minorities, that the possibility of maintaining peace in our time can be assured? Is there any realistic hope that any of this is possible given the narrow nationalist, the chauvinist, the racist and the expansionist outlook of the ruling clique in Washington? Is there any realistic hope of that, given the reality of the economic crisis that exists in the United States today? What are the prospects for any expansion of human rights in that country? What are the prospects for even keeping those human rights which have existed over the years?

Let us look at the situation with women in the United States. Today, the struggle for the Equal Rights Amendment, a struggle in which generations of women in the United States have been involved, is facing its worst possible period. Ronald Reagan is perhaps the first President in modern times to publicly oppose the Equal Rights Amendment. President Reagan has around him people like Jesse Helms who openly say that women have no rights, they must go back home, return to the kitchen, become once again the house slaves and kitchen mechanics. People like Jesse Helms even go to the extent of saying that women do not have the right to wear trousers and must only be seen in dresses. This is part of the new reality facing the women of the United States — a reality that they are certainly going to continue to resist.

Today an unbelievably large number of people are out of work in the United States, with official figures proclaiming over nine and a half million workers unemployed. In such a situation workers of the United States involved in any industrial dispute must face the real possibility that all of them could lose their jobs, as the air traffic controllers recently discovered to their cost.

Reagan Attacks Unions
But, even worse than that, Mr Reagan and the people around him have moved to the incredible stage of decertifying trade unions, so that even the right to join trade unions and be certain that those unions will be allowed to continue to exist, even that right is now being removed in the United States.

120

Minorities and the poor are in a similar situation. This can be seen from the attitude of the Reagan Administration to desegregation and to busing, an attitude which creates an atmosphere that allows crimes to be committed every day against poor people in general but against Blacks and other ethnic and national minorites in particular. With schools being closed, hospitals being closed, old people's homes being closed, with cutbacks taking place on food stamps, on medical care, on student subsidies, on farmer subsidies, and so on, it is now very clear that rights which previously existed and which the poor and working people of the United States had begun to take for granted are being taken away under this present administration.

It is very clear that the human rights picture has begun to undergo a slide backwards. Far from consolidating or going forward, the picture is that of a backward trend. And what of the question of peace versus war? With a Ronald Reagan in the White House it would seem that war is almost inevitable, it would seem that war is almost a certainty at some point in the future, and perhaps in the near future. The arms industry, which is not a defence industry but a war industry, is escalating again; it is today being built up to massive proportions. At exactly the same time as schools, hospitals and old people's homes are being closed and farmers and students subsidies and food stamps are being cut and millions are out of work, $214 million are being spent on arms.

Future of Mankind in Peril

A massive arms build-up is once again facing the people of the United States and threatening the future of mankind.

In the 1930s, when Hitler and Mussolini emerged, the rationale was the same, the argument was that armaments are necessary in order to keep out the Communist threat. Once again they are dishonestly pretending that the arms industry is good for jobs, when what they really mean is that the arms industry helps to ensure that the sagging profits of the transnational corporations involved in munitions are again allowed to overflow.

Comrades, with a philosophy that is essentially fascist, with a philosophy that believes that no people have a right to self-determination, that no people have a right to develop their own process, that no country has a right to operate or to exist except in conditions approved by this United States Administration, the prospects for war are real. Professor Richard Pipes, one of the people very close to Ronald Reagan, is on record as saying that the socialist world system must be made to collapse, that so far as this United States Administration is concerned there is no room for peaceful coexistence, that these two systems cannot and will not be allowed to coexist, that one or the other must go.

Few Prospects for Peace
With people like that, with a philosophy like that, with a world view that

121

negates the existence of the socialist world and the national liberation movements, a view that says that the people of El Salvador do not have a right to choose their own way of life and to struggle to reclaim their country from oligarchy, with a philosophy like that, comrades, what are the prospects for peace at this time?

With a philosophy that says that the people of Namibia do not have a right to independence and even after the United Nations passes a Resolution, as it did in 1978, declaring that the people of Namibia must be allowed to proceed to independence forthwith, the United States then attempts to rewrite a mandate coming from the rest of mankind, what are the prospects for peace?

This Reagan Administration supports every criminal aggression committed by Israel, their client state. They arrogantly proclaim that the Palestinians have no right to their own homeland, that the people of Palestine do not have a right to exist but Israel has the right to do whatever it wants in that part of the world. Zionist Israel can go into Iraq and bomb reactors if they wish, then go into Syria and bomb the people in the Golan Heights if they wish, all the while marauding in Lebanon where they commit murder on a daily basis, and that is justified because they are allies. Or consider South Africa where millions of Black oppressed peoples are daily having to face up to the torture and death of an outlaw apartheid system. Reagan has no problems with this because Souty Africa is an ally and there are massive US investments in South Africa which justify maintaining any amount of double talk and double standards.

Whole Peoples' Rights Ignored

Comrades, here you have a philosophy which says that the socialist oriented countries in the world have no right to exist; that the people of Angola do not have a right to choose and develop their own process but must have Savimbi foisted on them, that the people of Mozambique, the people of Nicaragua, the people of Libya, the people of Grenada do not have a right to develop their own processes, and if they choose to try to develop such a process then they would be subjected to the total barrage of propaganda destabilization, economic warfare, violent terrorism and the ever-present threat of mercenary or marine invasion.

Here's a philosophy that says that even their allies in Europe do not have the right to develop their own countries in their own way, or to use their own money for what purposes they see fit. Thus, when the EEC Countries offered to send humanitarian assistance through the Red Cross to war victims in El Salvador, President Reagan dispatched emissaries to the EEC trying to block such humanitarian assistance. Likewise when the new French President — François Mitterand — was about to form his Cabinet and decided to invite three Communists to join that Cabinet, Reagan challenged the sovereignty of the French government and contemptuously insulted the people of France by protesting this right of their newly elected President to decide who his Ministers must be.

Comrades, this is a philosophy that says that the countries of the Third World do not have any right at all to develop their economic resources in their own way unless it is substantially tied to private enterprise, unless it remains dependent on the continued exploitations of the transnational corporations. This is a philosophy that rejects the New International Economic Order which so many of us in the Third World are struggling to bring about so that our countries can have fair and equal terms of trade among other similar and just rights. It is a philosophy that says that the New International Economic Order must not be allowed to come about so that the poorer countries of the world must continue to live in the vicious cycle and circle of exploitation, under which every year the prices of our primary products go down while the prices of their manufactured items go up. To Ronald Reagan, such exploitation is nothing less than justice.

Comrades, in the discussions which have been raging now in the United Nations around a new regime for the resources of the deep sea, the United States has consistently maintained a position that the deep sea resources must be exploited by the transnational corporations and used by them for their own benefit and in the interest of their own profits. Just about everyone else in the entire world has come to the conclusion that an international authority must be set up to exploit the resources of the deep se so that these resources beyond the legal jurisdictions of all countries can be used to help to end poverty, illiteracy, ignorance, disease and other such crimes against humanity. But as usual the ruling elite in the United States is holding out on the side of their rapacious transnationals.

Right to Life: Most Important of All

Comrades, with this sort of situation, it seems to us that the prospects for peace, and therefore, the prospects for the most important human right of all, the right to life, are not very good. Reagan's logic seems to be that the arms industry is good for business and is an answer to his economic problems. But if you believe that the manufacture of arms is good for your business then, logically, you must encourage war if you want to remain in business, otherwise you will reach the inevitable point where there are more arms available than people who are willing to buy those arms, at which point only another war will give you the opportunity to keep on expanding your business and economy. In other words, arms can only be stockpiled up to a certain point and thereafter they have to be used, and that is one of the major predicaments that humanity today finds itself facing.

Comrades, it is our very firm belief that progressive lawyers cannot be neutral in all of this, that progressive lawyers must take a partisan position on this question. They must take a stand. Progressive lawyers have a duty and an obligation to deal with the prevailing world reality and, as we know, the reality is frightening.

Some Alarming Statistics:

In the area of military expenditures alone, I have some figures which I want to read to you very quickly. Half the resources at present allocated to military expenditures *in one day* will suffice to finance a programme for the total world wide eradication of malaria. *In just five hours*, the world's military expenditures are the equivalent of the overall UNICEF's budget for child care programmes. The number of people working in the military sphere, including the armed forces, is today twice the total number of all teachers, physicians and nurses in the world.

Approximately 25% of the world's scientific personnel is engaged in military activity. It is estimated that some 60% of the overall scientific research and scientific expenditures is absorbed by military programmes. The value of such research projects if five times greater than that of the projects devoted to health protection. Countries in Asia, Africa and Latin America allocate 5.9% of their gross national products to weapons and military expenditure, whereas they devote only 1% to public health and 2.8% to education. Furthermore, only 1% of the military budgets of the developed countries could overcome the existing deficit in international assistance for financing and increasing food production and creating emergency reserves.

Expenditures for military activities in a year during the middle 1970s would have financed, among many other things, a vaccination programme against infectious diseases for all the children in the world, a programme for the eradication of adult illiteracy in the entire world, a supplementary food programme for 60 million pregnant women and a classroom increase for 100 million pupils.

Comrades, the reality of these figures is truly shocking and must be something that, as progressives, we have a duty to consider and reflect upon, and the fact is that these military expenditures are occurring at this time, notwithstanding he awful problems of hunger, of malnutrition, of illiteracy and of unemployment which the Third World faces.

It has been estimated, for example, that the rate of growth of the gross national product of underdeveloped countries dropped from 4.8% in 1979 to 3.8% in 1980 and to 3.2% in 1981. Every year the figure falls and, as if that was not bad enough, the annual rate of growth of the lowest income countries in the underdeveloped world was only 1.8% during the 1960s and 0.8% during the 1970s. These figures mean that the lowest income countries representing one quarter of the world's population will require some 400 to 500 years to reach the present existing per capita income levels of the most developed capitalist countries.

Worsening Trade Relations
The share of the underdeveloped countries in the world's exports, excluding

fuel, was reduced from about 25% in 1950 to less than 12% in 1980. The continuing deterioration in trade relations between primary products and manufactured items which was sharpened by the increase in oil prices has contributed to the emergence of a huge, chronic deficit in the balance of payments of oil importing underdeveloped countries amounting to some $53 billion. The external debt of the Third World is estimated to have reached, in 1981, the enormous figure of over $524 billion and the tendency points to a continued increase in a brutal, vicious circle of debt service payments with growing interest rates and more debts.

Workers, Women and Children Hard Hit
The reality in the Third World, Comrades, is a frightening one and that reality is as bad for the workers as it is for the children and women of the world. According to the ILO, for example, in 1980 there were some 455 million workers in the Third World amounting to over 43% of the working age population. During that same year, 46% of the labour force in Latin America was affected by open unemployment or underemployment and since then the situation has gotten worse.

In 1979, there were 75 million children under the age of 15 years who were working in the world, especially in underdeveloped countries, and in many instances they were doing exhausting and always underpaid jobs. Thirty-five per cent of the world's labour force is composed of women and although they represent a little over one third of the total labour force, they receive only one tenth of the world's revenues. Women make up one third of the workers but the money they get between them is just about one tenth of all the income that is going around.

When we consider this reality in the world, and when we consider, too, the attitude of some of our own people to solutions to these problems and their idea of what a model country is, we can better understand why this world reality needs to be explained together with the reasons for it. Because the sad fact is that for many people in the Caribbean today, the United States still has an image of being paradise on earth, still has an image of being the country where everyone, once you are willing to work hard, can become a millionaire overnight, still has an image of being a very stable and secure democracy.

Revealing FBI Statistics
I found some very interesting statistics coming from the Federal Bureau of Investigation (FBI), and these statistics have to do with crime, and therefore will be very relevant to a lawyers' conference. In the United States:

— every two seconds a crime is committed,
— every four seconds larceny is committed,
— every eight seconds an assault and robbery is committed,
— every twenty eight seconds a car is stolen,
— every forty eight seconds someone is beaten up,

125

- every fifty eight seconds a hold up takes place,
- every six minutes a woman is raped,
- every twenty three minutes someone is murdered.

These are the statistics of the model society and of what stability and security and democracy means for many, many people in the United States.

In 1980, the FBI again declared:

- rape cases rose to 82,000,
- 500,000 people were robbed,
- 650,000 people were held up,
- 23,000 murders were committed.

That is the country of great human rights, the country of ideal democracy. In Grenada, today, when a murder takes place that is almost like saying that war has broken out somewhere in the world. It is such a rare event.

Develop a Progressive Perspective

Comrades, in your deliberations over the next two days I urge you to bear in mind as you address this question of 'Human Rights in the 80s' and as you develop a perspective for progressive lawyers on human rights, that the most critical variable to take into account is this prevailing reality in the world and the prevailing reality in our Caribbean region, as part of that world.

Knowing as we do what the realities are for most of the poor people in our countries, the perspective we develop must be a perspective that, firstly, focuses on the absence of human rights for the majority of the people, a perspective that aims to look at human rights in the context of developing those rights for the majority of our people who continue to be poor and over exploited, in this part of the world and, indeed, in many other parts of the world.

Secondly, and arising out of the first point, the perspective we develop must be a perspective that addresses the material realities and deprivations of the people and ensure that the realities of poverty, hunger and illiteracy, of discrimination, of lack of electricity, pipeborne water, housing,, jobs, of legal inequality, are realities which we face up to and try to find solutions for.

Thirdly, comrades, in developing this perspective we must aim to look in a very serious and scientific manner at the ways in which laws are really made, at the ways in which rights really come about.

Laws and the Balance of Forces

We must recognise, that governments are composed of men and women who make laws according to the prevailing material realities in the country, and who make laws according to the prevailing balance of forces between the exploited and the exploiters. We should recognise also that the official slogan of the establishment that, 'What we have is a government of laws and not of men', is much more myth than reality.

A few years ago, Anatole France gave perhaps the classic answer when he said, 'the law in its majestic equality forbids the rich and the poor alike from sleeping under bridges.' Obviously, the question of who sleeps under bridges in reality is really the question to focus on. The question of whom the law is really aimed at in the first place and whom the law catches is what really tells you what kind of law it is and how the law came about. If you examine people who are in the jails in different countries, I think it gives a very good idea of the reality in that country with regard to laws on the statute books.

Comrades, we must never forget that it is the struggles of the working people which won them their human rights in the first place, and it is precisely our struggle today that will ensure that these rights continue. And in today's conditions it seems to me that our struggles must have three specific aspects:

Firstly, we must ensure that those rights and those laws which have brought benefits but which have been taken away are in fact restored;

Secondly, we must ensure that those laws entrenching rights which are now on the statute books in fact remain there. We must jealously guard them and ensure that no one tries to remove them, thus weakening the strength of the working people and further eroding the rights which they have won;

Thirdly, we must in a conscious and systematic way, struggle for an expansion of the existing rights.

Finding New Human Rights

The majority must now be able to enjoy the human rights which they have never had. We must put new human rights on the law books. We must struggle for new human rights that will deal with the real needs of the people in housing, jobs, health care, education and so on. We must find ways of ensuring that these human rights become entrenched in the constitutions and laws of our countries. The struggle for these new rights must start from the premise that there can be no equality before the law if real concrete social and economic human rights are the preserve only of a privileged minority. When we examine some of these paper rights that are entrenched in all constituions, the right to freedom of expression, for example, we see right away that this right can really only be fully relevant if people are not too hungry, or too tired to be able to express themselves. That right can only be relevant if appropriate organs of popular democracy exist, through which the people can effectively participate, receive reports from their leaders, make decisions, and be trained for eventually ruling and controlling their society. This is what democracy is all about.

When we speak, likewise, of the right to work, as some constitutions speak, that right surely can only be relevant if one can get a job. Otherwise, it is a meaningless so-called right.

127

Further, that right can only be relevant if the working people have the legal right to form and to join trade unions of their choice. And this in turn raises the question of the speed at which trade unions can be recognised, assuming in the first place that there is on the books a law compelling employers to recognise any union that is the choice of the majority of their workers. And we know that in many countries in our region and beyond that such a right does not exist. A right to work, likewise, must surely include a right not to be arbitrarily dismissed, otherwise what is given in the right hand can be easily taken away with the left.

In Grenada we also believe that the right to work includes the right to know what is happening in your enterprise or workplace. In fact, we believe that it includes the right to help make decisions, the right to examine the books, the right to know what the production targets are, the right to know what the possibilities for profits are, and the right at the end of the year when profits are made as a result of the sweat of the workers, the right also to share in those profits. All of that, it seems to us, is part of the right to work.

And comrades, the right to life is also meaningless if secret police and mongoose gangs are able to kill, maim, brutalise and torture people without any legal remedy, without any resort to the courts, without any justice being given to those being killed or brutalised. What is the point of speaking of the right to life if the legal and judicial system cannot provide remedies to enforce this right? What is the point of speaking of this right to life if health facilities in the country are so costly that it becomes impossible for the poor and working people to be able to receive proper health care?

The Right to Dignity

The right to dignity, the right to live a life of dignity, can only be a meaningful right to the extent that the basic needs of hte population are met, to the extent that legal and social equality are being worked towards, to the extent that the people as a whole have the right to decide on the question of war versus peace, and have the right to decide whether they want to go to El Salvador to fight and die for the transnational corporations and the tiny ruling minority who perceive that to be in their interest. These questions are questions which the people themselves must discuss and be involved in taking decisions about. Otherwise, that right too becomes another paper right.

Thank you very much!

13. Turn the Words Around!

First Conference of Journalists from the
Caribbean Area, St. George's, Grenada, 17
April 1982

For us in Grenada to host this conference is both an honour and something of
a strange experience. *An honour*, in that to have so many fine professionals
and honest men and women among us is always a heartening and strengthening stimulus, *but strange* for us in that we have, since our grasp of freedom in
March, 1979, been on the receiving end of so much vile and false journalism,
so many lies and slanders, such profound hostility from the media barons of
the hemisphere. So for us there is a kind of irony in your presence, for you
represent the opposite of that brand of mercenary and bought-out mafia
journalism. You represent hope and integrity to us, an alternative kind of
journalism and the professional courage to stand up to lies and disinformation.
We salute you and embrace you as *comrades in truth*, for just as truth is your
tool, your trademark — so it is the vital essence and integral ingredient that
is contained in all the organs and aspects of the Grenada Revolution. In
coming to Grenada and attending this conference you are demonstrating your
willingness to stand up with us against falsehood, and for that alone we thank
you on behalf of our Revolution and our people, from the depths of our
hearts.

We are particularly impressed by the level of unity achieved by the conference organisers and sponsors. We see here the combined strength and
wealth of experience of the International Organisation of Journalists, the
Federation of Latin American Journalists, the Press Association of Jamaica,
our own Media Workers' Association of Free Grenada and of dozens of
individual but as yet formally unorganised journalists from throughout the
region. If ever any of our people grew in the slightest way despondent
throughout the three years of organised and co-ordinated media-assault that
has continually bludgeoned us, this conference and its participants will
certainly go a long way towards dispelling any such feelings.

We welcome you here in the spirit of co-professionalism, recognising that
each of you have a dynamic, original and significant contribution to bring to
this conference which we see as a crucible for democratic journalism in our
region. We are not conscious of any aristocracy among you, any media-
peerage, and that again fills us with hope and encouragement, for we have
often been the butt of blows from some of the most powerful vested interests
and press magnates of the region, and indeed, the world. What you incontro-

vertibly demonstrate to us is the other side of journalism, the part that has been prepared to treat us with fairness, equity and an open mind, to come and share our process, talk to our people and see for yourselves. You have, in short, shown us the democratic tradition of journalism in the Caribbean, the tradition we must fight to strengthen and extend.

Imperialist Stranglehold of Information

Comrades, the widespread and relatively successful campaigns of negative propaganda carried out by the Caribbean and North American media against Nicaragua, Cuba, and Grenada, the freedom fighters of El Salvador and all other progressive and peace-loving forces of our region are facilitated by the unjust, irrational and undemocratic nature of the present world information order.

An examination of the current situation in the field of international information and communication reveals a number of glaring imbalances.

Firstly, there are considerable disparities in the world-wide distribution of the media. Whilst, for example, in Europe and the USA, for every 1,000 inhabitants there are 312 daily newspapers and 696 radio and 301 television receivers, in the developing countries for the same number of inhabitants there are merely 29 daily papers and 83 radio and 22 television receivers. This massive difference is in the first instance a result of colonial dependence, for the former colonial rulers did nothing to develop a national information system in the regions they exploited.

Secondly, this backwardness in the field of information is a fundamental reason for the fact that the international exchange of information is only a one-way process. Basically, a veritable flood of information flows from the major imperialist cities to all corners of the globe, whereas there is a mere trickle in the opposite direction.

Today, the imperialist media businesses, to all intents and purposes, still control and regulate the flow of information from, to and between the developing countries. The four major capitalist newsagencies, *UPI, AP, AFP* and *Reuters* have an output of 33 million words daily. The ten largest Western foreign broadcasting services are on the air 5,200 hours per week, i.e. an average of 750 hours daily, and an increasingly large proportion of this is in the national and tribal languages of the developing countries. The big US television companies control more than three quarters of the international television market.

Thirdly, this 'cultural imperialism' is not merely a formal problem but also in essence a question of content. For ultimately it is not a question of how much information is broadcast through how many channels from where and from whom, but rather what information and with what objectives, is broadcast over national frontiers.

Work for the New World Information Order

In view of the wide-ranging problems associated with the transboundary role of the media, it is understandable that for a considerable time now, questions of information and communication have been the subject of increasingly intense international discussion. A growing number of countries, including Grenada, are asserting loudly and clearly that the time is now ripe to democratise the international information system and to free it from the vestiges of colonial rule. Such countries are also asserting that it is imperative to eliminate psychological warfare and cultural neo-colonialism from intercourse between states and peoples. These universal democratic and anti-imperialist objectives have been reflected in the demand for the establishment of a new world information order (NWIO), which has been posed by the socialist and the developing countries in UNESCO and the UN since the middle of the 1970s.

What are the aims behind the setting up of a new world information order? Firstly, the most important task consists in guaranteeing that in the ideological struggles of our age the mass media make an active contribution to the maintenance and consolidation of *peace*, to *disarmament and detente, international understanding* and the resolving of the *global problems* of humanity. An essential condition here is that the international exchange of information is arranged in line with the principles of international law as anchored in the UN Charter, and that in particular principles such as equal sovereignty and non-interference apply fully to international information and communication.

A further aim in setting up a new world information order consists in organising a more balanced, comprehensive and freer exchange of information on a democratic foundation, an exchange which is free of the various forms of psychological warfare and cultural interference in the affairs of other states and peoples. For this, it is necessary to curb the influence on those sections of the media which even today continue to abuse freedoms in the international dissemination of information, and for the voices of democratic and progressive forces campaigning for peace and social progress to attain increasing prominence. This entails, in turn, building up the information capacity of the progressively-orientated developing countries which at the moment cannot participate sufficiently in the international exchange of information.

International Principles Are the Basis of the New Order

However, in order for these objectives to be attained, it is necessary that all participants in the international exchange of information act in accordance with the universally accepted principles and norms of international conduct and relations.

One of the resolutions adopted at the 21st UNESCO General Conference held in Belgrade in 1980 expressly states that the basic principles laid down in the UN Charter — namely, ban on use of force, equal sovereignty, non-interference, self-determination, peaceful settlement of disputes, co-operation, fidelity to treaties, must form the basis of a new world information order. These principles form the general framework for the international activities of the media. They represent the yardstick for the policy of states in the information field in line with international law and form a starting point for the concrete process of drawing up specific norms for the international exchange of information, a process embarked upon with the adoption of UNESCO's 1978 declaration on the media.

They must be seen within the framework of the aims and principles of the UN Charter in their totality and indivisible unity, and taking into account the political, economic and social conditions existing in any particular society. Thus, in the case of the new world information order, it is not only the right to freedom of expression laid down in Article 19 of the 1966 International Covenant on Civil and Political Rights that is relevant. Equally important are such rights as the right to education, cultural activity or participation in public affairs. Guaranteeing the freedom of the press is of absolutely no use for instance to an illiterate whose society denies him the right to education. Furthermore, the right to freedom of expression is inseparably bound up with duties and corresponding responsibilities. Thus, today one of the moral obligations of a state is to prevent war–mongering propaganda, in the same way that the responsibilities of journalists include writing for the cause of peace and showing an active commitment to the ending of the arms race and a switch to disarmament.

Numerous international bodies have repeatedly condemned propaganda advocating the use of force and war, racism, apartheid, colonialism, neo-colonialism and other breaches of international law. For example, according to Article 4 of the International Convention on the Elimination of All Forms of Racial Discrimination of 1965 and in line with Article 20 of the 1966 International Convent on Civil and Political Rights, states are obliged to forbid by law appeals to war and racialist propaganda. To too, we would argue that deliberately false reports, slanders, smear campaigns, hostile tendentiousness and subversive campaigns which undermine international security and are aimed against good-neighbourly relations between states, must also be regarded as contravening principles of international law.

Preserving sovereignty over national information in a situation where international information and communication are constantly growing in volume is one of the central issues in the establishing of a new world information order. From the principle of equal sovereignty the following rights accrue to individual states:

> to set up, develop and organise their own independent information systems tailored to national aims and interests;
> to map out their own national information policy, to lay down priorities and to create a corresponding legal framework;
> to utilize the media as an instrument of national development, to help

the formation, preservation and consolidation of a cultural identity and the education process, as well as to represent, free of discrimination, their legitimate interests and their outlooks, aims and values in the international arena;

within the framework of their legal system, to forbid the dissemination of information which represents a threat to international security and jeopardizes their national sovereignty, their economic stability or their cultural identity.

These rights derive from the right of peoples to self-determination. In the view of tact that many developing countries still do not possess an adequate information system, the UN and UNESCO have repeatedly pointed to the urgency of setting up such systems. The UNESCO International Commission for the Study of Communications Problems (MacBride Commission) similarly attaches major priority to the solving of this problem.

The obligation to respect the sovereign rights of states in the field of information is a principle aimed in the first instance at excluding the use of the media to interfere in the affairs of other states and peoples. In any event, in line with international law, states are bound to refrain from every kind of interference and to outlaw every form of subversive activity emanating from their temerity. This is expressly stated, for example, in the Declaration on the Inadmissibility of Intervention and Interference in the Internal Affairs of States adopted by an overwhelming majority on 3 December 1981 during the 36th session of the UN General Assembly. This declares that states have the right and duty 'to combat, within their constitutional prerogatives, the dissemination of false or distorted news which can be interpreted as interference in the internal affairs of other states or as being harmful to the promotion of peace, co-operation and friendly relations among states and nations.'

It is extremely important for example to enusre, through preemptive legal provisions, that the introduction of direct satellite television, envisaged by experts in the second half of the eighties, is prevented from becoming a source of international disputes merely because a few states choose to ignore generally binding norms. In this regard, the UN Committee on the Peaceful Uses of Outer Space has been working on an appropriate convention for the past ten years, the adoption of which has so far been blocked by the US.

Comrades, having laid out the principles upon which this new world finromation order is premised we must ask what are the practical means for setting up the new order?

Practical Ways to Achieve the New Order

We want to suggest that today, there are three principal tasks which are closely related to each other: *Firstly*, all Democratic, peace-loving and progressive forces in the information field must be mobilised for peace and disarmament. This is no longer just a statistical necessity; it has now assumed the character of a universal commandment and a moral imperative, given the real threat to peace and the looming possiblity of a final war that now faces all of humanity. *Secondly*, the principles of a new world information order must be implemented. *Thirdly*, increased support in the field of information must be extended to the developing countries.

UNESCO has played a particularly prominent role in this process over the past few years. The 1978 declaration on the media, the 1979 report of the MacBride Commission, and the foundation of the IPDC in 1980 have not only created a world-wide awareness of the issues involved, but also represent milestones in the eventual establishing of a new world information order. These events have provided a major impulse. Thus, in 1983, to mark the fifth anniversary of the media declaration, a world congress is to take place to analyse the implementing of this document and Grenada intends to make a contribution to this congress.

Comrades, the struggle for a new world information order spearheaded by the world's democratic forces and stoutly resisted by the transnational media monopolists and mafia in the West must be seen within the context of the developing international class struggle which has gathered momentum in recent times with the successes of in particular the anti-colonialist and national liberation forces in the Third World.

Imperialist Attempts to obstruct the New Order

This information battle has been characterised by three consecutive phases on a world scale although in the Caribbean region elements of all three are taking place simultaneously.

In the beginning, imperialism attempted to shake the anti-imperialist orientation of public opinion in the independent and liberated former colonies by utilising its own media to penetrate the national information arenas of those countries. However, these direct 'experts' of cultural and informational imperialism did not bring the desired results in several of the newly liberated territories.

So, imperialism then tried to erect all sorts of obstacles to the creation of the independent national press, radio and television of the young states. However, material assistance, from the developed progressive forces made it possible to push ahead in this area although much progress in developing media infrastructure in the Third World is still to come.

The third phase − the most dangerous, sophisticated and subtle phase was then introduced to bolster the first two phases, under which the Western press monopolies have set about attempting to control the information services of the Third World from *within* by themselves occupying key positions or through influencing key but unpatriotic, reactionary and self-seeking nationals in management and editorial decision-making positions to disseminate great quantities of their biased and distorted news, or through bribing and/or manipulating journalists and their professional organisations and even through creating phantom organisations of journalists.

We Must Fight Back

Thus, it is necessary for the world's democratic movement of journalists to organise a broad programme of multilateral assistance and co-operation to journalist colleagues in the young states and to their journalists' associations in order that they may confront the assault of the imperialist press mafia and more rapidly create and strengthen national information media serving the cause of independence and progress.

This assistance and co-operation can be manifested by expanding the varied contracts between the IOJ and its national unions, by providing more active assistance in the training of journalists and by raising their qualifications, through a permanent exchange of opinions on different levels, more intensive information work and the dissemination of scientific knowledge about journalism as well as socio-political and specialised progressive publications that will help to develop such co-operation.

Hence, the importance of exchanges of delegations and groups of journalists, and joint participation in various journalists' initiatives and in meetings on subjects of interests to journalists as a whole cannot possibly be over emphasised, given the tremendous potential of such activites to the development of a new world information order.

Comrades, having set out some of the major principles that are required to bring about a new and honest dispersation in the international flow of information that would ensure both authentic, relevant, educational and truthful news for the people and full integrity and job-satisfaction for media workers, I must, unfortunately, now descend from these heady heights to the real and cruel world imperialist, monopoly, mafia journalism that still engulfs, stifles and represses our region and the world.

Propaganda Destabilisation

I start with the concept of propaganda destabilisation. Comrades, the word 'destabilisation' is not *our* word, neither is it a concept that belongs to us or a form of behaviour practised by us. You would remember it is a part of the lexicography of the United States Central Intelligence Agency, coined by one of their ex-directors. And yet now it is a word that every Grenadian knows, for our people have known exactly what it means on their pulses and nerves ever since the first dawn of our Revolution. They have experienced destabilization in all its insidious, violent and most treacherous forms — economic, political, diplomatic and violent destabilisation — but its manifestation that has become as much a part of our lives as a bowl of callaloo soup or the scent of nutmegs, is the reality of *propaganda destabilisation.*

Our people can tune into one of a dozen stations and hear reports, purportedly about Grenada, but in truth about a fictional country that has never existed. They can buy newspapers that print such blatant lies and disinformation as to create the screenplay for the most fantastic and vulgar of Hollywood melodramas, notwithstanding the remarkable record ex-Hollywood actors have sometimes seemed to demonstrate in that particular field of endeavour. If they take with any degree of seriousness at all the extraordinary barrage of reports in the regional and North American press about military bases and activity here, then instead of the peaceful, verdant and productive island on which they live, they would behold as their homeland a stark militarised zone of tar and concrete which would appear like an uneasy combination of Pearl Harbour, Chelsea Barracks, Cape Kennedy, West Point and the Panama Canal Zone — with fighter planes as numerous as our butterflies and nuclear submarines in flotillas like shoals of sprats! In fact, the absurdity of the propaganda caricature of Grenada has reached such a point of high farce and such levels of hallucination and absurdity as to have completely refuted itself.

However, rejection of the lies of the media mafia is now easy for our people in Grenada as we have set in motion in our country a profound level of mass mobilisation and mass education — which we believe to be twin aspects of the same process — that has made our people constantly vigilant and concerned to unravel, understand and defend the *truth* of events. We have said before that we hold the truth itself to be revolutionary and we shall stand firm by its side. Propaganda destabilisation and the systematic manipulation of falsehood, as practised by journalists unworthy of the name and media interests who have only corruption and decadence to defend, is perhaps the most sophisticated form of lying that human society — or perhaps it would be more accurate to say *anti*-human society — has ever generated. We have witnessed examples of this grisly phenomenon over the last few years in our continent, perpetrated and orchestrated by the CIA, that would out-Goebbels Goebbels, that most monstrous purveyor of the lie. But the unleashed force of an organised people, a conscious people, a vigilant people, a united people, a people who are educating themselves and each other through their political process, a people who are stopping not only to *listen*, but also to analyse, criticise and discuss everything in their country from the budget to calypsoes to public health to events in El Salvador, Namibia or the Western Sahara, cannot be deceived or fooled so easily. They stand as interpreters and protectors of the truth. In the same way that they patrol and guard the beaches of our country from physical attack, they are also guardians of the truth. In the same way that they are training themselves to repel any mercenary or imperialist incursion, they are also, through an accompanying process, training themselves to dispel the lies and slander that insult the truth of their progress and distort their Revolution.

But although imperialist propaganda destabilisation has out-lied and out-libelled itself and exposed its own rotting carcase in the process, honest and dedicated journalists clearly have a huge responsibility and obligation to hasten its final and inevitable self-destruction, for it has caused enormous and bloodsoaked damage throughout its rabid lifespan, and continues to do so in its throes of death. In Grenada we have carefully analysed the extent of its devastation in Chile and Jamaica through such newspapers as *El Mercurio* and the *Daily Gleaner* respectively, and knowing what was set loose there, nothing the imperialist press can invent and say about us can ever give us any surprises. We have read page after page of lies about us, ingeniously concocted by the hirelings of some of the richest media merchants in the world — about *us*, whose population would only amount to heads counted in a small North American city! *The Boston Globe, The Washington Post, The New York Times, The Christian Science Monitor, The Miami Herald, The Wall Street Journal, The Los Angeles Times, Newsweek, Time* — why should they spend so much time, labour and printer's ink writing about our tiny nation and composing more and more fantasy about our process?

In West Germany, shortly after our Revolution, *Bunte* Magazine told us that we had a lightning-erected Soviet missile base, with warheads aimed at neighbouring islands, perched somewhere like a fairy castle on the rugged peaks around the Grand Etang which you would have passed when you crossed over the central ridge of our island on your way from Pearls' Airport to St George's. Then, after a long, taxing and strenuous campaign to raise money to pay for our New Internatonal Airport which will have *one* 9,000 runway, the British Broadcasting Corporation obligingly informs us that in fact we are putting down *three* runways, thus wishing that exhausting process on us again twice-over! Indeed, with the recent reports in the London *Daily Telegraph* of yet another secret submarine base at Calivigny on our South-East coast, you might be excused for blinking your eyes and for a moment *not* believing you are in the National Conference Centre of Free Grenada but on a Hollywood film studio watching the filming of one those old Z-rated movies that Ronald Reagan used to enjoy acting in so much in his younger days. However, the extraordinary reality is, that while these fantastic stories circulate unashamedly in the imperialist press, and make out our beloved island to be a sinister haven of international intrigue, our people still work and produce in their gardens, factories and farms; our tourists enjoy our beaches and waterfalls and go for rides in mini-mokes all over our island; six hundred American medical students continue to apply themselves seriously to their studies, and our people in thie busloads take Sunday afternoon excursions, have picnics, collect shells thrown up by the dredge at Hardy Bay and fly their kites with happiness and pride over their international airport project which they recognise correctly as the most important and vital economic project that our country has ever undertaken.

Comrades, we know that the CIA has direct access to over 200 newspapers. We also know that it puts out its *Bi-Weekly Propaganda Guidance* to radio stations right through our continent. We know of the twisted techniques it uses to control those conservative newspapers in 'flashpoint' countries it needs to destabilize progressive governments. We know how the newspaper editors and owners concerned are promoted overnight to the Board of Directors of the Inter-American Press Association at the outset of this destabilizing process, for the sake of artificially boosting the prestige of their rags. We have observed this clearly again in the case of *El Mercurio* in Chile, and more recently, in the case of Oliver Clarke, the publisher of the Jamaica *Daily Gleaner*. We have noted the way in which progressive type-setters and designers on these target newspapers have been summarily dismissed and replaced by misguided elements, who, by using word-association techniques, pictorial insinuation, emotive symbolism and the juxtaposition of negative images with photographs of progressive leaders, have attempted to spread disorder, demoralisation, distrust and fear amongst the readership of these journals.

We also know the editors of the largest and wealthiest newspapers in the Caribbean were invited to Washington in May, 1981 by the United States International Communications Agency (USICA), the propaganda arm of the US State Department, for a crash course in these honourable professional techniques, and how a few weeks later the ignoble concept of the Free Press under imperialism was further dignified with identical front page editorials pouring ridiculous but sordid lie after lie, comma for comma, full stop for full stop on Grenada in the columns of the *Gleaner, The Barbados Sunday Sun*, the *Barbados Advocate*, the *Trinidad Guardian* and the *Trinidad Express*. In this we saw the clumsy and unethical hypocrisy and dishonesty practised by the Caribbean proxies of the major US press goliaths. Their lack of deftness shows that they still have a lot to learn from their USICA masters and teachers, and we can confidently expect a return seminar for a little remedial education for Mr Gordon, Mr Clarke and their backward classmates.

USICA and IAPA: Enemies of Democratic Journalism

Perhaps at this point it would be instructive for us to consider USICA and IAPA a little more closely. USICA was born from its mother organisation, the United States Information Agency (USIA). The Deputy Director of this illustrious organisation, one Thomas C. Sorenson, said in the 1960s that:

> The USIA is the psychological instrument of the US Government overseas, just as the State Department is the diplomatic instrument of the Agency for International Development (USAID), the economic assistance instrument, and the Central Intelligence Agency (CIA), the intelligence instrument.

And as you can see this is quite a constellation, comrades! So let there be no doubts as to the motives of the USICA seminar for the Caribbean media-chiefs. For this 'psychological instrument' is openly waging war on the minds of the Caribbean and Latin American masses, taking many leaves from the US Army's *Field Manual on Psychological Warfare*. In what is perhaps the zenith of cynicism, this enlightened document, required reading for all propaganda destabilizers, says quite bluntly:

PEACE . . . IS THE CONTINUATION OF WAR BY NON-MILITARY MEANS

Psychological activities are those carried out in peace time, or in places other than war theatres, in order to influence the feelings, attitudes and foreign groups in a manner favourable to the achievement of the policies of the United States.

And even though many of our Caribbean editors and newspaper owners went running to their master's voice in Washington bursting with enthusiasm, it is important to remember that the 'country team' in any US Embassy will contain not only military attaches, a CIA station chief, USAID heads and a Peace Corps co-ordinator — but also the head of the local USICA mission, who is aiming his psychological arrows constantly at the political and economic power structures, trade union leaders, opposition prospects, editors, broadcasters, educators, community leaders and anyone else likely to serve his ends.

USICA's grim twin is IAPA, whom we met earlier as the kindly sponsor of the destabilization blitz in Chile and Jamaica. This organisation, which has a truly impressive record of orchestration of outright slander, lies and scurrilous calumny was again the progeny of the US State Department from whence all good and pure destabilizing instruments come. It was first formed in 1926 as the *First Pan-American Congress of Journalists*, and seized in 1950 by the CIA after it had passed to the leadership of a group of indepen-dent-minded journalists — a state of affairs, of course, intolerable to US State structures. Since then it has single-mindedly dedicated itself ot a crusade against truth, and has been decorated many times for its intrepid attacks upon journalistic honesty and integrity.

Comrades, Grenada is a free area which is liberating itself from the false perspectives and distorting moulds of imperialism. Our people are developing the critical consciousness and powers of discrimination to detect propaganda destabilization whenever and however it threatens them. It is a strange contradiction that the attempts at destabilization hurled against our country by newspapers and radio are themselves *steeling our people* and sharpening their critical sense, making them more able and committed to identify, resist and beat back the lies. Every slander thrown at us presents a mental manoeuvre for our people, an exercise which strengthens their consciousness and mind muscles. In this sense, the propaganda destabilizers are unwittingly doing our people a favour, for they are creating within the minds of our people a determined mental militia which launches back a hundredfold of truth for every single falsehood aimed at our country. Having lived through an apprenticeship of lies daily striking our shores, our people are building the fabric of resolution and truth which they are offering to the world. For here in Grenada, *falsehood shall not pass*, even though it is the daily bread of imperialism.

Democracy and the Caribbean Press

Comrades, in order to seriously consider democracy and the press, we need to examine the situation in which the majority of Caribbean journalists apparently find themselves locked. The working journalist is a true producer. He follows and hunts the news, he hustles for stories, he uncovers the submerged truth of events, he blasts open secrets and corruption with his investigative dynamite. Alongside his colleagues who produce and print the newspapers, he is the *worker of news*. And yet his product is not his. His work is valued solely in terms of how he contributes towards making profits for the owner of his medium, which is a commodity to be bought or sold at a market place like a pound of saltfish or a pile of mangoes. While he strikes out towards the truth, the owner of his words and column counts up his dollars and looks for ways of making more. And if prostituting the truth is the way forward towards that end, then so be it!

So how then, does the honest journalist, whose work is alienated, relegated and despised, act! We have seen some courageous resistance in relation to our own country, when the calculated and co-ordinated swapping of falsehoods and vitriolic anti-Grenada editorials launched through a corrupt section of the Caribbean Press by the USICA, was met with a determined and principled act of protest by some of your Trinidadian colleagues, but many other regional journalists would prefer to work on in their own way, in their own individual niche, and continue to interpret that existence as 'the freedom of the press', even though their stories are cut or warped, even though their opinion in the enterprise in which they work is counted for nothing, even though they have no control over their working conditions, even though they have no say in the political direction of their newspaper, even though their just wage demands are treated with the same scorn as their skills and opinions, even though the decisions affecting their newspaper are taken over the clinking of glasses filled with *Chivas Regal Scotch* at a luxurious country club. While the true journalist works with the people, searching out the truth of their real lives and problems and writing stories seeking to expose the conditions bearing down on their own hope for progress, their employers machinate with the forces of falsehood, the media-monsters of the CIA and Inter-American Press Association, the anti-people, anti-progress robots who are completely and unscrupulously machiavellian in their appetite to distort all reality and shape it in the moulds of the voracious multi-national corporations.

These are the forces who claim to have sanctified the principles of Press Freedom, who control the region's editorials, who prefer to print the computerised calumny of 'top Pentagon officials' to the real views and naked words of the Caribbean people.

Let us take for example the *Trinidad Guardian* of Wednesday, 3rd March of this year. You would have seen the elegant headline emblazoned across the front page with the original, well-chosen words, *GRENADA BASE OPEN TO REDS*, where one American Fred. (Fred. S. Hoffman), a journalist, quotes another American Fred. (Dr Fred. C. Ikle), a US Under-Secretary of Defence, with more unsubstantiated lies and slander about how our International Airport is to become 'an airbase available to the Soviet Union'. If the hard-working Caribbean journalist or the bemused Caribbean reader begins to scratch his head in bewilderment at where *his own people, his own aspirations, his own country* begin to fit into this network of Freds and international scandal, it would not be unreasonable. His own land, his own issues, his own problems have been leap-frogged, set aside and deemed irrelevant. His voice is nothing, the screaming and shrieking of the US State Department is clearly more important to the *Trinidad Guardian* than his Caribbean existence. And yet this so-called 'democratic press' always seeking, as it so often tells us, to present all sides of the story, in the case of the March 3rd article, as indeed many other articles *refused to print* the letter of response sent by the People's Revolutionary Government two days later, and up till now, has not even had the democratic manners to send back an acknowledgement.

We in Grenada were not surprised at these proceedings, neither have we been surprised at the dozens of other similar outpourings of lies and garbage which characterise the columns of the *Trinidad Guardian* or the *Trinidad Express*. This is not to say that we are not also continually disgusted at the growing intensity and desperation of these utterances, but we have made our customary analysis of those who seek to defame us, and we understand their motives, for we understand the real power behind these pages. These papers which proudly boast their independence, in fact speak with the same voice and the interests of the same class. Jointly, there are eighteen directors on the boards of these two newspapers. Of the ten about whom information exists, they have interlocking directorships in 47 other companies, including national. regional and multi-national business corporations such as insurance and stock-broking companies and several banks, namely the Bank of Commerce, the Royal Bank of Canada, Barclays and the locally-owned National Commercial. Clearly, journalistic integrity and democratic aspirations do not go hand-in-hand with such interests, and should the journalist of such enterprises wonder who he is truly serving, the facts are there before him.

Is it surprising that such forces would attack, with so much bile and bitterness, the advances of the Grenada Revolution? Is it surprising that the knowledge of a proud and free people in an island just across the sea, who are claiming their right to control and direct their own destiny, build their own economy and cast away tyranny into the furthese memory of history, should provoke such passionate and maniacal fear among these paper barons? A poor people gaining wealth through participation and organisation, a people casting their own moulds, a people resolved to finish with mimicry and fear. No wonder they are frightened, for the spectre that haunts their drunken nights, the image which dances at the bottom of their Martini glasses, the shiver that shakes their flesh in their air-conditioned offices is the vision of the free people of Grenada building a new life on the ruins and wreckage of the system they uphold, and the terrible thought that the readers of their own newspaper will one day, sooner than they fear, boldly take a parallel road.

141

This is why these newspapers, whilst printing millions of words of lies about our process have printed nothing aobut our new revolutionary grass-roots democracy here in Grenada, and why you will read pitifully few lines about our mass organisations, our workers' Parish Council, our Zonal Councils. And you will find next to nothing about these remarkable and vibrant structures of our people's power — our organs of popular democracy in other newspapers up and down the region that are owned and managed by the same parasitical cabal. Ken Gordon, for example, of the *Trinidad Express*, is also a transnational media magnate, with a part ownership in the *St Lucian Voice*, the *Barbados Nation*, and the late, but not lamented *Torchlight*, which he used as a base of slanderous and destabilizing operations here in Grenada.

Because we do not fear the lies of the imperialists and their proxies, we allow into our country *every day* their newspapers and magazines with all their distortions against us. Any day on the streets and in the newspaper shops of the country, you can buy the *Trinidad Express*, the *Trinidad Guardian*, *The Bomb*, *Challenge*, *Target*, the *Barbados Advocate*, *Time* or *Newsweek* magazine but every week, notwithstanding our best efforts, you cannot buy on their streets our national newspaper *The Free West Indian*. Yet, they are the ones who speak of press freedom.

I want to give you the benefit of some research done by our Media Workers Association. They analysed the 19 month period from June 1980 to December 1981; to be more concrete they did a content analysis of a section of Caribbean press coverage during that period for the following newspapers; *Trinidad Guardian*, *Trinidad Express*, *Vincentian*, *Voice of St Lucia*, *Dominica Chronicle*, *Barbados Advocate*, *Barbados Nation*, and occasional copies of the *Jamaica Gleaner* and the *Trinidad Bomb* newspapers. What this analysis showed is that during this 19 month period, these papers carried some 1,570 articles on Grenada during this period, which works out to an average of nearly three articles per day. Some 60% of these were editorials or other comment and the remaining 40% was 'straight' news. About 60% of these articles were negative towards the Grenada Revolution being either downright lies or subtle and not so subtle distortions. Furthermore, 95% of the PRG's rebuttals to many of these scandalous and libellous articles were never published.

It is clear that no other topic has attracted such vast coverage in this section of the Caribbean press over the last three years. And comrades will, of course, note that only some newspapers in a handful of islands are included without reference to radio or television coverage and also that the vast press and other media coverage in the rest of the Caribbean, Latin America, North America and Western Europe is excluded altogether from this analysis. There is no doubt that the Grenada Revolution has been very profitable for the media magnates and saltfish mafia of the region.

So what do we in Grenada raise in the place of the great democratic sham of the imperialist press? Where do we seek the forms of our press democracy? We uphold the freedom of the majority of the working people, who form the mass of our population, to express their views and their right to have access to the mass media which serves their interests, which reflects their struggles and aspirations, their perceptions and opinions. We vindicate a media which is a tool to help organise our people, for without that constant activity and participation there is no democracy, no collective strength. We add that our media must inform our people honestly and seek to educate them, it must provide them with constructive criticism for the examination of problems and the formulation of solutions, with the opportunity to advance proposals and ideas that will help to form the country's domestic and foreign policies. As such, it is crucial that the people's letters and complaints are openly printed for public comment, and conversely in the spirit of the principles of Emulation, that the most outstanding of our workers receive appreciation and recognition through our newspapers, radio and television. To implement these principles, there are nine regular newspapers published in Grenada, in place of the only one rag that was being printed before the Revolution. And a new newspaper, *Fedon*, the voice of the People's Revolutionary Armed Forces is to begin publication in the next few days. Their owners are the masses and their mass organisations. Look and scan with every means you have, comrades, you will find no directors of foreign banks editing or managing *The Free West Indian, Women's Voice, Fight, The New Jewel, The Pioneers Voice, Cutlass, Fork, Media Workers Voice*, or the *Workers Voice*. There is a newspaper serving all the major elements of our society: our youth, our women, our trade unionists, and our children, as well as our national newspaper, *The Free West Indian*, which binds these constituent parts together.

Comrades, we cannot tell you, neither would we presume to tell you, to duplicate our experience here in Grenada, in your own countries. Your means of democratising your media will arise out of your *own* conditions, your *own* struggles, your *own* definitions. But every inch of ground gained in your workplace is a liberated area for the entire Caribbean, every assault upon organised lying is a blow for truth which benefits every working person of the Caribbean, every defeat of the press barons in things great and small means a few steps forward for all our people. Words *are* weapons, and the vested interest of the Caribbean media are pointing them not only at us in Grenada, but at any oppressed or scrunting group that begin to stand up for a new and better life. Comrades, we must *turn the words around*, aim them back at the exploiters and begin to free our Caribbean Journalism of the despair and tyranny which holds it in a vice, and permits no democratic advance. You are the writers, you hold the weapons. You have the power to create your own notions and structures of Press Freedom that will expose and obliterate the terrible untruths that have made it, in the mouths of the ruling class of the press, the greatest and hollowest falsity of our age.

Journalism and the Struggle for Peace

Comrades, although there may be differences between us in some matters, there is one issue in particular upon which, above all, I am certain that we stand absolutely united. I am referring to the question of *Peace*, and the common commitment that we share to make our region a *zone of peace*. Perhaps such an assertion has even greater significance at this present time, when the forces of the North Atlantic Treaty Organisation (NATO), led by the hawks of the United States of America, are preparing once more to turn our Caribbean Sea into an armed lake. Like an overgrown child at his bathtime, President Reagan is about to drop into what he believes is his bathtub, his fleet of toy battleships and aircraft carriers filled to the brim with plastic planes and clockwork marines. I speak, of course, of the soon to be realised military manoeuvres code-named *Ocean Venture 82*, which are shortly to strike our region.

Such huge military rehearsals, so perilously close to our shores, and in fact *including* the shores of our comrades in Cuba and the occupied earth of Puerto Rico, only demonstrate one more time the proximity of war and the blasé, imperial and Monroe Doctrine-like attitude of the United States to our region and waters. The impunity with which their carriers of war float around our Caribbean is only encouraged by those governments which say that a shipload of American sailors in port bringing in thousands of dollars to their foreign exchange justifies their presence in our seas. Let us be clear that such money is nothing more than the wages of war, the cost of prostituting our sisters, the mercenary price paid to harass and threaten our region, to militarise it and turn it into a potential theatre of war and as such it can never be justified!

In this context, it is crucial that our regional journalists accomplish their sacred mission to be the propagandists of peace. Mere sabre-rattling has developed into the rumbling of aircraft carriers and the hissing of nuclear missiles, and these are the noises we shall be hearing more and more in our region while the present US warmongering continues. Any journalist that seeks to preserve peace and help to secure a future for humanity has a decisive role and responsibility *here* and *now*, that of monitoring the warlords, keeping on their tail, never losing sight of them, constantly supplying detailed and exact information on their movements and violations, and keeping continually vigilant to their threats and provocations.

In our own region we have had a particularly admirable example of such investigative power by some of our journalists. For years in two islands of the Caribbean, Antigua and Barbados, a transnational munitions company was secretly developing and testing a lethal artillery device on behalf of the South African racist government. This giant howitzer was not only used to lob and explode a nuclear warhead some five miles into the upper atmosphere, but also to shell and murder our African comrades in Angola during the abortive South African invasion into that sovereign state while the brave Angolans were fighting their Second War of Liberation. The foul and clandestine work of this transnational company, which operated under bogus respectability as the *Space Research Corporation*, was unmasked by courageous and outstanding journalists both in Barbados and Antigua. Their probing work had important consequences, for it resulted in this poisonous company being ejected from both islands. As such, it was a blow not only for the preservation of peace in our region and an expulsion of the racist scientists of death, but also a victory on behalf of the oppressed and struggling people of South Africa, for every deprivation of weaponry the Pretoria regime suffers, gives more hope and inspiration to the South African liberation forces and brings their inevitable victory a step forward. It must be emphasised that our quest for peace here in the Caribbean and the exposing of warmongering and bellicose initiatives provoked by imperialism in our *own* region by our *own* journalists, is not only good for our own dignity, but as a global significance, for in the age of thermo-nuclear arms the threat to peace even in a speck of the world like two very small islands barely seen on a world map is a threat to peace for the entire world.

In this epoch, the eyes of the world are staring squarely at our region. They see our Caribbean as a flashpoint, a trouble spot, with an intensity that we have never experienced before. The struggle of our heroic neighbours, first in Nicaragua and now in El Salvador and Guatemala, has made our region the world's focus, the target for international journalism. The future of humanity is being fought out on our doorstep, and the need for accurate, pro-human democratic and progressive journalism in such a scenario is unprecedented in our region. The integrity of Caribbean journalism has never been so necessary, so fundamental, so critical as it is now. The warmongers and tyrants know well that the honest journalist, no matter what his personal ideology may be, is an obvious and natural ally of the national liberation movement. He is recording resistance to oppression, the struggle for bread and justice, the hope and aspiration towards a better life. Whether it was Herbert Matthews, an American, covering the struggle of Fidel and his comrades in the Sierra Maestra, Wilfred Burchett's reporting from Vietnam, the dispatches and articles by Basil Davidson from the liberated zones of Guinea-Bissau, Angola and Mozambique, or John Reed's inspiring words from revolutionary Russia in 1917, the journalist is the crucial link between the fighter for freedom and peace and the man or woman reading a newspaper in any street in any city or village in any country.

This is plainly why the ex-five-star general of the defeated US Army in Vietnam, General Westmoreland, is now openly declaring that in any future conflict involving the United States, the American and International press must be restricted, and must not have open access to the battle zones. He knows, perhaps better than anyone, how much American public opinion was turned against the US Vietnamese adventure through the day-by-day reporting from the front line by newspaper, radio and television, and how the American people grew sickened, appalled and ashamed by the vile brutal actions of their own soldiers, by the defoliation and chemical warfare. Westmoreland and others of *his* ilk understand only too well how American parents — many of them poor — were watching with increasing horror the futile maiming and permanent destruction of their own sons on the television screen while standing in their own living rooms, or how ordinary Americans who talked glibly about the great American ideal sat transfixed as they watched the newsreels showing the cold-blooded torture and executions of young men who were supposed to be Viet Cong suspects. Clearly, after that war, journalism could never be the same again, and nothing did more to resolutely change American public opinion and put it against the war, despite the continued frothings and splutterings of the warlords.

In the same way, in June 1979 in Nicaragua, when the American public saw a news film of the arbitrary and merciless killings of an ABC correspondent by one of Somoza's National Guard, there was a horrified and incredulous outcry through America which quite clearly made it extremely difficult for the US hawks to take the option they wanted of direct military intervention in Nicaragua. This event was to prove very significant for the eventual Sandinista victory. And we could compare a situation, as in Nicaragua or El Salvador, where the press are able to cover the war, despite the immense difficulties, to a situation where they cannot. In East Timor, the FRETILIN soldiers of national liberation have been waging a six-year war with irresponsible courage, against the Indonesian armed forces, who invaded their country a week after it achieved its independence following centuries of Portuguese Colonialism in 1976. East Timor, an enclave on an island in South East Asia, has been sealed off from journalists by an air and sea blockade, and receives scant publicity and little reporting. Consequently, the just struggle of its people has never received the kind of international solidarity of other struggles for peace and justice that have been more prolifically covered by international journalism. The result is that a heroic people continue a massive struggle in virtual isolation, and carry forward their drive towards freedom under a serious disadvantage — a vacuum of press coverage.

So comrades, in this present period, when national liberation struggles and the demands of the poor and working people dominate our region and much of the world, it is the right and responsibility of the journalist of integrity to move to cover them, to report upon them, to photograph, film and record them, to spread out the news of their people's struggles from Namibia, from El Salvador, from South Africa, from East Timor, from the Western Sahara, from Palestine. For their cause and the cause of all oppressed and struggling peoples march side by side with the cause of peace. There can be no true peace while the lives of these heroic people with justice on their side are dominated by tyranny or circumscribed by oppression.

Our times are full and echoing with the insane talk of war. In the United States there is the attempt by the disciples of the monstrous industrial-military complex to legitimise the concepts of 'limited nuclear war', the 'First Strike' option, the dangerous concept of 'linkage', the Reagan Doctrine of total uncritical support for international outlaw regimes like Zionist Israel and racist South Africa because they best represent the global expansionist and warlike ambitions of the neutron warlords, and many journalists are falling into the fatal trap of favourably publicising, and thus giving credence to this madness. Clearly, freedom-loving and peace-loving journalists must take the firmest possible stand against such jockeying with the future of our earth, our humanity and everything our people have ever wrested from their history and everything we have ever built for our children. On this fundamental question of peace, disarmament, detente and peaceful co-existence, we must stand united and nothing must tear us apart, for over and above everything else it stands as the most vital issue of our day, the first issue and the last issue: the right to life itself, for any and all of our peoples.

Journalists Must Promote the Cause of Peace

Faced with this historic responsibility, how can progressive journalists counter such vile propaganda designed to whip up fear and hysteria and create an artificial and erroneous public opinion among the people of our Americas? How can they exercise their responsibility to the ideas for peace and disarmament shared by a growing majority of mankind?

We wish to suggest a number of ways that democratic and progressive journalists using their pens and microphones can wage ideological struggle against the forces of reaction, misinformation and mystification.

Tell your readers and your listeners that peaceful coexistence is a necessity, indeed, that there is no alternative to world peace, that detente is advantageous to all countries, that the right to live in peace is the most basic human right, the guarantor of all other rights.

Explain to your readers and your listeners that the objective of international relations should be disarmament, not arms races and show them how the colossal amount of resources now being squandered on arms should be used to solve the great universal problems of hunger, poor health, illiteracy, substandard housing, etc.

Expose to your readers and your listeners that the drift towards war and military intervention is not in the interest of the peoples of our Americas but only serves the military-industrial-state complex's greed for ever greater profits from the manufacture and sale of weapons.

Highlight in your news reports and commentaries all proposals for disarmament, all disarmament conferences, the activities of the growing peace movement around the world and the efforts to have the Caribbean declared and recognised in practice as a Zone of Peace.

Expose in your papers and on your radio and television stations the lies against the Cuban Revolution, the Nicaraguan Revolution, the Surinamese process, the Grenadian Revolution and the truth and reality of the reasons for the struggles of the oppressed peoples of El Salvador, Guatemala and elsewhere.

We in Grenada believe that the peoples of the world have the fundamental right to obtain an objective idea of reality with the help of clear and precise information and at the same time the right to freely express their opinion

through the mass media. Connected to that is our view that today's journalists have a great responsibility to help make information broadly accessible
to public opinion and to enable public opinion to directly participate in the
work of the mass media. This places on the journalist a responsibility to exercise professional honesty, respect for human dignity and defence of dignity
and defence of universal human values and in this context we strongly
support the efforts of UNESCO, the IOJ and the World Democratic journalists movement to establish an international code of journalistic ethics based
on the following responsibilities and ethical standards:

1) The journalist is responsible for what he writes, publishes or broadcasts.
2) The journalist has a duty to defend peace and non-recourses to force in
   the resolving of international disputes.
3) The journalist has a responsibility to struggle against all forms of discrimination and racial, social or religious intolerance.
4) The journalist has a responsibility to minutely verify the information
   commented on or intended for publication or broadcast.
5) That journalists who engage in publishing or broadcasting cheap sensation-
   alism, vulgarity, pornography, lies, false information, hoaxes and scandals
   violate the lofty principles of professionalism, manipulate public opinion
   by diverting its attention from the real and important issues and prostitute
   themselves to reaction and its greed to make profits from such journalistic
   abuses.
6) That the journalist has the duty to preserve the honour of his profession
   and to maintain in relations with his colleagues a balance between the
   spirit of healthy competition and professional solidarity.

And never for one moment be tempted to believe that to achieve such an
international code of ethics does not involve just as great a struggle as that
for a new world information order. Indeed, they are one and the same thing.

The Emperor Visits the Region

Comrades, before concluding I wish to take this opportunity to restate
Grenada's views on the one news event which has surpassed all others in
recent times in the coverage it received from the Caribbean mass media —
President Reagan's visit to our region last week.

The character of this visit and the inflammatory remarks made by
President Reagan constituted a fundamental insult to the people of Barbados,
the people of the Caribbean and the regional journalist community.

Firstly, Reagan ignores Mr Michael Manley, opposition leader in Jamaica
during his one day visit there, then shortly after landing Barbados, on the
soil of a sister CARICOM nation, he launches a vehement attack on Grenada,
another member of the Caribbean Community.

During his four-day stay he insultingly refused to drive in a car provided by the Barbadian people, or eat Barbadian food or accept the quality of Barbadian health care. This illustrious gentleman who fancies himself as a 20th Century Emperor not only takes with him a royal entourage of hundreds of courtiers and minions armed even with their own toilet paper but also a battalion of swarming Western newsmen who enjoy free access to all the places and events that the Emperor graces with his presence while Barbadian and Caribbean journalists are harassed, bullied and denied their national and professional rights to cover the visit by Reagan's crew of racist security goons.

This insult, this imperial arrogance, this wanton and contemptible disrespect on the sovereign soil of our region, comrades, deserves the strongest condemnation from all democratic and independent minded people of *our* Caribbean.

And there are lessons that Caribbean journalists and Caribbean journalism must glean from such experiences, for what we witnessed last week are the characteristics of an insensitive millionaire who represents the interests of an imperialist ruling class whose so-called concern for the region's people is crassly opportunistic. Caribbean journalism therefore cannot set itself apart in some illusionary ivory tower of objectivity and not raise its voice against this and similar abuses, insults and disrespectful and imperialist practices against the independent, sovereign and freedom-loving people of *our* region. No! Indeed, Caribbean journalism has the duty and responsibility to side with exploited and oppressed masses of *our* region against monopoly control.

For as long as there are social classes in our societies, and as long as our region and the world is divided into rich and poor, haves and have nots, privileged and under-privileged journalism cannot exist and function outside of these contradictions.

It cannot be independent of society, it cannot be uncommitted to topical social problems because it would lose its purpose and cease to be journalism at all. On the contrary, only its close connection with society, with the forces of progress or the forces of backwardness do we find the substance and purpose of journalism's existence.

Fight Concentration and Monopoly Ownership of the Media

It is clear that one of the major challenges that will confront progressive and honest journalists in our region in the months and years ahead is the urgent task of demonopolising the Caribbean mass media, particularly the region's large newspapers with their myriad corporate and ideological linkages. And growing out of this effort will be the struggle to democratise the workplaces where journalists labour, i.e., to provide opportunities to participate in the editorial and management decision-making processes, to set productivity targets, to organise emulation and grievance committees and to share in the profits of the media enterprises.

And it must be emphasised that this issue of concentration and monopolisation of newspapers has relevance not only to Caribbean journalism but to Western journalism in general. Permit me here to refer to the findings and recommendations of a Canadian Parliamentary Commission that recently studied the state of the newspaper profession in Canada.

As much cannot be said for the concept of press freedom as the guarantee of responsibility. In a one-newspaper town it means nothing except the right of a proprietor to do what he will with his own. In a country that has allowed papers to be owned by a few conglomerates, freedom of the press means, in itself, *only that enormous influence with responsibility* is conferred on a handful of people. For the heads of such organisations to justify their position by appealing to the principle of the freedom of the press is offensive to intellect and honesty.

Today we are bombarded by information that is far greater in quantity, and more complex in nature, than we can digest. To be even moderately informed, therefore, we depend increasingly on the services of intermediaries who select and interpret for us.

The most generally important of these intermediaries are the newspapers. Their old and difficult obligations, to be accurate and fair and balanced in their reporting, remain. The increasingly difficult task is to make reports of complex matters both accurate and interesting, with the necessary brevity. To go below the facts to their significance, to give the truth by interpreting without distorting, is even more demanding of the journalist's knowledge and understanding, perseverance and patience. To be well done, journalism requires both penetration and breadth of mind at least equal to those of any other occupation.

The Commission emphasizes what it regards as the essentially professional nature of the journalist's work. The professional — the doctor or the lawyer, for example — places his special skills at the service of the patient or client, to deal with problems which the layman does not himself know what to do about. The professional is in honour bound to use his judgement to do what is best for the health or welfare of his client. The layman has a closely analogous need for the journalist's services: to select from the mass of available facts the information which is significant to most of our newspaper's readers and to present that information in a way that is accurate, understanding, comprehensible, interesting, and balanced.

In the days of head-on newspaper competition, and in a less complex society, it is natural that most journalists should think of themselves, and should be seen, as practising a craft rather than a profession. It is equally natural that the adjustment of attitudes to a changed society and the role of the monopoly newspaper should take time. What is sad is that the organisation of the newspaper industry is making the transition so very long. Many journalists are under-educated for their responsibilities. More are underpaid. Almost all lack the editorial leadership that would give them the understanding and the opportunity to perform the service that a free society now requires of them.

The Davey Committee said 11 years ago that the newsrooms of most Canadian newspapers were boneyards to broken dreams. Our investigations lead us to think that there are now fewer dreams to break. Some of the cynicism is the deeper one of not having had dreams. Journalist's confidence in their publishers is thin or worse. They are frustrated but, even more, confused. This malaise is, in the Commission's view, part of the price we pay for conglomerate ownership.

We certainly agree with these opinions and hasten to wish all success to the cemocratic journalists of Canada in their attempts to break the stronghold of the corporate mafia in the media as they strive to develop an honest and professional approach to the career of their choice.

All Success to the Conference

We in Grenada are humbled and greatly honoured at having been given the opportunity to host a conference of such historic significance and we wish the delegates and the organizers all success in their deliberations over the next three days. We sincerely hope that this conference will initiate an on-going process of dialogue and professional co-operation among the region's journalists.

Comrades, the 20th Century has been called the century of information. Never before has information played such an important role as today because today the mass media powerfully influence the minds and hearts of millions of people thereby contributing greatly to the general regional and international climate and the forming of public opinion.

All the greater, then, is the significance for the future well-being of our peoples the questions of how and for what prupose are the mass media operating and whether they serve the aims of peace, progress and truth or whether they spread discord, distrust and lies among countries and peoples. This problem clearly shows the broad scope of the responsibility that must be assumed today, tomorrow and the days ahead by journalism, and journalists in the Caribbean, Latin America and the world.

Again, in the name of our party, government and people, I welcome you to our struggling but proud country. We trust that you will receive the opportunity during your stay to see a bit of our country, experience the warmth of our friendly and peace-loving people and discover the truth of our new reality as our people struggle together in a united and determined way to build a society free of all forms of exploitation and injustice.

With the greatest of pleasure I now declare this historic conference formally open and wish for all its participants peace, justice, ever-increasing consciousness and job-satisfaction and success in your collective endeavours to hasten the day of the New World Information order.

151

14. Fight Unemployment Through Production!

Address to National Conference on Unemployment, St. George's, Grenada, 28 June 1982

At the beginning of this historic conference there are five brief points I would like to make by way of introduction.

First, unemployment is not the fault nor is it the wish and desire of our party, our government. In fact, as all comrades here know, we regard now and always have regarded unemployment as being a disease, a curse, a blight and a waste of very important and scarce human resources.

The second point is that unemployment for us in Grenada is a relatively new experience for our people, an experience created by capitalism. The Siboneys, the Caribs and the Arawaks, the first inhabitants of our soil, all worked in those days because if you did not work you could not eat. Likewise, under slavery, one *had* to work under conditions of degrading, criminal brutality and exploitation. One had to work under the whip.

It is only when slavery had ended and capitalism came around that we began to see unemployment emerging in our country, and that came about historically largely because agriculture was the mainstay of the economy and the agricultural land was owned by a very small minority and all the rest of the people had to find work on a few huge agricultural estates.

The third point is that our people have had a long tradition of working, and working hard and working honourably. Our people have been accustomed to work and working in the best tradition of hard, dedicated work.

All of this can be seen in many different ways. We can see it certainly in the fact that today when we look around at our own historic landscape and we look at Fort Rupert and Fort Frederick, as we look at the tunnel, as we look at the network of roads going around the hills of our country we know that it was our forefathers who built all those things. It was their sweat, it was their blood, it was their labour, their sacrifice which produced all of those historic monuments and important networks of roads.

We can also see this evidence of hard work by our people in terms of the work our people have done in several metropolitan centres, certainly London and England as a whole, in Canada, in the United States, our people who have migrated to these countries have in fact done tremendous work and in the case of England it is our people who are responsible to a great extent for maintaining the transport and health systems in this country.

The fourth brief point, comrades, is that there is more unemployment today in the capitalist world than in the past 50 years. The capitalist today is going through a major crisis and one of the major side effects of this crisis is this massive, unbelievable unemployment. It is estimated that today in the capitalist world, there are 25 million people out of work in the 24 most heavily-developed capitalist countries. And it is also estimated that by the end of this year that figure will become 30 million people out of work. In other words, some 300 times the entire population of our country are out of work in the capitalist world, and as you know comrades, imperialist propaganda attempts to hide and distort this reality. They try to pretend that there is no unemployment, or when they admit unemployment as they are more and more forced to do now, they say not only what they have always said that unemployment is necessary, unavoidable and they have moved to the ludicrous extent of trying to blame unemployment on the national liberation struggles worldwide.

These people try to blame their unemployment on what is happening in El Salvador, in Cuba, Nicaragua, Grenada, in Mozambique, Angola, in the Socialist World. That is the extent of the desperation that the capitalist world now has.

The fifth point, comrades, is that in Grenada we allow no concealment, we allow no secrecy, we allow no lies to fool or mystify our people. We come before our people openly, as always admitting this problem of unemployment and pointing out that together as government and people we have to find a solution to unemployment and that is why, comrades, we have this historic conference today. That is why today, we continue this whole task of finding a mass solution for ending unemployment, trying to fight unemployment through increasing production.

In setting ourselves the huge task of solving our traditional and inherited unemployment problem we can allow ourselves no brambling. For because unemployment for us is a mass problem, we are determined to find a *mass solution* to it. The people themselves, in particular *the unemployed themselves*, must be fully involved and engaged in finding the remedies that will cure joblessness once and for all in our society. So when we began this historic process of tackling unemployment, our first move was to organise an unemployment census which started on March 26th this year. This was followed by a series of parish conferences on the issue, first of all in St Patrick's, then St John's and St Mark's followed by St Andrew's, St George's, St David's and finally Carriacou. In broaching the problem in this participatory way, we knew that we were only beginning the first steps of a long *process* that could not be completed overnight, or in a few weeks. Democratic solutions, as we have learned repeatedly during the Revolution, do not happen that way. As an honest revolutionary and democratic government we cannot give unproductive jobs to our unemployed simply for the sake of giving them jobs and then watch them dig holes in the road and fill them up again, and then declare that we have finished with unemployment. Neither do we have the economic capacity nor the desire to serve out a weekly dole or freeness to the unemployed. Comrades, we can only honestly seek to solve unemployment by seeing it in the context of *economic construction, of the drive for greater production* — of the necessity to work harder in order to build our country. So any solution that we create must have the capacity of contributing to production, so that other jobs are created, and conversely any productive drive we make must throw up more and more possibilities of work for our people. In short, each job we create must generate dozens more jobs. Comrades, unemployment is both *your* concern and *your* problem as well as a national problem, so *you* especially are the people to attend to its solution. In the same way that we embarked upon an unprecedented democratic and participatory method in organising and framing our national budget which became a true People's Budget, we are taking the same road, already blazed for us by our budget process, in seeking to resolve the massive problem of unemployment. For we want a people's solution, a people's remedy, *a people's cure* that will come out of the very guts and experience of our masses, and which will therefore be a guarantee of its acceptability and succcess.

So this is why we are here today comrades, and this is why our process has brought us to this point. For by the end of the day we shall arrive at no magic formula, let us be very clear about that. What today will serve to achieve will be a pooling of ideas and information, a discovery of common ground between us, an itemisation of the insights and genius that our people have for creative ideas to solve their problems; and a definition of the precise nature and dimensions of the beast against which we are all fighting. Our struggle is continuing today along the road of the process of solution, so we must not think of today as a last act or finale. We are merely taking another step, but it will be a giant step, a massive step because it is a step being taken by *all of us together*, with our minds focused and clenched round the same evil, and our wills collectively determined to finish with it forever in our country.

Comrades, during the period of 1970s our economy was unable to create jobs for our people. The economy lacked the capacity as we exported our primary products which resulted in no value added, and we imported finished consumer products which only used up our foreign exchange.

To get the extra value and benefit, what was needed was to process our primary products such as cocoa, nutmegs and coffee, and also to process our fruits, vegetables and spices. However, the Gairy regime did not think of this, they were not interested in changing the 400 years of misery our people had suffered. First under slavery and then under capitalism the majority owned nothing but their ability to work, and they were forced to work at a subsistence wage.

Comrades, let us look at some of the figures of the labour force during the period of the 1970s under the Gairy regime. In 1970, the estimated unemployment was approaching 30% of the total work force. This was so despite the so-called boom in the economy during the 1960s.

Of course, as the Gairy dictatorship displayed its total incompetency in handling the economy, the situation worsened between 1970 and 1975 as all production fell, and unemployment increased tremendously.

After March 13th, 1979

Thus by the time of the March 13th Revolution, nearly 50% of the total work force could not find anything to do. The economy had not changed much over the previous 400 years in terms of providing productive employment for our people, This was even more destructive for our women and young people under 25, where the brunt of the unemployment fell.

When the people took power in 1979, the People's Revolutionary Government pursued its previous objectives of diversifying the economy and processing its primary products, while, always in our minds was the creation of productive employment — not just any employment, but productive employment — for our people. Our first priority was to increase the employment of women, especially our young women who were the hardest hit. Our first step in that direction was to decree equal pay for equal work in the state sector for all our women. This was not employment in itself, but it brought equality and justice to women by ending discrimination against them. And since then, on a progressive basis, more and more women have been brought into the work force. Today we have women workers at the Airport Project, women tractor drivers, more women in the National Commercial Bank, in the Fisheries Company, in the Agro-Industrial Plant, forming micro-co-operatives, etc.

Our other main priority was to provide jobs for the thousands of unemployed youth. Here, we ensured that whenever new jobs were opened up that the unemployed youth were among the first to be placed. It was this conscious policy that allowed thousands of youth to be employed in the International Airport project, on the roads, in the expanded and revitalised agricultural state farms, in fisheries and so on. Together with this, we embarked on a nation-wide campaign in 1980, our 'Year of Education and Production' to create more jobs through getting our youths to work co-operatively on the idle lands in our country. Our great slogan then was 'IDLE LANDS + IDLE HANDS = AN END TO UNEMPLOYMENT'. This campaign achieved reasonable success with the result that some 20 agricultural co-operatives with almost 200 members were established with the assistance of the National Co-operative Development Agency (NACDA) — an agency established by the Revolution to promote co-operatives.

And of course this programme of 1980 is continuing with a bang this year with our Land Reform and Youth Employment Programmes, which we confidently expect to make a major contribution to our twin goals of raising production while providing more jobs. Certainly, the enthusiasm of the 50-odd youth present at last Thursday's formal opening of the new La Sagesse Agricultural Training Centre leaves us in absolutely no doubt that the youth of our country are ready to 'Fight Unemployment through Production', in the firm conviction that production is the only REAL SOLUTION.

The 1982 Unemployment Census

The Unemployment Census was conducted in April and May of this year and aimed at identifying all the unemployed in the state. This is, all those who at the time of the census had no jobs. It was also intended to identify part-time workers, that is persons who on average worked less than two days a week and seasonal workers, that is those who worked for three consecutive months within the calendar year.

The census identified 7,040 such persons, including 6,640 who were fully unemployed, 229 part-time workers and 171 seasonal workers. The majority of the total unemployed was found in St Andrew's with 27½% followed by St George's with 27%, St Patrick's had 15%, St David's with 13% and the other three parishes making up the other 17.5%.

The census also confirmed another point which was generally known: that is that most of those unemployed are young people. About 64% of the persons met in the census were between 16 and 25 years old. This percentage got smaller as the age increased — only 18% of the total number of unemployed, seasonal workers and part-time workers were between 26-35 years; only 8% between 36 and 45 years and only 3% of the total were over 55 years. 52% of those actively seeking jobs are the 16-25 year olds, with 12% not seeking jobs, probably because of the frustration experienced or which they saw their colleagues experience. The other 36% of this age group, the 16-25 year olds, are either seasonal workers or part-time. Still, they also need to find full-time jobs to ensure security and a better standard of living.

The greatest number of unemployed by far, were found to be females. 72% of 4781 persons were females, and coupled with the fact that most of the unemployed are between the ages of 16 and 25, we see a real problem that these young women of our society face.

The parish which registered the largest percentage of female unemployed, happened to be Carriacou, where nearly 90% of the total number of unemployed counted in Carriacou were female.

Comrades, the data also indicated that we are still trapped to some extent within the socio-historical trap of sex discrimination, where men find it easier to bet a job. Although the male/female ratio in the population is roughly 1 to 1, we found that generally the split between male and female in the unemployed pool is 1 to 2, that is for every one man unemployed, two women are unemployed.

The ratio between the sexes in relation to the nuber of persons seeking jobs, suggest to us that for every one man seeking a job, there are two women. This is in line with the unemployment breakdown. However, when we examine persons not seeking jobs, we see that there are three times as many of our women as men who have given up the search. In terms of the educational background of the unemployeds, seasonal workers and part-time workers, less than 2% had no education whatsoever. Over 70% of the comrades have gone beyond class four and up to secondary education but did not go to secondary schools. We came across 18% of these comrades who had been to secondary schools — of course, we employ all our university trained cadres.

When consulted about which sector they would like to work in, whether state, private, co-operative or self-employed, the vast majority of comrades preferred the state sector, and in all parishes between 68 and 78% said they would prefer to work in the state sector.

Therefore, although 42% of the comrades displayed an interest in areas which are not directly productive, such as services and commerce, we must remind comrades today that jobs can only be created if we first produce goods, that is agricultural products, nectars, jams, juices, fish, etc. Only then, after such production can we talk about employing people in the other economic sectors which are not directly productive.

A New Concept of Work

Comrades, we have already spoken of the curse and brutality of our labour and the class of parasites it served in the days before we grasped our power and unfurled the flag of freedom in every village across our country. For March 13th, 1979, as in so many things, gave us a new direction, a new cause, a new concept of *work*. For as soon as our land became *ours*, as soon as we had severed its beauty from the ugly grip of the dictator, we knew that *work* itself would and must take on a new meaning for us. From being an alienated act of hate and despair, work suddenly had the promise of being an act of love and fulfilment. From being drudgery it began to take the shape of joy. We began to see the extraordinary spectacle of many hundreds of our people from every village in our land, coming out in happiness to perform *voluntary* and *unpaid* acts of work, in their *own* time and most usually upon Sunday mornings. We began to see drains and culverts cleared that had been clogged up by twenty-five years of sewerage and Gairyism. We saw roads repaired by the collective work of neighbours, overhanging branches chopped down, bridges built and walls decorated with the colours and words of freedom. We saw the parents of our school children and the children themselves taking over their schools while their teachers discussed the future of Education in our country at the National Teachers' Seminar in their hundreds during January 1980, and we saw the parents contributing in that one week over a million dollars' worth of free labour, of truly *free* labour. We saw the House Repair Programme depending on the voluntary help of neighbours of the houseowners and getting it too. We saw the maroon* coming alive again in

* Traditional voluntary act of collective work

157

Grenada! A new attitude had developed towards work. Work changed its very nature as the Revolution revealed its true meaning for us. For through our voluntary community work brigades and all the sessions of collective work that were carefully, or sometimes spontaneously organised, we were realising a truth that was new to us — that work is a liberator, work is what unites us, builds us, develops us and changes us. Without work we go nowhere, we achieve nothing. When our work is against us, only serving others who exploit and scorn us, we fall into despondency and frustration. *But with work on our side* we build a new world, a world which will truly serve the workers of the world.

Comrades, perhaps I could make this point clearly and forcibly by quoting to you the words of a man who was with us in Grenada just a few weeks ago, as a member of the delegation of President Samora Machel of Mozambique. For travelling with this great man were other outstanding men with a whole history of struggle and victory inside them. One such Mozambican leader, who unfortunately we did not hear speak publicly as the visit was so short, was Comrade Sergio Vieira, who travelled with the delegation as Minister of Agriculture. This comrade is recognised in his own country as a prominent poet and thinker, and he is the author of a particularly widely-read and influential pamphlet setting out the ideas for the creation of new men and women in his country Mozambique, with new, liberated mentalities, called *The New Man is a Process*. In the following way, the people themselves are creating their own future and constructing their own economy.

'*Work creates and liberates. Work is not punishment. When a person works there should be some result to his work. Work can never be a game! Work has to have a concrete result and have a social benefit. Work which has no benefit is not work. It is a demoralizing action*'. Comrades, there is much to be learned in these words which is very relevant to our situation here in Grenada. For here too, *our work must have a concrete result*, and that concrete result must be *more and more production*, which itself will create *more and more jobs*. That is why we are framing our slogan in this way: *Work is the mother of production, production produces/creates/throws up work!* For we can allow ourselves no non-productive work, no joke work, no disguised unemployment — for our task too in tackling unemployment is to unmask *that* and tear away the disguise. Production is both the cause and product of our work, and there can be no space for work which is merely ornamental or which stands on the sidelines of development like an interested spectator on the roads, watching the bands pass at Carnival.

Work, The Transformer

Why are we so concerned about unemployment? Why do we see it as such an evil, such a negative force in our society? It is because we believe in the future and because we know that our people are builders of the future — and because we know that if we don't work, then we can't build. We are working for ourselves and each other in Grenada now, and most importantly, we are working for our children, all our children. So we believe that every single Grenadian should enjoy that right and responsibility to be a builder and constructor of that future. While a Grenadian remains unemployed it means that he or she is denied the right to build that future, to participate in the construction of that planned and real civilisation that we are mapping out for our children and our children's children. We would not deny anybody in our country that right and responsibility, which is why we believe so strongly in the right to work, and why we have to set out on this long process to *ensure* that every single one of our people can proudly say: 'I am the builder of Grenada. I am a part of that fuel that will drive my country forward.' For when we understand the nature of the *dignity* that the Revolution is bringing to our people, we see that the right to stand up as a working person, the right to achieve excellence in work, the right to be emulated for that excellence, the right to be exemplary in punctuality, efficiency and productivity – all these are the new rights that the Revolution has brought us with respect to work, rights that are a part of the great treasure that is March 13th. And it is these rights which contribute to the new notion of dignity and independence that our people are proudly demonstrating right across the land.

Unemployment therefore is an attack on that dignity, but more importantly it is an attack on our resolve to achieve greater production, which will give us the true material basis for that dignity. Unemployed workers mean less land under the plough, less processing, less manufacturing, less exporting, and therefore less foreign exchange, less ability to buy those things we *really* need from abroad like tractors, medicines and vital spare parts. And yet with all the loss in production that unemployment brings, we still have to feed the unemployed, to care for them, to educate their children, to hospitalise them when they are sick. Like anyone else they still need housing and recreation, and they must still participate in and take the social wage that is there for all our people. Although, in short, they are not producers, they are still consumers, and so they are inevitably taking out more than they are putting in, although this may be no fault of their own.

For work is a great transformer. Not only does work change the material reality around us – like it created a new city in Dresden in the GDR, like it is making concrete our dream at Point Salines – but in doing this it transforms the human being himself, or herself. For the serious application to the tasks of work, the discipline and sense of fulfilment that it brings, the sense of pride and purpose of contributing to building a new world – all this in itself creates a new mentality and a new type of person that must live in, contribute and bring his strengths to bear to that same new society he is helping to create.

The Fruit of New Jobs

Comrades, we in Grenada are struggling to be part of that new world, and to build it we must ensure that there is work for everybody, that nobody is excluded. At the moment we are a long way from that situation, for between 21 and 22% of our people are still unemployed, which means that some 7,000 of our brothers and sisters are not being allowed to make their full contribution. It is towards these Grenadians that we are resolving to reach over the next two to three years, to ensure work for all, and thus push up our productive capacity to create the possibilities of more and more benefits and a greater social wage for all of us. For the solution to unemployment lies only in increased production. We still have over seven thousand acres of idle and under-utilised land, and every two acres of this land can create at least one new job in agriculture for our people. This will cause the creation of a minimum of another three thousand, five hundred jobs in agriculture alone. Then we need to examine the prospects of the greater production that cultivated lands will bring, and the *fruit of more jobs* that will grow from that production, for example in the agro-industrial sector, with the production of more mangoes, more guavas, more bananas, more soursops, more tamarinds to process. The boxing plants will need for workers for more boxes for more bananas, the greater volume of fruit will need more transport, more trucks, more drivers, the docks will need more warehousemen, more stevedores, more forklift truck operators. All in all, the rise in production caused by the new jobs we create by putting more land under cultivation, will take us towards a one-job-per-acre situation and in the case of bananas, one and a half jobs per acre. If we include the further jobs created in all the sectors connected to and spinning off the production from the newly cultivated land we get 7,000 acres creating over 7,000 new jobs! Comrades, this is why we say again *work is the mother of production, production produces/creates/throws up work*; and we can only fight and win the battle against unemployment through greater production.

In addition to our agricultural thrust, we shall see the expansion of our fishing fleet, and its greater efficiency through the land-to-sea radio equipment that we shall soon be receiving from our friends in the German Democratic Republic. We shall also be encouraging the expansion of further light industries, particularly in the area of garment-making. For we need to turn resolutely towards new forms of work and new methods of production, in order both to diversify our products and diversify our type of work. All this will need new and requisite forms of education and training, something we have already successfully started with our fishing school. For what we have seen in the Fisheries sector is that our training facilities have developed alongside our growing capacity to catch more fish and process more fish. All this growth has begun to create a genuine fisheries industry in our country, which is not only contributing to feed our people and beginning to give us some more valuable export earnings, but it is, of course, creating more and more jobs in that sector. And this growth has caused many of our people to

take fishing far more seriously. It is causing our fishermen to look at themselves in a more organised way and to combine together and form fishing
co-operatives. For a spirit of co-operation and working seriously together in
a planned and organised way, will always cause the creation of more jobs than
the dog-eat-dog, violent individualist competition of the capitalist way of
production, which might have a few winners, but at the expense of many
losers, many victims. And the worst casualties are the rejected unemployed,
those who are left behing in the race to dominate, crush and push out of
the way.

A Legacy of Discouragement

We would all know comrades, that in our country we have inherited from our
particular history many reasons and factors which have encouraged
unemployment. Conditions of work were so bad under the dictatorship that
many workers actually preferred unemployment to staying in lowly-paid
jobs where they were expllited not only by their employers, but also through
a situation whereby they paid a large proportion of their salary as dues to a
corrupt union, whose leader only used its funds to build his own hotels, host
decadent parties at his Evening Palace and lay up accounts for his inevitable
defeat and flight to the heart of imperialism! Who would prefer, if one was
able, to drop out of such work, and perhaps fall back on some gardening, or
sewing or a little washing and ironing or whatever you could get? Also in
Grenada we have a legacy of unwillingness among many of our people to
work the land. Again, conditions historically have been so bad on many of
the private estates that our people have always identified agriculture in
terms of that particular form of production. What is significant now, however,
is that the Revolution has introduced new forms of production, organisation
and management in working the land, in particular through co-operatives,
whereby organisations and ownership are participatory and collective, and
whereby the co-operators are working for themselves and for each other. This
democratisation of agriculture has clearly attracted many of our young
people back to the land, and of course NACDA guarantees to find the
resources to assist serious co-operative ventures to start and continue, and
this is as true in the agricultural sector as it is in other areas.

In addition, colonialism continually floated the white collar in the dreams
of our people, so that work was valued in how far you could escape from the
land, rather than how well you could work it. Non-productive work in an
office was seen as the ideal, with the desk, the paper pad and the pen far
more worthy of respect and aspiration than the hoe and the fork — and
colonial education was based squarely on this premise. The six sizes and
shapes of Henry the Eighth's wives became more important than our own
size and shapes of our bananas or mangoes. Little Miss Muffet sitting on a
tuffet became more significant than the sister who sat on a wooden stall
cracking nutmegs, and Sir Francis Drake's pirate boat — *The Golden Hind* —

took precedence over our schooners and fishing boats from Windward, L'Esterre, Petit Martinique or Gouyave. This is why education for us now must mean production too, and this is why we place so great a value upon education, and why we have put the Centre of Popular Education at the centre of our educational thrust to raise the cultural and skills levels of our people. So that when the time for more specific work training comes, then they can be more ready, more able and more receptive to commit themselves to it and to succeed. This is also why we have resolved to integrate real production into the curriculum of our schools, so that they cease to be centres of irrelevant education that take our children's heads out of their own land and earth and send them chasing after Brooklyn, Toronto or London, but instead become genuine production centres where all the growing brain power of our youth and students is focused upon how to produce more for our country — and thus how to find more work and prosperity for our people.

Production the Key

For we have inherited an economy that *doesn't* teach us to educate ourselves — and those are confines and walls that we must break through, for they force us towards importing rather than producing. But the reality is that *if we don't produce then we can't import*, and so our emphasis must *all the* time be on *what else can we grow ourselves*, what else can we make ourselves, what else can we process ourselve and how much of all *these* things can we consume ourselves, rather than all those imported items that give our economy such daily licks and blows. For while we depend upon other countries' products we are like cast-asides and orphans in the world, motherless children without our own production. For dependency in any form is very dangerous for us, and can jeopardise any progress we may be making. When we import equipment and machinery from abroad we *must* be able to maintain and repair it and this again shows the crucial need for training. To have foreign equipment obtained at great cost sitting idle until a mechanic or technician from its country of origin can come and repair it, is another sure sign of our dependency and underdevelopment, something which can only be changed by permanent training, the acquisition of new skills and the mastering of the science and technology that we use on a daily basis.

Real Employment

Comrades, during our People's Budget process of January, February and March we spoke about the need to eliminate what we call disguised unemployment, labour which receives a wage but which is unproductive, which is wasted, which does not create wealth or contribute to development.

And our call was echoed by our people all over the land in the parish and zonal councils on the economy leading up to Budget Day.

This disguised unemployment was and remains a major concern of our people, because they recognise that the provision of unproductive jobs through political patronage is part of the destructive and wasteful colonial and neo-colonial legacy inherited by the Revolution, designed to keep us in a state of permanent poverty.

Our people have correctly pointed out that some sectors of the public service are over-loaded, that some of these workers could be better placed somewhere else, that they should be re-deployed in a productive or a potentially productive sector.

For it is our working people who have to pay the cost and carry the weight of disguised unemployment in the same way that they have to support the totally unemployed. Our disguised unemployed too, need to be freed from the mockery of work they are presently engaged in, so that they can make a real and genuine contribution to production and national development.

In three short years, the Revolution has made it possible for thousands of hitherto unemployed sisters and brothers to make such a patriotic contribution because the Revolution has created countless job-generating projects.

Formerly unproductive workers in the Ministries of Construction and Health, who have been redeployed on roads and other new projects like the Sandino block and tile making plant and the expanded telephone system, also now have the opportunity to contribute meaningfully to the production process.

In 1982 the forward movement to rid the economy of unemployment continues. Despite critical problems, we have still been able to create jobs in our economy and re-deploy people. For example in the Ministry of Health we have created over seventy new jobs although the critical budgetary problems have made it necessary to re-deploy people.

To give a concrete example of this redeployment into areas more productive, we can also use the Ministry of Health. The hospitals are now producing food for themselves. For example, instead of laying off workers at Princess Alice Hospital, in the month of May alone the hospital's farms produced 510 pounds of cabbages which not only made this hospital self-sufficient in cabbages for May, but also allowed them to sell 180 pounds of cabbages to the General Hospital.

The General Hospital itself is also producing — re-deploying its workers to produce, there are 100 banks of potatoes now, and during May they produced 50 pounds of cucumbers, 8 pounds of lettuce, 25 pounds of sweet pepper, 30 pounds of callaloo, 25 pounds of green peas among other products that this hospital has produced, to preserve the jobs of workers and produce directly.

Richmond Hill and Princess Royal are also involved in agricultural production to save money, and also more and more so to re-deploy those workers, thus saving their jobs.

Comrades, a tour around the country on any working day would reveal a startling sight that could convince even the scientists, the critics and the doubting Thomases. What is taking place today is that in every parish in our land, involving hundreds of our people who were once jobless, is the most widespread activity geared towards social and economic development that our nation has ever known in its history. What you can see on such a tour are dozens of capital projects that have and will continue to create jobs for masses, projects which cost hundreds of thousands and in some cases millions of dollars. Let me give you a few examples.

So far this year over $3,660,000 has been spent on our international airport, a project where 250 Grenadian workers find meaningful and productive employment.

Over 100 workers are now producing jams, jellies, nectars, pepper sauce and other food products at our new Agro-Industrial Plant in True Blue.

In Corinth, St David's and Bonaire, St Mark's dozens of workers are productively employed in the construction of two new primary schools.

With seven hotels and restaurants, the Grenada Resorts Corporation, a production of the Revolution, today employs over 100 workers while our new fishing fleet and fishing company has given employment to some 70 of our people.

In our sister isle of Carriacou over $1 million dollars is being spent in bringing electricity to the entire island and $264,000 has been laid out already this year for the continuing resurfacing of roads. In Petit Martinique a new $24,000 health centre is going up, the Marketing and Importing Board outset is expanding and an electrification project has just begun. All this, of course, means new jobs have been created for the people of Carriacou and Petit Martinique.

But, comrades, perhaps the most dramatic evidence of this stepped up economic activity can be seen in our massive road construction and resurfacing programme presently under way all over our country.

Under the auspices of the Ministry of Agriculture and the Productive Farmers Union, 32 miles of feeder roads have been laid with cliff sub-base since July, 1981 and another 20 miles will be prepared before this $2 million project is completed. Here alone 240 jobs have been created and valuable voluntary labour has been provided by patriotic farmers all over the country, who understand what these feeder roads would mean for opening up new lands to agricultural production.

But this is not the only feeder road project. In fact $7.5 million in funds provided by the Caribbean Development Bank will go towards the complete paving of 15½ miles of feeder roads in our agricultural parishes of St Andrew's and St David's. This project currently employs 56 workers, while 60 more have found employment on the $560,000 Westerhall Redgate project and the $300,000 Davey Project Road in St Patrick's.

Of course, not to be forgotten is the huge Eastern Main Road that by next year will link St George's to Grenville with a beautiful new highway. Over 100 of our people are now employed on this project.

And comrades, we can continue this list but time on this occasion does not allow for a lengthy catalogue. However, we cannot overlook at this time one particular project with direct bearing to the strengthening agriculture, the motor of our economy, and which is indicative of the Revolution's new thrust to create employment. I make mention of the La Sagesse Agricultural Training Centre which opened last week, with 50 students who will learn a wide range of agricultural sciences and ways of applying theory to practice in the service of increased production. At the end of this training these students will become workers in agricultural co-operatives and elsewhere in agriculture.

Plans are also under way to open three more such training centres which will teach 200 additional students by the end of this year, and which will bring 500 acres of productive land under cultivation as part of the practical application of the scientific skills acquired in the classroom.

Comrades, there is no doubt that the revolution has created jobs, and not just any job, but jobs that are directly productive, real jobs that produce goods and services, thousands of new jobs in three years. In fact, more jobs than were created in the first 9 years of the 1970s.

By the beginning of 1981, the total number of unemployed had fallen to about 28% of the work force. Thus jobs had been found for about 22% of those previously unemployed along with others who were just joining the labour force. So our successes in the field of employment have been impressive and unprecedented in the history of Grenada and the English-speaking Caribbean.

A Democratic Solution to Unemployment

But we must never rest on our victories. We must never grow complacent. The relentless struggle against unemployment continues.

So comrades, what is our way forward from here in the mighty task before us – to remove unemployment from our country. We have started a process which is democratic in nature, which will involve all of you here and thousands of other Grenadians. For in fighting and organising to end unemployment we shall be using centrally our democratic structures and mass organisations. They are our problem-solving infrastructures and our means of mass consultation, and just as they provided the organisational basis for the making of our People's Budget, so they shall form the structures through which we shall finish with unemployment. This is because we believe that people's participation is a must, is *essential* to solve the people's problems. If we attempted to solve unemployment by bureaucratic methods with no popular involvement, we are convinced not only then such a method would be wrong and unacceptable to our people *but that it would and could not work*, because the most important people in this entire venture – the unemployed themselves – would not be involved. So we are calling upon the mass organisations, the National Youth Organisation, the National Women's Organisation, the trade unions, the Productive Farmers' Union to be deeply and integrally a part of the vanguard in this national campaign against unemployment. Your members are involved in the problem. So it must be your task and responsibility to contribute towards finding the solution. We see it as your task primarily to help in the organisation of the unemployed, so that they can find work themselves with the backing of the mass organisations. We envisage that your members will seek to identify the possible areas of projects alongside your unemployed brothers and sisters as well as helping to mobilise support for projects already existing in their own villages or other parts of their areas. In addition, the mass organisations must assist their unemployed comrades in the formation of co-operatives, and lend their organisational expertise and experience to those comrades interested in the co-operative principle, but who are inexperienced in the actual day-to-day organisation, administration and maintenance work necessary for the planning and efficient running of such structures. The mass organisations must be firm and reliable means of support and infrastructure to the unemployed, must be there at all times to lend comradely help to the comrades' search for work. In particular, and here the role of the trade unions is especially paramount, our mass organisations must continue to encourage the unemployed comrades to gain as much *education and training* as they can obtain, as well as stimulate their own educational and training schemes, in order to increase the technical capacity of our unemployed to make them more *useful* future workers, as well as raising their general grasp of necessary agricultural and industrial skills — so that when they begin to work they will already have attributes and abilities that will make them more productive in the building of our production and economy.

The Role of the Private Sector

The private sector, too, has a significant role to play in this great challenge to finish with unemployment in our country. We hope and trust that they also, along with the mass organisations and Trade Unions, will keenly contribute their long experience and practised expertise to this vital process for our people and the future of all of us. At this stage in the development of our economy, it is generally true to say that our private sector has, over the years, achieved greater skill levels in economic and managerial organisation than we have presently in our public sector. Clearly, the brothers and sisters in the private sector are veterans in this respect, and have a lot to teach us and give us. They are in no way left out of our economic thrust and strategy, and we see them taking a crucial and responsible role in our present battle against unemployment, for we are on the same side. Within the ranks of the Private Sector many too are practitioners and businessmen with sympathisers and significant capabilities in raising and mobilising funds for schemes and investments that will create more jobs and thus create more production, and we welcome them into the heart of our strategy to cure our country of joblessness — for we are all doctors in this process. We can see, for example, in the area of garment manufacturing, how great a contribution is being made to fight unemployment by the private sector, for this particular industry is highly labour-intensive and is providing many jobs for our people — particularly our sisters, for as we have seen, our women are the principal sufferers from the disease of unemployment in our country. We feel strongly that similar strides could also be made by the private sector in the area of shoe-making, wood-working, furniture and food-processing — all of which would both cut down on our import bills and provide jobs for many of our people through direct production. So comrades from the private sector, we are asking for your contributions and your advice and suggestions, for you are and always have been, in the mainstream of creation in our country, and we would certainly want this to continue.

The Parents of Progress

So these are the basic points I wanted to make to you this morning comrades. As you continue in your crucial work, I am confirmed yet again in our Grenadian belief in collective consultation, collective discussions, collective wisdom which always emerges from assemblies such as these. For with so many proud, independent and free minds exchanging and combining, giving and receiving, criticising and deciding, *together and more together* every day, every week, every month, we are creating an intellectual and democratic unity which will form the basis of all our social activities and progress. For comrades, all of you are the parents of progress, the mothers and fathers of national development, and as such you are making our economy not only productive but also reproductive. With your insights, ideas and collective genius you will cause the birth of more jobs, more production, more wealth and carry our country forward to more happiness and freedom for all our people, whereby every Grenadian will be able to say: 'Look, I have a job. I am a producer for my country. I am a builder of Grenada, I am a constructor of a new land of courage, love, hope and productive achievement. I am a part of the new society we are all trying to build.'

15. Heirs of Marryshow

Address on Marryshow Day, 7 November
1982, St. George's, Grenada

The great Grenadian whom we are honouring today, in every sense of the word can be described as a genuine original. Our dear and veteran comrade, Cacademo Grant, who worked, organized and struggled side by side with this man, once had this to say about him: 'Marryshow was truly a great man, a man you would like to be near. Those of you who didn't live one day with Marryshow, then you didn't live a satisfactory life.' Comrades, T. Albert Marryshow is physically with us no longer, but his inspiration and example is something we must invoke every day of our lives, his undying commitment and love for the people of *his* and *our* Caribbean must burn in us continually, his presence must always be inside us and alongside us. In this way, remembering our brother Cacademo's words, we can at least begin to lead satisfactory lives, — lives, like that of Marryshow, that give everything to our people.

Why is the memory and example of T.A. Marryshow so vital for us now in Grenada, and now throughout the Caribbean region? It is because Marryshow was the creator of a tradition, a set of principles and attitudes that since March 13th, 1979 we have struggled to implement, consolidate and extend. In a sense, of course, Marryshow, himself was also the inheritor of a great tradition. He grew from the earth of Fedon, a great revolutionary who fused the humanism and hatred of tyranny sweeping from the French masses in 1789 by way of the great Haitian upsurge, with the fury of the rebel slave ground down in his own island by slavery and British colonialism. The huge courage of Fedon and his comrades in 1795 gave birth to Marryshow in 1887, and perhaps we should note that almost a century divided them, and that Marryshow's birth in 1887 was in fact almost the mid-point in time between Fedon's Revolution and our Revolution. So in every sense, comrades, he was also a continuer, a link, a great bridge between two massive blows at imperialism.

This great son of our soil was also a son of the working people, born just a stone's throw from here in Lucas Street in St George's. There was nothing special about his birth, he inherited no money or property, his only inheritance was that great fighting tradition of Fedon that runs in the blood of every Grenadian. Alongside his great contemporary, Tubal Uriah Buzz Butler, he lit the way for all of us present in this commemoration in his honour tonight. Apprenticed to a carpenter, he later shifted trades and became a compositor and then a trainee printer. But Marryshow soon found that his love for words and writing was uncontrollable, and as a teenager he turned to the tool and weapon that was going to serve the Caribbean people and cause them to marvel at him and admire him for the rest of his days — his pen.

The Man and His Pen

Here was a man of complete eloquence, whose power of speech was only matched by his power with the written word. As he levelled his pen at them, colonial administrators and governors who had sat behind the most expensive desks in England and idled their way through Oxford and Cambridge universities through right of birth, quaked and trembled. And yet Marryshow had no university education, not even a secondary school education. He learned to read and write without the benefit of electricity, he had no money to buy books, he had no access to vast libraries, bookshops or museums. He learned his brilliance from the streets of St George's and the great hills and forests of our beloved Grenada. He studied the hearts and hopes of his people.

His first great influence was the man whose newspaper he began to work for at the age of 17 years in 1904 — William Galway Donovan, the editor of the *Federalist and Grenada People*. And what a fantastic combination that was! Here was W.G. Donovan, half black Grenadian and inheritor of Fedon's mighty struggle, half Irishman, and inheritor of Wolfe Tone, of O'Connell, of the Fenians and the great Irish rebels and republicans, who like the Caribbean people had spent centuries trying to free themselves from the British colonial stranglehold and who are still fighting, up until now! And here was Donovan and his paper, which in its very title, was articulating the great dream of Marryshow — a united, federal Caribbean, *one* Caribbean, one indivisible people. Again comrades, the more we look at our history, the more we see the connections we have with the rest of the struggling people of the world, the more we realise our destiny remains integral with the fortunes of the oppressed of the world.

And Marryshow more than anyone before him realised this and expressed this. By 1909, at the age of 22 he was editor of the *St George's Chronicle and Grenada Gazette*, and by 1915 he had helped found *The West Indian*, and stayed as editor of that pioneering journal for nearly twenty years, headlining on *every single* issue the slogan that was to be his watchwords for the rest of his fighting life! *THE WEST INDIES MUST BE WEST INDIAN!* And yet his unquestionable commitment to the Caribbean did not make him simply a regionalist. In 1917, he wrote a ferocious and historic attack on the racist state of South Africa, in his *Cycles of Civilisation*. And never forget that at this time there was no world-wide movement against Apartheid, no United Nations, no great cluster of independent African States to support him. The man he was attacking, General Jan Smuts, one of the early architects of the emerging Apartheid state, was seen by the ruling class of the British Empire as an important ally, and bastion of the Empire, and Marryshow's great defence of the African people came in the middle of the 1914-18 imperialist war, when millions upon millions of people from all over the world were uselessly dying.

Such words from an impertinent, unknown black man in an outpost of the empire would have been seen as treason. And yet none of this deterred Marryshow, man of Grenada, man of the Caribbean, man of the rising world, from his defence of justice and truth, and his undaunted assault on all things racist, oppressive and inhuman. In fact, in 1917, when the pillars of the ancient order were being torn down in Soviet Russia and when Lenin was directing the Russian masses to storm the palaces of the Tzar, T.A. Marryshow was sitting writing words in a small island in the Eastern Caribbean, a forgotten and remote part of the British Empire. And the words pouring out from the great Grenadian's pen read like an extraordinary prophecy of what has happened in Ghana, in Mozambique, in Angola, in Guinea Bissau, in Libya, Zimbabwe, in Cuba and Grenada – and what will storm through South Africa and Namibia in the months and years that are approaching.

Here are his words written in 1917 after he had heard and read about the great events taking place in Russia in 1917, a revolution which took place exactly 30 years after Marryshow's own birth:

> Africa! it is Africa's direct turn. Sons of New Ethiopia scattered all over the world, should determine that there should be new systems of the distributions of opportunities, privileges and rights, so that Africa shall rid herself of many of the murderous highwaymen of Europe who have plundered her, raped her and left her hungry and naked in the broad light of the boasted European civilisation. Africa would then be free again to rise her head among the races of the earth and enrich humanity as she has done before . . .

Comrades, thus spoke Grenada in 1917. Thus speaks Grenada in 1982.

Man of the Caribbean, Man of the World

T.A. Marryshow never forgot the rest of the world as he spent his life struggling for a united Caribbean. In his own words, he was an enemy of the old style bramble politics, or as he called 'parish pump politics', and his anti-parochialism was manifested in his ceaseless struggles to unite the Caribbean, culturally and politically. As founder and President of the *Grenada Working Men's Association* formed in 1911, he became a prominent figure in Caribbean Labour Organisations, and his evergy and commitment was instrumental in setting up the *Caribbean Labour Congress*. As president of this body in 1946 he persuaded it to take a supportive stand on the Federation. In every forum in which he participated he condemned the political tribalism that put territory against territory and one section of working people against another. It made no sense to him, he saw it as reactionary and foolish – his whole life was dedicated to unifying and bringing together all of his people, who had been scattered and separated by the interests of British imperialism.

In 1921 he travelled to London, using his own money and under his own initiative. He sought out the colonial office, marched in with all the dignity and independence that marked his entire character, and brought his eloquence to bear on the men behind the desks at the hub of Empire. At that time, the legislative councils of the Caribbean islands – with the exception of Barbados and Jamaica – had no *elected* members, and were all appointed by the British governor. Marryshow spoke not only for Grenada, *not only for his own island but for the entire unfranchised Caribbean.* As a result of his reasoning and argumentation, achieved without pleading or begging, the Wood Commission came to the Caribbean, and as a direct consequence of Marryshow's mission, a measure of representative government was achieved not only for Grenada, but also for the other Windward islands, the Leewards *and* Trinidad.

And it is important to remember, as Book I of our locally written CPE Adult Education Reader reminds us, that this historic victory of representative government for our region came as a direct result of dozens of years of struggles by T.A. Marryshow dating back to his formation in 1917 of the Grenada Representative Government Association.

The creation of a representative section of the legislative council meant that T.A. Marryshow became the elected member for St George's and stayed in that seat for 33 tireless, brilliant and self-sacrificing years, until his death in 1958. He had struck a great blow for democracy throughout the Caribbean, and given the people a foot in the door of freedom, a door which was to be thrown open fully on March 13th, 1979 by the struggles of our people. But of course, the emphasis of his public and political life was firmly upon creating a structure of regional unity, which found expression in his vision of *FEDERATION.* It was a noble, democratic vision which sought to re-integrate a divided people to bind our islands together in one fraternal, united mainland. From 1929 when he attended the first regional conference on regional integration in Barbados, through the years until the West Indies Conference of the Caribbean Commission in St Kitts in 1946 and the Montego Bay Conference in 1947, Marryshow personified Caribbean oneness, he was in himself the symbol and dynamo of unity, the 'Father of Federation'. In 1953, he was the advisor to the Federal Conference in London, and played an integral role in the Planning Conference for Federation in Jamaica in 1957. In 1958, when what had been just a compelling idea in his brain became a political reality and he himself became one of his country's two federal senators to the Federal Parliament, he could only utter the unforgettable words – 'This is my dream come true. Today, I am member of that august body that I dreamed into existence.'

The Marryshow Standard

Marryshow died in the same year, 1958, and over his bones grew division, faintheartedness and a withdrawal to insularity. Suddenly there was no Marryshow to heal these wounds and bind the parts of the whole together once more. And so, comrades, we have to continue his unfinished work, to bring together again everything that was lost. That is not a mere sentimental or nostalgic gesture for us in Grenada, it is a part of our blood, ours mixed with Fedon's, mixed with Butler's, mixed with Marryshow's. It is a part of the responsibility of the tradition handed down to us, part of the task passed to us from the giants of our history who have laid the foundations for us and our progress.

For when we consider Marryshow, we see an extraordinary man who grew from the ordinary earth that we all share. In a way, we can see him as the *most ordinary* of men who grew from the most ordinary of backgrounds. And yet this working class boy of St George's became the greatest journalist and prose stylist of his age, became the founder of our country's first labour movement, became in himself the standard of honesty, integrity and truth. One of the greatest singers of his generation, the mighty Paul Robeson, told him his voice was one of the most magnificent he had ever heard; that he should become a professional singer. His poetry was compared to that of the great black American, Paul Lawrence Dunbar. He was a sportsman, a humourist, a democrat and a struggler for human progress: and perhaps the nearest to a complete human being that our region has ever produced.

He was not only a firm anti-colonialist, he also firmly refused to compromise his principles regardless of the consequences, a quality which always got him into the bad books of the British colonialists. In fact, up to 1921, the British never called his name but only referred to him as 'this dangerous radical.' And what a nice compliment that was! This strong kind of principle continued right through his life.

During the late 1940s the colonial system was challenged by a worldwide struggle which campaigned for placing all colonies under the rule of the League of Nations (later to become the United Nations). The British therefore elaborated a scheme to get the West Indian colonies to say to the UN that they wanted to remain with Britain instead of obtaining independence. In pursuance of this trickery and deception, the British requested Marryshow to go to The Hague in Holland to read such a statement for them. Of course, Marryshow with his customary courage and uncompromising attitude to colonialism, bluntly refused, and so it fell to Grentley Adams to go before the Security Council to try to make out the British case that West Indian countries wanted to stay as colonies.

And so comrades, in honouring and remembering him yet again tonight and as we do on this date every year, what does his message from the past bring us at this present moment, how is he speaking to us now? He is demonstrating to us and telling us a standard, that we, as Grenadians and Caribbean people, must seek to emulate. If we pause and examine ourselves and our

Revolution by the Marryshow standard, we can, of course, find many places where we have fallen short, but we can also find other places where we are proud to have touched him. We know he would have approved of our declaration in the early hours of March 13th, 1979 that our Revolution, 'is for work, for food, for decent housing and health services, and for a bright future for our children and grandchildren.' He devoted his own life to those things, and we were merely carrying on his concerns and those of Fedon and Butler. We felt his closeness on July 14 and 15 of 1979 when we hosted the Grenada Summit and conferred with the Prime Ministers of St Lucia and Dominica. His same spirit of Caribbean solidarity was present at that meeting, when all three Prime Ministers spoke of the creation of one, united Caribbean, and when it was decided that travel restrictions between our islands would be eased, and in the future between our shores, passports would be irrelevances. T.A. Marryshow was with us when we signed the Declaration of St George's, telling the region that we would erase the traces of colonialism in our countries and move *forward together in a non-aligned policy* towards peace and progress. And his spirit travelled with us to Lusaka in Zambia a month later. Following his example of a rejection of parochialism and national selfishness, we spoke not only for ourselves, but also for Zimbabwe's independence and for all small island states, not only in the Caribbean, but throughout the Commonwealth, the islands of the Pacific, the Atlantic, the Indian Ocean and any other small national territory like ourselves which had been set apart by both geography and imperialism. We asked that there should be more assistance for states like ours from the bigger and richer Commonwealth countries to give us free access to their markets, that they offer us greater financial help with less debt traps, that they create a Basic Needs Fund for the small island states, that they help us to be more self-sufficient in our energy supplies, and less dependent upon their oil by giving us the technical assistance to help us discover our own energy sources.

Not Only For Ourselves

Comrades, we spoke not only of Grenada and for Grenada. We wanted nothing for ourselves that our neighbours and brothers and sisters in the neighbouring islands couldn't enjoy too. We have never said that only Grenada matters because for us that would be impossible as the heirs of Marryshow, Fedon and Butler. We have always believed and still believe that what is good for us is also good for the entire Caribbean, although we would never force our view on our sister islands. But, we know, we all suffer from the same underdevelopment, the same scars of colonialism, the same trade imbalance, the same exploitation by the transnational corporations that try to suck us dry. And so, what we labour to find for ourselves, we shall labour to find for the rest of the Caribbean.

And the fact is that three years after the Lusaka Conference the mighty presence of Marryshow still accompanies us when we travel around the world to seek assistance, co-operation and friends and allies, who will help us without trying to dictate to us. When Comrade Coard was in London last month at the Commonwealth Finance Ministers' Conference, we saw the same pattern, the same insistence that Grenada fights for the entire Caribbean, that we saw with Marryshow's lone journey to London in 1921. There we spoke out for all small island states in the manner of Marryshow. We proposed that the Commonwealth appoint a panel of experts to conduct a special survey of the problems of small island states, recognising that over half of the nations of the Commonwealth fall inside this category – including Grenada, St Lucia, Barbados, the Seychelles, Tonga, Kiribati, Ascension Island, Bermuda, the Bahamas, Montserrat and St Vincent. Comrade Coard, like Marryshow of old, was fighting for all these countries, battling to secure more favourable repayment periods from the International Monetary Fund in Toronto a few days later, fighting to improve the situation of our small farmers and their counterparts right through our Caribbean, Marryshow's Caribbean.

T.A. Marryshow was with us too comrades, when we were in Paris a few weeks ago, inspiring us in our conversations with President Mitterand of France. We could feel his joy when the generosity the French government was expressed in substantial aid from their Fund For Aid and Co-operation, secured *not only for us*, but for six of our closest neighbours too. This was the *first time* ever this fund had reached out towards the Eastern Caribbean, being normally directed to former French colonies and the Portuguese-speaking nations of Africa. As this month's *Caribbean Contact* declares and acknowledges:

> Several million dollars' worth of economic aid will start trickling into the Eastern Caribbean early next year as part of the effort by France's new Socialist government to step up its aid to the Third World. This bonanza will be largely thanks to Grenada!

And we could add not only thanks to the Grenada of today but thanks to the Marryshow tradition, for we are simply carrying on his work, his sustaining love for the Caribbean – and not by words alone, for indeed Marryshow was a man of magnificent words, but every word was matched with a deed, with a real, concrete action. He did not simply compose elegant sentences and write emotional poems to Caribbean unity. He lived that unity, worked tirelessly for it, travelled oceans and continents to bring it nearer and finally, if only temporarily, he helped to bring it about. That is our way too comrades, our tradition, our commitment. And that is what we pledge to continue and consolidate on this day, the day when we remember Marryshow.

Unite or Perish

Comrades, like Marryshow, we recognise the strength and necessity of workers' organisations and have promoted their regeneration and re-invigoration by scrapping all the dictator's anti-trade union laws and giving the choice to all workers to join which trade union they please.

And Marryshow was also a great housebuilder. Next time you walk along the Carenage look at those houses next to the Empire Cinema. And next time you walk along Tyrrel Street watch the houses opposite the University of the West Indies centre — they are the houses that Marryshow built, workers' houses, and for just three dollars a month for twelve years, the houses were theirs!

Think what Marryshow would have done with our Sandino Plant, with our pre-fabricated houses from the government of Venezuela, with the no-interest loans of our House Repair Programme! We built them in the spirit of Marryshow. He promoted sports for all, like the Revolution does and he built parks. He was cheering with us in Tanteen when our Netball sisters played like lionesses this August, and he will be singing with our National Performing Company as they tour the USA right now and during the next month and he will undoubtedly soon be laying the bricks of our House of Culture.

And because he loved beauty, culture and sport, Marryshow was a man of peace. He knew that *peace* is the ideal of every working person. He was with Comrade Louison in La Paz, Bolivia, at the OAS conference when we first put forward our determination that the Caribbean shall be, and must be, a *zone of peace*, when we articulated the principle of ideological pluralism and friendship and co-operation between all nations of the Caribbean and of the wider world. He would have understood our concept of the *wider Caribbean*, that languages and national boundaries and the different identities of the ex-colonial powers must never be factors that separate the *one people* of the Caribbean Basin, whether they are from the Bahamas or Suriname or Jamaica, from Mexico, Panama, Nicaragua or El Salvador, from Curacao, Haiti or Cuba, from Guatemala or Grenada — one people, one history, one Caribbean nation!

Tonight we remember comrades, what Marryshow's mentor, W.G. Donovan inscribed upon his newspaper, something that reached right through Marryshow and came directly to our Revolution, the remarkable words — '*Better a naked freeman, than a gilded slave.*' Tonight as we remember these words, we also remember that just as we do not interfere in the internal affairs of other nations, so we will accept no bullying, no intimidation, no interference, no bribery, no blackmail or whitemail from any person or government. We are certain that if Marryshow and Donovan could look around this meeting tonight and through the villages of our own country, and certainly be confident that they see no gilded slaves in Free Grenada! Only free men, free women, free children in our small island, a world of freedom.

A Vital Upcoming Period

Comrades, the next three weeks will be vital for us. We have over one hundred activities leading up to Bloody Sunday, two major regional conferences here in Grenada, and the meetings of the heads of the Organisation of Eastern Caribbean States and the heads of the CARICOM states. And as we know the existence of these regional structures in themselves owe a huge amount to the vision and lifetime's work of Marryshow, which makes them of particular significance to us, as there is undoubtedly a huge amount to be done to carry on Marryshow's work.

For us in the People's Revolutionary Government, the continuation of Marryshow's visionary work is the priority for these meetings — to boldly extend and sustain his efforts, to build on his foundations, to make these meetings genuinely *meaningful* to the lives of the poor and working people of our Caribbean. We are not going to cuss or fight any other nation; we are going with our heads and hearts open to build upon our history, like Marryshow went to Barbados in 1929, like he went to St Kitt in 1946 and Montego Bay in 1947. We go to St Lucia and Jamaica in 1982 to continue Marryshow's work, to find real answers to the massive problems facing our people.

What can we do *as a Caribbean people* to help our farmers sell their products? What can we do *as a Caribbean people* to develop much more just and equitable terms of trade with the European countries? What can we do as *a Caribbean people* to secure better prices for our cocoa, our bananas, our nutmegs — or our arrowroot, our sugar or our bauxite? How can we bring closer the New International Economic Order? How can we begin to control the massive imperialist cultural onslaught on our people's minds and consciousness? We shall be recommending plans to develop a regional maritime transport system, recalling the days when we had the *Federal Maple* and the *Federal Palm* plying between our islands.

We Shall Defend UWI

We shall be resolutely defending our regional university, the University of the West Indies, arguing that it must stay intact for the benefit of all Caribbean people, as it is a part of our Marryshow inheritance that we cherish and hold dearly. We shall be putting forward proposals for much greater cultural and sporting interchanges. We shall be recommending ways of promoting much deeper friendship and understanding between our people, and putting forward a policy of bulk-buying of certain expensive imported goods for the region, so that we can collectively cut our import bills and ease strain on all our budgets.

In other words comrades, we are approaching these meetings in the Marryshow tradition, with positive, unifying proposals. We want nothing to do with sectarianism, conspiracies or cliques, we want an agenda which serves our people, the Caribbean people, and confronts and seeks to resolve their multiplicity of problems. We remember the words of the man whose life and work we are celebrating today:

> A West Indies in a world like this must unite or perish. This is not the time for parish pump politics. We must think nobly, nationally, with special regard for the first fundamentals of a West Indian unity, and a West Indian identity.

Comrades, we go to St Lucia and Jamaica with these words ringing clearly in our minds.

The Intellectual Worker

As you know comrades, for you have been at many openings and public sessions — Free Grenada has been the venue of many Caribbean conferences. We have had conferences of Caribbean workers, Caribbean and American lawyers, Caribbean trade unionists, Caribbean journalists, just to name a few. Later this month we shall be hosting two more regional conferences. One will be the first ever international conference to be held in our sister island of Carriacou, on the subject of Education and Production, in which we aim to demonstrate the excellence of Camp Carriacou as a Conference Centre, while emphasising the meaning behind our slogan, that *Education is Production too!* The other is a conference of Caribbean Intellectual Workers, some of the most remarkable and talented people of our region, who will come together here in Grenada to discuss and affirm the cultural sovereignty of the Caribbean.

Historically, intellectuals, or what we used to know as the 'intelligentsia' — authors, journalists, artists, poets, and scholars — have seen themselves as alienated, apart from the ordinary working people of region. As such, they tended to distance themselves from the people's struggles, living abroad or in ivory towers of dreams and sheer individualism. This conference is designed to help to create intellectual workers out of intellectuals, to form a policy and a plan of action that will make cultural and intellectual work, in the words of one of the conference's organisers, the brilliant Barbadian novelist George Lamming, 'an essential part of the lives of all our people'. We shall be host to many outstanding minds and imaginations: from Michael Manley of Jamaica to the great Caribbean poet, Martin Carter of Guyana, from Paul Keens-Douglas to the Minister of Culture of Nicaragua, Ernesto Cardenal, from Trevor Farrell to George Beckford and Don Robotham, from the 1982 Nobel prize winner for literature, Gabriel Garcia Marquez of Colombia, to the legendary Harry Belafonte who was last here 1955. Scarcely have so many extraordinary Caribbean people come together for such an event, and comrades, they are coming together in Free and Revolutionary Grenada!

So earlier on this evening we formed a *Committee of Grenadian Intellectuals*, which will formulate its own programme and proposals for bringing

177

the Arts, all aspects of National Culture, and scholarship, closer to our people, so that intellectual work stands beside manual and productive work and takes us towards the same ends and objectives: the full economic, social and political emancipation of our people, and a way of life which imitates none, which mimics none, which is slave to none, but which reflects the originality and genius of our struggling people and our developing nation. Thus our intellectuals, like our workers, farmers and fishermen, will be producers too, and catalysts in creating and reflecting a new life for our people, as well as guardians of our culture who ensure that the imperialist cancer cannot penetrate and destroy the new values and definitions we are building for ourselves through our own unique process.

A Very Special Day

Without doubt, today is a special day in many ways. It is the day of T.A. Marryshow, but it is also a day in which we also remember great events and other gigantic people. Today is the 65th Anniversary of the Great October Socialist Revolution, that epoch-making event in Russia in 1917, which has paved the way for so many enormous changes, not only for the Soviet people, but for the entire world. In 1917, as Marryshow wrote his *Cycles of Civilisation*, he knew of the massive blow struck against backwardness and tyranny in Russia. Listen to Marryshow as he expressed his joy in his unforgettable language and style as he beheld the triumph for the masses of St Petersburg and Moscow an ocean and a continent away. 'A great spirit of Democracy and Socialism is coming to do God's work of levelling up and levelling down.'

Today, we also commemorate Palestine Liberation Day, and we are happy to have a Palestinian comrade with us, who has given us the latest information of the heroic struggles of their people against the murderous Zionist aggression backed up to the cowardly hilt by US imperialism. We can hardly find words to express our shock and shame at the barbarous forces that massacred your people in Beirut. We mourned with you for the loss of your innocent lives but we also clench firmly our Caribbean fists to fight on with you. We can only say that your agony was also our agony, but that your certain and inevitable victory and joy will also be ours.

Our Party, our People's Revolutionary Government, and our Free people are with you. Last month we marched through our streets in solidarity with you, and one day, just as you are visiting free and revolutionary Grenada, we shall be visiting you in free and revolutionary Palestine.

Our Culture is Our Dignity

Comrades, in our presentation this evening we have truly traversed the world. In dealing with Marryshow, this is inevitable, because of his worldliness, his universal vision. But let me end by saying that his day, Marryshow Day, will from this year, also be known as *National Day of Culture* in our country. Marryshow, as we have noted, was a cultured man, and a true forerunner of the organized intellectual who strives to use his brain, his art, his scholarship to serve his people. He would have been the first to sponsor and take part in the intellectual conference on culture and sovereignty we are hosting later this month. For our culture is how we live, how we produce, what we grow, how we make our democracy and freedom, how we change and transform our earth, how we organise our hopes, dreams and aspirations, how we love one another. And how, as we change the world, we are changed ourselves, into new men, new women, new Caribbean people.

The great man once said and it was on March 13th that he said it, comrades, as if he already knew what that would mean for us. March 13th 1950, in the Market Square where have had so many of our own meetings:

> From earliest times I had thought in terms of human dignity, that a man no matter how poor could lift himself and become somebody in the world. I read avidly in my youth, and the quotation: 'I never did believe, nor do I now believe that Providence ordained one set of men, spurred to ride and the others saddled to be ridden', had a profound influence and inspired me!

Our culture is our dignity, the dignity the Revolution has brought us and the dignity it sustains in us. We are sovereigns of our dignity, of *our pride in being we*, and we are proud of our consistent victory over the forces that try to make us their imitators, their mimics and their puppets. Our Revolution has put on the agenda of the Caribbean people a new way, a new view of ourselves, a new determination in our destiny. For this we thank and honour T.A. Marryshow, the Prince of West Indian journalists, the father of the West Indian Federation, the oldest statesman of West Indies, and all those Caribbean masses, our ancestors and their ancestors, that have brought us to the freedom of being what we are and being what we are, determined we shall be, and determined we shall walk in a conscious, organised, productive and united way along the glorious new path that will bring peace, happiness, justice and social progress to all of our free and patriotic people.

16. One Caribbean!

Address at Rally to Commemorate Bloody
Sunday, Seamoon, St. Andrews, Grenada, 21
November 1982

In the name of our Party, our government and free people I welcome you all
to this 9th commemoration of Bloody Sunday, and I would like you to welcome and recognise all of our distinguished guests who have joined us on this
occasion.

In 1979, the first year of the Revolution, when we commemorated Bloody
Sunday, we made the tremendously historic announcement that the International Airport Project, which had been a dream for over 30 years, was
about to start with the assistance of revolutionary Cuba.

Today, comrades, we can record with pride, and considerable satisfaction
that in spite of imperialism's desperate efforts to stop the construction of our
International Airport, the project nonetheless continues to proceed on stream
and reasonably on time.

Today we have already completed filling up Hardy Bay and have even
started to pave a section of what used to be Hardy Bay. Our Terminal
Building has begun to go up and in 1983 it will be finished, while fuel storage
tanks with a capacity of 1½ million gallons are being constructed and should
also be completed in 1983. The new access road to the International Airport
is already under way and by 1983 that too will be finished. Only last week we
signed a contract for the communications equipment — the navigational aid,
the radar and all the other important equipment we will need to ensure
that the airport proceeds on time.

You may recall, comrades, that last year when we commemorated Bloody
Sunday, we announced that 44 million dollars had been found to ensure that
the project would continue on stream throughout 1982 and beyond.

Foreign Friends With Us Again

At last year's Bloody Sunday commemorations, we had a number of distinguished delegates, guests and friends from overseas who were here for the
3rd Caribbean Workers' Seminar, the biggest of the three held to date, and for
our first International Solidarity Conference when over 112 people from 41
countries and from all 5 continents of the world came to show support for
our process and to be with us on Bloody Sunday 1981.

It is with a deep sense of pride and satisfaction that we can look around us on this platform today and once again see so many friends, who have come to attend two more significant conferences being hosted by our country – the *Caribbean Conference of Intellectual and Cultural Workers* which started yesterday and which has tremendous significance for developing the cultural aspirations of our region's people, and starting in Carriacou tomorrow afternoon, the conference on Education and Production, which will look at Grenada and the Caribbean's work/study experience. We certainly look forward with great anticipation to the deliberations and results of these two major conferences.

Comrades, today, we have with us a comrade who has been serving his own people and the people of the world in a major crusade for peace, a comrade of great artistic talent who has put his career on the line, who stands with firm principle, who has the courage of his convictions, an unparalleled internationalist, a major figure on the international stage – welcome once again to Free Grenada Comrade Harry Belafonte.

Also, comrades please recognise the representative from a sister nation, which like ourselves achieved its freedom, and its liberation in 1979 only some three months after we had done so. Welcome once again the fraternal representative from revolutionary Nicaragua, Comrade Ernesto Cardenal.

I want to also acknowledge the presence of Comrade Dudley Thompson of Jamaica, Comrade George Lamming, outstanding novelist, Comrade Asad Schuman, Minister of Health of fraternal Belize, Comrade Edward Lamb, all of the delegates and all of our guests from our Caribbean sister nations who are here with us, many of whom have come to Grenada on several occasions and who therefore are absolutely no strangers to our free people.

The Intellectuals Conference

Comrades, we believe that this *Conference of Caribbean Intellectual and Cultural Workers* is of historic importance because of the major issues that the delegates have been focussing on; such as the critical question of the communications media, of the success of planning and politics and how they all relate to the general question of sovereignty and of cultural sovereignty, in particular.

These are critical questions for our people and for the people of the region and we are convinced that the answers they will come up with will greatly assist the people of our region and will ensure the responsibility of intellectual workers in serving all our people.

We have had a particularly significant experience with our own intellectual workers. We have seen during the budget exercise this year, for example, the tremendous role that our own intellectuals, our top technicians, our leading managers of state enterprises can play in helping to lift the consciousness of our people.

We have also seen how in going out among the people and talking to them

181

at the Zonal and Village Councils, these intellectuals themselves were able to benefit from that experience. In Grenada we certainly need no convincing that intellectual workers have a major role to play in helping to build the people's consciousness, and through regular contact with the masses ensure that their own consciousness is advanced.

The Education Conference

The Education and Production conference, which starts in Carriacou tomorrow, is also a conference for all the people of our region because its main focus is the question of integrating work and study, so that education may become more relevant. The work/study approach means that the people benefit in a meaningful way from the education which they receive, so that when they come out of this school system they will be able and ready to face the real world and to make a contribution to production, to building the economy, our democracy and our Revolution.

Education: A Major Area of Focus

The Education and Production conference, therefore, has tremendous strategic value for us. Education after all has been and continues to be one fo the major areas of focus of our Revolution. That is why in the first few months we embarked on this wide-ranging campaign to wipe out illiteracy in our country. That is why today in the second phase of that programme, our Centre for Popular Education is now embarking on Adult Education in the evenings on a voluntary basis.

That is why, comrades, we are ensuring that more day care, day nursery and pre-primary facilities, and more primary and secondary schools are being constructed in our country, so that more and more of our people will have the opportunity of receiving the benefits of an education.

That is why the number of children in secondary schools has moved from 11% before the Revolution to some 35% more after the Revolution.

That is why so much time and effort is spent on ensuring that the teachers in our country are trained to provide a scientific education to our children. That is why the ratio of teachers to students was reduced so dramatically, from one teacher to every 51 students before the Revolution to 1 teacher for every 30 students today.

And that is also why so many of our students now, once they have gained the necessary qualifications are able to walk into free university scholarships, which moved from a figure of some three in the last year of the Gairy dictatorship to over 109 in the first six months of our Revolution, to over 300 today.

The CARICOM Conference

But comrades, the main focus of our Bloody Sunday commemoration today must be a report to the people of our nation on the CARICOM conference which turned out to be a massive, resounding victory for the government and people of Grenada.

It is absolutely correct, comrades, that every single one of the objectives which we had set ourselves before we went off to Jamaica for the conference was fully accomplished.

The Hunters Became the Hunted

It is also true that those people who had set themselves up as hunters before the conference, became the hunted during the conference.

Those who had hoped to be the prosecutors of Grenada, became the prosecuted. And this was not done through any wild actions on the part of our delegation which included comrade Unison Whiteman, our Foreign Minister, and Comrade Chris De Riggs, our Minister of Health. It was simply because we had agreed from weeks ago in discussing our preparations for this conference that all we needed to do was to take a sober and steady course, to rely on truthfulness, honesty, firmness and principle and not opportunism.

We had decided not to allow ourselves to be side-tracked into any mud-slinging matches with the agents of imperialism, not to be drowned by any kites or red herrings whch were being flown, not to get involved in any divisiveness but instead to concentrate and focus on the issues, on the concerns and real needs of the people of our Caribbean.

And that plan of ours was outlined in Suriname for the first time during our visit some weeks ago, and repeated at a delegates' NWO meeting, on Marryshow night in Grenada, at the Organization of Eastern Caribbean States heads of government meeting in St Lucia and repeated further on several occasions in different press statements and press conferences before the Jamaica summit. We were confident that all we had to do was to stick to that plan.

We know that this question of trying to isolate Grenada and pretending that Grenada had a human rights problem was not a question on the minds of the people of the Caribbean. We knew that if all of these so-called 'free' newspapers, the Guardians and the Gleaners and the rest of them, had taken the trouble and the pain to go out to the people of the Caribbean and to conduct a poll among the people, that even if they asked 500 questions not one of the answers would have shown that the people of the Caribbean were against us here in Grenada. This is why these elements can never isolate the Grenada Revolution because the people of the Caribbean stand with the Grenada Revolution and what we are trying to do.

The Caribbean People's Real Concerns

The people of the Caribbean were and still are clearly concerned about the question of jobs. They want to know how it is that so many of them are out of jobs, how every week a few hundred more of them are losing jobs.

They want to know how it is that even in their own countries where there are elections and so much talk of free this and free that and free the other, that every week when they are being dismissed that not even the trade unions are allowed to come to their defence because laws are passed in some of these countries ensuring that workers have no rights.

Comrades, the people of the Caribbean are concerned about this international capitalist crisis which causes the prices of our goods to keep dropping every day: sugar, cocoa, nutmegs, bananas, arrowroot and bauxite.

They want to understand how come our goods keep falling in price but yet every week when we buy items such as cars, trucks, tractors, food in cans, fertiliser and so on, all of the things that we do not produce, those prices keep going up.

Our Caribbean people are looking for answers to these questions. They want to know hwo they could maintain closer contact with each other.

We have found in every Caribbean country this great desire and appetite to travel to different islands. But yet the price is so prohibitive that very few of our sisters and brothers are able ever to leave their own islands.

Comrades, consider that in 1970 the cost of an airline ticket to Dominica was somewhere under $200;* today the cost is some $550, another $60 in tax and about another $90 in taxi fare. So to go from Dominica to Grenada today will cost about $700 and our people want to know what can we do to solve this problem. How can we ensure that our people maintain contact with each other? What creative ways can we find of reducing this high cost of travel? Can we, for example, get hold of *Federal Palm* and *Federal Maple* type boats once again and in this way ensure cheaper inter-island travel?

The questions of sporting contacts, of greater cultural exchanges, of more training opportunities are what the Caribbean masses had and have on their minds. And that is why during the conference we raised these questions. We presented documents trying to focus on these issues. We tried to ensure that whenever contributions were made on our side those contributions were aimed at strengthening and deepening the regional integration movement, not disintegrating it.

We tried to focus on the issues and areas where we could ensure greater co-operation among the countries of CARICOM in the interests and for the benefit of the people in the CARICOM region. We tried to look at concrete ways in which collectively we could prepare ourselves better before we go out there to international conferences. We tried to focus on ways in which together we can bulk-buy a number of key items like drugs and goods that the people of the region need.

* These prices are quoted in Eastern Caribbean currency

Firm Mind and Clean Conscience

We tried to focus on relevant and practical areas of co-operation. And it was with this understanding, sisters and brothers, that we faced our antagonists at the conference. And we confronted them too with the conviction that coming out of the great tradition of Marryshow and Butler, no Grenadian representative could ever sink to the depths of trying to destroy CARICOM. We went to Jamaica with a clear conscience, with a firmness of mind and purpose and with the deep conviction that the people of Jamaica and the Caribbean would be ready for our message and that message we were going to deliver.

And so, sisters and brothers, comrades, the attempt to isolate and discredit our country failed miserably. The attempt to throw us out of CARICOM failed miserably. The attempt to pretend that there was an issue of human rights violations in Grenada got a lot of licks. Tom Adams' attempt to amend the treaty was hit for six. The attempt to foist the narrow bourgeois view of human rights upon the people of the region didn't just get a six, it got a twelve!

Our delegation's plans to support and to propose steps to strengthen the practical co-operation among the people of the region received widespread support. Our plan to ensure that CARICOM survived was also massively successful. Our intention of ensuring that whatever else happened among the people of Jamaica and the region, that we preserved the image and reputation of our Revolution was another massive success.

We can say comrades, in all truthfulness, with the greatest sincerity and honesty that, in fact, the CARICOM conference was a massive victory for us. But today as we stand here commemorating Bloody Sunday, what is more important than just simply saying we had a successful conference is to say also that apart from being a success for the people of Grenada and the Grenada Revolution, the women, the youth, the farmers, the workers, the broad masses of Caribbean people were victorious also.

A Victory for Principle

Our victory was a victory for principle over opportunism, for the forces of progress over the forces of reaction and imperialism, for the concerns of the people and not the concerns of a tiny minority ruling clique living in the capital of imperialism. Our victory, comrades, was a victory for the human rights of the majority of our people in the Caribbean — the poor and working people — and a defeat for the human rights of a minority that continues to exploit that majority.

It has to be seen, therefore, that what was being waged, in Jamaica this past week was a major political and ideological struggle. When you consider who were Adams and Seaga fighting for? Who were these people pushing a case for? Whose interests were they defending? When you ask these questions, comrades, you begin to see the real meaning of this CARICOM Heads of Government meeting over the past week.

When people in the middle of a conference of this type are able to argue with all of their force and their might for a definition of human rights that only stresses elections but ignores the right of workers to strike, ignores the right of our people to jobs, ignores the fact that in their own countries and in the case of one of them, over 300 people were murdered during the course of last year without any recourse to law or justice; when you see these elements fighting hard against the principle of ideological pluralism, you must understand where they are coming from.

Because we were fighting to confirm once again the important principle that in this region there is and there should be tremendous ideological diversity and difference, that people were entitled to believe in a different way of building their own countries, economies and political processes. We were arguing what was a fact of life all around the world, but Messrs. Adams and Seaga were fighting with every ouce of energy they could muster to say that the principle of ideological pluralism or diversity was not a principle we could accept in CARICOM.

Support Growing for Zone of Peace

Now, if you are against that principle that a people have the right freely to choose their own way forward then what you are saying is that you do not believe in freedom, independence or national self-determination. That is what Seaga and Adams are saying by this disbelief.

Take a concept like *the zone of peace* which many democratic organisations up and down the Caribbean are today fighting for; this principle which calls for our Caribbean Sea to be declared a zone of peace, independence and development is supported by just about every significant organisation in the region. *The Caribbean Congress of Labour, The Caribbean Conference of Churches* and just about every single political party, and every serious organisation in the region have come out in support of this principle which says that no one has the right to put their military bases in other people's countries against their consent, that no one has the right to force colonialism on any people who want their independence and no one has the right to use pressure and threats and economic aggression against any country.

And yet you had Seaga and Adams fighting with every ounce of energy they had against this principle of a zone of peace, fighting hard on behalf of their masters' self-proclaimed right to send their warships up and down our Caribbean Sea to try to frighten and terrorise and bully the people of our region.

When you see that happening, comrades, you get a clearer idea of what they are fighting for. When you see these people fighting hard to bring Haiti into CARICOM while at the same time fighting to keep Suriname out, it tells you really where they are coming from. These elements were actually saying that Haiti was a democracy but Suriname was a dictatorship — Haiti, a country universally regarded as an international latrine where people are being killed and where people cannot get foot to eat. These elements were saying,'no problem with that'. That is their conception of democracy just like it is the conception of their masters.

Bowing and Kneeling to Uncle Sam

So comrades, when we examine these questions we get a very clear idea indeed of what these people were really representing, whose interests they were really fighting for, of the extent to which their brainwashing has them so totally and completely in the corner of the mighty United States, to whom they virtually kneel down and genuflect and bow and scrape because to them the United States is the beginning and the end of the world. These are the people who dare to try to point an accusing finger against the Grenada Revolution. These are the people who were bold and brave and fresh enough to try to accuse our free people of needing human rights.

And when in meetings with the people of Jamaica and with the leaders of CARICOM we were able to explain our concepts of human rights and democracy, Adams and Seaga discovered that it was an entirely different wicket that they had to bat on.

Because they discovered then that the people of the region were not only interested in what we had to say but they were enthusiastic about what we had to say, that they were not only not hostile to the Grenada Revolution but were fully in support of the Grenada Revolution. And all of this came as a mighty shock to these reactionaries, because they had begun to believe their own propaganda. They had already believed that the lies and distortions that they were planting in the *Guardians* and *Gleaners* and *Advocates* in the region had fooled the people. And when they discovered that the people were not being fooled, that the people were able to see the truth, then they had to turn around and move totally and completely on the defensive.

When these people presented their case on elections and human rights violations, they started off making a lot of points about how the people of the region wanted this Westminster parliamentary democracy system, how the people must have a chance to decide and that if the people are not able to decide then you don't have democracy. In our response we said that when we speak about human rights we don't just speak about political and civil human rights in the limited narrow way but we also talk about the social, the cultural and the economic human rights that the people are also entitled to and that the Universal Declaration on Human Rights speaks about.

Human Rights for the Majority Too
We don't just speak about their kind of limited human rights but we talk about the human rights that the majority has never been able to enjoy, the human rights that they believe only the minority is entitled to: the human

187

rights to a job, to decent housing, to a good meal when the day comes, to be able to form and to join a trade union, to be able to get pipe-borne water inside of your house, to get electricity in your house when you press a switch, to be able to ensure that you can live a life of dignity and decency. All of these human rights have been the human rights for a small minority over the years in the Caribbean and the time has come for the majority of the people to begin to receive those human rights for the first time.

And when we speak of democracy, we told them, we don't just see the question of elections as being democracy but we see democracy as having much more than just a tweedledum and tweedledee election, more than just a rum and cornbeef convention, more than just a five seconds in five years right to put an X.

We said that if elections is something that comes as part of a process every five years which ensures that the people are able to rule, then democracy of, for and by the people must be much more than just putting an X once in every five years.

The Five Parts of Democracy

So we made out the case, comrades, that democracy must at least have five minimum parts and each of the five is important. We said that if you have a democracy, first of all, the representatives of the people, the politicians must be responsible. Responsibility must be the first component. The politicians must work according to a plan that the people accept and not a plan that they decide to set on their own. They must make sure that on a regular basis through their contact with the people they tell them whether they are happy or unhappy with what they the leaders are doing. Responsibility therefore is the first aspect of democracy.

We pointed out secondly that a democracy must also have account-ability. If there is no accountability, if the people had to wait for five years before the politician went back to them to account then you didn't have democracy. If for 4 years 11 months 3 weeks 6 days and 23 hours the people had to keep their mouths shut then that can't be democracy. So we were saying for there to be accountability the people must be able to have the right on a regular basis (at least once a month) of ensuring that the political leaders go and face the people and tell the people how the work plan is going, how you are carrying out their mandate, and their ideas. The politician must inter-mix with the people, must ensure that the opinions, views and changing moods of the people are considered, or else you have no democracy.

We pointed out thirdly, comrades, that if you are talking about demo-cracy, then you have to develop mechanisms and organisations and institutions through which the voices of the people can be heard. You must ensure that on a regular basis the people through their own grassroots organ-isations are able to meet and look at the problems of the country, come up with solutions and then implement the solutions which are found for these problems. If you don't have mechanisms for people's participation and people's control, then you don't have democracy; what you have is a minority elected dictatorship.

We pointed out to these elements during the conference that in Grenada every single month thousands of our people come together in different villages around our country in their Zonal councils, Workers' Parish councils, women farmer and youth councils and there they are able to discuss their own problems, receive reports from the leaders of mass organisations on how the programmes of the revolution are going, get reports from the top managers in the country — whether it is the manager of the electricity company or of the telephone company or the price control inspector or the public health inspector — on what they are doing and how well they are spending tax payers' money.

We pointed out to these people that every single month the very top leadership of the party goes before the people in these monthly councils and accounts to the people on what they are doing. We pointed out to these people that these organisations are no joke organisations but are real, living and developing organisations, which bring real benefits to our people, such as when the workers in a parish council in August of 1981 demanded that the government find $1 million to buy 26 new buses that the workers could get to work on time and the children would be picked up and brought to school on time.

We pointed out to these elements that all our people were entitled to join the mass organisations in our country; that our NWO, starting from virtually scratch before the Revolution, now has over 6,500 women, or nearly one of every three eligible women in our country, that over 8,000 of our youth are in the NYO and 9,000 of our children in the Pioneer Organisation, that any woman, any youth, any child is able to join these organisations.

We further pointed out to them that every month these organisations meet and discuss the problems of our women, our youth and children, that every 2 years there are free and fair elections where the women and the youth elect their own leaders after reports on the programmes and the constitutions of the organisations are discussed at length by every single woman and youth who belong to the organisations. We said, if you want an example of accountability, of responsibility, of participation — come to Grenada and see our mass organisations in action.

We had to point out to these elements that whereas they were crushing the workers in their countries that our Revolution, coming from the Gairy dictatorship with an inheritance of 50% of our people out of work, has in just 3 years moved to just 14% being unemployed — 36% of our working people no longer unemployed.

We had to point out to these people that when every day the cost of an injection was going up in their own countries and our own little, free Grenada suffering under greater economic pressure than them, we had free health care for the people of our country and twice as many doctors to give that free health care.

189

While the mighty United States was closing down its schools, we were opening up new schools and today in our country 35% more of our people are enjoying free secondary school education and 3,500% more are enjoying university education which is free of cost to our people.

While they were crushing the workers in their country and going before their bourgeois parliaments and passing laws to legislate how much money workers must get, we in free revolutionary Grenada have moved from under 40% of our workers unionised to about 80% of all the workers now in a union of their own choice.

The Right to Life is No. 1

We had to say to these people that while they were saying that the first human right was the right to a bourgeois election, the first human right is the right to life and therefore we protect and preserve and promote the life and the health of our people.

While they cock-fight the people with elections and call that democracy, for our people in Grenada the main components of democracy — responsibility, accountability, mechanisms for our people to participate, benefits for our people — guarantee that every single day of the week we in Grenada practice democracy and we are by far the most democratic country in the CARICOM region.

But the greatest lesson of all we had to teach up there was when we said to Adams: 'All right, you say let the people decide, you say it is the people that are important. We agree with all that. Let us therefore instead of just talking about elections regard this question of human rights in the same way as the United Nations regard human rights, as being a mixture of 5 different things: political human rights, civil human rights, social human rights, cultural human rights, economic human rights. Let us take all of these human rights, put them into one big basket, then draw up a questionnaire on a sheet about human rights and let us bring that sheet to all the people of the Caribbean in all the countries, and ask the people to tick off what they call human rights. Let them say which one they want more of, which one they are not getting, which one they feel is the most important and when we get this big basket of human rights questions answered let us come back and publish it for the people of the region and the world to see'.

And comrades, when we said to Adams: 'Let us take a poll', his response was that under no circumstance would he conduct a poll in his own country. In other words, only elections is democracy.

And as you heard, comrades, a number of American Congressmen were in the hotel next door to where the Caribbean delegates were staying, and so every 5 seconds these American parliamentarians could come across and peep at Seaga and Adams to make sure they were behaving like nice obedient boys.

Every morning at breakfast one of them had to go over to the Americans to take the morning instructions, every lunch time one had to go down and report how the morning went, and at night another set had to go across and tell them how the rest of the afternoon went and plan strokes for the next morning. It was that amount of vulgarity that obtained in Ocho Rios and that is the final piece of proof of the extent to which the United States imperialism was trying to dictate this conference for Seaga and Adams. But what these people didn't understand is when you come out of a tradition of Fedon, and Marryshow and Butler and when you go through a 1951 revolution and a 1973 revolution and a 1979 revolution there is a thing called revolutionary tactics that you learn and collective revolutionary experience that you gather as a people.

When these elements talk about free press and human rights and detainees we have to look at them and laugh because we know we never tried to fool our people or any other people. When they ask us about democracy and elections we say elections will come in a way most relevant to our situation, but one thing is certain and it is that Westminster parliamentary elections and Westminster parliamentary democracy is dead and buried in Grenada.

Ten Papers with One Voice

When they talk to us about freedom of the press we have to say to them that your 'free press' is the same kind of 'free press' that we can hear and see up and down the region with different newspaper names but with the same voice speaking. They might look like 10 different papers but it is the same handful of big capitalists who own them all.

When they talk about detainees we said to them that when our revolution came, we could have lined people up in the streets and shot them down, or we could have done like you and pretended that the people run into the hills and then gun them down and say it was a 'shoot out' or an 'accident' or an 'attack on the police first' or 'we really don't know how it happened'. That is how 300 murders happened in one of your countries last year, that is how in one lady's country 13 people were killed in one year and you still can't hear about court results because everything is an accident and a shoot-out and nobody heard. But because of the humanitarian nature of this revolution, those people who were out to use violence against this revolution were not shot but instead were detained. For these elements all detainees are to be buried six feet deep because their preference is shoot them down in the streets.

When they talk about free press we have to point out to these people that before the revolution there were two papers in this country: *The West Indian*, which was really Gairy's voice, and *Torchlight*, which was really Cromwell's* voice. But since the Revolution today there are really over twelve different newspapers in our country apart from the *Free West Indian*. There is our party paper, there is *Scotilda*, the women's voice; *Fight* the youth voice;

* D.M.B. Cromwell, a major shareholder in the *Torchlight*

Workers' Voice, speaking for the urban workers; *Cutlass* speaking for the agricultural workers, *Fork* speaking for the small and middle farmers, there is the *Media Workers' Voice*, there is *Fedon*, speaking for our Revolutionary Armed Forces and so on. Today, the people in their sections and in their groupings are now able to come out and speak for themselves, through their own voice. We say that is what we call freedom of the press.

So comrades, we look forward with the greatest anticipation to next year's CARICOM conference in Trinidad and Tobago, the 10th anniversary conference which will take place in July. And it is true, there was some tremendous statesmanship exhibited by a couple of the leaders during this conference. We don't want to embarrass any of them so we won't call names, but I have in mind right now three leaders, and in particular one of them who spoke out early during this human rights debate and made a critical point that CARICOM is about the unity of our people, that the most important question is to keep CARICOM alive, that everybody will never be able to agree on the same kinds of things, that people have a right to disagree and to build their own processes in their own way free from outside interference. And that man's contribution was decisive.

I think of another leader who also made a decisive contribution, who said that as far as he was concerned there were issues that were raised for bilateral discussions, and what he wanted was a bi-lateral discussion with Grenada to explore the problem so he can understand what we are saying and where we are coming from.

The Greatest Hypocrites: Reagan and Cronies

There were some people in Ocho Rios who understood the importance of a united Caribbean, who were honest enough to say that a revolution means a rupture and a break with the past, that a revolution means that a change has come, that a revolution must mean some dislocation, that a revolution in the interest of a majority must involve the ruthless crushing of a violent minority.

There were some who were willing to understand these things and to state these things. There were some who knew their history and who knew that the greatest hypocrites of all were Reagan and his cronies.

Because has Reagan ever been interested in elections and democracy? When did Reagan ever call on Haiti to hold elections? When did Reagan ever call on the butcher Pinochet in Chile or on South Korea to hold elections? Is he calling upon racist South Africa to hold elections? No! Even when Allende in Chile had in fact won power through elections what did the American President Nixon at the time do? Nixon, Kissinger and Helms sat down the night after Allende won the elections in September 1970 and they worked out their plan of aggression and destabilization against President Allende.

Allende didn't say 'no more elections'. He didn't arm working people or try to close down the reactionary paper *El Mercurio* as he should have done. Allende relied on the parliamentary form that they wanted him to rely on.

But because he was a socialist and was independent and was bringing benefits and justice to his people, the American elite went out of their way to crush him ruthlessly. And the criminal they put into power has yet to be told by the so-called democratic United States to call an election.

There were people in that room in Ocho Rios who understood that when the United States revolution took place 200 years ago it was much more violent, bloody and far-sweeping than most revolutions have been. There were people who understood that after the American revolution there were 600,000 counter-revolutionaries who remained loyal to the king. The revolutionaries sent 100,000 of them into exile, and 60,000 of them across the border to Canada. The counter-revolutionaries had no right to vote, right to teach, to preach, to own property or hold office. All of their printing presses were confiscated. In fact one famous family – the Fairfax family of Virginia, owned 6 million acres of land (the whole of Grenada is 85 thousand acres and the whole of Jamaica is 2.8 million acres), and the revolutionaries took every inch of that land and gave it to the small peasants of the United States.

In the American revolution, those who were not exiled were jailed. Many died in jail and many more were shot. It was a bloody, violent occasion and period. And they didn't call an election in 2 weeks or 2 years after they took power. They took 13 years to call their elections. What the American revolution did will make the Grenada Revolution look like a tea party and yet these criminals are talking about the Grenada revolution taking away human rights.

And on top of that, sisters and brothers, the American revolutionaries were bold and brave enough to entrench and institutionalise for all time the universal right of any people to revolt whenever their government became oppressive. The American revolutionaries did that, not the Grenadian revolutionaries.

NJM Always Defended the People
Their revolution, unlike ours, was made by outside arms. Because not even our worst enemies ever denied the fact that when 46 of us went off to the Green Beast barracks and took power on the morning of March 13th with bare chests and half-dead weapons, and then put out a call on our radio station, we were confident that our people were tired and wanted no more, that our people trusted us, that our people knew that we were no dry weather politicians, that rain or shine, licks or bullets or death, the New Jewel Movement was always there and would always come forward to defend them. Our people understood that.

We had to tell these jokers who are accusing us of exporting revolution (as if revolution is like butter or saltfish you could export!) that 46 of them should go and attack a barracks somewhere, and let us see how much people would come out and defend them!

Struggle for Regional Unity

So comrades, our task now is to continue that struggle for regional integration and unity, continue that struggle for practical co-operation, continue to avoid the divisions and the divisiveness of United States imperialism, continue to struggle for regional institutions, in particular, the University of the West Indies which some of these elements are threatening at this time.

Our duty now is to continue to struggle for greater people-to-people contact among the masses of the region, continue to struggle to raise consciousness among the masses of the people of the Caribbean, continue to struggle for the closest possible links with all of our Caribbean sisters and brothers, whether they speak Spanish or English or French or Dutch or even American, and continue to struggle for the closest possible links with the people of Latin America, in general.

Our duty is to continue to struggle to have our Caribbean Sea declared a zone of peace, independence and development in practice. Our duty is to continue to struggle against imperialism, to continue to build our Grenadian revolution, to continue to walk in the shadow and the footsteps of Fedon, of Marryshow, of Butler, and ensure that we as the Grenadian people, small as we are, will forge that meaningful link to ensure the unity of our people.

17. For the Cultural Sovereignty of the Caribbean People!

Address at the Opening of the Caribbean Conference of Intellectual Workers, St. George's, Grenada, 20 November 1982

I want to start by extending a very warm, fraternal welcome to all of the distinguished delegates and guests who have honoured us here today by their presence. We certainly believe that this *Caribbean Conference of Intellectual and Cultural Workers* is a milestone and an extremely historic event. We certainly believe it is going to have a major impact on helping us in our own task of ensuring the fullest cultural development of our own Grenadian people.

Also I want to apologise, comrades, for reaching this late. But, as I am sure you would have heard, we were attending the CARICOM *Heads of Government Conference* in Jamaica and notwithstanding our very best efforts to get back yesterday, we could not. We had to overnight in Port-of-Spain, and were only able to come in this morning. But I am sure that comrades would be glad to know that even though it has taken us this long to return to our beloved homeland we have come back with a convincing victory over the forces of reaction that were hoping to isolate us.

Today, when we speak of cultural imperialism, we are describing a world-wide menace. We are talking about a process at work not only in those parts of the world which have for centuries lived under the heel of more powerful nations.

Today, nations which in the past have colonised and subjugated other peoples, destroyed or sought to destroy their cultures, are themselves facing the danger of cultural imperialism.

Creeping Coca-Cola Culture

But the form that this age-old process takes, in this the late 20th Century, is far more refined, far more scientific, has far more resources at its disposal than ever before in the history of mankind, and it is therefore far more devastating.

Today, no corner of the earth is safe from the creeping ravages of the Coca-Cola culture. In the Western World, concerned and conscious citizens look on with horror at the contamination of their young people by the shallow export culture beamed out to all mankind from the headquarters of imperialism.

But there is perhaps no region of today's world that presents so dramatic a picture of the process of cultural imperialism as does our Caribbean. The Caribbean is a laboratory of cultural imperialism because it offers such ideal conditions; our geographical fragmentation, aided and abetted by continuing political fragmentation, which in turn is one of the major objectives of cultural imperialism; to keep us well apart and, if possible, always at each others' throats, so that we might never come to realise the strength that lies in our unity.

The history of our region provides a most interesting and tragic example of culture in the service of political and economic domination.

The '*New World*', so-called, begins with the conquest of the Amerindian. In some places he was exterminated outright; elsewhere his culture was so hopelessly wrecked as to render him easy prey to every conceivable form of exploitation.

When that dirty work was done, our region became the arena for yet another brutal collision between the economic interests of Europe and the human rights of a people less equipped than their aggressors for self-defence – Africans uprooted and transported thousands of miles from the fount of their cultures.

A Culture Viewed With Contempt

Upon the ashes of the Amerindian, the African forged a new culture in this part of the world, a new set of responses to the physical environment and to the challenge of survival.

For centuries this Caribbean Culture, this culture of the masses of Caribbean people has developed in limbo, unrecognised, unrecorded or at best viewed with contempt. This culture is yet to gain the approval of the very people who are creating it and practising it – the masses of Caribbean people. And this, above all, this weak self-image of our culture, lays us wide open to domination. Our people can be so softened up, so drugged by the hypnosis of American television, American advertising and capitalist consumerism, that some really have no objection to becoming the backyard of the US.

Our cultures have never had the opportunity of developing to the point where they become a bulwark of our sovereignty. Education for Caribbean people has never meant the application of human knowledge to ensure the viability of our people's way of life. Education has meant the selection of an elite to be assimilated into the lifestyle and thought patterns of those whose interests lay in dominating us.

Education has meant a mutually impoverishing divorce between the culture of the educated and that of the masses. The political dimension of this fact is that our elites have been accomplices to the subjugation of our people.

Early in the 20th Century, from within the ranks of this educated elite, the intellectuals of various parts of the Caribbean, there first came the impetus towards asserting the validity of our African-based Caribbean cultures.

Negrismo, Haitianism, Negritude — movements taking place over the 1920s, 30s and 40s — all were manifestations of the uneasiness of Caribbean intellectuals in their second-hand European culture and their rejection of the policies of assimilation used by the various colonising powers as part of their overall strategy of domination and exploitation.

These Movements Did Not Change Caribbean History

These movements produced a fine flowering of literature and no one would wish to underestimate this legacy. Nevertheless, these movements cannot be said to have changed the course of Caribbean history.

These are important forerunners of the new developments that this body of intellectuals here today represents. We must build upon the work of our forerunners by taking stock of what they have achieved. But by examining their shortcomings we avoid errors of a similar kind.

A major weakness was that their ideas remained locked within the tight circle of an educated elite. Theirs was essentially a dialogue with the white world, not with the masses from whom they had sprung. Indeed in the case of the Negritude movement among French Caribbean intellectuals, the forum was Paris! These movements for the enthronement of Caribbean culture never touched the Caribbean peoples who were the creators of this culture.

These early movements involved Caribbean intellectuals most of whom were themselves irreversibly the products of cultural imperialism, members of the colonial bourgeoisie which was totally assimilated to European culture. These intellectuals who had been removed by colonialism from the all-important living contact with the masses, and who could now only make piteous gestures of identification with their own culture. This contradiction has produced some beautiful literature which we count as part of our cultural heritage today.

But perhaps the most significant weakness, and the one from which the others derived, was the political immaturity of these movements, their failure to deepen their political perspective of culture.

These movements of intellectuals were basically a response to a political situation — the situation of colonialism, and specifically a protest against racism and cultural domination. But the movements failed to develop any real combative power and became narcissistic, spinning around in race and culture until they had no further to go.

One notable exception however, and this we must adknowledge, is our Martiniquan comrade Aime Cesaire, foremost poet of the Negritude movement, who took the struggle onto the political plane even after the cultural movement had lost its impetus.

But Negritude as a collective response of intellectuals to the problem of cultural domination remained largely an artistic movement, a literary response to a political problem, a response which was not sufficiently informed by a political awareness of the problem.

The Effects of the Black Power Movement

One generation later came Black Power, affecting primarily this time the English-speaking areas of the Caribbean

The Black Power Movement achieved more of an impact upon the direction of Caribbean history, because its philosophy had a stronger political base which kindled the consciousness of the masses.

It is true to say that after Black Power, the Caribbean will never be the same again. The movement has contributed to the process of changing the status of Caribbean culture.

The Black Power Movement has contributed to transforming the Caribbean, largely because so many of its adherents later continued to develop politically. A large cross-section of the progressive forces of the Caribbean are comrades who first became engaged in political struggle through their involvement with the Black Power movement. This is true of the entire leadership of Grenada's New Jewel Movement.

We must acknowledge all the stages through which our struggle has passed, and we must recognise the limitations of the historical context within which these movements occurred.

A vision of sovereignty is provided toady in the process of the great Cuban Revolution, and in the younger processes of Nicaragua and Grenada.

I want to offer an example of this vision which shows the marriage of politics and culture in one Caribbean experience. In 1981, the great Cuban poet, Nicolas Guillen received the Jose Marti Award. In a ceremony held in the Palace of the Revolution he made a very brief statement:

> In Cuba we have great poems, some of which have travelled beyond our national boundaries. Poems which are engraved on our lives, and bear permanent witness to our human progress: the agrarian reform programme for example, is one of the greatest poems in our history; the popular literacy campaign, higher education for all, the national-isation of the means of production, once in undeserving hands, is also a poem of infinite value: and all these make up the great poem that is the Revolution, the revolution triumphantly led by Fidel Castro.

And then Guillen read a poem of thanks to the Revolution:

> *When I see myself and touch myself,*
> *Only yesterday Johnny-who-had-nothing,*
> *And today Johnny-who-has-everything*
> *I turn my head, look around*

And ask myself and touch myself
I have, let's see,
I have the pleasure of going everywhere in my country
Owner of all that is in it,
I did not have or couldn't have before.
I can say crop.
I can say bush
I can say city
Army I say
Already mine forever, and yours, ours a spreading radiance
lightning, star, flower.

Today we have the advantage of witnessing this unfolding of revolution-ary culture within our own region. Indeed, today's movement of intellectual workers springs directly out of the Cuban revolution. It was the Casa de las Americas, the great Cuban house of culture, which one year ago convened for the first time the Conference of Intellectual Workers for the sovereignty of the peoples of our America. Your conference which opens today upon the soil of Free Grenada is a continuation of the initiative that was launched at that historic gathering.

The Challenge Which Confronts Us

Where lies the way forward? This question will no doubt be focussed upon during your deliberations of the next three days. But it is important to concentrate on the challenge which confronts us now. There is an important document, prepared for President Reagan, which outlines a strategy for dealing with your category of workers in the Caribbean.

I quote:

> The war is for the minds of mankind. Ideological politics will prevail. . . . Education is the medium by which culture retains, passes on and even pioneers its past. Thus, whoever controls the educational system determines the past . . . how it is viewed . . . as well as the future. A campaign to capture the intellectual elite through the media of radio, television, books, articles and pamphlets, fellowships and prizes must be initiated, for consideration and recognition are what most intellectuals crave, and such a programme would attract me.

This is the way intellectuals of the region are perceived by the American Administration and the agencies they employ.

Our educated class is made up of men and women who are up for sale, and who can be bribed by the offer of scholarships, grants, and the oppor-tunities for publication of their work. 'Consideration and recognition are what most intellectuals crave.' We wish it were possible to make this document known to every teacher at all levels throughout the region. We need no further definition of cultural imperialism than these strategies which are outlined here.

The Intellectual Mercenary

There is a man who will fight in any army, anywhere, at any time. He demands a certain price for his skills, and asks no further questions. He is called a mercenary. The intellectual may also be a mercenary; that is a man whose relation to his work is determined entirely by his personal interests in the promotion of a career. In this respect, the historian, the economist, the writer may be no different from the type of soldier we have just mentioned. A revolutionary struggle has the duty to help rescue men and women from this fate. All of you here are intellectual workers who have had to wrestle with this problem, since capitalism surrounds you with markets which are always ready to buy and hire your skills, and at a price poor nations cannot pay. It is to your credit that you have remained where you belong.

In our context you have to ask yourselves, in whose interest, on behalf of which class do you carry out your social function as teacher, researcher, actor, writer?

In our view, there are at least two armies, the military army and the cultural army. The revolution must be defended; but we cannot train young comrades in the use of weapons to create and defend a revolutionary struggle unless we can also make it clear to them what is the meaning, the true nature of that struggle. This task of defending and clarifying the meaning and context of a revolutionary struggle must be the task of our cultural army. And it is indispensable. Without it every military victory remains a sterile victory, where the 'freedom of the press' allows the transnationals to shape the tastes of the people.

Cultural Development in Revolutionary Grenada

The Grenada Revolution is young. It is barely 3½ years old. But already it presents a living example of the regenerating impact of political process upon cultural development.

The cultural development of our people since the Revolution is due to a vital process of change which only political revolution can set in motion. This process of change has two aspects — they complement each other; they come together to produce a strong, revitalized cultural identity. The cultural regeneration of our people comes out of a twin process of increased self-expression and increased education.

Where does our culture reside, the culture that we can call our own? It resides among the masses of our people, the people whose way of life is a submerged and disrespected sub-culture — the masses of the people, whose norms and values have never made it into the law-books or the education system, whose voices are silenced by the authoritative words and images that dominate all the organs of communication and discussion in the society, from the newspaper to the Parliament.

Today in Grenada, the long-submerged culture of the masses of the people is rising to the surface of our history through the development of structures which unlock the voices of our people from centuries of oblivion.

Today in Grenada we are building organs of democracy and the right to speak, *all* over the country, in every nook and cranny of Grenada, Carriacou and Petite Martinique — not in St George's alone, not in one barricaded building in the capital, not in one gilded and velveted room, not around one polished table with room for only a handful of men to sit and decide on our behalf, but everywhere in our country and for everybody in our country.

Our media, too, have been infiltrated by voices which they have never accommodated before. Our people are firmly taking control of their newspapers, their radio, their television. Our people will never again be controlled by the media.

A Band of Faithful Mongrels

We make no apology for interpreting the freedom of the press in Free Grenada to mean liberating every possible medium of communication from the stranglehold of a minority which in turn is manipulated by powerful foreign interests. We make no apology for moving swiftly, and with the consent of the majority of our people, to silence our local representatives of the reactionary Caribbean press, that band of faithful mongrels who all this week have been wagging their tails and yapping in unison at the command of their headquarters. Identical editorials, identical lies and distortions, manufactured in one factory and then off-loaded onto your free and independent newspapers across 1000 miles of Caribbean Sea. If that is freedom and independence of the press, then we will have none of it in our free and independent Grenada.

Our people today have channels of expression which were not open to them before, and so, inevitably, the culture of our people emerges out of its age-old limbo.

But at the same time that we institute mechanisms for the release of our people's culture, we must guard against the notion that culture is something to put away in a glass case or preserve in a bottle. It is perhaps quite incorrect to use the word 'preserve' when we talk of culture. We speak, rather, of the *defence* of our cultures.

We cannot speak of liberating our culture if all we mean is taking it out of one cage to put it into another. Our culture has to develop into a strong frame of reference, a strong rallying-point for our people in today's world, in tomorrow's world.

In all the formerly colonised countries of the world where the masses are still kept in a state of ignorance while a small elite are given access to education — an education which is imported wholesale from another culture — the folk culture or the culture of the people remains in a state of under-development, unable to give the people real confidence, real power, real viability in the modern world. On the one hand the culture of the people is cut off from the light of modern knowledge, and on the other hand the educated classes are cut off from the culture of their people.

Simple but Dangerous Solution

This problem is not insoluble. The solution, in fact is so simple as to be dangerous — dangerous of course, to the headquarters of the *Guardian*, the *Express*, the *Advocate*, and the *Gleaner*. To arm the Caribbean people with their own culture, to rescue the culture of the Caribbean people from its present role of amusing American tourists, to turn this culture into a living force which can fire the masses of Caribbean people with self-pride and independence — this is one of the truly dangerous developments in Grenada that place us in the shooting range of President Reagan and his pack of hunting dogs of the Caribbean Basin.

For our culture to grow to its full stature, the people, *all* the people must have access to education. There are thousands of illiterate people in some of the very Caribbean countries which are used as bases for attacks on Grenada. No one is concerned about their human rights, their right to education, and our attackers do not see our literacy campaign as an increase of our people's human rights.

Our people must have access to education, but this education must be fashioned in our own image, this education works *through* our culture and not against it, through *our* reality, through *our* priorities, through the values which bind our people together.

I would hope that our visitors have the opportunity of viewing some of the materials and learning of the activities of our Centre for Popular Education while they are here in our country. The CPE is only one aspect of the massive development of education for all in our country since the Revolution. Opportunities for education and training have increased a hundredfold — education and work training relevant to *our* needs, our situation.

Knowledge in the Service of the People

For the first time in our history knowledge is being made available to the people who hold the keys of our culture, knowledge which does not come in the alienating forms of colonial education.

An important part of this process of cultural regeneration is the new contact between the educated elite and the masses, facilitated by our Revolution.

Members of these two traditionally separated classes today meet and take strength from each other within the ranks of our mass organisations, and in our new political process in general. In the NWO, sisters who have university training or who work behind a desk must collaborate in community work with sisters who never finished primary school and who know how to work the land for a living. They must respect and support each other. In our People's Militia a man or a woman who is a teacher in civilian life must take orders from a squad leader who not so long ago was one of his/her students. In our political education classes or study groups, the educated and the under-educated pool their ideas, and their life experience to the benefit of both, to the achievement of deeper insights for both.

For, yes, we have political education, and we have the honesty to call it political education. The television network of our Caribbean Basin doesn't call its canned-in-the-US programmes 'political education', it doesn't call its massive onslaught of advertising on the minds of the people 'political education'; it doesn't even call its slanted newscasting 'political education'. The news media of the Caribbean don't admit that they are engaged in political education, with their blanket of silence on developments in Grenada, interrupted only be prefabricated editorials on us, and reports on Soviet MIG fighters that are unloaded in crates on the St George's wharf.

Yes, the political education of our people is a major aspect of the defence of our culture. For our people must be able to see behind the smokescreen created by the US-controlled media in the Caribbean. They must not be blinded to the realities of the forces which seek to control our destiny. Our people must have the facts, the power to analyse their own situations and make choices.

A Confident Flowering of the Arts

What choosing power do the majority of Caribbean people have after years of being hammered with images of American TV analyses of the world situation seen through the eyes of American interests? What choice does the majority of Caribbean people exercise, given the subtle, insidious imperialist political education that they receive?

The awakened consciousness of our people, their newly-won access to self-expression on the one hand, and to education on the other, already have borne fruit in the regeneration of our culture.

In the first place, we are witnessing in Grenada a confident flowering of the arts — a wealth of creativity in poetry, song, music, drama and dance. At this moment our National Performing Company is on tour in North America, after a most successful tour of England.

The steady growth of Grenadian literature is particularly note-worthy. Grenada has no representation in the impressive hall of fame of Caribbean literature because of the traditional under-development of our education system and the lack of self-awareness of our people. But in the 3½ years of the Revolution alone we can boast that never before have so many Grenadians put pen to paper, never before have the voices of so many Grenadians been recorded in print.

The growing self-knowledge and pride of our people is something which strikes the attention of all who visit our land. The growth, too, of new dimensions of culture — new attitudes, new behaviours, new routines which we take for granted.

Grenadians are Walking in New Ways

For culture is the arts and the deeper processes which throw up the arts. All of our shared habits, all of our collective responses to our common situation, all of these are culture. And today in Grenada our long-submerged culture is surfacing to the light of day, but it is also growing new leaves, new flowers. We are walking in new ways that are *our* ways.

* The oldest grandmother living in her little house on her plot of land in a rural village, putting on her hat to come out at seven o'clock in the evening to participate in her Zonal Council meeting, for she wants to keep abreast of all that is going on, and because she has her piece to say, and takes it for granted that everyone must say his or her piece.

* The youth whose life pattern included liming on the bridge for hours on end, who new takes on the discipline of attending meetings and participating in community work — for who must be responsible for the building and protection of the community but the people who live there?

* The young of middle-aged sister who steps forward to participate in the defence of her revolution, calmly manipulating an automatic rifle or controlling the anti-aircraft machine, guarding the beach with the rest of her sisters and brothers.

* The young Pioneer who has to be stood upon a chair to reach the microphone in order to deliver a solidarity message or recite a revolutionary poem before a gathering of 10,000 people.

* The young people returning willingly to the land to ensure that we grow what we eat through programmes of the Revolution such as the Co-operative movement and the new farm schools.

* The women and men of our country sitting down to discuss what should go into the nation's budget and demanding that we cease the folly of wasting precious foreign exchange on commodities which we do not need, commodities that are considered life blood by people as poor as ourselves in other Caribbean countries, where the media allows the transnationals to shape the tastes of the people.

Taking Destiny into Their Own Hands

All of these images of cultural regeneration, images of a people taking their destiny into their own hands. This, comrades, is what is threatened by cultural imperialism, which aims at the very opposite, focussing our individual energies upon a foreign ideal which militates against our own development as a people. And because of this threat, Intellectual and Cultural Workers of our region have a real responsibility to ensure that this threat is defeated.

We know, of course, that imperialism is well organised and rich in human and financial resources. Yet it is clear there are things that our intellectual and cultural workers can do.

Firstly, intellectual and cultural workers have to respond by becoming organised and united regionally.

Secondly, intellectual and cultural workers must move creatively and energetically to forge closer links – direct links – with the Caribbean masses, and help them to raise their consciousness so that they would not be misled by the lies and distortions of imperialism; so that they would be better able to understand the new revolutionary values and processes that are being built in the Caribbean today.

Thirdly, intellectual and cultural workers must forge in reality the link between People's Politics and People's Culture.

Fourthly, intellectual and cultural workers must unite in strength to expose the warmongers and the merchants of neutron death. And in this context they must struggle hard to ensure that the Caribbean in reality becomes a zone of peace, independence and development.

Fifthly, intellectual and cultural workers must struggle for *real independence* for our people.

And, because we know that this historic conference aims at achieving these objectives, among others, we are doubly happy to be your hosts during this period.

LONG LIVE INTELLECTUAL AND CULTURAL WORKERS OF OUR CARIBBEAN, LATIN AMERICA AND THE WORLD!

LONG LIVE THE STRUGGLES OF OUR PEOPLE FOR THE FULLEST CULTURAL DEVELOPMENT!

LONG LIVE THE STRUGGLES OF OUR PEOPLE FOR THE RIGHT TO BUILD THEIR OWN PROCESS!

LONG LIVE THE STRUGGLING PEOPLES OF THE CARRIBEAN AND LATIN AMERICA!

FORWARD EVER! BACKWARD NEVER!

18. Long Live the Women of Free Grenada!

Address to the First Congress of The National Women's Organisation, St. George's, Grenada, 6 December 1982

Our party and government salutes this historic first congress of our National Women's Organisation and this outstanding tribute to the free, fighting women of free and revolutionary Grenada.

It has been a long, hard road to this day. This fifth anniversary, this historic first congress has not come about easily, without a tremendous amount of sacrifice, a tremendous amount of struggle on the part of the leading women of our country.

We can see this struggle in several different ways. We can recognise the great achievements of our fighting women if we just pause to consider the fact that when this National Women's Organisation was formed five years ago on December 10th 1977 we were talking about 60 of the leading women of our country getting together. A few years later on March 13th, 1979, the dawn of our Revolution, there were only 120 women in the NWO. And even as late as December 1980 the figure stood at only 1,500 in 47 groups around the country. Yet by December 1981, as a result of that massive mobilisational drive that ran from July to December, we are able today to proclaim to the world that our NWO now stands at 6,500 strong.

Sacrifice and Suffering Brought Achievements

And comrades, as Comrade Phyllis was pointing out, this achievement came about as a result of tremendous suffering and exploitation of the women of our country — exploitation from slavery, through colonialism, Gairyism, GNP-ism, neocolonial independence — exploitation and suffering which saw the women of our country without jobs, with some 70% of them unemployed before the Revolution, exploitation which left our women without dignity having to subject themselves to sexual exploitation in return for work, exploitation which left our women without any security, without any maternity leave, without the right to join trade unions, without the right to equal pay for equal work, exploitation which saw the women of our country with no opportunity for developing themselves individually and collectively, with no opportunity to participate in a democratic way in the running of their own country.

This exploitation left the women of our country with no peace but only with harassment as a result of the brutal beatings of their husbands, sons and brothers and as a result of the brutal humiliation that they themselves had to be subjected to at the hands of Gairy's green beasts, secret police and mongoose gang.

All of this exploitation and suffering never for one moment daunted the courage and fighting spirit of the Grenadian women who always came back fighting. At every stage of our history from slavery, through colonialism and Gairyism we have been able to see this struggle and fight on the part of our women.

Let's consider the recent past — the last 12 years. Who can ever forget the glorious marches of 1970 led by the nurses of our country, marches that were not called to get better wages for themselves but marches and demonstrations called because of their concern over lack of bandages and medicines and aspirins and basic facilities in what was being called a hospital but could better have been described as the third department of La Qua's Funeral Agency. Who could ever forget that year and the struggle and courage of those nurses.

And who can ever forget 1971 when the women farmers of our country came out in their thousands protesting Gairy's attempt to grab their Nutmeg Board and Nutmeg Association from them.

Who could ever forget 1973 when the women of our country were in the forefront of the people's struggle against Lord Brownlow, that foreign parasite who believed he could come to our country and lock up our beaches claiming it was part of his property!

Who could ever forget the large number of our women who went to the airport in April 1973, after Jeremiah Richardson one of our first martyrs — was murdered by a police bullet — and faced the guns and pressures of Belmar and his henchmen.

Who can forget the massive turn out of our women at the People's Convention on Independence in May 1973, and at the People's Congress in November of the same year! Who can forget their fighting spirit then when they called on Gairy to resign and when they elected a National Unity Council in order to effect a smooth transition to power of the new Government!

Who can forget the glorious saga of our fighting women in our streets in January 1974, when for 21 days one third of our population marched every single day calling upon the dictator to resign.

Who can forget January 21st 1974, when our women had to face the bullets, bullpistles and sticks of the Mongoose Gang and the criminal elements in Gairy's armed forces and the courage and dignity with which our women stood up and fought back!

Who can forget throughout that period of 1974 and 1975, the daily acts of heroism that our women performed: hiding and burying gasoline to ensure that the leadership could move around the country during those difficult months; ensuring that the newspaper of our party always came out regardless of its suppression by the Gairy dictatorship; week after week finding paper, moving the roneo machine around from house to house to avoid detection; writing the articles and typing, producing and distributing the newspapers.

Who can forget all of that heroism! Who can forget the tremendous acts of self-sacrifice and courage played by one of our great national heroes, an elderly sister in her 60s, a sister who hid members of the party in the underground days and who every single Saturday morning would leave her house on Lucas Street and go outside with bundles of newspapers and pass those papers in a hidden form to different bus drivers going to St Patrick's and St Andrew's.

And who can forget that fateful Saturday morning while carrying out her usual revolutionary task of distributing the paper how this sister was unfortunately crushed by a bus after slipping and falling! Who can ever forget the outstanding, unparalleled qualities of Sister Edith McBain, one of the main heroes of the Grenada Revolution!

Our Women Played Their Role on March 13th 1979

And, as we know, comrades, plus courage was shown not just before the Revolution but also after the Revolution. If the women of our country had not come out in their tens of thousands on Revolution morn, if they had not brought water and food to the revolutionary troops, the new troops freshly created from the youth and unemployed in our country, if they had not come out and cooked the food and joined their menfolk in going to the police stations to ensure that the white flags of surrender were put up, maybe March 13th could have had a different meaning.

And who will ever forget after the Revolution the historic rally on June 19th 1980, when we were commemorating Heroes Day as we know the women of our country were in the majority at that historic rally, and when the bomb went off and those murderers who had planned to wipe out the leadership were able to sit back and count the totality of their destruction, what did we find: 97 of our people sent to the hospital, 80 of them women, 40 hospitalised, 36 of them women; 3 murdered, all of them women. today, once again we salute the memory and the sacrifice of Laurice, Laureen and Bernadette.

Today, comrades, we also think of the heroic role our women played in tracking down those vicious counter-revolutionaries who, not satisfied with their work on June 19th 1980, proceeded on November 17th of the same year in one single night to murder five of our patriots, all young sons of our Revolution. And when the People's Militia and the other sections of our Armed Forces under the leadership of General Austin decided to look for them, and when revolutionary justice was handed out to them, the women in our militia were again in the forefront.

Today's first congress, therefore, symbolises and reflects the rewards and achievements for all of these sacrifices and struggles. And the reward is a very rich one, comrades. We have seen it in the regional and international support for this first congress and for the NWO in general which has come from all around the world from peace-loving, democratic and progressive organisations hailing the achievements of the NWO and welcoming this historic day.

We have seen it by the presence today of comrades from the socialist world, in particular from the Soviet Union and Cuba, by comrades who have come from Europe, and from Asia where the fighting people of one particular country, in February 1978, buried feudalism in their own country once and for all and began a process of socialist construction and since then have been harassed night and day — we welcome the delegate from the fighting people of Afghanistan.

We can see this reward today, comrades, in the presence of our sisters from the United States and Canada, from Central America and from the Caribbean. So there is no doubt that the NWO and this first congress has been amply rewarded by the presence of so many outstanding fighters, the finest representatives of the women of their own countries.

Widespread National Support for the NWO

But we must also mention the great local support that the NWO and the first congress have received by our own people of Grenada. The massive number of solidarity messages from so many different organisations of youth, students, workers, farmers, from ministries and government departments, and from state enterprises. All sections of our people have come out and demonstrated in a concrete and practical way their support and love for the women of our country and their leading mass organisation. They have also demonstrated their support, in part, through material offerings they have given to this Congress.

Comrades, we can speak today with the fullest confidence, absolute honesty and the firmest conviction of the rise of patriotism amongst the women of our country, of the growth in consciousness among the women of our country, of their greater commitment and dedication, of their almost unbelievable unity.

We can also see the greater internationalism of our women, the growth in their self-respect and dignity, in their self-confidence, in their ability to express themselves, to give vent to their ideas and views and to give expression to their cultural and political creativity.

Today, we can certainly remark on the level and quality of organisation of our women and compliment them for the ever increasing exercise of people's power in our new democracy. And what a fantastic training in democracy our NWO sisters have had over these past few months in preparing for this Congress.

The NWO is a fully democratic organisation. This can be seen by the fact that entry into its ranks is open to any woman over the age of 14, as well as by its respect for the right of its members to decide its programme and policy. The NWO also insists that every three years all members have the right to elect their National Executive and to ensure that these officers are accountable and responsible throughout their three-year term.

In every sense we have seen over these past months a fantastic exercise in democratic participation by the women of our country. This has not been a case where the President of the NWO suddenly descended on this conference centre one December morning and said that this is the programme for the next three years, as is the traditional pattern of many so called democratic organisations.

An Activity in Democracy

Contrary to that approach, the executive of the NWO over a period of several months, firstly prepared a draft outline of the programme for the next three years, circulated this programme in typed form to every member of the NWO and then for a period of several months, hundreds of discussions at group, parish and delegate levels analysing the document, criticising and evaluating it, searching for new ideas, for clearer formulations and more concrete perspectives were held.

The result of this activity in democracy has been such that the original draft programme has undergone tremendous changes and the final version which was read here this morning by Comrade Phyllis Coard represents, in fact, a document that has been put under the microscope, subjected to numerous discussions by all NWO members and undergone a number of concrete changes. I would like now, comrades, to look at a few of the changes, because I think it is very important for us to see the practical importance and value of democracy and democratic participation.

In the first draft it was stated that the main problem facing women was jobs, but after very serious discussion at group, parish and national levels, the women had a closer look at that analysis and decided that instead they should speak of two main problems and two main tasks. The analysis that produced that change was fundamental because what the sisters concluded was that it was not enough in our context and conditions to simply speak of unemployment as being the main problem. Rather, it was necessary to examine at the same time how to go one step further, and look at how we can solve unemployment in a productive way that could benefit the country at large.

Coming out of that analysis, the sisters were able to go back and do a lot more concrete research, work out figures on the likely availability of jobs over the next three years, examine what kinds of skills would be required in the workforce over the next three years, analyse whether or not those women presently out of jobs were likely to fill the jobs coming on stream, and if not look for the type of training necessary for those tasks: jobs for our women, yes, but because of the increasing complexity of the economy and the new skills needed, the second priority linked to the first priority must be training and education for the women of our country. That is how it came about that the programme speaks so concretely about political education, academic education, social education, skills training and leadership training.

Comrades, our party and government certainly want to give our total support to this new formulation and analysis. It is our confident expectation that over the next few years we will wipe out unemployment in our country but in order to do that in a fully productive way we must ensure that as the new jobs are created our people have the necessary skills to take up those new jobs.

The more than 23,000 people before the Revolution who were out of work has now become 5,600, 4,000 of them being women, the vast majority of whom do not have primary school leaving certificates or special skills or training for most jobs.

But while on the one hand that is the reality facing us, on the other hand, the needs of the economy are very different. We estimate, for example, that in agriculture 2,500 jobs are likely to be created over the next three years — jobs for tractor drivers, soil scientists, farm managers, agricultural economists, accountants, co-operative farmers, extension officers and so on; jobs that demand skills for the modernised agriculture that we are in the process of building.

It is the same in construction, comrades. The 2,000 new jobs we expect to be created in construction over the next three years will require plumbers, electricians, masons, carpenters, painters, architects, mechanics, surveyors, soil testers, engineers, and so on. But the most cursory examination will show that most of the unemployed women today do not now have the necessary skills or training to take up these jobs.

It is not far different in tourism where at least another 500 jobs should be created in the next three years particularly when the new international airport and new hotels and restaurants come on stream. And again, these new jobs will all require a certain measure of skill.

With our industrial expansion too, we will be looking for people who can not only read and write, but who also have the ability to use modern equipment and technology. In all areas, therefore, it is quite clear that the answer is no longer to simply say that if we find jobs for the unemployed then the problem is over, because the question that will increasingly remain is what kind of jobs and what kind of skills.

Therefore, comrades, if we are to scientifically prepare for the future, it must be correct that our main priority must be to provide the appropriate training and education for those still unemployed in order to ensure that they are able to take up the jobs once they come on stream. And there are other examples of how the draft programme was affected by thorough discussion.

Another analysis was made by the sisters which I think is extremely important. They said that even if the training is provided we will still have the problem that many of those unemployed sisters have children, and most of them do not have the means to hire help to look after the children, and many cannot get voluntary help, and therefore the question of the day care centres and pre-primary and nursery facilities also became major issues.

When they analysed the question in detail they discovered that it was not just about the number of jobs and the type of training required for those jobs, but also about where the children would be put when those sisters take up jobs for the first time in their lives. And the answer to that question is not easy.

The sisters, therefore, concluded correctly that because day care centres are very expensive they would have to better maintain those that we have. They would have to put more voluntary labour into maintaining the existing plant.

They are pointing out, secondly, that one way in which we can ensure that we build more day care centres is if the furniture and toys required for the existing ones are built by the women of our country on a voluntary basis. They are pointing out, thirdly, that in order for those we have to continue operating and for more to come on stream, the women must give of their time voluntarily in order to look after the children in the day care centres. Furthermore, they are pointing out that it is critically important to expand and deepen their international work and through this means seek ways of receiving internationalist assistance in the form of equipment and materials for the construction and equipping of these centres.

Collective Input and Wisdom

The point is, comrades, that out of the discussions a very concrete analysis resulted and its concreteness shows that a realistic approach is being taken to this question of day care facilities. The democratic discussions have led to a more elaborate and concrete document and one that is much more valuable because it reflects the collective input and wisdom of all NWO members.

Also, as a result of the discussions, more concrete ideas have come up with regards to legal reform, the solution of social problems, price control, culture and sports, all areas where women face problems. In fact, as the result of a national survey among 700 NWO members, a debate that was going on for some time within the organisation was finally answered. This survey established that the women of the NWO also wanted to be involved in sporting activities. And this in turn led to a decision that from next year and over the next three years, the NWO will give high priority to organising sporting activities for the women of our country. And I feel that too is very important for our women.

The discussions also revealed that a number of the problems faced by the organisation are problems which can be solved by the women themselves. They identified, for example, a shortage of quality full-time workers for NWO organising work.

And one of their creative solutions to this problem is the proposal to develop new committee structures at the national parish and group levels. At the national level the approach will be not just to rely, as they had done in the past, on the members of the national executive who are greatly overworked but to develop instead a number of national committees with a national executive member leading each committee.

At the parish level the idea is not just to rely on the parish executive members of the NWO, but also to have those members develop and lead a number of parish committees that would share the work. And at the group level to develop group committees also aimed at diversifying and sharing the work among more sisters.

As to the problem of inactive members, a problem faced by all organisations that have grown large, where you discover that very often it is a minority of women who are every day engaged in concrete work, the way in which our NWO sisters have handled this problem is to recognise that inactivity very often relates to a lack of interesting activities and a sufficiently exciting programme, and therefore, ultimately it relates to a lack of effective leadership at the group level.

Proposed Training Courses

Their proposed solution to this problem is to develop three new types of training in order to train the new political leadership at the middle and base level, the cadres required to get the groups going with vibrancy and active participation of all members.

One of these training course will concentrate on political education talks, where every month, 12 members of each group will be singled out and a political education talk will be given along with a written hand-out, after which it will be the responsibility of these 12 sisters to take this knowledge back to their groups.

A second method of training will be a two-hour leadership training programme every fortnight, over a three-month period. And, finally, a third method will be a combined political ecucation and leadership training course over six months, utilising one weekend in every month.

I have absolutely no doubt, comrades, that if this programme is maintained, with its correct emphasis on political education, and leadership training, then by June of next year already we would have seen a tremendous impact on the quality of work, and on the level of organisation, within the NWO.

We are convinced that this programme, because of its seriousness and its correct identification of the major problems, will increase even more the quality of organisational skills that the women in the NWO already possess.

Expansion of our Women's Human Rights

Comrades, we see all this activity over the last few months, all this discussion as being genuine democracy, as being the way in which real democratic participation should take place. We see this as being a real expansion of the

213

human rights of our women.

In many other ways, the NWO and the Revolution have expanded the human rights of the women of our country. The equal pay for equal work decree was an expansion of human rights. The prohibition of sexual exploitation by men in return for jobs was also a new human right, The Maternity Leave Law which stipulates that for three months during and just after pregnancy that women are entitled to such leave, and are entitled to have their jobs back at the end of such pregnancy, that too was another real expansion of the human rights of our women.

The Community Health Brigades that the women have been developing in order to improve the health conditions of their families and themselves are too an expansion of the human rights of our sisters. The benefits received together with other workers, through the National Transport Service, the Rent Law, the increased workmen's compensation, the Third Party Insurance law which ensures that buses must now be insured for at least $100,000 so that in the event of accident there will be reasonable compensation for the family, the free milk programme, the housing repair programme – all of these programmes which the women, together with the men of our country, have benefited from are, in our view, real expansions of the human rights that the women of our country have been able to enjoy for the first time.

New Class Formations

I want to focus for a while on the question of jobs, looking at this question in the context of the growth, the role and the importance of the working class women of our country. Obviously, the more workers that come into the workforce the greater should be our production. The speed at which we can bring more workers into production will help to determine the pace at which we can make the transition from the path of socialist orientation to that of socialist construction in our country.

As more and more women come in from the working class and assume positions of leadership in the National Women's Organisation, and receive scientific training as leaders, then more and more the new working class that develops will be a more mature, more class-conscious and more organised working class. So this question of the expansion of the women workers in our country is really a very, very important question for us here in Grenada.

We have done an analysis of 275 of the 300 plus delegates who are attending this Congress. A poll was done of these sisters and they were asked to answer a questionnaire with various questions like where they are working, how long they have been working there, their social class background and that of their families and so on. And from this analysis we have been able to discover that of the 275 delegates who were polled 180 of them were employed in one way or the other, and of this 180, 67% of them were members of the working class, the rural working class or they are NWO part-time and full-time workers.

From the urban and rural working class there are 91 delegates in that figure of 180 who are employed. That is 50.5% of all of the employed delegates are from the urban and rural working class. Add to this 30 more delegates who are NWO part time and full time workers (16.5% of the total) and we have a grand total of 121 of these sisters coming directly from the working class or 67% of all of the delegates who are present.

Now, that is a highly significant development. These figures are extremely revealing because they confirm a number of things which we have been thinking more and more about. They confirm first of all that the economy has in fact been growing, something that has been independently established by the World Bank, among others. They confirm too that many more jobs have been created for our unemployed people, particularly our women, and most of all they confirm the development of new class formations in our country.

If we compare the social class background of the mothers of these delegates with their own, you begin to see how important these figures are. Because what these figures also show is that over one quarter of all the mothers of these delegates are housewives as opposed to only 4.7% of the delegates themselves being housewives; that only 29.8% of their mothers were working class as compared to 67% of the delegates being working class and that only 2.2% of the mothers were intellectual workers as compared to fully 25% of the delegates being intellectual workers.

In one short generation, we are able already to see a very fundamental change and development taking place in the overall class formations in our country and in particular, the working class. The development of the working class carries tremendous implications for increasing production and for building the new society.

Comrades, I want to end on a point that was raised by your comrade President — the question of the internationalist work that our women have to do and the critical question of peace. Women, just as men, and, perhaps women even more than men, because women are the childbearers, have a great responsibility to ensure peace.

We believe the NWO has, in fact, begun to assume more of its internationalist responsibilities. More and more solidarity days are being held with different struggling peoples. More and more political education talks are being given. More and more members of the NWO are members of the Grenada Peace Council. For example, Comrade Claudette Pitt, International Relations Secretary of the NWO is an executive member of the Grenada Peace Council. The NWO is a member of the Women's International Democratic Federation, the largest and most progressive international women's organisation. The President of the NWO, Comrade Phyllis Coard, is a member of the Continental Women's Front against Aggression, and earlier this year a National Solidarity Campaign with the peoples of El Salvador, Namibia and Angola organised by the NWO commanded a lot of enthusiasm and received a lot of support from our people. In fact, $8,000 were raised for the struggling freedom fighters in El Salvador and 500 boxes of clothing were sent to the refugees of Angola and Namibia.

It is our view in the party and government that this work has to be deepened and strengthened because it is extremely important for the women of our country. It is important because the National Women's Organisation wants progress and happiness for all of its members. It wants security, progressive development and long life for the children of our country. But all of this cannot come about in the context of an unstable peace, where threats are being made against our process and other revolutionary processes, where tension prevails in the region. Therefore, peace is the first requirement to ensure these objective needs are met.

What Development Really Means

If we look at this question in terms of development, we can say that development implies a growing economy, more jobs for the people, more benefits in the areas of education, helath care, housing, water and food. Development means more infrastructure for the country: physical infrastructure like the international airport, the main roads, the feeder roads, the new telephone plant, the new electricity generators and so on. Developing also means the social infrastructure where we can emphasise health and education; the structure where we have the democratic organs that allow our people to participate in running the country; the economic infrastructure where we have the planning mechanisms, the military infrastructure where we are developing a strong armed forces based, in particular, on the people through their militia. But all of these aspects of infrastructure are really very important when finally compared to the most important aspect of infrastructure – the peace aspect. Because if we don't have peace, if world war descends tomorrow on mankind, it would not greatly matter what work we've done on the physical, the social, the political, the economic or the military infrastructure. In the final analysis, all of those infrastructures could get wiped out in a few seconds.

The Critical Importance of World Peace

And that is why it is so important for us to ensure that the women of our country concentrate in practice on raising the consciousness of all of our people on the critical importance of world peace, on the need to end the arms race, on the importance of disarmament and detente, on the need to ensure that those people who are manufacturing neutron bombs are completely exposed, on the need to support the people of the Soviet Union on their public declaration that they will never be the first to use nuclear arms.

We need to support the Soviet Union and other socialist world countries in the tireless efforts which they have been making to promote the concept of peaceful co-existence, a concept developed by Lenin many years ago, a concept which was continued and developed even further by the late Leonid Ilych Brezhnev, another foremost champion and stalwart for peace.

We need, in practice, to get the women in our NWO to understand the importance of having this Caribbean declared a Zone of Peace, Independence and Development. They must understand that such a declaration means an end to military bases set up without the consent of the people in a particular country; an end to aggressive military manoeuvres that threaten the peace of the region; an end to the use of mercenaries against other people's processes, the right of all peoples to build their own process in their own way, after their own image and likeness, free from all forms of outside dictation, free from all threats, free from the big stick.

This must be something that is concrete in the minds of our women. Because, if we are able to get these aspects of the Zone of Peace principle accepted, in practice, think of what it would mean for Cuba, for Nicaragua, for the revolutionary process in Suriname, and for our own revolution in Grenada.

Real Necessities for the Present

We have to begin to see these concepts not as abstractions but as real necessities that the present period demands. Establishing a Zone of Peace Independence and Development means guaranteeing the right of all colonial peoples to become fully independent and free. If that was fully accepted think of what it would mean for the patriots of Puerto Rico who are today still fighting for their independence.

If the right of a people to shake off oligarchs, and dictators, as part of their right to self-determination were accepted, think of what it would mean for the peoples of El Salvador, Guatemala, and Honduras, people fighting against military and other dictatorships who although oppressed yet see tremendous support being given to their oppressors by the United States, in particular.

Think of what it would mean for us if this Zone of Peace declaration really became accepted in practice and put an end once and for all to all forms of propaganda destabilization, economic aggression and destabilization, political and diplomatic isolation, military threats and the use of military force against any other country.

Think of what that would mean for the prospects and possibilities of peaceful and progressive development for all of our people in Grenada!

So comrades, this question of peace, of getting to understand more and more what is meant by the Zone of Peace, of getting the women in the NWO to really internalise all of its concepts and begin to speak more and more to our people about its importance is something that we can never underestimate.

Importance of Ideological Pluralism

Linked to the zone of peace is the important question of ideological pluralism. What this concept of ideological pluralism really says is that everybody has a right to choose their own way of developing their own country, that everybody has the right to decide their own social, economic, cultural and political forms and to develop their countries in their way. A major struggle is still being waged to get these concepts accepted.

The recent CARICOM Heads of Government meeting was a classic example of the difficulties of getting these concepts accepted, because there were people at that conference who were opposed to these fundamental principles. And some of these people having been exposed before public opinion in the Caribbean are now pretending that they never had any disagreement, and that Grenada is making up something on them. But as all of our people know, comrades, we in the People's Revolutionary Government and the New Jewel Movement never tell lies. We rely only on the facts and the truth. Some of these elements today are trying to get some of their friends in the so-called free press to pretend that at the conference the questions of a Zone of Peace and of ideological pluralism (and I expect that soon they will add the question of the University of the West Indies) were never discussed.

But the fact is that these matters were discussed, and it is important for the people of Grenada and the people of the region to insist that all of their representatives make a public stand on these critical questions. The people have a right to know where their leaders stand on this question of a Zone of Peace and on the right of all people to develop their own countries in their own way. This kind of exposure therefore must be done.

We certainly continue to say in Grenada: yes, to the Zone of Peace, yes, to the principle of ideological pluralism, yes, to the need to keep the University of the West Indies as a regional institution, and we have no doubt that all of our people, all of our workers, farmers, youth, and women will fight for these principles.

We know that our people will reject all attempts at ducking and covering up. We know that our people are going to insist that our Party and government continue to demand that the Caribbean in fact is declared a Zone of Peace.

We are confident that our people and, among them, our women will continue to support the just struggles of the peoples of El Salvador, Guatemala, Honduras, Haiti and Chile. Our people will continue to support the revolutionary processes going forward in Cuba, Nicaragua, and Suriname, will continue to give our fullest support to the fighting people of Mozambique and Angola who are today facing the threat of direct invasion from South Africa, will continue to support the people of Palestine in their just claim for their own territory, will continue to support the people of East Timor, the people of the Western Sahara, the people of Namibia, the people of South Africa and all of the National Liberation Movements around the world fighting for peace, independence, justice and social progress for their people.

We have absolutely no doubt that the free, fighting women of revolutionary Grenada with pens in their hands when necessary, with machines and tractors when necessary, with cutlasses and forks when necessary, with their organs of people's power when necessary, and with their guns when necessary — will fight to safeguard our revolution, to build it and push it forward.

Confidence in Our Heroic Women

We know that we can rely with the greatest of confidence on the heroic fighting women of Grenada. We know we can rely on them to safeguard and defend every nutmeg pod in our country, every cocoa tree in our country, every single sapodilla in our country and the grains of hair on the heads of all the elderly and young people in our country.

Today, we salute the National Women's Organisation and their First Congress. We salute the work of our women over the years in production — our women agricultural workers, our women farmers, our women construction workers, our women in co-operatives and our women teachers. We salute the tremendous work the Ministry of Education and Women's Affairs has played over the years and in particular the role which has been played by Comrade Jacqueline Creft as Minister of Education.

Today, we salute the creation of the new Ministry of Women's Affairs for the first time in the history of our country and the history of the English-speaking Caribbean. We also salute the outstanding leaders of the NWO for their tremendous courage, discipline, dedication and self-sacrifice. We commend them for their outstanding organisational qualities, for the scientific work which they have done over the months and years to ensure that the NWO is today what it is. And in particular, we salute the tremendous work that has been done by Comrade Phyllis Coard, the President of the National Women's Organisation.

We salute today, comrades, the memory of Edith McBain, of Scotilda, of Laurice, Laureen and Bernadette, and so many unknown and unsung martyrs and heroes who died in the cause of justice and freedom over the years.

Today, we are confident that the National Women's Organisation will go forward with the tasks which you have set, that you will continue to make progress in production, education and training; that the priorities which you have set in political education, skills training, and academic education through the CPE will be followed; that the internationalist work which you have outlined for yourselves will strengthen your responsibilities not only to the Grenada Revolution but to the world revolutionary process and to the struggle for peace and progress and against imperialism. We are confident that our women in the fighting NWO, conscious of their duties, will go forward and will carry out these historic tasks.

219

19. 'Every Grain of Sand is Ours!'

Radio/TV Address to the Nation, 23 March 1983, St. George's, Grenada

Tonight on behalf of our Party and government I have the responsibility of informing our people that our Revolution is in grave danger and that our country is faced with its gravest threat since our glorious March 13th Revolution. From the evidence in our possession we are convinced that an armed attack against our country by counter-revolutionaries and mercenaries organised, financed, trained and directed by United States imperialism is imminent and can come any day now!

Only a few days ago — on March 17th, to be precise — at our 1983 Budget Plan presentation I revealed the analysis of our Party that the warmongering Reagan was becoming increasingly desperate and in that desperation the possibility of military intervention against the revolutionary processes in the region — particularly Cuba, Nicaragua and Grenada — seemed inevitable.

This seemed the only way out for the fascist clique in Washington because their arrogant designs for regional and world domination continue to fail. The continuing economic crisis in the United States and its effects, the increasing successes of the popular liberation movements particularly in El Salvador, the continued deepening and strengthening of the revolutionary processes in Cuba, Nicaragua and Grenada, the total collapse of Reagan's so-called Caribbean Basin Initiative, and the growing popular opposition in the United States and internationally to his mad nuclear policy have made imperialism more desperate and determined to halt revolutionary processes in this region.

Less than 36 hours after we PUBLICLY REVEALED what our intelligence sources and our analysis suggested; less that 36 hours after we alerted our people to this possible danger, an all out invasion of Nicaragua was in fact launched. A large contingent of Somocista counter-revolutionaries — armed, trained, financed and directed by the CIA — were dropped by airplanes into Nicaragua, only 120 miles from its capital.

It is important to note comrades, that this invasion came exactly three days after the statement by the US Chief of Naval Operations, Admiral James Watkins, that the time had come 'for the United States to put some teeth behind our rhetoric'. In other words he was saying that the United States must back up its threats with military action.

We now have concrete intelligence information which confirms the view that the revolution will be faced with military aggression from imperialism. With the attack against Nicaragua, the dangers facing us are more real and urgent.

For some time now, our intelligence services have been gathering information on counter-revolutionary groups who have publicly declared their intention to overthrow revolutionary governments in the region. What we have discovered as a result are the following facts:

1. That the key counter-revolutionaries have been meeting more frequently in recent times;

2. That several of these corrupt, opportunist and reactionary elements who aspire to grab power have begun to resolve their leadership differences with the aim of creating a more united counter-revolutionary front;

3. That their co-ordination with the CIA has stepped up;

4. That they have received direct assistance from the CIA in the form of money, arms and training and they have also received offers of transportation, logistical support and supplies and an undertaking that immediately on launching the attack their declared counter-revolutionary government will receive US recognition;

5. We have been able to discover the name and full background of the main CIA case officer responsible for co-ordinating the present plot; we know his name, where he has worked before, his previous activities and which other revolutionary processes he has attempted to subvert in recent times.

6. Another CIA case officer involved in this operation is known to have been involved in directing and masterminding the operation to assassinate the leadership that resulted in the murderous June 19th 1980 bomb blast.

7. These elements have established direct links with the Cuban Exile Group which was responsible for the Air Cubana disaster and with Somocista counter-revolutionary elements who are right now involved in the invasion of Nicaragua.

8. With the assistance of the CIA, these elements have been able to get some of the criminal elements they hope to use in the invasion of our country — trained in Miami in some of the same camps in which the Somocista counters and various other mercenaries have been trained.

9. As part of their planning process, the CIA helped to allocate different sets of these criminal counter-revolutionaries for the physical attacks against Nicaragua and Grenada and they decided several weeks ago to attack during this precise period in order to coincide with the massive military manoeuvres taking place in our region at this time and as a culmination of the major propaganda offensive of Reagan and his chief lieutenants against the revolutionary processes in the region.

10. The main base of operation and activity of these elements is one of our neighbouring territories, only a few miles away from Grenada.

11. As a result of all this work on our part we have been able not only to uncover actual plans to overthrow our Government and turn back our Revolution, but also the approximate number of men they hope to use, the

approximate number and type of arms they possess, the kind of logistical support they hope to receive. We know, comrades, the targets they intend to destroy. We know many of the persons they plan to arrest, those they plan to kill and how they plan to strike terror and fear among the broad masses. 12. It is necessary, sisters and brothers, to doubly emphasise that we know the actual period in the near future that they are hoping to use to launch their murderous attack.

Sisters and brothers, bearing in mind all of these facts, considering the clear and disturbing pattern of United States intervention and aggression in our region and the world, noting the invasion of Nicaragua now taking place, we have concluded that the danger which we face in this period is real and imminent. When the President of the United States of America, who is also Commander-in-Chief of the armed forces, states publicly and clearly that tiny Grenada is a threat to the national security of the mighty and powerful USA, and when his top advisers and military personnel indicate that the time has come to put 'teeth into their rhetoric' then it is clear that Goliath has finally turned his full attention to David.

When the Commander-in-Chief of one of the most sophisticated, most advanced and largest armed forces in the world, chooses to classify a small, proud and determined people as a threat to his national security then this must be cause for serious concern.

We have to ask ourselves why would Reagan's most senior officials, including his Vice-President, George Bush (former chief of the CIA), his Secretary of State William Schultz, his Secretary for Defence Caspar Weinberger and his Deputy Secretary for Inter-American Affairs, Nesta Sanchez, all choose to make slanderous statements, if this were not to provide the justification for this planned aggression against our country?

The United States Government has a well documented history of dealing with countries which it has deemed threats to its national security. The United States has intervened militarily in this region alone well over 100 times in the past 100 years to protect its so-called national security interests.

And, although the information on this current threat is by far the most detailed and specific that we have had of any plot, and although this threat is by far the most dangerous that we have ever faced, yet some of our people are saying that there have been occasions when we have had cause for justified concern that our Revolution was threatened. That is true comrades, and we just admit it, but what is important for us to stress tonight is that on previous occasions, we forced our enemies to change their plans at the last minute because we were successfully able to mobilise regional and international public opinion in our defence. In other words, we were able to alert the world to the danger that we faced and the world stood up with us.

Informing International Public Opinion

The best example of this that I can give you tonight is the 'Amber and

Amberines' manoeuvre conducted by the United States in August 1981 off
Puerto Rico as a full scale dress rehearsal for an invasion of our country.
Once we had received concrete proof from the lips of the man in charge of
the operation – Rear Admiral McKenzie – that this manoeuvre was a trial
run for the actual invasion of our beloved homeland we immediately went
on a political and diplomatic offensive to alert the world of the threat facing
us, to call for international solidarity and to request our friends to pressure
the United States not to carry out its aggressive plans. We informed the
United Nations, the Non-Aligned Movement, the Organisation of American
States and other regional and international organisations of the grave
situation. We also informed peace loving and friendly governments, political
parties, pressure groups, and other organisations of the danger.

In fact, literally hundreds of cables, telexes, telephone calls, letters and so
on were made to virtually all parts of the world. It was fortunate for us that
the conscience of mankind and the force of world public opinion on all
continents responded readily to our call. In fact, at a recent summit, the head
of a particular government informed us of his government's concern at the
time of the 'Amber and the Amberines' threat and the action which he had
taken at that time in calling in the US Ambassador resident in his country to
demand an explanation. This particular country is tens of thousands of
miles away from us.

As a result of these and other experiences, we now fully understand and
appreciate the tremendous importance and impact of international public
opinion and on this occasion we are again taking the necessary steps to alert
and mobilise regional and international public opinion.

But comrades there is another very important lesson which we have also
learnt and that is: whenever our country is in danger, whenever our
revolution is threatened, we must always go all out to give our people all of
the facts, to fully alert them as to the precise nature of the danger and to call
upon them to mobilise and organise themselves in defence of our revolution.

Ready for the Ultimate Sacrifice

That is why, apart from mobilising international public opinion to stand up
with us at the time of the 'Amber and the Amberines' threat, we also
mobilised our people to respond decisively with the successful 'Heroes of
the Homeland' manoeuvre which demonstrated to the world that in the
defence of this land, in the freedom of our sea and sky, we stand as a proud,
united, conscious and vigilant people ready and willing to make the ultimate
sacrifice.

Sisters and brothers of our beloved Revolutionary homeland, again in face
of grave danger we need to call our people to arms. Once again, we have to
shoulder our fundamental responsibility to defend what we fought for and
won after many years of bitter struggle. We must never forget that the only
way in which we can ever guarantee that international public opinion comes

to our defence is if we can continue to demonstrate to the world that we are willing as a united people — every single one of us — to stand up firmly on our own two legs with arms in our hands to fight and to die, if necessary, in the defence of our beloved homeland. This land is ours, every square inch of its soil is ours, every grain of sand is ours, every nutmeg pod is ours, every beautiful young pioneer who walks on this land is ours, it is our responsibility — and ours alone — to fight to defend our homeland.

Over the past few days, our people have demonstrated a genuine spirit of internationalism. In the many solidarity statements with heroic Nicaragua coming from all sections of our working people, our women, our youth, the sense of fraternal anguish and shared identity comes very clearly across. But even so, comrades, we must be self-critical and we must admit that we have allowed ourselves to slip into complacency and a degree of overconfidence, in responding to the present situation. Some sections of our people, while recognising that dangers do exist, allow themselves to believe that Grenada will not be invaded because we are a small island or because we share no borders with hostile neighbours as Nicaragua does. Some also feel that because ours is the only revolution that has not yet faced direct military attack from outside, we will continue to be lucky, and some even go as far as to say that with victory on the horizon for our sisters and brothers in Nicaragua, imperialism will not have any mercenaries to send to Grenada.

Not Lose Sight of the Dangerous Reality

However, comrades, we cannot under any circumstances, and particularly in light of the concrete information we now have, lose sight of the dangerous reality at present. The Seychelles islands and Comoros islands, smaller in size and population than Grenada, were both subject to invasions from the forces of imperialism in the last few years.

We should also remember that prior to the 1961 Playa Giron or Bay of Pigs invasion of Cuba, which resulted in crushing defeat for counter-revolutionary forces supported by United States imperialism, there were some Cubans who believed, for all kinds of similar reasons, that there would be no invasion of Cuba. But it came, and today the Cuban revolution is invincible because our heroic Cuban comrades — like our heroic Nicaraguan comrades today — have learnt the lessons of history and the need for permanent vigilance and preparedness of their people. We in Grenada cannot — like ostriches — bury our heads in the sand and ignore the lessons of history.

Sisters and brothers of our Revolutionary homeland, how do we respond to the present threat? Our fundamental duty is to defend our homeland, to be psychologically, politically and combatively prepared to handle an attack in whatever form and at whatever time Reagan and his warmongers may choose to land on our shores.

This means that for those of us who are not yet in the Militia — we must join now!

For those who are inactive — we must reactivate ourselves and begin training in a serious, disciplined, consistent and revolutionary manner!

There is a role for everyone to play in defence — the elderly as well as the young. We must remember that Reagan and his warmongers will not choose who to kill! The bullet does not spare the young or the elderly.

Our Main Task

There are trenches to be dug, vehicles to be driven, food to be cooked and distributed, first aid assistance to be organised, the care of the young and elderly to be guaranteed, and many more specific tasks to be accomplished.

In addition to our *number one task* of recruitment into the Militia, there are other measures to be taken to strengthen our defence capacity.

There will be immediate recruitment into some sections of the People's Revolutionary Army and Grenada Police Service.

Our Peoples Revolutionary Armed Forces will stage a massive military manoeuvre from April 21-24. This manoeuvre, which we are calling 'Jeremiah Richardson Defence of the Homeland Manoeuvre', will again demonstrate to imperialism that we are a united, strong and vigilant people who will never give up!!!

Sisters and brothers of our Free Revolutionary Homeland, let us ensure that Reagan and his warmongers never ever turn back the forward march of our people and revolution. The work that we are doing today in the building of a people's economy and the construction of a new infrastructure is laying the basis for a secure future for all our people.

Let us do everything in our power to ensure that that secure future is not unduly disturbed by the terrible loss of life, property and the mass suffering and destruction which any invasion that we are not prepared to withstand is bound to bring.

Towards the Glorious New Day

Notwithstanding the uncertainty posed by this present threat, let us continue to work with discipline, determination and serene confidence towards the glorious day when there will be no unemployment in our country, when each and every family will have a decent living, when every man, woman and child is guaranteed their total right to education, health and social security.

As we prepare to deal with this imminent threat, let us remember that our sisters and brothers, the brave sons and daughters of Sandino's Nicaragua are continuing their fierce struggle to crush the forces of counter-revolution and United States imperialism.

According to inside reports, 500 well trained counter-revolutionaries were parachuted into Nicaragua days in advance of the main force and are right now being supplied by planes coming from Honduras. At the same time,

1,500 more are now inside Nicaragua on their way to join the advance group of 500 and a further 2,500 plus are concentrated on the border with Honduras, awaiting their turn to massacre innocent women and children in their vain hope to turn back the heroic Nicaraguan Revolution.

While we in Grenada must unhesitatingly and firmly condemn these acts of aggression against our sisters and brothers of Revolutionary Nicaragua, we must at the same time, in a clear, resounding and unequivocal voice, join the rest of progressive mankind in condemning the active involvement of Israel and Honduran army personnel, including the direct bombing of key positions in Nicaragua by Honduran military forces, in this open and barbarous onslaught on the sovereign soil of Nicaragua.

Our Permanent SolidarityWith Nicaragua

It is clear to us however, that no amount of arms and weapons of war can hinder the onward march of the revolutionary process taking place in Nicaragua and we once again affirm to the sons and daughters of Sandino our full, unswerving and permanent solidarity.

Let us take careful note of the fact that these counter-revolutionary elements were sent in advance of the main force — just like had happened in their attacks on the Seychelles and Comoros islands. Let us also observe that they are receiving regular supplies by enemy planes and that more elements were waiting to move it. Let us observe these facts, learn the lessons and apply them to our situation.

With our information, with these examples, both historical and present, we ought not to be taken unprepared. That would be a crime against our past, present and future. Let us together ensure that we come out of this period stronger in unity, fortified in spirit, firmer in our determination, more organised in our democratic structures, so that we will be able to respond to future threats like a second nature because of our constant preparedness.

Sisters and brothers, in your name, even at this late hour, we issue another call for sanity. We want to repeat that our preference is for peace and normal relations with the United States administration. We understand very clearly that only an environment of peace will allow us the opportunity to continue to develop our economy, raise our academic and skills levels and our political consciousness and bring more and more benefits to our people.

We do not want war. We have never wanted war. But equally we are not prepared to give up our birthright or to allow others — no matter how big and powerful they are — to shape our destiny for us or to tell us what we can do, when we can do it and how we must do it.

Our enemies had better try to understand the deep pride and dignity of our people and the courageous way in which we have always faced up to difficulties. They will do well to recall the heroic history of struggle and resistance of our people from the days of Fedon through Butler and Marryshow right up to the present. They had better remember the vanguard role of our glorious Party — the New Jewel Movement — which mobilised, organised and led our people through the years of terror and repression of the Gairy dictatorship right up to the seizure of state power and the dawning of the new day of liberation and freedom which came to our country on March 13th, 1979.

Proud, Peace-loving and Courageous People

There is no doubt that we are a peace-loving people but there is equally no doubt that we are proud and courageous people who will always fight to defend our dignity, our freedom and our homeland.

What is needed from us as a people at this time is to be more self critical, to make sure that we never allow ourselves to slip back into complacency, to make sure that we are always as ready to defend our homeland as we are to continue to build it, to make sure that we never again allow our Militia duties to be taken lightly, to make sure that once we regain our fighting strength and vigour of (August 1981) when we were responding to the Amber and the Amberines threat we do not allow ourselves to ever lose that vigour and strength again. Our watchwords must forever be:

Calm and calculated in the fulfilment of our daily tasks
Always vigilant
Always willing to work
Always ready to study
Always ready to produce.

yet always ready, prepared, confident and assured of victory whenever and however Reagan and his warlords strike!

20. Forward to Peace, Genuine Independence and Development in a United America — Our America!

Address to Protocolary Session of Organisation of American States, Washington USA, 1 June 1983

We meet here at a time when the world and in particular the developing world which we so amply represent, is faced by an alarming array of social and economic problems which we must collectively confront in an effort to attain genuine progress and development for our peoples. Yet this is also a time when genuine efforts are already emerging from among us to resolve the social, economic, financial and political problems with which we are confronted. These efforts represent a reserve of determination and will which is part of our American heritage.

A century and a half ago, the great Liberator, Simon Bolivar, the father of Pan-Americanism whose bicentennial we celebrate this year spoke to patriots throughout the Americas of the importance of unity in the struggle for progress. In his famous Jamaica letter written in Kingston in 1815, he stated, 'Surely unity is what we need to complete our work of regeneration' and in 1819, delivering an address at the inauguration of the Second National Congress of Venezuela in Argentina, came the famous lines: 'Unity, Unity, must be our motto in all things. The blood of our citizens is varied: let it be mixed for the sake of unity'.

Today, 150 years later, as we seek to attain peace, justice and progress for the people of the Americas, we must respond to those echoes in the corridors of history. Indeed, even while we speak of the need for unity and the integrated development of our people, we do so with the knowledge that while we have shared historical experiences, the specific character and development of each State is different. Our unity is therefore based on mutual acceptance and understanding of each other's right to develop its own process as it deems best for the progress of its peoples.

In this region, we are a diverse people, of Indian, European, Asian and African origins, with an array of cultural and social patterns. What we acclaim and must cherish is our unity in the diversity that we represent.

The destiny of our English-speaking Caribbean is inextricably linked with that of our Spanish-speaking brothers and sisters. Not only Simon Bolivar, but also other great thinkers of our time have recognized that our future lies in the unity of our peoples. In the early 20th Century, the Grenadian Theophilus Marryshow, the Father of West Indies Federation said:

A West Indies in a world like this must unite or perish. This is not the time for parish pump politics. We think nobly, nationally, with special regard for the first fundamentals of a West Indian unity, and a West Indian identity.

As Simon Bolivar fought at the beginning of the 19th Century for the unity of Latin America, so too Marryshow fought at the beginning of the 20th Century for the unity of the Caribbean. As inheritors of these great traditions, we have a duty: that is, as we approach the 21st Century, doing so with collective experience of national independence and with an anti-colonial perspective, our duty must be to harness the strength of unity that we represent and that we genuinely embody. For only in unity can we earnestly fight to overcome the seemingly monumental difficulties of our region, 'Our Americas', as Jose Marti, that great Americanist thinker, entitled our region.

In this regard we in Grenada place great significance on the signing of a Treaty in December 1982 which established formal relations between the Caribbean Community (CARICOM) and the Organization of American States. The basis for institutional interaction and exchange is most certainly being strengthened within our region.

Our American continent must not only be united, but we must have peace: a peace which brings economic and social justice, equality, and greater independence and freedom for all those down-trodden and oppressed.

Our entire region has a history of struggle for independence and freedom from domination. We cannot forget the first great Revolution in our hemisphere, when on July 4th, 1776, the Congress of the United States declared that 'These United Colonies are and of right ought to be free and independent States.' The people of the United States fought bravely for their freedom, against colonialism and exploitation, so that in 1783 England lost all her original colonies in North America. Throughout our region the struggle for independence, progress, peace and genuine development has gone on. It has never stopped. We are experiencing a natural historical continuum between these brave early struggles for independence and self-determination on the one hand, and the epic struggles of the people of our Americas on the other hand, of which the heroic and unconquerable people of Central America deserve singular mention.

We must continue to offer all our support for the achievement of real justice, economic well-being and social equality for all our people. For it is in attaining justice and equality that we can begin to realize peace, meaningful peace. Yet another son of the Americas, Benito Juarez, helped to fashion a workable reality for us when he said: 'Respect for the rights of the other is Peace.' If we truly aim at peace and development for our region, at the individual development of each country and our collective progress as well, we must respect the rights of the sons and daughters of Sandino to seek their solutions to the problems of poverty, unemployment, illiteracy and under-development which have plagued their country for over a century since the attainment of independence in 1838.

We join international public opinion in supporting initiatives by the people of Latin America to the problems of our region. Contadora represents a significant step towards finding a solution to important dimensions of the problems in Central America.

It offers concrete hope for finding a negotiated solution to our problems, and additionally reemphasises the importance of peacefully settling disputes through dialogue and without resorting to the use of force or interference in the affairs of our neighbours.

Mr Chairman, today, the peoples of Central America, indeed the peoples of Latin America and the Caribbean, must be allowed to decide what process befits their particular experience.

Nicaragua has had a difficult past. For decades, its integrity has been trampled by the interventionist boot and from 1936 to 1979, by the unparalleled tyranny of a family dynasty. Despite the popular and definitive character of the Sandinista victory of July 19th, 1979, the Nicaraguan people are not being left to develop their own process in peace and to find solutions to the problems which have plagued the country. This is a matter of grave concern to Grenada. Moreover, Grenada shares in the broad international outrage at the provocation to which Nicaragua has been subjected over the last week. Similarly, and with equal seriousness, we decry the tremendous loss of life and the overall regrettable state of affairs in Central America.

We oppose any attempt to give support to those whose objective is to destabilize the Sandinista regime and to promote strife and discord in Central America. What matters is the future of the people of the Latin American region as perceived by the people themselves. The region cannot be held to ransom or made to adhere to values and systems which others choose. The people of Central America will look at the experience of almost two centuries of their independence, decide for themselves why poverty and under-development have pursued them so relentlessly and seek their own negotiated solutions to their problems.

I reiterate my country's support for the French-Mexican Declaration of 1981, an effort which seeks to bring together for dialogue all the truly representative forces in El Salvador.

Mr Chairman, Grenada again calls for peaceful solutions to all the region's border disputes, another legacy of colonialism which continues to adversely affect our peaceful and integrated development. The territorial integrity of Belize must be respected and the Belizean people left to pursue their own path to peace, progress and genuine development.

We also seek to ensure that all vestiges of colonialism are removed from our region. The foreign policy of Grenada is unequivocally anti-colonial. Our support for peace, independence and development automatically assumes opposition to the colonial situation which has so divided our peoples. We extend full support to the Argentinian people in their struggle to retain the Malvinas Islands. It is an issue about which we cannot be apathetic. The

Non-Aligned Movement has consistently supported Argentina's claim to the islands. Consistent with the United Nations resolution on the issue, and in the interest of a peaceful and speedy settlement, we call upon Great Britain to return to the negotiating table with Argentina.

Even as we concentrate on themes of unity and peace for the development of the region, we are aware of the severe economic and financial problems facing our countries. A report prepared by the IDB shows that the GDP of Latin America and the Caribbean declined by one percent in 1982. Some of our countries have had to seek rescheduling of foreign debts. We have felt the adverse effects of fluctuating international markets for our primary products. Now more than ever, we feel the urgent need for restructuring of the international monetary and financial institutions to make them more responsibe to the needs of our developing countries.

Our interdependence is a fact of our existence as developing and over-exploited countries of the American continent, and we are deeply aware of the need to co-operate in order to secure social and economic benefits for our people and to secure peace in our region. We sincerely hope that the meeting to be convened in Venezuela later this year will generate new and workable solutions to the region's deep economic and financial problems.

Because peace, independence and development are necessary for the progress of the peoples of the entire region, Grenada is particularly concerned about our relationship with the United States of America.

My government has consistently sought to establish and to maintain normal and mutually respectful relations with our powerful northern neighbour. It is an unfortunate historical fact that every effort on our part to achieve this has been ignored or rebuffed.

As a member of the Inter-American family, Grenada's purpose is to solve the social and economic problems which confront our people. We pursue a foreign policy of Non-Alignment which for us includes a real and ongoing diversification and expansion of our relations.

This explains our active involvement in the concerns of Latin America, seeking solutions to the problems of our Small Island States, advocating self-determination in a new political and economic framework, and acceptance of the principle of ideological pluralism.

I reaffirm what representatives of our government and people have said so many times before: that Grenada constitutes no threat to the United States. We repeat that the new International Airport is a civilian project vital to the economic development of our country. It has been discussed and considered by successive Grenadian governments for the past quarter century and no less than six voluminous studies and reports have been done on its feasibility. The runway is the same length as St Lucia's and smaller than that of Barbados. It is also a project which past United States and Canadian administrations have recognized as vital to the development of our tourist industry. We have received assistance for the project from countries throughout the world; and its importance to our economic development is unquestionable.

Our particular vision of the Americas is one which recognizes the right of member states to choose their own destiny and this same vision of ours accepts the possibilities of peaceful coexistence, diversity and a variety of political systems. It is in this ideological spirit that we embrace Venezuela, Cuba, Nicaragua, Mexico, Barbados, Martinique and Suriname as all legitimate sons of the Americas. We cannot in principle subscribe to the attempt to isolate any member of our hemispheric family.

Pluralism is a reality of our region. We exist with different systems, different solutions, different approaches emanating from the common search for peace, true independence and meaningful development.

On another issue, Mr Chairman, we cannot express support for the US Caribbean Basin Initiative, since it deliberately seeks to exclude our country and others of the American family from economic benefits given to the region. The unity of our peoples must not be compromised by attempts to divide us. We who have a history of colonialism already understand what it is to be divided by language and culture. We already know what it is to be fighting off the colonial legacy of mistrust. If assistance is to be given to an area designated the 'Caribbean Basin', then it must be given to all the countries of the area without discrimination.

In this regard, we take the opportunity to express our additional concern over the United States announcement that $4.4 million will be made available as scholarship assistance through the OAS to countries of the Caribbean Basin, excluding Suriname, Nicaragua and Grenada. The vision of an organisation with a people united in a common drive towards development precludes the toleration of such divisiveness, and an organisation which by its very existence gives substance to the dreams of Bolivar, must, we feel, not allow discrimination against any member state. This is a danger to our regional movement.

Mr Chairman, distinguished Ambassadors and representatives, the unity of our region must prevail. Member-states of the Organization of American States, represented at the Third Special Inter-American Conference, stated in a preambular paragraph to the 'Protocol of Buenos Aires' that

> the charter of the Organization of American States signed at Bogota in 1948, set forth the purpose of achieving an order of peace and justice, promoting solidarity among the American states, strengthening their collaboration and defending their sovereignty, their territorial integrity, and their independence. Our unity must be based on principles of justice, genuine independence, liberation, peace, and mutual respect.

The countries of our Organization of American States must demonstrate respect for the principles of legal equality of all nation states, mutual respect for sovereignty, territorial integrity, ideological pluralism, non-interference in the internal affairs of other states and the rights of each country to develop its own process free from all forms of outside dictation and pressure. Above all, our countries must work together actively in the promotion of peace, for without peace, our dreams of development will remain mere dreams. Without respect for internationally accepted principles, Central America will have no peace and will be doomed to continuous turmoil.

Grenada has always envisioned the attainment of peace in our region, and our Organization of American States has helped to give substance to that dream by unanimously adopting the IX General Assembly of the Organization of American States a Resolution aimed at declaring the Caribbean region a Zone of Peace.

Let us all, inheritors of the compelling vision of Bolivar, Benito Juarez, José Marti, Marryshow and all those other heroes who fought for peace, progress and freedom, work together in this our America to ensure concrete and long-lasting solutions to the real problems of the region — to poverty, unemployment, illiteracy, disease and transnational exploitation of our resources. The vision of an America peaceful by virtue of its integrated development is still vibrantly alive.

Grenada reiterates its commitment to the Charter of our organisation. Our nations must proceed without confusion believing that we will achieve the goals agreed to in our Charter.

Mr Chairman, distinguished Ambassadors and representatives of our America, if we lose the war on poverty and underdevelopment and allow ourselves to move back into the darkness of enslavement, we will have to blame not the weapons of the enemy, but our own divisiveness.

Forward to peace, genuine independence and development in a United America — Our America.

21. We Proudly Share the Noble Dreams of Martin and Malcolm

Address to the Sixth Annual Dinner of TransAfrica, Washington, 8 June 1983

First, I want to thank Mayor Marion Barry and the people of Washington DC for the presentation of the keys to your historic city. This honour to the government and people of Grenada is something that we will always cherish.

I am greatly honoured, and greatly moved, to find myself here tonight in the presence of a gathering such as this one; a gathering of some of the finest sons and daughters of the heroic Black American people.

To you I bring greetings from the government and people of our small, brave and freedom-loving island nation of Grenada. I also wish to congratulate you on this your 6th Annual Dinner and to express my pleasure for the opportunity to share these precious moments with you.

Your history and ours have at times been so closely intertwined as to be near inseparable. We can point to Caribbean-American figures such as Marcus Garvey, for while he was born in the Caribbean he has spent many of his more productive years living and working in the USA. By the same token, *our* Harry Belafonte is also your Harry Belafonte. Many, many eminent and distinguished black Americans are Caribbean-born or of Caribbean parentage. We point to a few examples such as Malcolm X and Sidney Poitier, Kwame Toure (formerly known as Stokely Carmichael), and Ciceley Tyson. In fact in the case of Malcolm, his mother came from a small village in Grenada, called La Digue. It is certain that some of you here tonight also share this distinction of Caribbean-American heritage.

The history, the problems and the aspirations of the masses of people of Africa, the Caribbean and Black America are extraordinarily similar. And that is why TransAfrica is an organisation with so much meaning and relevance to us all. Tonight, I salute the policies and recommendations that TransAfrica has initiated and the work accomplished on behalf of the people of Africa and the Caribbean.

Indeed, tonight's event is a timely testimony of your tenacity, your fierce independence and judgement of will and your dedication to justice, equality and freedom for us in the developing world. Consistent with the above, we are certainly happy to endorse TransAfrica's recommendations of June 1982,

that the United States, given its immense leverage with South Africa, should adopt a policy of escalating economic and political sanctions against that country with the aim of bringing about an end to apartheid and the independence of Namibia.

The links between our people and the 30 million Black people of America go far back into the chronicles of the European assault on our ancestral land and our common struggle against racist oppression and the enforced transportation of our ancestors to the Americas.

The struggle of the Black American people has been a constant source of inspiration to the liberation struggles of the peoples of the world. In every corner of the earth where people are struggling or have struggled to win their freedom, the names of your great leaders are honoured, and people draw strength from your struggles and your victories.

We know the role that the example of your fighters and the ideas of your thinkers have played in the liberation of their ancestral country, Africa. No one can deny the influence of people like W.E. Dubois, Paul Robeson, Langston Hughes and Martin Luther King, on the awakening of the political consciousness of Africa. The independence movements in Africa sprang directly out of the Pan African Movement, which in turn, owed a great deal to the spread of liberation ideology from Black America and the Caribbean.

As regard Black America and the Caribbean, your fighting history has had a most significant bearing upon the course of Caribbean history, bringing with it an interesting interaction, a cross-fertilisation of our two destinies.

I must also say that our country, Grenada, with the same fierce determination as that of African states and Glack America, has embraced Africa's number one priority: full, unconditional liberation and self determination for Southern Africa. In the exercise of this embrace and endearment of Africa, thousands of our people have warmly received in Grenada President Kenneth Kaunda, President Samora Machel, and Sister Sally Mugabe – the courageous and inspirational wife of President Mugabe and a leader in her own right.

Let me also, at this time, reiterate our firmest support for the African National Congress (ANC), the representative political organisation of the black people of South Africa and SWAPO, the authentic representative of the Namibian people.

Let me also restate our conviction that the government and people of Mozambique will defeat the aggressions against them and that the government and people of Angola will continue to consolidate their revolutionary process.

But sisters and brothers, to be very open and frank, what worries us about the Southern African struggle is not just the brutal, aggressive and expansionist policies of South Africa, but also the attitude of the powerful USA administration to the conditions of misery and suffering in that part of the world. The warm and friendly relations between the United States and South African governments in defiance of the UN is really an affront to humanity. The open hostility of the United States Administration to Grenada, while at the same time embracing South Africa, underlines the serious hypocrisy of the present Administration and has painted an image that does no justice to the greatness of the American people.

In Central America what we are experiencing is the extension of the same attitude that again negates the interests and aspirations of the people of this region and the course of history. After all, the entire region, including the USA, has had a history of struggle for independence and freedom from domination. How can the American Revolution and war of independence be ever forgotten? Revolutionary upheavals in Central America and the Caribbean today are only the continuation of these struggles, with different forms in some respects, but fundamentally the same in essence: 'the struggle for National Liberation, Peace and Justice.'

Because this is so, the question arises: What is the way forward in these troubled parts? We in all honesty think that *only* the people of Central America can solve their problems. Contadora, the much debated initiative, advanced by Mexico, Panama, Venezuela and Columbia must be seen as a step in the right direction, and therefore given the fullest support. Recognition of the right of the people of Central America to themselves solve their problems through dialogue and negotiations replacing violence and outside interference must be given a chance to prevail. This is a fundamental demand because the people of Central America have bled for too long.

Consider the case of Nicaragua, whose people have suffered so much during this century from military invasion of their country, through the many years of the brutal and corrupt Somoza dynasty, to this day of CIA backed and trained counter-revolutionaries and mercenaries. What crime have they the Nicaraguans committed? The only crime that they are guilty of is the same committed by the American colonies in their war of independence: the struggle for justice and self-determination.

We join with most of humanity in demanding that the people of Nicaragua be given a chance to build *their* country and their future in peace along the path that they choose.

As regards El Salvador, let me once again state boldly our support for the French/Mexican Declaration of 1981 which is aimed at bringing together the different representative forces of El Salvador for dialogue.

The failure of the United States Administration to support these initiatives, which are the only realistic options for peace and social security in Central America, is really unfortunate and regrettable, and it brings to the surface once again the image of this Administration as being insensitive to the just aspirations of the peoples of the Third World.

At home in Grenada our people have a similar perception of the United States Administration. This has come about as a result of the strained relations that have existed between our two Governments, since our March 13th Revolution. Our people have never failed to contrast the poor state of relations between the United States and Grenada today with the embrace that the brutal, and corrupt dictator Eric Gairy received from successive US governments before the Revolution.

Up till very recently, our requests for dialogue have been met consistently with economic, political, diplomatic and military pressures on our young Revolution.

From the first days of coming to power, the United States pursued a policy which showed no respect for our national pride and aspiration, and sought constantly to bring the Revolution to its knees. Many of our efforts to build a new economy have been undermined by the United States in multilateral institutions such as the IMF and World Bank, and as you know, bilateral assistance has not been forthcoming. In 1981, our regional institution, the Caribbean Development Bank, was offered $4 million for basic human needs projects, on condition that Grenada be entirely excluded. Another example of this policy is to be found in the US sponsored CBI, which excludes Grenada from being a participant, for purely political reasons.

We have faced tremendous adverse propaganda, especially against our new international airport project. We faced military pressure in August 1981 from a naval exercise 'Operation Amber and the Amberines' designed to intimidate Grenada. They have not agreed to our request for an exchange of Ambassadors; and even letters which I wrote to President Reagan in 1981 — proposing normalisation of relations and early high level talks — have not been responded to.

These actions by the United States Administration over the last four years constitute definite unfriendliness towards our young Revolution and young nation. On reflection and analysis, we conclude that such an attitude exists principally because Grenada has taken a very decisive and firm step on the road to genuine national independence, non-alignment and self-determination. This is certain. It is also certain that nations and peoples everywhere, with international legal and public opinion on their side, are more and more taking their own destinies in their hands, and fashioning their own realities. The 1776 American Revolution was history-making testimony to this fact. The sovereignty of a people is non-negotiable, and for us in Grenada, inheritors of a deep sense of pride and independence — not an iota of our rights is negotiable.

It is also apparent, that Grenada is perceived as part of Washington's geopolitical designs. The numerous private and public assurances given by my government that we constitute no threat to the national security interest of the United States of America, or for that matter, of anyone else, should have been adequate long ago. However, once again in your presence here tonight, we repeat these assurances and reemphasize our efforts towards secure, friendly and mutually respectful relations with all our neighbours, including the United States of America.

A third issue has been national elections. The new Grenada, like your country, was born in a great revolutionary act of liberation. The American Revolution gave itself a period of 13 years to consolidate before holding the first elections. In South Africa there is no electoral process for Blacks, who are the majority of the population. Why isn't the United States Administration withholding its massive support for South Africa until democracy is instituted for the millions of disenfranchised Blacks there? And let us recall that despite the fact that the government of President Salvador Allende of Chile, was duly elected and instituted by the approved parliamentary processes, yet none of this deterred a previous US Administration from violently overthrowing this regime and liquidating its leadership and thousands of its people.

Sisters and brothers, friends, despite all of these clear inconsistencies, these painful and damaging actions against Grenada, this clear pattern of unfriendliness, we remain fervently committed to the normalisation and improvement of relations with your government, for this is in the best interests of our two peoples. In these very days we are engaged in an earnest search for meaningful dialogue at appropriate levels and as far as Grenada is concerned we are willing to go into talks with an open mind and without preconditions. For us the true bottom line is — let us talk now.

Domestic developments in Grenada are satisfying. Many achievements are being recorded and temporary dislocations are being resolved.

The most significant achievement in four years of revolutionary transformation is the development of institutions of popular participatory democracy through which the legacy of backwardness and underdevelopment is being wiped out in Grenada, and real material benefits are coming to our people. Over the past four years unemployment has been dramatically reduced. In fact, unemployment has been reduced from 49% to 12% and we have introduced free health care and free education for all of our people. Our form of democracy in Grenada has already achieved four main aspects to date. These are: participation, accountability, responsibility and material benefits. A fifth and final component of our new democracy, electability, is already being experienced by our people through their mass organisations where fair and open elections are held on a regular basis and in due course this process will also be extended to the national level.

But sisters and brothers, among our proudest achievements is the development of *institutions of popular democracy*. Participation in trade unions and other mass organisations has grown by leaps and bounds. New organisations of women, farmers, youth and workers have been formed and existing ones have grown stronger.

A system of monthly *Parish and Zonal Councils*, open to all citizens, ensures free, regular discussion of issues, permanent contact between government and people and strict accountability and responsibility of the leadership of the government and party.

Of course, the Revolution like all previous revolutions has brought disrupting and temporary dislocations in Grenada. A small number of persons have had to be detained, some press freedoms have been limited and elections have not yet been held. Our government understands the difficulties these situations pose.

However, it is important to repeat that all revolutions involve temporary dislocations and, for a period, it is always necessary to restrain the abuses and excesses of a violent or disruptive minority in the interests of consolidating the revolution and bringing concrete benefits to the long-suffering and formerly oppressed majority.

The People's Revolutionary Government and the people of Grenada have regarded development of the economy, improvement of the standard of living, expansion of education and employment, development of the popular organisations and the improvement of the country's defences as matters having priority over constitutional reform. The time has come, however, to take the process of the formal institutionalisation of the Revolution a stage further and commence work on the preparation of a new constitution. We take this opportunity to announce tonight that a Commission was today appointed in Grenada and charged with the task of formulating a meaningful democratic and workable constitution for our country.

The Commission comprises: Allan Alexander, State Counsel and former High Court judge, a distinguished Trinidadian lawyer of gread experience and prestige; Richard Hart, outstanding historian and lawyer, and the present Attorney General of Grenada; Ashley Taylor, an outstanding Grenadian lawyer. In addition to these three eminent jurists, one representative to be selected by the Grenada Trades Union Council, the umbrella organisation for all Labour Unions in our country, and one other representative of the other mass organisations of farmers, women and youth in our country. In this way, the views of all classes, strata and sections in our country will be represented on the Constitution Commission.

Taking into account the views of our people, including all minority views, the Commission has been mandated to formulate within a period of 24 months, a constitution relevant to the needs of our vibrantly developing society.

After the findings of the Constitutional Commission have been submitted to our government, the Draft Constitution will then be discussed in detail by the people of our country. These discussions will result in a second draft which will include the ideas of the people and when a referendum is held and all due process completed a new people's constitution — the first in our history — would have come into existence.

This new constitution will define all dimensions of our electoral process and in particular will institutionalise the systems of popular democracy which have been introduced by our government and which have given such depth and meaning to the term participatory democracy.

Because of the momentous nature of tonight's announcement, I want to crave your indulgence to read the terms of reference of the Commission:

1. To obtain information on alternative forms of political constitutions and the ways in which political constitutions work in practice in other countries.
2. To receive and consider written and oral representations as to matters which should be provided for, and the form and structure of a constitution for Grenada.
3. To receive and consider the views and proposals of all classes, strata and interests of the Grenadian people.

239

4. To prepare for public consideration and discussion a draft constitution and participate in public and other discussions thereon.
5. To consider and assess written and oral proposals for improvement or alteration of the Draft Constitution received from organisations, groups or individuals.
6. To prepare for the Government, with such notes and other supplementary material as may be appropriate, a final draft constitution for approval by the people of Grenada in a referendum.

As we strive to bring social and economic benefits to the people of our country, we look forward now to an event of tremendous significance to our economy, to our people, to our future development – the opening of the new international airport. Those of you who have visited our country know just how important this project is to both our peoples. And those of you who have not done so, will soon have the chance – as I now invite you to join with hundreds of others who will be on the inaugural flight from Washington to Grenada on the day the airport opens – March 13th, 1984. Certainly if you can make it this will give you an opportunity to travel to the most widely publicised International Airport the world has ever known. Let us thank those responsible for all the free publicity.

We certainly look forward to welcoming on that inaugural flight as many of you as possible. We will welcome you with the greatest pleasure and look forward to your sharing with us the tremendous joy of that important event.

Sisters and brothers, the unity and solidarity of our people is of great importance. We see it as our duty to support every initiative for the unification of the peoples of the Caribbean who are not only part of the same geographical formation, but who share a basically common history and culture – the history of slavery and colonialism, the culture which we have forged from the legacy of Africa.

As we take initiatives aimed at finding solutions to the problems of small-island states; as we focus upon the need to find more efficient and less costly transportation services between the islands of the Caribbean region; as we repeatedly issue the call for the Caribbean region to be declared and recognised in practice as a Zone of Peace, Independence and development; as we host conferences of labour leaders, journalists and intellectuals who discuss the problems of the region; we are guided always by the vision of the Caribbean as one people, aiming together at genuine peace, independence and development.

Brothers and sisters, the economic achievement of the poor and dispossessed peoples of the world is a matter of great concern to us. We cannot support a system in which transnational corporations, interested only in profit, bolster racist regimes like that of South Africa, and contribute to the suffering and hardship of millions of our brothers and sisters.

The existing international economic order makes a mockery of dreams of development for our struggling peoples. We must support the establishment of a New International Economic Order, aimed at the ownership and control by developing countries of their economic resources and at a system of international trade based on just prices for our exports. The 1982 agreement on the Law of the Sea is an important achievement and should be recognised as such by all countries sensitive to the problems of underdevelopment, since it seeks to ensure for developing countries a just share of the resources of the sea.

Grenada continues to give support to the North/South dialogue and the need for the resumption of the global negotiations convinced that the world's industrialised countries have a responsibility to assist with the establishment of a just and equitable international economic order which is objectively in their interest as well as in the interest of the developing world.

But no new international economic order is possible, no development can take place in any area of the world without the necessary social infrastructure of world peace. By far the most important struggle in the world today is the struggle for peace.

The very existence of humanity is threatened by the insane drive to stockpile weapons of mass destruction. Think of the tremendous waste of one country's spending US$3 trillion on arms over the next five years. And this, when there are so many people jobless, when there are so many starving, illiterate, unemployed people all over the world.

Statistics show that the cost of one modern tank could pay for the construction of 1,000 classrooms for 30,000 children in developing countries; that the price of a Trident nuclear submarine equals the cost of keeping 16 million children from underdeveloped countries in school for a year *plus* the cost of constructing 400 large living complexes to house two million persons.

These startling figures certainly give added impetus to the ever-strengthening call of the world's peoples for peace in this hemisphere, and make even more sadly ironic the hunger and deprivation of so many millions of people the world over.

Grenada calls for an end to the arms race, for serious negotiations aimed at strategic arms limitation, for a move towards genuine disarmament. Increasingly, the people of the world are realising the need to speak out against warlike and confrontationist policies, to insist that there be dialogue aimed at establishing a lasting peace.

Together we must insist that the policies on Southern Africa, on Central America, on the Middle East, and on the Caribbean, be aimed at ensuring peace, justice and progress for the peoples of these regions.

Sisters and brothers, we call upon you, as an important foreign affairs lobby of the United States, to continue to analyse the actions of your country in the world today.

If the world is to be at peace, if the suffering and deprived peoples of the world are to attain some programme of progress and justice, the United States must, as a world power, pursue policies which show a clear understanding and appreciation of the problems of developing countries. Sisters and brothers, friends, your country must approach these problems, not with arrogance and condescension, but with sensitivity and empathy. This would augur well for world peace and would lead to better relations among all the nations of the world. The April 1983 Report of the Linowitz Commission on the Inter-American Dialogue shows a great deal of recognition of this need for understanding, co-operation and dialogue. The peoples of our region, and the peoples of the United States cry out with one voice for peace, for sanity, for justice, for dignity.

Bearing in mind the importance of dialogue and understanding to the proper conduct of international relations and the tremendous importance of peace to our dreams of development and progress, we once again reiterate our genuine interest in establishing normal bilateral relations with the United States Administration; we remain open to honest and genuine proposals for dialogue at appropriate levels. We must show, in our mutual approach to the Resolution of our difficulties a spirit of inter-American equality and respect.

Grenada cherishes the vision of a new Caribbean civilisation, free from oppression and exploitation, where the conditions will exist for every man, woman and child to exercise to the fullest their human potential.

Finally, sisters and brothers, friends, we proudly share with you the noble dreams of Martin and Malcolm for an America free of racism and discrimination; for a world free of hunger, poverty and strife; for a future free of want and despair.

With sincerity and humility, we thank you for your kind invitation to be here at this time, for your past, present and future support, and for the warmth and hospitality you have unhesitatingly showered on me and my delegation.

We invite you, to soon visit our friendly country so that we may reciprocate your gracious cordiality and show you the revolutionary achievements of our people.

LONG LIVE FRIENDSHIP BETWEEN THE PEOPLES OF THE UNITED STATES AND GRENADA.

LONG LIVE PEACE IN OUR AMERICAS AND IN THE WORLD.

TOGETHER WE SHALL OVERCOME.

FORWARD EVER, BACKWARD NEVER.

Appendix 1
Fascism: A Caribbean Reality?

Extracts from an Address to a Seminar Organised by the
Oilfield Workers Trade Union, Trinidad, October 1975

What I propose to do is to look at Grenada in terms of the various faces
[of fascism] that we have spoken about. Let us try to see how many of these
faces of fascism are present in Grenada. First of all, look at the question of
absolutist rule. Look at the question of the maximum leader. There is no
more maximum leader in the Caribbean than Eric Matthew Gairy. Perhaps
not even Baby Doc can surpass him.

We must see this both in terms of what he says of himself and more
crucially in terms of how his supporters see him. So that for example, no
cabinet decisions of any kind, and I mean any kind, can be made if Gairy is
out of the island. He is president for life of the ruling political party, and he
aspires to be Prime Minister for life, or maybe later, President for life of the
country.

The evidence in Grenada, with respect to totalitarian rule, extends to all
aspects of human relations. It is true of the politics, it is also true of the
unions. Gairy has been maintaining a very consistent policy, which has been
stepped up from 1973, of trying to take away the membership of the other
key unions on the island.

There are some 16 registered trade unions in Grenada, but only about
five are worth talking about and Gairy has been trying to poach workers
from these from about 1973 onwards, particularly from the Technical and
Allied Workers Union. In fact, there was a strike called by Technical and
Allied in May 1973 which had nothing whatsoever to do with the question
of workmen's wages, nothing to do with the question of better conditions,
but was called solely for the purpose of reminding Gairy that the union still
had the ability to turn the lights off and to remind him not to poach. The
strike in fact was engineered by one of Gairy's right hand men, a minister
in the government, who was then also legal adviser to the union and president
of the Trade Union Congress.

Now, this year, there have already been four different but related efforts
by Gairy to further control the activities of Trade Unions. Sometime in
February this year, Cable and Wireless began the building of a micro-wave
station and about two months after the project was underway, the workers
asked the Technical and Allied Workers' Union to organise them. But a few
days after the president of the Technical and Allied Workers' Union had

enlisted the workers, Gairy arrived on the scene.

Driven to the scene by the foreign manager of Cable and Wireless, Gairy told these workers that he alone had the right to organise workers employed in any public capacity in Grenada. Nobody else had that right, he insisted, as he had been given that right since 1961, although he didn't say who gave him that right. And therefore all these workers were going to have to join his union or they were going to find themselves without a job. The workers, almost to a man, resisted but he nonetheless got the manager to arrange for each of them to get a dollar a day extra.

At the end of the week virtually all the workers on that project refused the increase and were showing the greatest solidarity with the union. But do you know what that union did eventually? The union turned around and agreed with the Gairy proposal that the question of recognition be submitted to the Trade Union Congress. That was the reaction. And predictably, the Trade Union Congress said: Gairy's union is in charge. The actual agreement reached was a compromise allowing for the joint recognition of both unions with the union dues being paid to the TUC. I need hardly say, however, that in this situation the Gairy union soon won out.

The situation at home is complicated by the fact that we don't have the kind of militants among trade union leaders that Trinidadians have. There is, for example, no George Weekes, and that makes a fundamental difference. At home, to give one example, the unions apparently are only now hearing about a Cost of Living Allowance, and are only now, in a few cases, beginning to negotiate for that. And when they ask for an increase in wages they don't ask for 147%, they ask for 30% or 35% hoping to get 15 or 10. So, I mean it's that level of union organisation and backwardness we are dealing with.

There is a place in Grenada called the Grenada Yacht Services — a marina for foreigners with all their nice yachts and so on — and there are some workers there whom Gairy tried to organise but the workers refused to join his union. The result was that he had a number of them sacked with the collusion of the management.

Then there is the situation with the Nutmeg Association workers. The Nutmeg Association in Grenada is, after the government, the single largest employer of workers on the island. As you may well know, nutmeg is the most important industry in Grenada is, after the government, the single largest employer of workers on the island. As you may well know, nutmeg is the most important industry in Grenada, and Grenada produces the world's second largest amount of nutmegs. Only Indonesia produces more than we do.

Now, there are three large processing stations on the island, and something like 18 receiving stations and these workers were unionised by the Commercial and Industrial Workers' Union. But in July, Gairy acquired the Nutmeg Association and one of his first acts was to replace many of the unionised workers by his own workers. So that through this mechanism of control, workers are constantly being divided, they are unable to see any dynamism or militancy in the leadership of the other unions and in concrete terms they recognise that whenever Gairy wishes to move to victimise them he can do so with impunity. It means that the spirit of these workers is being dampened and stifled. And this kind of worker can very easily become de-classed and fall prey to the lure of fascists or neo-fascists.

Now, all of you have heard about Parliament in Grenada — a fiasco and a farce. There are 15 seats, 14 are held by Gairy, one by the opposition GNP. In the last elections in 1972 the GULP claimed 58% of the votes and gave the opposition 42. Now, how 48 and 42 works out to be 14 to one is a matter, I suppose, for mathematical geniuses. But in any event that is the reality.

The radio is another good example. There is one radio station that is totally controlled by the government and only their voices can be heard. In fact, in a speech last year, after we began agitating for radio time, Gairy said that for the NJM to ask for radio time was the same like his asking us to be allowed to write an article for our newspaper. So, as far as he is concerned, the radio is his personal property.

Regarding newspapers, well, of course, you have heard of the Newspaper Law, which I will deal with a little later on.

Outlaw and Disorder

Let me come to the question of the legal and constitutional face [of fascism] ; Grenada is also well-known for its repressive laws. All the usual ones like State of Emergency Acts, Public Order Acts, Explosives Acts and various such devices that Comrades here are very familiar with, we also have in abundance in Grenada.

We have, in addition, something which was passed last year which was called Shops-Regulations of Opening Hours-Act. Now, that was designed to make sure that all shops kept their doors open. Remember last year there was a general shutdown and business places had closed down. So what Gairy did was to pass this Act demanding that business places stay open. This year, following on the footsteps of Antigua, and after the Privy Council had given its very famous pro-establishment judgement, Gairy passed an Amendment to the Newspaper Act. Now in Antigua they were asking for $10,000 so he decided that he wanted $60,000; he wanted six times more. Grenada of course is richer and independent to boot, so we must demand more. This sum was eventually reduced to 20,000. And therefore to legally print a newspaper in Grenada now, you have to put up $20,000, additionally you have to sign a bond; and also you have to pay an annual licence fee of $500. This law had the effect of closing down the other opposition papers. The GNP's newspaper was closed, another group called the UPP also stopped printing and *The Torchlight* likewise stopped publishing until they were able to comply with the law. Only our newspaper continued, and still continues, to publish the facts.

They have just passed a very interesting law, a law which on its face might not appear to be dangerous. This is an amendment to the Jury Act. And what they have done by this law is to disallow jurors from sitting in any civil cases. That might look simple enough, it might look harmless enough. It is very far from that. What this jury law is designed to do is to make sure that in libel cases no jury sits. The background is that Gairy has a world record in the bringing of libel cases. Up to 1972, Gairy had brought no fewer than eight libel cases. And he has had about five brought against him. He is a man who likes the court. He has had something like 22 different debt cases taken against him. And one of the things he likes to boast about is that in one year he was charged some 35 times for road traffic and other offences. That is one of his smaller pleasures.

What this particular law is designed to do is to ensure that in libel cases there will be no jury sitting to determine the facts and come to a conclusion. You are going to have to deal with a judge alone who will have to be judge of law and facts. This law, in fact, seems to have been timed to prevent a jury from hearing a libel case, adjourned last week, which Gairy had taken against Michael Sylvester, a lawyer and former opposition politician. That gives you an idea of what I mean when I say this law is not nearly as harmless as it might appear.

Now, moving very quickly to the question of the judiciary — the judicial face. We have a situation at home where there is virtually no magistracy. The magistrates are almost totally non-functioning in the sense that questions of law are of no concern to the majority of them.

Many of you remember November 18, 1973, what we call 'Bloody Sunday., when six of us were beaten by Gairy's Secret Police in Grenville, where we were going to attend a meeting. Well, they kept us in the cell, bleeding, bottle-trimmed and in desperate need of medical attention that night, and the next morning we appeared handcuffed and barefooted before the magistrate, a man called I.I. Duncan, and were charged with being in possession of arms and ammunition.

Now, the law says that where persons are charged with summary offences bail must be granted, but Duncan stated that as far as he was concerned, no law could take away his discretion, he did not care what the law said; he was granting no bail. That is the magistracy. When we talk about magistrates who do not even pretend that there is something called 'law' which they must try to serve and uphold, you must come to Grenada to understand. It is nothing short of a comic pantomime going on in most of the courts today.

So far as the judge (there is only one in Grenada) is concerned, elements in the government had been expressing open hostility to the judge who used to be there up to a couple of weeks ago. He had given a number of decisions against the government which they were not happy about, and they have been applying all sorts of pressure to have him removed. In fact, this month he was removed, transferred to Antigua and a new judge has arrived. As I said before, judges must be judged more in terms of their class outlook rather than their personal integrity, though integrity is always an important consideration.

Police and Military Power

Next, the military side of fascism — the military face. Since 1967, when the GULP got back into office, there have been no less than ten different Commissioners of Police. Some years we might have two, other years only one and so on. Ten different Commissioners of Police in eight years! From 1954 to 1967 there was only one Commissioner; he somehow or the other managed to last thirteen years but once Gairy resumed office the new pattern took shape, And the vast majority of these Commissioners have been foreigners. Quite obviously, when you bring a foreigner in as Commissioner he has no loyalty to the country, no responsibility to the people, so he either does what he is told or he goes and for that very reason he is a lot easier to control and to remove when he becomes too 'manish'. So over the years they have just been chopping and changing Commissioners with the regularity of the seasons.

Right now the Commissioner of Police is from Nigeria; he has been there with a Deputy Commissioner, also from Nigeria, for the last three months. This seems to have been the result of some arrangement worked out by Gairy with General Gowon before he was overthrown sometime last year. Gairy had gone to the Pan-African Congress in Tanzania, which again is quite an amazing thing when you think about it — imagine Gairy as a Pan-Africanist, and all dressed in white. And coming back from the Pan-African Congress, he stopped off in Nigeria to beg a return passage home and to work up this deal with Gowon. A safe prediction is that our Nigerian brothers are very unlikely to last the duration of their two year contract.

Now, beyond that, there is the question of constant victimisation and promotions based on patronage and for 'brutality services' rendered. A police force in fact, which the Duffus Commission of Enquiry, held last year into the events in Grenada, found to be entirely lacking in morals and discipline. This was the finding of that Commission of Enquiry. Along with the police force, there had been up to 1974 the secret police and the infamous mongoose gang.

Now, as long ago as May 1970, in a very famous speech entitled 'Address on Black Power', the same speech that Comrade Belgrave was referring to when he said 'If yuh neighbour's house on fire wet yours', Gairy claimed in effect that there were two Erics in the Caribbean, a fast one and a slow one, and he was not the slow one. Yes, in that speech in May 1970, he announced that he was going to recruit 'the roughest and toughest roughnecks' he could find — that's the exact quotation — in order to meet steel with steel. And he also promised to create what he called 'Voluntary Intelligence Units for the Protection of Property'. And this, according to him, was to come from the propertied and monied classes, people who were going to come forward to protect their interests from the spectre of Black Power.

Now, since May 1970 he has created in fact a Night Ambush Squad, a Special Secret Police Squad, then he formed what he called Police Aides and finally they formed what they called Volunteers for the Protection of

Human Rights. As you recognise, this is similar language to Mussolini and Hitler. They are saying that these Volunteers for the Protection of Human Rights, all two thousand of them during their heyday, were volunteering only to protect the human rights of the government and the human rights of supporters of the government. And in fact, their methods of attack were nine out of ten times designed to make an impact. It was not a question of catching you in the dark and beating you; these beatings had to take place in public, in the full view of everybody. Obviously, they were trying to tell Grenadians something about their future. They were not hiding, it was open, it was public, it was brutal.

And, even up to two or three months ago, on July 18, one of our comrades, Kenrick Radix, was beaten and chopped up in the middle of St George's. Yes, two or three months ago, by some of these same people who are now posing as members of a Defence Force. They are once more preparing for war.

And when you talk about a Defence Force in Grenada, you are not talking about a Defence Force like you have in Trinidad where, at least so far as the law books are concerned, it is legal. In Grenada, that Defence Force has no legality whatosever. Our laws provide for a Grenada Volunteer Constabulary and for Rural Constables. But there is no provision under the law for this Defence Force, so like the Secret Police it is again an entirely illegal creation that operates illegally but has the full force, backing an effect of the 'law'.

Now, this Defence Force continues to be comprised of criminal elements. In fact, one of the things that the Commission of Enquiry found is that no less than sixty four members of the so called 'Police Aides' had criminal records. Some of them had as many as 34 previous convictions. And many of these same people are now in this Defence Force. So when we are talking about legality and illegality we must understand that no real attempts are made to disguise, to clothe or to hide institutional illegality and brutality in Grenada.

Who Owns What

Le us move on Comrades, to the economic face of fascism as it appears in Grenada. Now, Grenada is no different to the rest of the Caribbean, except Cuba. Like the rest of the Caribbean, the controlling class has struck an alliance with would-be local capitalists and local compradors. Opposite to that class there is of course the broad base of workers – the working class. Here you find that unemployment in Grenada today is something like 50% of the work force. If you add underemployment to that, the figure would probably pass 65%. Even official documents in 1970, when it was supposed to have been a boom year because of tourism and a great deal of construction activity, put open unemployment at 17%. The government, of course, hides behind what they call 'the crisis' of 1973 and 1974.

They are unable to do anything about unemployment, so they have been saying that 'Jewel' created the crisis and therefore 'Jewel' must solve the unemployment problem. And 'Jewel' is not even in office yet!

If we look at the class structure, what we find is that the producing class of wage-labourers, people engaged in agriculture, in the few factories that we have, in manufacturing and so on, these people are doomed to a life of social misery, degradation and exploitation. The few parasites at the top of course live in great luxury. In between these two come the middle strata. As with the rest of the Caribbean, they have one main social function, and that is to provide the supportive machinery for the state, the international bourgeoisie and the local compradors and capitalists. Their main function is to consume and that is what they are doing. But in addition to consuming they provide the apparatus of control for the ruling class.

Now, there are exceptions to this within the middle strata. There are, in the Grenada situation, many elements of that middle strata that can be neutralised and there are certainly elements of the middle class who are, quite frankly, as fed up with capitalism as the working class. In other words, they can be won over to the working class. And efforts, in our view, have to be made to do precisely this.

When we look at the question of foreign control of the economy, what we find at home is that the multi-national corporations dominate and control the areas of banking, insurance companies and tourism. There are five international banks operating there. There are no fewer than 66 registered insurance companies in Grenada — *sixty-six*! But yet they tell us that we are poor, small, worth nothing, and without money and all that. And yet they have 66 of those companies in Grenada. What are they doing there?

In the hotel business, of the 15 or so hotels, one of them, Holiday Inn, alone controls 60% of the total bed space available. In agriculture, there is a monopoly by Geest of our bananas. With cocoa and nutmegs, we ship these raw crops up to England where they are processed, packed into tins and shipped back to us. We are not engaged in any form of agro-industrialisation.

When our cocoa farmer picks his cocoa pod off the cocoa tree, he has to sell it to the Cocoa Association which in turn sells to agents in England. These agents then sell to manufacturers who package or tin the cocoa, call it *Ovaltine* or Chocolate or *Cadburys* or *Fry's* or *Milo* or whatever and return it to be bought at five or six dollars a tin. A straight case of dependent economy — an economy totally controlled by outside forces.

The few compradors (if we can so call them) we have at home do not even understand the basics of capitalism. They seem incapable of understanding that with a little money, a little organisation and a few ideas money can be channelled in agro-industry. They seem totally barren of ideas and are mainly concerned to break off 95c profit or a dollar profit or whatever they can get on a tin of corned beef or a pound of saltfish, put that in their pockets and then call themselves 'big capitalist'. But perhaps it is as well that they do not understand!

Comrades, from all of this we can conclude that neo-fascism is fairly well entrenched in Grenada. Entrenched, not in the sense that people are consciously and publicly and actively articulating a philosophy of fascism, that is to say, they are not saying they are fascist, but what they are doing tells us that they are fascist or neo-fascist in outlook. And this in reality is the only way to assess and judge fascists and fascism.

It does not matter what comes out of the mouths of politicians, it is a question of what they do in practice. It is what their social practice is, that will determine whether objectively they are or are not fascists, regardless of whether they believe subjectively that they are the greatest democrats since Locke or Rousseau. And this, Comrades is the situation in Grenada in terms of fascism.

Appendix 2
'We Have the Right to Build Our Country After Our Own Likeness'

A Last Interview with British Journalist, Victoria Brittain, St. George's, Grenada, September 1983

Victoria Brittain: *You have repeatedly accused the CIA of threatening Grenada's security – is this an immediate threat now?*

Maurice Bishop: It is difficult to say how immediate the threat is. I think that the threat is always going to be there, in the sense that this United States administration, generally speaking all United States administrations but I would say particularly this one, is very hostile to any progressive or revolutionary regime. Their primary approach is to invest the stamp of legality only on regimes which fully support them and fully carry all lines that they wish. And therefore, for a government like ours that is so determined to maintain an independent non-aligned path, obviously we are going to have problems with them at all turns.

The reality is, that right for the first days we did have certain experiences with the United States, and with the CIA in particular. In the very first days, when Ambassador Ortiz (who was then ambassador to Grenada) came to Grenada, he warned us against having relations with Cuba, which of course we rejected. *Newsweek Magazine* in the first three or four weeks of the revolution, said that the National Security Council had met, and had actively considered some kind of blockade against the country.

Two months later, I made a national address in Grenada where I disclosed a CIA plot against us, which had been leaked to us by someone who had very good links with people in the CIA, and this plot was in the form of a pyramid, so we called it a CIA pyramid plan. It was the usual kind of thing. At the bottom was the propaganda, in the middle was economic aggression, at the top was the military threat, the terrorism, the assassinations etc., and we have seen all aspects of this particular plot, in fact, put into effect over the years. We have had experiences where even the farmers in our country, who belong to a sub-regional farmers association, WINDBAN, Windward Islands Banana Association, have been deprived of rehabilitation assistance following the hurricanes, while the farmers of the other islands in the association were in fact granted assistance.

We have had attempts by the US to deprive us of money even through the Caribbean Development Bank, which is a regional institution, and which by its Charter cannot discriminate against any of its members. So, I am afraid that the overall attempts at destabilisation on the propaganda, economic and military fronts has really been quite widespread. On the military front there was the 1980 bomb blast in Queen's Park, which was an attempt to wipe out the entire leadership, using technology that was completely alien to our country. From the interrogations and admissions made by people who were arrested afterwards, it is clear that there was a US link to that plot.

In February this year, the end of February, the *Washington Post* carried this long article disclosing a CIA plot against us under Carter and again under Reagan. It seems that Carter approved propaganda, Reagan approved economic aggression, and on top of the propaganda also added what they called certain unusual and unspecified components. One doesn't know what that is. I assume it means assassinations etc. In any event that plot is fully disclosed in the *Washington Post*. Then most recently in March, we had occasion to alert our population again about another major threat. So my overall answer is that while we have nothing particularly concrete about the absolute immediate period, we continue to assume that the general plans which have been drawn up in the first days, and which we know surfaced only recently again, would in fact continue.

Your calculations seem to be that by having a very high international profile – as in your recent visit to the United States – you can shame the US into not carrying out these kind of plans. Is this correct?

That is part of it. The United States visit is a little more complicated than that, but certainly I would accept that formulation in part. I think it is also a way, from our point of view, of ensuring that we have the opportunity of getting our view across to the widest possible cross section of the American people. We accepted an invitation from TransAfrica which is a highly respected African and Caribbean lobby, and the Congressional Black Caucus. We also met over 50 congressmen and senators. It gave us opportunity to meet with different sections of the media, of meeting with bodies like the Council of Foreign Relations, which is made up largely of former secretaries of state and so on, and also weeks of trying to get our view across to the broad masses, the ordinary working people of the US.

We also think the question of normalising relations with the US was really a matter of principle. That really, is the only basis that civilised countries can conduct rleations in 1983 – through diplomatic relations and exchange of ambassadors, particularly when you are talking about countries that historically have had such links and relations and therefore to ask the question of who it is in power, whether it is Reagan, is it a Republican or Democrat is really neither here nor there. It is fundamentally for us a question of principle. We think it is very important to establish these relations, to normalise relations and therefore not to find any difficulties that this administration is putting in the way of normalisation. We think it is only going to cause trouble to achieve that.

When you look at the experience of other countries you are close to in spirit either they end up as semi-autarchic kind of position like Cuba and Vietnam or like Manley in Jamaica they get overthrown. What makes you think that Grenada's experience can be different?

We think in many respects our country does have a peculiar situation. We think that this is not the only respect in which we are going to create history. We think our country is also going to create history in respect of the particular path that we are going to choose that we are choosing rather, to build social- ism. You are talking about a very small country as you know, little over one hundred thousand people, a little over one hundred and twenty one square miles, in terms of natural resources not particularly well endowed. You are really talking about a very small country with a very small population and on top of that they are largely untrained, and to attempt to speak of building socialism in this context really is a very novel thing. No one in the world has tried it before, and in that sense I think what we are going to attempt to do in Grenada from that point of view will have some very rich experiences for many of the countries in the future.. Frankly, that is the way in which I see the question of our attempt to do what you describe. I, on the one hand, affirm a principled and independent and imperial foreign policy that is non aligned. On the other hand maintaining those trading ties. In our view the present balance of forces in the world, generally speaking, is making it easier for more and more countries in the Western world to accept that small, poor, developing countries do have the right to diversify their foreign relations and economic relations. And to the extent that that becomes more and more accepted world wide, to that extent it becomes easier, but in any event, we think it's the correct path and we are struggling for it.

In your speech to the non-aligned conference in New Delhi you made a strong plea for a return to basic principles of non-alignment, and for an end to the arms race as Mrs Gandhi and Fidel Castro have demanded. Will this Third World view be seriously heeded by the West?

Well, our view really is that obviously the question of peace is the number one question in the world, particularly in this day and age. Having regard to the fact that you are really playing for keeps, that nuclear weaponry means nuclear annihilation and, therefore, it is a question that all countries do have to focus on. We genuinely believe therefore that even though we are a small poor country, that we have a right to get our own views on this question heard. I think it is important for us to struggle for a greater acceptance of the nature of this potential confrontation that the world faces. I think that, too, we must not underestimate the peace movements. Right there in Britain, for instance, there is this massive demonstration by so many people. They are against the deployment of nuclear weaponry in their country, that they are against the return of the cold war, that they are for peaceful coexistence and detente and so on. I think that is true in Holland, West Germany, France, right across Western Europe and inside the US itself. I think in a sense if we look at things dialectically, that is really what we are to focus on, and recognising that there is a struggle which we have to engage in, I think what we need is to look for the young shoots to see where there is room for hope and to try to work and build on that, so that over time more and more people will become convinced and persuaded that what we are talking about is not at all eccentric, it really is reality, it is life itself. After all, if you examine a question like the question of acceptance of a need for unemployment, the argument of the capitalist, and more so the classical capitalist, is that unemployment is something you can never really do without. It must be there and so on: I think more and more people, having regard that they have to face that on a day to day basis, are coming to realise that it doesn't have to be so, and shouldn't be so, and they do have a right to work and a right to live. I think more and more people are coming to accept progressive sentiments, progressive ideas, progressive prescriptions, progressive solutions. In part, I think it has to do with the very contradictions within capitalism, which of course exacerbates all of these antagonisms. It is the same way in which we have to see the whole peace question, we have to see to the struggle. A very critical and decisive struggle which we have to engage in and regardless of whom is unable to understand a particular period. We have to struggle to get them to understand, and I think in a sense it is a weakness of progressive forces in the world that they have not yet been able to find a correct formula to gain a wider acceptance and understanding of what they are saying. I think it really is our duty to try to find the simplest, but at the same time starkest, ways of getting across our message so more and more people come to understand what we are saying.

So your optimism is based on the fact that Western governments don't really represent the majority opinion in the West? There is the gap, and that is where your optimism and your hope lies?

Certainly the Reagan administration is not a hundred per cent majority sentiment in the United States, that is quite clear. He's just about a thirty per cent government. I think that is true for many many of the Western governments. The whole history of coalitions in countries like Italy and so on, even when election results appear to be very dramatic, very often when we look at it it has to do with the structure of the first-past-the-post system than the real expression of a democratic view by many individuals in the country. So I think yes, that is part of the answer but I think in a sense even more fundamentally what I am saying is there are many people in those countries who already recognise the danger, who already are open to progressive solutions and prescriptions, and I think more and more people will become so disposed, particularly in the context where the world capitalist crisis continues and therefore I think dialectically we have to see this as a struggle we have to continue.

Looking back to the beginning of the four years, are you surprised at how little help you have had from the West and how much antipathy you generated?

I don't think frankly it was a shock. We pretty much expected that some countries in the Western world were likely to maintain that position. One or two particular countries from time to time have been a little bit of a surprise. Even there I don't think much of a massive surprise or anything like that. Certainly the overall response and reaction of the US frankly was no surprise to us, after all, the US is the formulator of Monroe Doctrine in 1823. The formulator of the Roosevelt corollary in 1904. The US one hundred and thirty five times invaded countries in this region over the last one hundred years. Frankly there is no reason for us to be shocked or surprised at their attitude and response and therefore I think in overall global terms it has not come as a surprise or shock. We try however, to act always in the most principled way we can, try to get across to middle ground elements in the different countries of the world and of course to reach public opinion generally and as a small country nonetheless, we have the right to try and build our own process in our own way. We have a right to choose our own friends. We have a right to diversify our economic and international relations just like their countries have that right. We have a right to seek our own development. We have a right to build our own country after our own likeness and image and not after somebody elses. We try to get that meaning across.

I think honestly we have had some success in that way. On many occasions we ourselves have been surprised when we quarter-expected a particular move in one direction and found it didn't come, and very often we have discovered from talking to people afterwards it has not come because people have listened to what we have said, analysed what we have done and genuinely come to the conclusion that really in Grenada what we are trying to do is to bring about our own development in all aspects, socially, economically, politically, spiritually, for our people. Therefore we have the right to pursue that course, that really we pose no threat to anybody, and I think that from time to time even when we did not quite expect to win, we have found we have won some little struggle, even with the international financial institutions. Very often it has come about precisely from maintaining that principled course, but at the same time really spending a lot of time trying to persuade, in particular the middle ground elements. That what we are doing is something we are very sincere and genuine about, and really has relevance to our situation and poses no threat to anybody else.

How much of your problem of US antagonism do you think has been exacerbated by the Central American crisis?

It is very difficult to say. The fact is that even before the Central American crisis quite became what it has become in terms of the high profile around the world at this time, Grenada was already under threat and already under tremendous pressure. We already went through all facets of the destabilisation of the CIA pyramid plan as organised for us. I think that even outside of that crisis, that would have continued. I would say that what this particular period does is make much more dangerous our own situation obviously, because when you have a situation when they have all of these thousands and thousands of troops, hundreds of ships and planes and whatnot, and manoeuvres off the coast of Atlantic and Pacific coasts, off Nicaragua, bases being built inside of Honduras and the use of Honduras as a gendarme territory to squeeze the Nicaraguans to try to overthrow the revolution, then all of these things obviously create a great deal of tension in the region and lead to an overall atmosphere of instability, and that is precisely the kind of situation where aggressors would normally thrive. Therefore we have assumed that this period does pose greater dangers for the revolution. We have attempted to do some extra mobilisation of our people in this period so as to meet whatever threat comes about.

Talking about mobilisation, it seems to me that the problem of mobilisation now is apathy rather than any kind of actual middle-class opposition or anything like that. Is that right?

The apathy that you describe or you may have sensed that is around would be more of a surface thing rather than any kind of ground swell position from the masses. My personal view is that people are as enthusiastic today as they were four years ago.

Certainly, there is a tremendous amount of additional work that everybody in the country is engaged in. Even ordinary members of the population, ordinary sections of the masses would have a diary that might have 14 things in it, they have to do every week. Some meetings of the mass organisation, some meetings on the organs of popular democracy, community work maybe on a Sunday morning, Militia on a Wednesday or a Thursday. The masses themselves are really overburdened. Those who require CPE units phase two stage two would then have to go out on Tuesday nights and Thursday nights for six hours and so on. And I think the truth is that this obviously has led to a certain sense of tiredness on the part of certain sections of the population and therefore from time to time you may find that a particular event may not be as well attended as another one might be, a few weeks later. In that sense you may get a suspicion of apathy. I frankly don't think it is that at all. I think what has happened is that the work has deepened as it has broadened, that more and more people are engaged in more and more areas and tasks, that the work has also become much much more complex and therefore has required a lot more energy, a lot more thought being put out and this naturally has been quite taxing on large sections of our people and I think this is the kind of sense you may get from time to time and may misread as apathy. I don't think it is apathy at all. I think people are much more involved and much more engaged now, but they are much more involved and much more engaged in a structured and a systematic way.

Could you explain the reasons behind the recent appointment of a constitutional commission?

In terms of the constitution commission the realities are the following. We believe that the time has come after four and a half years of experimenting with a new democratic form, a new democratic structure to begin to institutionalise that form. We do not believe that we have yet reached the stage where we can fully institutionalise these forms. We think there is still a greater period of acceptance and experimentation required. But we think we are fast approaching that stage which is why we feel now is the time to open up the discussion about the new constitution. That obviously among other things will have the task of entrenching the new constitutional forms, the new democratic forms that have been worked.

Now you know the constitution commission has the task of consulting with a wide range of our people. They have the task in the next two years of bringing back the first draft of that constitution. It is only after they bring back that draft and then the draft gets changed and amended and so on, bearing in mind the criticisms of the people and suggestions and amendments of the people, that you are going to see a finer new constitution and it is our of that process, as far as we are concerned the whole national elections will come, because obviously one of the things the constitution will do is set the perimeters for elections, a framework for when the national elections are held, provide for unicamerol or bicamerol legislators on the ways in which the organs of popular democracy and mass organs are going to fit into the national framework. I mean all of these questions are questions for the constitution. We really see this as being a long process, we see this as being something the people need to be involved and discussing over a good bit of time. They need to be able to relate to their ongoing experience. What is already clear to us is that within the mass organisations the people have finally found a form with which they are happy, in a sense that they can go to these meetings of the mass organisations, they can meet in a spirit of equality, they can raise matters they wish, they know the main organisations are open to any sections of the population and therefore in that sense they are from a form and a structure that they can relate to.

Likewise, with organs of popular democracy, we have found the same thing. It is not like that when they go down to a parliament, sit in a room that can only hold forty people and applaud if you want to applaud when someone speaks and then walk out afterwards. Here, they can go into a building barefooted if they wish, sit down among their peers, discuss any problems they wish, have representatives, the management or whatever of telephone company, electricity, water, public health come to them ask them any questions they wish, look at all of the major programmes, say the question of the national insurance scheme or the question of the Centre for Popular Education programme or the question of the Militia or milk dis-

257

tribution. They can discuss all of these matters. They can meet with a top member of the leadership and therefore they know the accountability and responsibility is there and again in that sense they are obviously much happier with this democratic form than what used to exist.

But equally we are still very much in a process of experimentation. We may move from parish councils to zonal councils. We are now moving to mini-zonal councils, those have actually just started. From there we go to village councils. We still have a long way to go in fully developing the form itself, the structure. Likewise, we started off with the broad discussion with a structural agenda where leaders of the mass organisations and the trade unions will give reports on their areas of work. Then you get a speech from the top leadership or you might get before that a manager of one of the public utilities coming and then you would go home after asking questions. Now we are moving to the stage where we are making these zonals into workshops. So after a few speeches they break into workshops, look in much more depth and detail and then they come up with really concrete answers and these are presented back to a full plenary of the zonal. From there we want to move to establish standing committees in each zonal and mini zonal. These standing committees will have particular areas of responsibility for monitoring the economy, for monitoring the CPE programme, for monitoring the Militia, monitoring military distribution or community work or other tasks.

More and more of these things are evolving and every month out of our discussions and analysis of what took place a month before we are trying to add something new to ensure that the experience of the people and the training in self rule is deepened from day to day. But we think that nonetheless we have reached a point where we are coming very close to very broad popular acceptance by all the people and a greater understanding of what we are trying to do. That is why we feel the time has come for us to embark on this constitutional exercise.

All these things you describe represent such a threatening example to other countries around with more elitist leaderships, that it is hard to see how you are ever really going to get accepted by other countries around and that includes America.

Well, it took several hundred years for feudalism to be finally wiped out and capitalism to emerge as the new dominant mode of production and it will take several hundred years for capitalism to be finally wiped out before socialism becomes the new dominant mode. The struggle is the same with our neighbours. Most people who are unprepared to accept any form of change not only resent it but resist it in very open forms. I think you are going to find that there will be this difficulty amongst some of the leadership in neighbouring territories. We think that the key is to get across the message to them that we pose no threat to them and we are not interested in toppling their governments. We are not interested in imposing what we believe on them, that is the first thing. Secondly, we do really want to engage in as many areas of co-operation as we can. I think we have demonstrated that in a million different ways. Wherever we go we struggle not just for Grenada but for either the OECS territory sub-regional grouping or the wider CARICOM.

We never try to seek our own selfish interest. When I did a state visit to France last year that is when the French government chose to announce during the visit that FAC (Fund for Aid and Co-operation) is to be extended to seven OECS territories and that obviously came after discussions. So I think we have demonstrated that in our struggle for the small islands, the struggle for the zone of peace, is many many struggles, but what we think is even more important than all of that is the way we are able to communicate with the people of the region and there I think we have had an extraordinary impact. The realisation is that every time I for one make a visit abroad, and indeed many leaders of the revolution, we are able to communicate with the masses in the neighbouring territories. We are able to get them to understand what we are trying to do, and I think it is true to say that our experience over four and a half years has revealed that among the masses of the Caribbean there is no hostility. Of course among small sections there is, and in fact there is a tremendous amount of sympathy and in many cases active support, that they understand this is a new experiment. They understand that we are trying an alternative pattern of socio-economic and political development aimed at raising the quality of life for our people. They are willing to give it a chance to see if it succeeds and in fact they are very open to what we are doing. That has been our concrete experience. The hostility has been largely fabricated particularly in the media. They write all these fantastic editorials so on the one hand you have all these extraordinary stories coming up when their own people are coming to the country every day, every week and they are seeing for themselves a totally different reality and that is giving the lies to these people and exposing the nature of this mafia media. From our point of view it is an important way of raising the consciousness of the Caribbean masses and we think that frankly we are winning the struggle. We really think so.

So the Human rights attack was just a sideshow?

Absolutely. These elements are talking about human rights in Grenada. Where are all the editorials against Gairy? You know we had many disappearances in this country and where were the editorials then? These elements are talking about human rights in Grenada. Are we seeing editorials against Haiti? Are we seeing editorials against those countries that are murdering people every day and their own police? Information services are putting out figures that indicate that it is murder. Is not a right to life the first human right, but they don't write any editorials then about that. It is all ideological, a political struggle they are engaged in, and I think the people in this region of ours have come to understand that when you have five, six, seven, eight of these newspapers on the same Sunday on the same front page, carrying the same headlines, the same number of full stops and commas, identical editorial against Grenada they recognise as contrived. And that is also helping to expose these elements. I will give you a true example. It happened a few years ago. A number of these journalists in Trinidad for example, came out and passed a resolution against our newspapers, the *Trinidad Guardian* and the *Trinidad Express*, who have done this together with the major newspapers and the Jamaican newspapers. But when things like that happen in the final analysis, it is in our interest because it gets people to understand a little more clearly what is the true meaning and nature of this media as practised by these elements, in whose service they are. While they pretend to be 10, 15 and 20 newspapers and five, six, seven, eight radio stations it is really just one voice, the same voice speaking all the time. People are beginning to understand these things.

In a recent New York Times *article, one of the points made was that the population was seeping away, whereas I had though in fact it was the opposite. What is the reality?*

Like you I thought it was opposite and not only thought it, I know it's the opposite. The fact is of course, there has been some migration in the usual way but far from it being greater than the past it is exactly the opposite. I will tell you something. There was an interesting survey done a few months ago, maybe a year by now. It was a front page in the *Caribbean Contact*. They did a survey of all the islands in the region, including I think Puerto Rico but certainly all the English speaking islands, trying to establish which ones among the youth were willing to stay in their countries and help to build it, and which ones wanted to go. The survey showed that among the Grenadian youth over seventy per cent wanted to stay and were unwilling to leave. The next nearest island was under forty per cent. It is highly dramatic. These are the results of a survey not done by us.